Rooted in Rock

Rooted in Rock

New Adirondack Writing

1975–2000

Edited by Jim Gould

With Forewords by Rick Bass and Jacqueline F. Day

THE ADIRONDACK MUSEUM/SYRACUSE UNIVERSITY PRESS

First Edition 2001
04   05   06   6   5   4   3   2

Acknowledgment of permissions to reprint material in this volume
may be found at the end of the book.

The paper used in this publication meets the minimum requirements of
American National Standard for Information Sciences—Permanence of
Paper for Printed Library Materials, ANSI Z39.48–1984.∞™

Library of Congress Cataloging-in-Publication Data

Rooted in rock : new Adirondack writing, 1980–2000 / edited by Jim Gould ; with
forewords by Rick Bass and Jacqueline F. Day.—1st ed.
    p. cm.
    ISBN 0-8156-0701-6 (alk. Paper)
    1. American literature—New York (State)—Adirondack Mountains. 2. Mountain
life—New York (State)—Adirondack Mountains 3. Adirondack Mountains
(N.Y.)—Literary collections 4. New York (State)—Literary collections. 5. Mountain
life—Literary collections. 6. American literature—20th century. 7. Adirondack Mountains
(N.Y.) I. Gould, Jim, 1958–
PS548.N7 R66 2001\
810.8′097475′09048—dc21   00-049605

Manufactured in the United States of America

To Colleen Patricia Burke Gould, my rock,
and Corey Patricia,
and Molly Catherine

Contents

Rick Bass

Rick Bass has authored more than eight books of fiction and nonfiction set in the outdoors, including Winter: Notes from Montana, The Ninemile Wolves, The Deer Pasture, In the Loyal Mountains, *and* Platte River. *Bass is one of America's finest writers; his articles and stories have appeared in national publications such as* Esquire, The Paris Review, *and* Outside *magazine and have been widely anthologized, appearing in* Best American Short Stories, O. Henry Prize Stories, Pushcart Prize, *and others. He lives in northern Montana.*

I think it can sometimes be a mistake for any writer or storyteller, or a writer's readers, to consider that that storyteller speaks "for the land" or for "the bear," or "the wolf," or "the otter," or "the loon." Everything in nature speaks through its actions for its own self with magnificent eloquence; there are only those of our species who either know how, or care, to listen, and those who do not—but certainly in the instance of this collection, I think the case can be made clearly that indeed most of these writers are speaking for the land.

I'm fascinated by the manner in which this book seems to be representative of a phase in the human community, a maturation of the many voices that have always been coming from this region, coming from every windblown shutter, crack, and crevice, as they come from nearly all strong or unique places—the partnership of landscape and human art or storytelling as inseparable as any other primal bond. The first voices were exploratory, establishing tentative borders and boundaries—sometimes fearful, other times reverential; but increasingly, then, as humans wove our own history in with the lives of the forests and rivers and animals, not merely celebratory but advocacy-based: assuming, like adolescents entering adulthood, a greater awareness of one's responsibilities, after having spent so many teenage years preening and braying about one's self-important rights.

I'm struck by the way in most if not all of these stories there is a graceful and tacit balance, an understanding, of the mature and dynamic relationship between our shared rights and responsibilities; and of the poignant, bittersweet realization—sometimes spoken, other times implicit—that not all resources are infinite or even renewable—wildness, or wilderness, chief among them.

Perhaps not all interests are represented here, nor all voices—surely there is undiscovered in the Adirondacks a runaway circus bear trainer hiding out with a story to tell, a manuscript as thick as a phone book; or a world champion kazoo player who fashions his or her instruments from the limbs of native birch; or a real estate subdivider who tithes all of his or her profits to Greenpeace—but just as surely there is evident in this collection the successful democratic attempt to include, rather than to exclude. As such, the book, while certainly about celebration, and informative about a broad spectrum of the ways-of-life of a region, is as representative of community dialogue, even when the correspondents are unaware of or unknown to each other, as any place could hope for. And this book is a fine sampler of tolerance, too, for what better defines tolerance than the presence of many and varied voices?

Despite the astounding diversity present in this great doorstop, boat-anchor of a project, I'm also interested in and both amused and comforted by what seems to me like a prevalence of the same redundant themes—reassured by them as one is by the constancy of themes among the four seasons, which, despite our having only four to choose from, nonetheless present us daily with an infinitude of variety.

As with the children's half-globe liquid-filled shake-up toys that one turns upside down and then rightside up in order to watch the snow falling upon some intricate winter-scene held in the palm of one's hand—the same scene seeming slightly different with each shake, and yet always comfortingly familiar—we see, again and again in these stories, the emergence of repeated elemental truths for the region.

Recurring messages in this collection include:

An affinity for the community of others, with community's delicate dance of not-too-far-away but not-too-close, either;

The affinity, no, the reliance, we have upon the nations of animals: bear, loon, otter, deer, moose;

The weather, certainly—always, here or anywhere, the weather, and the orchestra of the seasons, of which the Adirondacks are blessed with all four (or five, if one wants to count the extended mud season of March and April);

And the archetypal cycles, too, of extreme paucity resting often uneasily right next to astounding excess, in both the cycles of wild nature as well as the community of humans. Extravagant opulence looming right alongside extreme economic deprivation, with a kind of hand-to-mouth, hunter-gatherer hardscrabble existence commonplace for so many of the residents.

Other common themes, infinitely varied but all somehow familiar, include the natural tension between city rats and country rats. It's a number that almost anyone who knows the region hears murmuring through his or her bloodstream, the statistic that 90 million people live within a day's drive of this wilderness—and still another prevalent theme is that of the increasing political and civic engagement—the town meeting; the comment-and-response to management proposals; all the unpleasant, even tedious chores that are the true sweat-work of citizens living in a democracy that is built upon free speech and the absence of political or cultural oppression.

And again, in this collection, I propose, it is a sign of the maturation of a community—in this case, a very large community—that there is such evidence and instance of so many members willing to give, in addition to their taking: advocacy on behalf of a land that has, for better or for worse, accepted the speakers, the storytellers, into the land's place-among-things.

I am a resident of a similar backwoods, northcountry landscape, the Yaak Valley in northwest Montana, a place that is surely "wilder" than the Adirondacks, due as much as anything to having one-tenth the human population, and due also to a far greater abundance of the kinds of wild creatures that, in the words of Doug Peacock, "can kill and eat you." (The unprotected regions of the Yaak being country which, despite being wilder, has paradoxically no permanent protection for its grandeur and wildness whatsoever—no layer of security or forethought or planning; only reckless and impulsive youth, in that regard, or perhaps adolescence.) As such, I feel a shared appreciation for the buggy, swampy, rainy lands depicted herein, in which only a certain type of individual, not always attractive or even intelligent, is comfortable, much less drawn and committed to the place.

This book is again a celebration, and I sense both between the lines and from personal experience that the tales of darkness and despair are downplayed here—there's a real good reason those 90 million people keep the place at arm's length, a full day's drive away—and that in this collection, from a standpoint of verisimilitude, there's perhaps not quite enough description of the mental and physical depressions brought about by the yearly cumulative effects of too much precipitation and not enough sunlight; nor of the true and often humorless hordes of the many species of bloodsucking insects that can and do despoil entire seasons for every mammal in the woods, humankind included and perhaps foremost; nor of the rank hostility and baleful uncommunicativeness of many of the backcountry's inhabitants.

And perhaps that is as it should be, in a celebration; and anyway, there won't be any quick fixes for these things, if ever. There will for a long time, I suspect, continue to be troubling conflicts that attend us wherever we pause and then settle within sight and hearing of others of our kind. Why should the needs of humans in the Adirondacks, or the unprotected wilderness of Montana's Yaak, or any other wild place, be any different in that regard?

As long as there is big wild country—I mean, really big spaces—to buffer our tiny squabblings and differences, and our tiny, passionate declarations and defamations—all of which are, even in their most strident or eloquent moments, but small stepping stones across some broad and as yet not fully charted river of history—there will be dissent, failure, joy, hope, greed, worship, awe, community, despoliation, restoration. This book, I think, profiles that diversity well.

Evident and constant, then, from even a casual or entertaining reading of this brick of Adirondack history—the span of some twenty-five years held in our two hands like something almost geological—is the need, through it all, the flow of time, and the riding of humans upon its back, as if on some small raft being carried always along, that whether through foresight or planning or any other mechanism, we must keep the biggest, wildest places—the wilderness—intact, against which we can lean our backs during times of tribulation and experiment, as well as in times of celebration.

These are gardens, or cores, or anchor-points of what the land was like when we first came to it, and first began to be shaped and sculpted by it. Reminders of what we, as well as our predecessors, once felt, looking into a deep and dark forest, or at an uncut mountainside. A stillness and a resonance both, stirring in our hearts—one which often launches the viewer into song, if not worship; a landscape that can help perform again and again, day after day, one of the greatest and simplest of miracles, which is to inspire us to think about something other than our own selves, and our own hungers and fears and needs. The wilderness is, in this regard, nothing short of an utter blessing, and deserving, always, to be cared for and treated as such.

My gratitude goes to all the different correspondents in this mammoth testimony to the remembrance of this basic and necessary truth.

Jacqueline F. Day

Director, Adirondack Museum

The Adirondack Museum is located at the center of the Adirondack park, a vast mosaic of state and private land that forms the largest public park in the contiguous United States. Since 1894, close to half of the Adirondack Park's six million acres have been protected as "forever wild" by the New York State Constitution. The changing face of the Adirondacks as a wilderness is one of the central themes of the Adirondack Museum.

Since the museum opened to the public in 1957, its exhibitions and publications have explored the complex interaction between people and the land as well as changing cultural attitudes toward nature. The American experience of the wilderness has been, in part, defined in this region where the reality of every day life and work was transformed through the myth-making imagination of its artists, writers, and other observers.

Jim Gould, in the introduction to this publication, writes that the bedrock of place-based writing is commitment to a landscape. I think that this collection of new writing from the Adirondack mountains would have pleased the museum's founder, Harold K. Hochschild, who had a deep love for the mountains, and a lifelong interest in its people. Hochschild was the author of *Township 34*, one of the classic works of Adirondack history. He was also the chairman of Governor Rockefeller's Temporary Study Commission on the Future of the Adirondacks and a committed advocate on behalf of the Adirondack environment. Since 1957 the Adirondack Museum has sought to stimulate interest and curiosity in the Adirondacks by providing perspectives on the past and on the present.

My thanks to everyone involved in this publication. Special thanks go to editor Jim Gould and to the writers in these pages who speak for the land and enliven the dialogue about the Adirondacks and its people.

Jim Gould

Like any anthology, this one is no more than a literary snapshot in time. While comprehensive, it does not purport to be all inclusive. Its limitations and biases will be apparent to the careful reader. Still, it is my hope that the collection's shortcomings will move readers to identify and celebrate other worthy writers in the Adirondacks.

An editor's debts are many. I want to acknowledge the generosity and patience of each contributing writer. All agreed to be a part of this project without significant compensation.

The vision and support from the staff of Syracuse University Press as well as the Adirondack Museum, particularly from Jackie Day, director, and Alice Gilborn, publications editor, were abundant throughout the project.

The good folks at Paul Smith's College were helpful from the start, and their support was made manifest in ways too numerous to list. Special thanks for administrative assistance and research go to Kellie Tavernia and Lynn Whalen. Needless to say, without nurturing from my colleagues and the extended community associated with Paul Smith's, the College of the Adirondacks, this important work of culture and community would not have been realized. Adirondackers all, they include Jack and Mary Jean Burke, Jon Dallas, John Quenell, Sue Halpern, Frank and Jeanne Hutchins, Pete and Simone McConville, Michael Wilson, Ellen Rocco, Joan and Sandy Weill, Sue and Bill Sweeney, Neil Surprenant, Ted Mack, Curt Stager, Paul Sorgule, Stu Buchanan, Kathy and Sean McHugh, Dan Spada, Ray Curran, Sheila Hutt, Charlie Alexander, Kirk Peterson, Jim Tucker, Cali Brooks, Mike Rechlin, Naj Wikoff, Gary Chilson, Maurice Kenny, Craig and Ruth Smith, Brian Mann, Amy White, Nathalie Costa, Sam and Julie Churco, Connie Prickett, Nancie Battaglia and Ed Finnerty, Stephanie Ransom, Fritz and Janet Decker, Kate Lanigan, Heidi Kretser, Tim Tobin and Mary Roscoe, Andy Keal, Bruce and Connie Landon, Sarah Lewin, Jay and Joanne Swartz, Arlene Day, Lisa Grigoriadis, Anne Trachtenberg, and the late and much beloved Lynn Boillot. Special thanks to the Turners at With Pipe and Book, Jerold Pepper at the library of the Adirondack Museum, the folks at North Country School and Camp Treetops, and the dedicated members of the Adirondack Citizens Advisory Committee on the Feasibility of Wolf Reintroduction, especially Mike DiNunzio, Anne Green, Phil Hamel, Bill Hutchens, Peter O'Shea, Clarence Petty, Sheila Powers, Sonny Young, Nina Fascione, Bob Inslerman, John Green, Bob Brown, and Howie Cushing.

And let me not forget to thank the one author who has almost singlehandedly raised the national profile of the Adirondacks. Bill McKibben has generously shared insight, enthusiasm, and many miles of trails in the dozen or so years of our friendship. It's a debt I'll not likely be able to repay anytime soon.

Finally, I owe an enormous debt of gratitude to Constance "Mike" Quenell, project manager and copy editor extraordinaire, who somehow kept thousands of details in line as we marched toward our deadline.

The Case for a True Adirondack Literature

What is Adirondack literature? Paul Jamieson, editor of *The Adirondack Reader*, the first comprehensive anthology of writing on the Adirondacks, answered this question by gathering Adirondack writings from many genres—essays, letters, journals, travel sketches, memoirs, and fiction. The 525-page anthology has entries from ninety writers, on an assortment of topics, issues, and settings, ranging from Champlain's first view of the Adirondacks in 1609 to literary works that date into the late 1970s.

While the Jamieson anthology is exhaustive in its representation of writings *about* the Adirondacks, no more than four writers of the nearly 100 writers included are or were full-time residents of the region.

Does an authentic regional literature demand some kind of residency requirement?

Just for the sake of argument, let's say yes. In the last few decades, there's been a surge in regional publishing and writing in the United States. Literary works created by resident writers, to generalize, seem to possess a greater degree of authority, knowledge, texture, and experience, and are rooted in a distinctive setting.

The bedrock of so-called place-based writing is, above all, a commitment to a landscape and many of its elements—environmental, economic, cultural, and social, among others. "Commitment" is not used lightly here, as the level of commitment often reveals the depth of the quality and authenticity of the writing. In terms of commitment, it is equivalent to the difference between dating and marriage. Taking the metaphor a step further, Jamieson's anthology of Adirondack writing is akin to nearly 500 pages of one-night stands.

Since 1982, when Jamieson's anthology was published, evidence of a new place-based literature can be found in the Adirondacks. A resident population of writers has gained regional and national prominence using the Adirondacks as their primary subject matter or, at the very least, as a significant point of departure.

These writers find their subjects in their jobs, which reveal the vagaries of making a living in a largely inhospitable landscape. Subjects also include the compelling environmental arguments of Bill McKibben, rooted in the day-to-day concerns the author makes so vivid writing from his home near North Creek. There's the private and public struggle of finding balance between solitude and community that we see in the writings of Sue Halpern, Jon Dallas, and Anne LaBastille. And then, of course, there's just the written record of life here in these mountains: bag groceries with Betsy Folwell, paddle flatwater with Chris Shaw, join Tom Hughes in celebration of long winters, and explore with Curt Stager the behavior of black bears in the north woods.

The power of the written word is no stranger to the Adirondacks; it has had perhaps as much to do in shaping this landscape as did the Wisconsin Ice Shield. In 1837, the published reports by Ebenezer Emmons of his party's first known ascent of Mount Marcy brought an increase in travelers to the High Peaks and the central lakes region of the Adirondacks. William H. H. Murray's *Adventures in the Wilderness* in 1869 incited the new middle classes to escape the chaotic, smoky, and garbage-strewn cities of the Northeast and return to what they thought were their wild, pioneering roots. Fools or not, Murray's readers brought a kind of nature-based tourism to the mountains, installing arguably the first truly sustaining economic engine in the region.

Essays and features in the mainstream press by Charles Dudley Warner, George Washington Sears, Charles Hallock, Charles Fenno Hoffman, Seneca Ray Stoddard, and others—especially in opinion-shapers such as *Harper's Magazine, Atlantic Monthly,* and the *New York Times*—emphasized a backyard frontier; a wilderness that was wild, yet accessible; and a sparsely populated mountain region full of colorful guides, resourceful entrepreneurs, and archetypal woodsmen.

The message to their readers was clear: see the Adirondacks. But just as powerful was the subtext: save the Adirondacks. State surveyor Verplanck Colvin's vivid reports from the field gave the scientific backbone to his fellow writers' often-romanticized, yet compelling letters, editorials, and travel essays and sketches.

The result, of course, was the establishment of a park that's not quite a park, a wilderness that's not quite a wilderness. The numbers are undeniable, however. The six-million-acre Adirondack Park is larger than the combined acreage of Yosemite, Yellowstone, and Glacier national parks. With only 130,000 year-round residents in a stretch of woods larger than Massachusetts, it is as sparsely populated as any region in the continental United States. The residents of Saranac Lake, the Adirondacks' largest village—there are no cities—number fewer than 5,000. And then there's the water: more than 3,000 lakes and ponds and more than 15,000 miles of rivers and streams. And all of this only a day's drive from many of North America's largest population centers, where millions of readers thirst for places more distinct, sustaining, exemplary, and peaceful than their own homes in America's suburban and exurban landscape.

So why do the Adirondacks suddenly have, in just a few decades, the beginnings of an authentic regional literature? This may be due to a number of simple socioeconomic and cultural circumstances—like a larger, more stable professional and middle class. But I think there's something else going on here, too. This nascent regional literature is primarily the result of the fact that the Adirondack Park, which has seen sustained year-round human population centers for barely four generations, is beginning to mature as a culture, community, and region.

Culture, that amorphous but very real accumulation of a community's behaviors, beliefs, and the other products of its thought and work, has taken root in the region during the last quarter-century. And the institutions in the Adirondacks that foster culture have begun to emerge and thrive and help identify the landscape and its community's values. At the same time, they provide refuge and nourishment to those agents, observers, and recorders of culture, our writers.

In the Adirondacks those institutions suddenly, historically speaking, are all around us and have developed a solid and sustaining maturity. They include the Adirondack Mountain Club, which in the last decade celebrated its seventy-fifth anniversary; the Sagamore Institute, now more than twenty-five years old; Paul Smith's College, which recently celebrated its fiftieth commencement, and the Adirondack Museum, recently marking its fortieth birthday. The Lake Placid Center for the Arts, Pendragon Theater, the Adirondack Lakes Center for the Arts, and Historic Saranac Lake are all more than twenty years old now. Non-government organizations and not-for-profits such as the Adirondack Economic Development Council, the Adirondack North Country Association, the Adirondack Nature Conservancy, the Adirondack Council, the Association of Adirondack Towns and Villages, and the Adirondack Local Government Review Board are, after a few decades of awkward institutional adolescence, emerging into a more mature adulthood.

Let me emphasize just how young these community institutions are: follow the Hudson River from its source on a shoulder of Mount Marcy and only 300 miles downriver—in the same watershed—is Columbia University, which was founded in 1754. That's almost a century before Emmons climbed, measured, and named Mount Marcy, a full century and then some before the Adirondacks were surveyed and mapped by Verplank Colvin.

The other significant development in the last two decades has been the growth of publications featuring writing about the Adirondacks. Nationally, there's been greater coverage of the region in prominent magazines such as *Outside, Audubon, Natural History, Sierra, Backpacker, Orion, National Geographic,* and the *New York Times Magazine.*

Equally significant, the regional bimonthly *Adirondack Life* has developed into a perennial award-winning magazine and has given a consistent and quality forum for writers in the Adirondacks. Current and past editors Jeff Kelley, Chris Shaw, Tom Hughes, and most recently Betsy Folwell, have identified and nurtured emerging as well as established voices. The exceptional quality of the feature writing and essays is underscored by remarkable photography, illustration, and design. *Adirondac,* the magazine of the Adirondack Mountain Club, contributes similarly, although by contrast most of its contributors are unpaid and fledging. The small literary magazine, *Blueline,* was founded in 1979 in Blue Mountain Lake, in the central Adirondacks,

and published there for ten years. Although it is now edited from outside the Adirondacks at Potsdam State University and does not publish
solely Adirondack letters, it has also contributed to the region's literary
fabric. And it may be too early to tell, but two other publications—*The
Adirondack Explorer*, a monthly news magazine based in Saranac Lake,
and the new literary journal, *Barkeater: The Adirondack Review*, edited by Professor Jon Dallas at Paul Smith's College—could certainly
add greater depth and variety to Adirondack letters.

Equally important has been the role of two regional book publishers—North Country Books and Syracuse University Press. Each has
published dozens of titles focusing on the Adirondacks, and, with the
Adirondack Museum, Syracuse University Press, has been ambitious
in its aim to promote the history, politics, literature, and arts of the
region.

Although a different medium, North Country Public Radio, the
National Public Radio affiliate based in Canton, New York, covers the
Adirondacks with transmitters and is the only Park-wide media source
for daily news and community information. The station, understaffed
and underpaid like most public radio outfits, has done a remarkable job
of nurturing a local culture, particularly offering another outlet for regional writers. In 1998, they marked their thirtieth anniversary, and a
year later they opened the Adirondack Radio News Bureau at Paul
Smith's College. For the first time, a full-time radio journalist covers issues of culture, economics, and environment in the Adirondacks with a
degree of thoroughness and timeliness yet to be seen within the Blue
Line.

The emerging body of Adirondack literature mirrors the regional
writing—and greater awareness of place—we now see blossoming
among writers across the nation. Still, valuing community, place, and
landscape remains a minority position in the face of the dominant
mainstream culture. In other words, "local," "regional," and "provin-
cial" are often terms of lesser value, even derision, while anything national, international, and global is to be granted honor and prestige.
Even so, some eloquent voices have emerged from the hinterlands in
defense of those things closer to home.

In a collection of essays on the study of place in America entitled
Rooted in the Land, William Vitek writes that "generally missing in [a

discussion about preserving landscapes and species as well as small rural communities] is any mention of the places where we live as biological communities or the importance of human communities rooted in a storied landscape."

Kentucky farmer and writer Wendell Berry makes a similar point, arguing that really the only concern for any writer are things important to the author's community, no matter where that community is. Furthermore, as a writer, the most pressing challenge, he says, is to make readers connect with the writer's community.

One of Berry's disciples, Wes Jackson, puts it another way, calling on writers to "become native" to their landscape. In Jackson's most recent book, he writes, "It has never been our national goal to become native to this place. It has never seemed necessary even to begin such a journey. And now, almost too late, we perceive its necessity."

In the Adirondacks, what is beginning to set the region's body of literature apart is the compelling influence of community and commitment. We now see the landscape's human communities beginning to understand in a more complex and mature way who they are and what their collective and individual roles are in the viability of both the human and natural communities inside the Blue Line. In other words, they're becoming more vested, more rooted to the landscape.

How are the writers responding? The writers of the Adirondacks are there helping to uncover, define, and articulate those values and roles. Does residency automatically convey literary legitimacy or create skilled and compelling writers? Certainly not.

Does lack of year-round residency preclude compelling writing? No. (And, in fact, several examples are included here.) But the overwhelming evidence is that many of the writers in the region are writing with more authority and entitlement. And in contrast to the common usage of the term in American universities and colleges, these writers are the more authentic writers-in-residence.

With this anthology, they are welcoming you into their homes, onto their land, and into their communities. Enjoy their good will.

Rooted in Rock

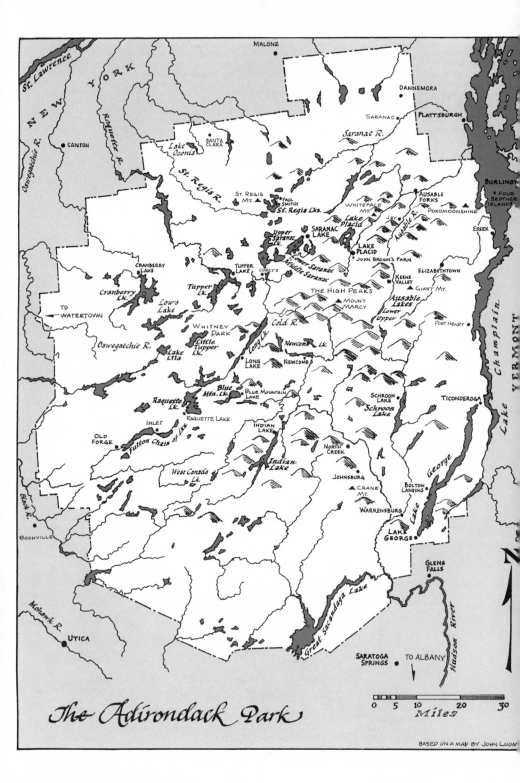

The Adirondack Park

BASED ON A MAP BY JOHN LUON

Christopher Angus

On the whole, Chris Angus would rather be paddling a canoe than doing just about anything else. Angus's first book-length work, Reflections from Canoe Country *(Syracuse University Press, 1997), grew out of his work as a columnist on environmental issues for newspapers in and around the Adirondacks. His work has appeared in the* New York Times, Albany Times-Union, Adirondack Life, Canoe, American Forests, *and other publications. A life-long resident of the Adirondack region, Angus is currently serving as the book review editor of* Adirondac *magazine and is writing a biography of Clarence Petty. Angus and his wife, Kathy, live in Canton, New York.*

The selections reprinted here first appeared in Reflections from Canoe Country.

Day Trip

I sit on the sand, swatting occasionally at August deerflies. My companions and I are deep in the Adirondacks, on the banks of one of its most popular rivers, the Raquette. The flies are of no account, for I am absorbing tales of these woods told by one whose memory stretches back four-fifths of a century. Clarence Petty, second-generation Adirondack guide, former member of the Civilian Conservation Corps (CCC), forest ranger, member of Governor Rockefeller's 1968 Commission on the Future of the Adirondacks, and long-time chronicler of and advocate for wilderness preservation in these woods, is clearly in his element.

Yet even as I listen, I cannot help thinking of another wilderness

1

trip, one immortalized by the writer John McPhee. In *Encounters with the Archdruid*, McPhee recounts his journey through the Grand Canyon with conservation's guiding light of the past fifty years, David Brower. How similar, I think, must be the reservoirs of experience of men like David Brower and Clarence Petty. And how very rare they are.

Floating the Colorado with the nation's preeminent dam builder as Brower did on that trip was symbolic of the many encounters that men like David Brower and Clarence Petty have had to face. Brower hates all dams because they destroy rivers. During the many arguments that ebbed and flowed during that Colorado float, Brower said: "I'm prepared to say, here and now, that we should touch nothing more in the lower forty-eight. Whether it's an island, a river, a mountain wilderness—nothing more. What has been left alone until now should be left alone permanently."

Those words might sound extreme to some, but, in fact, they were said a quarter of a century ago. A great deal of wilderness has been paved over since then.

Our day trip begins under clear skies at Corey's, the summer colony that had once been the center of operations for a handful of Adirondack guides, including Clarence Petty's father, at the turn of the century. From here, we pass through Stony Creek Ponds, down Stony Creek to the Raquette River, and on past Follensby Pond outlet to the boat launch on Route 3 outside Tupper Lake.

The excuse for this trip, as if one is needed, is to gather a handful of ardent Adirondack advocates together to explore the section of the river that connects with Follensby Pond. Privately owned and at risk of being broken up by developers, the fourteen-thousand-acre Follensby Park tract has become a symbol in the fight to preserve the Adirondack wilderness.

Our group is feeling somewhat relieved, almost giddy. Following three long, hard years battling to preserve endangered pieces of the Park like Follensby, we had finally witnessed the passage of the Environmental Protection Act of 1993 by the New York State legislature.

It is an imperfect bill. Precariously financed and reliant on a real estate transfer tax that is in turn reliant on the questionable resurgence of the state's economy, the Act nevertheless will allow the governor to give a list of proposed land acquisitions to the legislature every year as part of the budget process. Properties like Follensby Pond, Whitney Park, and the Heurich estate on Lake Champlain will be given priority by the state.

However, compromise at this level of state government can lead to some very creative results. Originally, Governor Cuomo wanted a fund of $271 million a year, the Assembly had sought $248 million, and the Senate Republicans proposed $100 million. What we will have in the first year will be $25 million and not just for land acquisition but for landfill closure, recycling, waterfront revitalization, historic preservation and parks, and a host of other projects.

But the deal is done for now, and we are canoeing with Clarence Petty. Victories in the battle to preserve the Adirondacks have been few and far between in recent years. We are here for fun and for at least a brief celebration of the likely saving of Follensby Pond. (Since that writing, the owner of Follensby Pond has withdrawn his offer to sell to the state and the future of the tract is now very much in doubt.)

Clarence is describing his transformation from avid hunter to, as he grew older, one who has greater compassion for the animals of the forest. Having witnessed and guided countless hunting and fishing expeditions in the early days of the century, he is a receptacle of Adirondack lore—the best sort of receptacle, one who loves nothing more than to spin the narrative for the enrichment of his companions.

I close my eyes and see clearly the Adirondacks of the 1920s as Clarence regales us with stories of twenty-pound trout, of early loggers and catastrophic forest fires. He tells of a freshly killed deer many decades ago that raised its head long enough to look its killer in the eyes and shame him into giving up the hunt forever. Could that hunter have been Clarence, I wonder? And was that long-ago shot the one that spawned his own enlarged understanding of the wild?

Speculation. I later read an interview with Clarence in Charles Brumley's fine history, *Guides of the Adirondacks*. In it, Clarence names the hunter in question, one Carlos Whitney, a huge man who had shot many deer. "It just shows you how people change," Clarence said. "I see this happening in people as they get older. I think they have maybe a greater respect for life than the young people."

Later, on the river, I stay close to his canoe. I want to see how someone who has paddled for more than eighty years handles his craft. As I suspected, his skill is masterful. Once, when I was new both to paddling and to the Adirondacks, my partner and I were having lunch on the shore when a beautiful cedar canoe came round the bend. Its occupants were both silver-haired, but they paddled with such complete serenity and efficiency, and in such relaxed harmony with the river, that we watched them go by in a kind of trance. They seemed almost a part of the woods, as though we had inadvertently witnessed a moose and her calf swimming upriver, rather than two men paddling. My friend broke the silence after their passing to remark, "Someday, I hope we will look like that."

That is how Clarence looks in a canoe. He belongs there. Perhaps he was born in a canoe or maybe a guideboat—it was known to happen among the Indians and the voyageurs, and, I suspect, the early Adirondack guides.

Following our lunch break, Clarence glances upward and suggests that we might want to hurry along a bit. He pulls his blue raincoat out and puts it on. In response to someone's question, he smiles and says, "Gore-Tex. You wouldn't believe what this jacket cost. Never would have purchased it myself. It was a gift, though, so I have to use it."

We launch our canoes and, sure enough, within twenty minutes the thunderstorm descends upon us with a vengeance. In an instant, the river is transformed. Sheets of rain pelt down driven by fierce gusts. Clarence is unfazed, paddling steadily, the rain dripping off the hood of his Gore-Tex parka.

We are not experiencing this storm alone. During the lunch stop, a group, including several very young girls, passes us. One of their canoes holds a novel collection of three paddlers, the middle of whom sits facing the stern, actually paddling against the others. The stern paddler is one of the youngest I have ever seen controlling a large craft. She cannot be more than eight or ten. Still, she seems to know how to handle her paddle, even if her placement of the crew is somewhat suspect.

I reflect upon these young girls, perhaps starting out on their own Adirondack journeys of discovery. They have much to learn, and I envy them the years ahead. The Adirondacks they will experience may little resemble those described by our guide this day. But unknown to them, they have made a good start. They have shared a thunderstorm with an Adirondack original, Clarence Petty.

The Osgood River

When I first saw the Osgood River, I was not impressed. Glimpsed a few times off the side of Route 30, it appeared small and too hemmed in by alders for my taste. But first impressions are deceiving.

As I paddled the little river that first time, my sense of completeness grew by leaps and bounds. Here was a river that met all of my requirements for an enjoyable paddle—a meandering stream and variable terrain, pristine surroundings, plentiful wildlife, and unexpected discoveries. I have yet to meet a more modest stream with more to offer. It remains one of my favorite trips anywhere.

The Osgood is the main feeder of Meacham Lake and is just fourteen miles long. It meanders through tamarack swamps and past steep piny eskers. There is a variety of vegetation, plenty of bird life, and interesting geological features. But the crowning glory of this little stream is the series of ponds whose short outlets cut through the esker. I have rarely experienced a greater sense of discovery in the Adirondacks than when I have followed a tiny side flow into one of the lonely ponds. Completely surrounded by the steep-sided eskers, these quiet pools boast magnificent stands of white pine and bestow a feeling of isolation that gives one a sense of the primeval.

A few years ago, I was camping beside one of these ponds with my wife. Our site was high above the water and the view we had out over the surface of the misting lake was intoxicating. As we sat staring out at the last, lingering, blue light before nightfall, drinking in the utter silence, we were nearly scared out of our wits by the screech of an owl that swooped down over our heads.

The Osgood can be navigated all summer long, though I prefer autumn or early spring before bug season. My partner and I once started from the highest possible point of navigation. As soon as we were fully committed to the quickly moving current, the river narrowed until alders from each side blended together, forming a tunnel. The word "tunnel" is an embellishment, for that implies an opening. In fact, we spent an unpleasant thirty minutes blasting through alders, our faces scratched and clothing torn. I wouldn't try it again.

Yet I so love this little river that I always hesitate a moment before recommending it to friends. After all, there are only so many good places to pitch a tent, and though the trip can easily be made in half a day, I much prefer to take longer and immerse myself in the surroundings. But, in fact, I have never met another soul, though this no doubt has much to do with when I choose to go there—early or late in the year and always midweek.

I am usually of two minds when informing others about my favorite spots—for obvious reasons. Telling a friend is one thing. Broadcasting a public notice through the media, another altogether. Still, I have known few paddlers who did not exhibit meticulous habits in the wild. Most have a reverence for such places and generally leave nothing behind them but ripples.

There will always be the exception, of course. But I firmly believe these exceptions are worth the cost to the alternative of closing the rivers completely. Rivers completely cut off from the eye of man, in perverse fashion, may suffer even greater depredations. In short order, they lose their admiring public. With the loss of awareness comes neglect. Large corporate owners and lumbering firms have been known to sell off such gems to developers at a moment's notice. Although the "forever wild" amendment has stood many challenges over the last century, vigilance will always be necessary, for little subject to the whim of man is truly forever—witness the present eagerness to drill for oil in Alaskan lands many had thought protected from such folly.

A few years ago, Earth First!, the radical environmental group, declared that the Five Ponds Wilderness Area south of Cranberry Lake should be completely off-limits to man. I could not disagree more strongly. I believe it is possible for people to visit these areas with minimal damage if—*if*—they are not allowed to use motorized vehicles and if other backcountry rules, such as proper disposal of wastes, careful tending of fires, and so forth, are followed.

But if no one is allowed to see a beautiful place, how long can it be before there is no one left to care about it? Out of sight, out of mind. Then the only people who know about the spot are those who disobey the rules and go there on their dirt bikes and in their 4 x 4s. A pristine river that people can see develops fierce partisans who will fight to keep it that way. A river that no one can see only develops developers.

Russell Banks

Russell Banks has been called one of America's finest fiction writers, and in the last decade he's been on somewhat of a roll. Three of his novels— Continental Drift, Affliction, *and* The Sweet Hereafter—*have been published to wide critical praise and translated into award-winning films. The author of more than a dozen books, Banks most recently taught writing at Princeton University. During the last two decades, he has been, with his wife, Chase Twichell, a seasonal resident of Keene Valley. There, in the shadow of the High Peaks of the Adirondacks, he was smitten with the Adirondacks; it soon became his permanent home as well as a setting for much of his recent fiction.*

His novel Rule of the Bone *(Minerva, 1995) is the story of a troubled youth in Ausable Forks, who finds his world populated with adults who are absent, violent, or preoccupied with finding their own way in a landscape that has little economic promise. His most recent book,* The Angel on the Roof *(HarperCollins, 2000), is a collection of short stories, many of which are set in the Adirondacks.*

In an another novel, excerpted below, we meet the personal injury lawyer Mitchell Stephens from The Sweet Hereafter *(HarperCollins, 1991), who has invited himself into the town of Sam Dent, a fictitious community in the northern Adirondacks that is coping with the deaths of many of its children from a recent school bus crash. The story's point of view, as well as its moral center, shifts throughout the novel to other voices in this small community, including the school bus driver, the father of two of the victims, and a teenaged girl who survives the crash only to find herself confined to a wheelchair.*

The second excerpt below, is from what many critics have called

7

Banks' most ambitious and compelling work—the story of the abolitionist John Brown. His farm outside of Lake Placid was the base from which Brown planned many of his antislavery activities, including those that resulted in his raid in 1859 on the government arsenal at Harpers Ferry. Cloudsplitter (HarperCollins, 1998), narrated by Brown's last surviving son, Owen, is a work of imagination based on historic fact, a recreation that is as much about race, fanaticism, and faith as it is about fathers and sons.

Mitchell Stephens, Esquire

Excerpt

Angry? Yes, I'm angry; I'd be a lousy lawyer if I weren't. I suppose it's as if I've got this permanent boil on my butt and can't quite sit down. Which is not the same, you understand, as being hounded by greed; although I can see, of course, that it probably sometimes looked like greed to certain individuals who were not lawyers, when they saw a person like me driving all the way up there to the Canadian border, practically, saw me camping out in the middle of winter in a windy dingy little motel room for weeks at a time, bugging the hell out of decent people who were in the depths of despair and just wanted to be left alone. I can understand that.

But it wasn't greed that put me there; it's never been greed that sends me whirling out of orbit like that. It's anger. What the hell, I'm not ashamed of it. It's who I am. I'm not proud of it, either, but it makes me useful, at least. Which is more than you can say for greed.

That's what people don't get about negligence lawyers—good negligence lawyers, I mean, the kind who go after the sloppy fat cats with their corner offices and end up nailing their pelts to the wall. People immediately assume we're greedy, that it's money we're after, people call us ambulance-chasers and so on, like we're the proctologists of the profession, and, yes, there's lots of those. But the truth is, the good ones, we'd make the same moves for a single shekel as for a ten-million-dollar settlement. Because it's anger that drives us and delivers us. It's not any kind of love, either—love for the underdog or the victim, or whatever you want to call them. Some litigators like to claim that. The losers.

No, what it is, we're permanently pissed off, the winners, and practicing law is a way to be socially useful at the same time, that's all. It's like a discipline; it organizes and controls us; probably keeps us from being homicidal. A kind of Zen is what. Some people equally pissed off are able to focus their rage by becoming cops or soldiers or martial arts instructors; those who become lawyers, however, especially litigators like me, are a little too intelligent, or maybe too intellectual is all, to become cops. (I've known some pretty smart cops, but not many intellectual ones.) So instead of learning how to break bricks and two-by-fours with our hands or bust chain-snatchers in subways, we sneak off to law school and put on three-piece suits and come roaring out like banshees, all teeth and claws and fire and smoke.

Certainly we get paid well for it, which is a satisfaction, yes, but not a motivation, because the real satisfaction, the true motivation, is the carnage and the smoldering aftermath and the trophy heads that get hung up on the den wall. I love it.

That's why I spent most of six months up there in Sam Dent, practically becoming a citizen. Not my idea of a winter vacation, believe me. But anytime I hear about a case like that school bus disaster up there, I turn into a heat-seeking missile, homing in on a target that I know in my bones is going to turn out to be some bungling corrupt state agency or some multinational corporation that's cost-accounted the difference between a ten-cent bolt and a million-dollar out-of-court settlement and has decided to sacrifice a few lives for the difference. They do that, work the bottom line; I've seen it play out over and over again, until you start to wonder about the human species. They're like clever monkeys, that's all. They calculate ahead of time what it will cost them to assure safety versus what they're likely to be forced to settle for damages when the missing bolt sends the bus over a cliff, and they simply choose the cheaper option. And it's up to people like me to make it cheaper to build the bus with that extra bolt, or add the extra yard of guardrail, or drain the quarry. That's the only check you've got against them. That's the only way you can ensure moral responsibility in this society. Make it cheaper.

So that winter morning when I picked up the paper and read about this terrible event in a small town upstate, with all those kids lost, I knew instantly what the story was; I knew at once that it wasn't an "accident" at all. There are no accidents. I don't even know what the word means, and never trust anyone who says he does. I knew that somebody somewhere had made a decision to cut a corner in order to save a few pennies, and now the state or the manufacturer of the bus or the town, somebody, was busy lining up a troop of smoothies to negotiate with a bunch of grief-stricken bumpkins a settlement that wouldn't displease the accountants. I packed a bag and headed north, like I said, pissed off.

Sam Dent is a pretty town, actually. It's not Aspen or Vail, maybe, and it sure isn't Saint Bart's or Mustique, where frankly I'd much rather have been at that time of year, but the landscape was attractive and strangely stirring. I'm not a scenery freak like my ex-wife, Klara, who has orgasms over sunsets and waterfalls and not much else, but once in a great while I go someplace and look up and see where I am, and it's unexpectedly beautiful to me: my stomach tightens, and my pulse races, and this powerful blend of fear and excitement comes over me, like something dangerous is about to happen. It's almost sexual.

Anyhow, the town of Sam Dent and the mountains and forests that surrounded it, they gave me that feeling. I grew up in Oak Park, Illinois, and have spent my entire adult life in New York City. I'm an urban animal, basically; I care more about people than landscape. And although I have sojourned in rural parts quite a bit (I've spent months at a time in Wounded Knee, in eastern Washington, in Alabama, where I won a big asbestosis case, in the coal-mining region of West Virginia, and so on), I can't say the landscape of those places particularly moved me. They were places, that's all. Interchangeable chunks of the planet. Yes, I needed to learn a whole lot about each of them in order to pursue my case effectively, but in those other cases my interest in the landscape was more pragmatic, you might say, than personal. Strictly professional.

Here in Sam Dent, however, it somehow got personal. It's dark up there, closed in by mountains of shadow and a blanketing early nightfall, but at the same time the space is huge, endless, almost like being at sea—you feel like you're reading one of those great long novels by whatsername, Joyce Carol Oates, or Theodore Dreiser, that make you feel simultaneously surrounded by the darkness and released into a world much larger than any you've dealt with before. It's a landscape that controls you, sits you down and says, Shut up, pal, I'm in charge here.

They have these huge trees everywhere, on the mountains, of course, but down in the valleys and in town, too, and surrounding the houses, even outside my motel room; they've got white pine and spruce and hemlock and birches thick as a man, and the wind blows through them constantly. And since there's very little noise of any other kind—almost no people, remember, and few cars, no sirens howling, no jackhammers slamming, and so forth—the thing you hear most is the wind blowing in the trees. From September to June, the wind comes roaring out of Ontario all the way from Saskatchewan or someplace weird like that, steady and hard and cold, with nothing to stop or slow it until it hits these mountains and the trees, which, like I say, are everywhere.

What they call the Adirondack Park, you understand, is no small roadside park, no cutesy little campground with public toilets and showers—I mean, we're talking six million acres of woods, mountains, and lakes, we're talking a region the size of the state of Vermont, the biggest damn park in the country—and most of the people who live there year round are scattered in little villages in the valleys, living on food stamps and collecting unemployment, huddling close to their fires and waiting out the winter, until they can go back outdoors and repair the damage the winter caused.

It's a hard place, hard to live in, hard to romanticize. But, surprisingly, not hard to love—because that's what I have to call the feeling it evokes, this strange combination of fear and awe I'm talking about, even in someone like me.

That wasn't what I expected, though. When I first drove up there, the day after the school bus went over, I was astonished by what I saw. Upstate New York, to me, had always been Albany, with maybe a little Rip Van Winkle, Love Canal, and Woodstock tossed in; but this was wilderness, practically. Like Alaska. Suddenly, I'm thinking *Last of the Mohicans.* "Forest primeval," I'm thinking. America before the arrival of the white man.

I'm driving along the Northway above Lake George between these high sheer cliffs with huge sheets of ice on them, and I look off to the side into the woods, and the woods come banging right back at me, a dense tangle of trees and undergrowth that completely resists penetration, and I start hoping my car doesn't break down. This is not Bambi territory. It's goddamn dark in there, with bears and bobcats and moose. Ten thousand coyotes, I read in the *Times*. Sasquatches, probably.

Of course, it was dead of winter then, that first time, and there was five or six feet of snow over everything, and daytime temps that got stuck below zero for weeks in a row, which only made the woods and the mountains more ominous. Trees, rocks, snow, and ice—and, until I turned off the Northway and started down those narrow winding roads into the villages, no houses, no sign of people. It was scary, but it was also very beautiful. No way around it.

Then I began to see the first signs of people—and I mean poor people here. Not like in the city, of course, not like Harlem or Bedford-Stuyvesant, where you feel that the poor are imprisoned, confined by invisible wire fences, life-long prisoners of the rich, who live and work in the high-rises outside. No wonder they call them ghettos. They ought to call them reservations.

Up here, though, the poor are kept out, and it's the rich who stay inside the fence and only in the summer months. It's like Ultima Thule or someplace beyond the pale, and most of the people who live here year round are castoffs, tossed out into the back forty and made to forage in the woods for their sustenance and shelter, grubbing nuts and berries, while the rest of us snooze warmly inside the palisade, feet up on the old hassock, brandy by our side, *Wall Street Journal* unfolded on our lap, good dog Tighe curled up by the fire.

I'm exaggerating, of course, but only slightly, because that is how you feel when you cruise down these roads in your toasty Mercedes and peer out at the patched-together houses with flapping plastic over the windows and sagging porches and woodpiles and rusting pickup trucks and junker cars in front, boarded-up roadside diners and dilapidated motels that got bypassed by the turnpike that Rockefeller built for the downstate Republican tourists and the ten-wheeler truckers lugging goods between New York City and Montreal. It's amazing how poor people who live in distant beautiful places always think that a six-lane highway or an international airport will bring tourists who will solve all their problems, when inevitably the only ones who get rich from it live elsewhere. The locals end up hating the tourists, outsiders, foreigners—rich folks who employ the locals now as part-time servants, yardmen, waitresses, gamekeepers, fix-it men. Money that comes from out of town always returns to its source. With interest. Ask an African.

Sam Dent. Weird name for a town. So naturally the first thing I ask when I register at a sad little motel in town is "Who the hell was Sam Dent?"

This rather attractive tall doe-eyed woman in a reindeer sweater and baggy jeans was checking me in, Risa Walker, who I did not know at the time was one of those parents who had lost a child in the so-called accident. I might not have been so flippant otherwise. She said, "He once owned most of the land in this town and ran a hotel or something." She had that flat expressionless voice that I should have recognized as the voice of a parent who has lost a child. "Long time ago," she added. Like it was the good old days. (Good for Sam, I'll bet, who probably died peacefully in his sleep in his Fifth Avenue mansion.)

She gave me the key to my room, number 3, and asked would I be staying longer than one night.

"Hard to say." I passed her my credit card, and she took the imprint. I was hoping that tomorrow I'd find a place in town or nearby, maybe a Holiday Inn or a Marriott. This motel was definitely on the downhill slide and had been for years—no restaurant or bar, a small dark room with scarred furniture and sagging bedsprings, a shower that looked as if it spat rusty lukewarm water for seconds before turning cold.

It turned out there was no other place in town to stay, and as I needed to be close to the scene of the crime, so to speak, I ended up staying at the Walkers' motel throughout those winter and spring months and into the summer, every time I was in Sam Dent, even when things got a little ticklish between me and Risa and her husband, Wendell. It never got that ticklish, but when the divorce started coming on, I was giving her advice and not him. Throughout, I kept the room on reserve, not that there was ever any danger of its being taken, and paid for the entire period, whether I used it or not. It was the least I could do.

The most I could do for the Walkers was represent them in a negligence suit that compensated them financially for the loss of their son, Sean. And that's only part of it, the smaller part. I could also strip and hang the hide of the sonofabitch responsible for the loss of their son—which just might save the life of some other boy riding to school in some other small American town.

That was my intention anyhow. My mission, you say.

Every year, though, I swear I'm not going to take any more cases involving children. No more dead kids. No more stunned grieving parents who really only want to be left alone to mourn in the darkness of their homes, for God's sake, to sit on their kids' beds with the blinds drawn against the curious world outside and weep in silence as they contemplate their permanent pain. I'm under no delusions—I know that in the end a million-dollar settlement makes no real difference to them, that it probably only serves to sharpen their pain by constricting it with legal language and rewarding it with money, that it complicates the guilt they feel and forces them to question the authenticity of their own suffering. I know all that; I've seen it a hundred times.

It hardly seems worth it, right? Thanks but no thanks, right? And I swear, if that were the whole story, if the settlement were not a fine as well, if it were not a punishment that, though it can never fit the crime, might at least make the crime seem prohibitively expensive to the criminal, then, believe me, I would not pursue these cases. They humiliate me. They make me burn inside with shame. Win or lose, I always come out feeling diminished, like a cinder.

So I'm no Lone Ranger riding into town in my white Mercedes-Benz to save the local sheepherders from the cattle barons in black hats; I'm clear on that. And I don't burn myself out with these awful cases because it somehow makes me a better person. No, I admit it, I'm on a personal vendetta; what the hell, it's obvious. And I don't need a shrink to tell me what motivates me. A shrink would probably tell me it's because I myself have lost a child and now identify with chumps like Risa and Wendell Walker and that poor sap Billy Ansel, and Wanda and Hartley Otto. The victims. Listen, identify with the victims and you become one yourself. Victims make lousy litigators.

Simply, I do it because I'm pissed off, and that's what you get when you mix conviction with rage. It's a very special kind of anger, let's say. So I'm no victim. Victims get depressed and live in the there and then. I live in the here and now.

Besides, the people of Sam Dent are not unique. We've all lost our children. It's like all the children of America are dead to us. Just look at them, for God's sake—violent on the streets, comatose in the malls, narcotized in front of the TV. In my lifetime something terrible happened that took our children away from us. I don't know if it was the Vietnam war, or the sexual colonization of kids by industry, or drugs, or TV, or divorce, or what the hell it was; I don't know which are causes and which are effects; but the children are gone, that I know. So that trying to protect them is little more than an elaborate exercise in denial. Religious fanatics and superpatriots, they try to protect their kids by turning them into schizophrenics; Episcopalians and High Church Jews gratefully abandon their kids to boarding schools and divorce one another so they can get laid with impunity; the middle class grabs what it can buy and passes it on, like poisoned candy on Halloween; and meanwhile the inner-city blacks and poor whites in the boonies sell their souls with longing for what's killing everyone else's kids and wonder why theirs are on crack.

It's too late; they're gone; we're what's left.

And the best we can do for them, and for ourselves, is rage against what took them. Even if we can't know what it'll be like when the smoke clears, we do know that rage, for better or worse, generates a future. The victims are the ones who've given up on the future. Instead they've joined the dead. And the rest, look at them: unless they're enraged and acting on it, they're useless, unconscious; they're dead themselves and don't even know it.

Cloudsplitter

Excerpt

We had left just at sunrise, under a cloudless deep blue sky with the morning star and a half-moon floating high beside us in the south like a diamond and a silver bowl. The road was somewhat mudded from yesterday's rain, but Mr. Epps expected it to be dried out by the time we got up into the mountains again, where, he explained, the road crossed mostly stone anyhow. After passing through the tiny settlement of Keene—a post office, general store, log church, tavern, and a half-dozen log houses huddled together and guarded by mangy, long-haired dogs that all seemed to be related—we crossed the East Branch of the Au Sable River and made our way easefully uphill past freshly plowed fields, switch-backing towards the notch that cut through the range of mountains which lay between us and North Elba.

I had not liked Mr. Partridge, and I told Father that.

"No," he said, "nor did I. I suspect he beats the woman and secretly mistreats the old lady. The man bears watching, though. Somewhere along the line," he said, "I fear we'll have to cut him down."

This, of course, I could not then imagine, for no one seemed less likely to oppose us and our work with the Negroes of Timbuctoo in any focused way than the lazy young man in whose house we had just stayed. But when it came to knowing ahead of time who would oppose him, the Old Man could be downright prescient. On a dozen or more occasions, I had seen him accurately predict which man from a congregation or town, to keep us Browns from fulfilling our pledge to rid this nation of slavery, would threaten our very lives, which man would simply turn away and let us continue, and which man would join us in the work. The Lord's Work, as Father called it.

"Well," said I, "at least the fellow was hospitable to travelers."

"I would not call it that."

"We're ten people. Nine of us and Mister Epps, and he fed and housed us all, and he let us enjoy his fire and shelter our animals. I'd call that hospitable, Father." Though I did not like Mr. Partridge, in those days I sometimes found myself feeling sorry for individuals that the Old Man harshly condemned.

"You don't know him as well as I."

"Tell me, then. Tell me what you know about Mister Partridge that I don't. Beyond his marrying a homely woman for her property."

"Trust me, Owen."

"Father, I'm trying to!"

We walked in silence for a while, and then Father said, "You remember when he came out to help me hitch the team to the wagon, while the rest of you were tending the beeves and sheep, and Ruth and Mary and the girls were inside the house?"

"I saw him out there, yes."

"Well, the man came up to me and asked for payment for our food and lodging. He presented me with an itemized bill, written out." It was an embarrassment to Father. Not because he had no money to give Mr. Partridge, he said, but because he had not expected it. If he had anticipated Mr. Partridge's charges, he would have negotiated an acceptable arrangement beforehand, and failing that, we would have camped someplace alongside the river. Mr. Partridge had surprised Father, and he found himself painfully embarrassed by it.

We resumed walking uphill in silence, with the wagon and team of Morgans in Mr. Epps's capable hands, clambering along behind us, Mary and Ruth and the girls all together now on foot and cheerfully admiring the spectacular vistas opening up on either side of the track, and, at the rear, the boys and our small herd of livestock. The road made its circuitous, slowly ascending way along the back of a buttressing ridge. The morning sun was shining full upon our backs now, and it was as if yesterday's brief snowstorm had never occurred.

"I must make a confession, Owen," the Old Man went on. I said nothing, and he continued. "It concerns Mister Partridge. The man's request for payment confused me. I told him that I could not pay him with money, because I had none. I'm ashamed to say that I gave him instead the clock."

"The clock? Your grandfather's clock?"

"Yes."

I was astonished. Except for his chest of books, Great-Grandfather Brown's mantel clock was Father's most valued household possession. Made of cherrywood, it was a treasure that had been entrusted to Father's care years earlier by his own father; it was perhaps his only family heirloom. It made no sense to me. How could he have handed it over to Mr. Partridge so easily? And in exchange for so little—a single night's lodging.

"I simply retrieved the clock from the wagon, unwrapped it, and passed it over to him, and he accepted it as payment quite happily and at once carried it into his house. Where I hope Mary and Ruth did not see it."

I looked back at the women. Ruth held her half-sister Sarah's hand, and beside her Mary held Annie's; the two women were themselves holding hands and chatting lightly to one another. "No, I'm sure they didn't see Mister Partridge carrying off Great-Grandfather's clock. They seem very happy," I added uselessly.

"They will know it soon enough. Oh, I am a fool!" he pronounced. "A fool!"

I did not know what to say, so, as usual, said nothing. Most times, when I did not understand something that Father had done or said, it was because he had acted or spoken more wisely than I. At such times, for obvious reasons, my best course was to remain silent and await the arrival of understanding. In this case, however, the Old Man had indeed been foolish, and by comparison I was the wise one.

Still, I remained silent. I loved my father, and respected him, even when he did a foolish or wrong thing.

By mid-morning, we were well out of the valley, and for a while the track turned steeply uphill. Mr. Epps, or Lyman, as I had begun calling him, got down from the box and walked beside the struggling horses, coaxing them on, and Father and I fell back and got behind the wagon and put our shoulders to it. The dense, impenetrable forests up here had never been cut, even those trees that closed like a pale against the road and the towering pines and spruces had begun to block off the sky from our view, covering us with thick, cooling, day-long shadows. Although we were now far above the greening valley, the air was still sufficiently warm that most of yesterday's snowfall had melted early and had run off the sides into small rivulets and brooks that dropped away from the ridge, disappearing into the forest, where we could see dark gray remnants of the winter snows, which looked permanent, practically, and glacial. The only birds we saw up here were curious little chickadees and siskins and the occasional screaming blue birds. None of the hardwood trees or low bushes had put out their buds yet, and the scattered thatches of grasses we saw lay in yellowed mats, still dead from last year's frost.

Nothing in the natural world appeared ready for the resurrection of spring. Worse, it was as if we were steadily slipping backwards in time, with May and then April disappearing behind us and darkest winter rising into view just ahead. Soon we were struggling through yesterday's unmelted, ankle-deep snow. It was cold and nearly dark here below the tall trees, as if earlier this morning, before crossing overhead, the sun, unbeknownst to us, had reversed its path and had descended and set behind us. Except for Father, we had shrouded ourselves with blankets again. A steady, high wind blew through the upper branches of the trees, raising a distant unbroken chorus of grieving voices to accompany our slow pilgrimage.

After a while, almost without my noticing it, the ground leveled off somewhat, and Father and I no longer had to stay close to the wagon to be ready to push it. Our little group had strung itself out practically in single file, as if we each of us wished to be alone with our morbid thoughts, with Father in his greatcoat up at the head of the column, and then the team and wagon driven by Lyman, and me trudging along in its tracks. Behind me came Mary, Ruth, Sarah, and Annie, picking their way through the snow in a ragged line, while stretching back for many rods walked the livestock, singly or sometimes two animals abreast, with Salmon and Oliver positioned among them to keep them moving, and back somewhere out of sight, Watson and the collie dogs brought up the rear.

The road by now had dwindled to a narrow, palisadoed trail barely the width of our wagon. It no longer switch-backed across the side of the mountain, and there were no longer the occasional breaks in the trees with views of the forested slopes and ridges below. Instead, plunging across slabs of rock and over snarls of thick roots, the trail ran straight into the still-darkening forest, as if down a tunnel, and had we met a wagon or coach coming out of the tunnel towards us, we could not have turned aside to let it rush past. It seemed that there was nothing ahead of us but slowly encroaching snow and darkness.

When, suddenly, as if struck by a blow, I realized that we had emerged from the forest. Light poured down from the skies, and the towering trees seemed to bow and back away. Dazzled by the abrupt abundance of light and space, I saw that we were passing along the shore of a long, narrow lake that lay like a steel scimitar below high, rocky escarpments and cliffs, beyond which there loomed still higher mountains, which curved away and disappeared in the distance. The enormous scale of open space, snow-covered mountains, precipices and black, sheer cliffs diminished our size to that of tiny insects, as we made our slow way along the edge of the glistening lake. Wonderstruck, gaping, we traced the hilt of the sword-shaped body of water and the long slant of its cutting edge to the point, where we exited from the gorge as if through an ancient stone gate.

We had passed through Cascade Notch, and below us lay the beautiful wide valley of North Elba. Off to our left, mighty Tahawus and McIntyre rose from the plain, splitting the southeastern cloudbank. To our right, in the northwest, we could see Whiteface Mountain, aged and dignified by its wide scars and pale gray in the fading afternoon sun. And between the mountains, spreading out at our feet for miles, lay undulating forests scratched by the dark lines of rivers and the rich, grassy meadows, and marshes that we would call the Plains of Abraham.

Lyman drew the wagon to a halt, and the family came and gathered around it and admired the wonderful sight together. We removed the damp blankets from our shoulders, folded them, and placed them back into the wagon. Then Father took himself off from us a ways and lowered his head and silently prayed, while the rest of us continued simply to admire the generosity and beauty of the land.

For a long time, no one spoke, and then, when Father had rejoined us, Lyman said, "We better keep moving, Browns, if we wants to get home by nightfall." He slapped the reins, and the wagon jerked forward along the rocky, narrow road, and we all moved back into line behind it, walking easily downhill into the valley, as the sun descended towards the hills and mountains beyond.

Richard Beamish

Dick Beamish grew up in Brooklyn and Albany before finding, as an adult, his true home in the Adirondacks. A journalist with a degree from Columbia University's Graduate School of Journalism, Beamish has been able to mix writing and conservation most of his professional life. He has served as director of communications for the National Audubon Society, the Adirondack Council, and the Adirondack Park Agency. Before that he worked as a reporter for the International News Service. For several years afterwards he was the manager and chief guide of a canoe and ski outfitting service in the Adirondacks.

He is currently serving as publisher, editor, and chief copy boy for the Adirondack Explorer, *a monthly tabloid newspaper covering the Adirondack Park. The essay below originally appeared there in 1999. Beamish lives with his wife, Rachel Rice, in Saranac Lake, New York.*

Adirondack Smithsonian

For some years I ran a canoe-guiding operation. For a week at a time, we'd accommodate a dozen or so guests, lead them on day trips along wilderness waterways, and provide a hands-on introduction to the Park. Halfway through the week, however, we'd give our paddling muscles a rest, pile into a van, and head for the Adirondack Museum.

On the edge of tiny Blue Mountain Lake Village (population 150), in the middle of a sparsely settled, wildly forested region the size of Massachusetts, you don't expect to find a museum that rivals the best of the

Smithsonian Institution in the nation's capital—rivals and in some ways *surpasses* that venerable enterprise.

Where else on earth can you find a setting like the one chosen for the Adirondack Museum? Its thirty-acre campus occupies the former grounds of a grand (and long-gone) Victorian hotel, at the base of a landmark mountain, overlooking an island-studded lake that resembles one of the nineteenth-century landscape paintings for which, among much else, the museum is distinguished. Outside, and in, this place offers an unforgettable trip back into the earlier Adirondacks.

"You can easily spend a whole day there, or even several days," we'd tell our guests beforehand. But not until they experienced it for themselves were they entirely convinced. For anyone seeking "total immersion" in the Adirondacks, and that's what our customers wanted, this was it.

They would spend the morning there, wandering from building to building, seeing how people lived, worked, and played in these parts during the past 150 years. They would lose themselves in the remarkable exhibits, some of which fill large buildings, that bring to life the history of mining and logging, boats and boating, and outdoor recreation. They would visit the log hotel, one-room schoolhouse, traditional hunting camp, Noah Rondeau's transplanted hermitage, Bill Gates's diner from Bolton Landing, the horse-drawn vehicles (fifty of them!) used for work and pleasure, a rich man's private railroad car, Adirondack rustic furniture and the Hudson River School paintings (many of the painters came north) that helped popularize the Adirondacks in the last century. And then, by early afternoon, we'd pull ourselves away to hike Blue Mountain, up the two-mile trail that begins across the road, for a stunning summit view of this land of lakes and mountains we'd come to know so much better thanks to the museum way down below.

How did such an institution take root and thrive in the middle of this wilderness park? When something extraordinary happens, it usually takes someone of unusual vision, resources and determination to make it happen. In this case that person was Harold K. Hochschild. A summer resident, Adirondack historian, and head of an international mining company, he not only launched the Adirondack Museum back in 1957 and made sure it flourished, in the late 1960s, Hochschild was also instrumental in creating the one other institution that binds the region together.

He chaired Nelson Rockefeller's Commission on the Future of the Adirondacks, whose principal recommendation was that New York State set up an Adirondack Park Agency to control development on the vast private lands of the Park, thereby preserving the character of the region in the decades ahead. It was, according to those who were involved, Hochschild's quiet determination that, more than anything else, made the APA a reality.

The Adirondack Museum is far larger today than when it opened forty-two years—and more than three million visitors—ago. But its quality and direction continue to reflect the values of its progenitor. The museum stands as a memorial to a man who has probably done more than anyone in this century—and his life spanned almost all of it—to give the Adirondack Park a regional identity.

Joseph Bruchac

Joe Bruchac, a Native American of Abenaki descent, is a storyteller and writer who lives in the small Adirondack foothills town of Greenfield Center, New York. Bruchac's poetry often reflects the two influences most central to his life—his ancestry and the landscape. Like the writing of many Americans, native and otherwise, his work often reflects the search for an identity and a home in a landscape that too often fails to satisfy either need.

His notable works include Tell Me a Tale, *a book about story and storytelling (Harcourt Brace, 1997), and an autobiography,* Bowman's Store *(Dial, 1997). His most recent book of poetry is* No Borders *(Holy Cow! Press, 1998). His most recent performance work,* Adirondack Tall Tales: the Bill Greenfield Stories *(Good Mind, 1999), is an audio recording on compact disc, with musical accompaniment by Adirondack fiddler and hammer dulcimer player John Kirk.*

The first three of the following poems are printed here for the first time. "Into the Cedar River" and "Coming Down From Hurricane Mountain" first appeared in No Borders, *and the prose piece, "Fitting the Ground to Plant," is from* Bowman's Store.

The Last Stand

Just one paved road then
led from east to west
across the Adirondacks.
We took it in the college bus.

24

September 1960 and so many things
then just begun, so many others
like the feathered seeds of milkweed
stirring in the wind.

The mountain forests had been cut over,
clearcut not once but more than twice
and though tall beech and pine lined roads
all were second growth except on one small hill
somehow the loggers missed, as if their eyes
were blinded by some ancient spirit
guarding that ridge near Saranac Lake.

Professor Hamilton's face seemed different
in the light that sifted down like pollen.
Wind sang the branches.
His voice grew quiet and even the sound
of our footsteps vanished in the cushion
of needles, centuries beneath our feet.

These pines, he said, were here before
the first white man stepped on this land.
I knew in that moment without speech,
the roots of those remaining few
might not be strong enough to hold their peace.

Yet, finding them in memory,
my heart is strengthened by their song.

Adali Wassak

In memory of Chief Maurice Dennis

His hands still move
with quick strokes,
his shoulders hunch

as he shapes the cedar
opening Bear's eyes
to the green light.

Under the pines
I stand beside him,
hold the crooked knife,
wait the moment
to turn the long pole,
balanced on the sawhorses,
holding it as firm
as his eyes
hold old stories.

A loon flies overhead,
circles down Moose River,
its call piercing, stronger
than the throb of diesels
from the road.

He does not look up,
but smiles, feeling its wings
within his chest, then
he tells me the tale
of the song he once heard
from the sky,
of the boat he saw,
pass overhead,
old Indians paddling,
the voices joining the clouds.

Turtle's shell rough
against my palms,
I turn the pole,
sun glinting bright
off the old man's glasses,
his eyes filled with a light

which sees further
than I have yet learned to travel,
through cloud and the grain
of years.

Carving

What you make
is shaped
by what you take away,
the way the gouge moves,
the knife edges
into shapes beneath.

Holding old steel
your grandfather left you,
the handle shapes
your hand to its strength.

The basswood trunk
is balanced on sawhorses
made of salvaged
rough pine 2 x 4's.

Beneath your feet
the shoots of a new tree
rise from the shade
where the old tree,
storm-lowered, fell.

After a day of such work,
standing on the old roots,
you come home, maybe,
with something more
than blisters

and shavings stuck
to your sleeves.

Your eyes have grown closer
to an old story
one you may not
have heard before,
but your hands
have begun to tell it.

Into the Cedar River

I cast my line
into the Cedar River,
watched it pull out of sight
as Adirondack rain began to fall
and thunder walked
over Panther Mountain.

A pulse touched
my fingertips and then
I stripped in line
until a brown trout
lifted from the water
as if seeking to fly
at the end of nylon leader
invisible as hands of wind.

A gust pushed me back
onto mica bright rocks.
I stumbled up the bank,
through rain thicker than breath,
carrying all that the river
consented to give me—

my memory holding the touch
of the trout's smooth fins,
as it left my hands
back into water
as tannin dark
as its vibrant skin.

Coming Down from Hurricane Mountain

John Cheney, the old Adirondack guide
told a story about coming around the corner
up on Hurricane Mountain
when he saw a panther.
It jumped right down in front of him, growling.
"What did you think then?" someone said to him.
"Thought I'd better shoot it," Cheney said.

And this evening, this evening,
coming down that old mountain
I saw two hawks.
One swooped low above my head,
wing feathers spread to hold the sky,
the second was in a spruce tree dead
and dry from the acid in the rain.
Both of them led my sight away
from the gouged earth below
where backhoes and dozers
worked to widen an intersection,
the road flowing
a black dead river.

Then I thought of old
Adirondack John
Cheney's words again.

Fitting the Ground to Plant

There is a story about corn. It is one of the stories that my grandfather never told me. There was hardly any mention of Indians at all when the old men gathered around the potbellied stove in my grandfather's general store, sitting in the wooden chairs my grandfather had made of pine cut from his woods. Even though more than one of those old men, like my grandfather, had the dark tanned skin and features that hinted at something more than the Scotch-Irish or French ancestry that most of them claimed, they were careful about how they mentioned Indians. One never knew who might be listening.

But I think of this story as one of his stories, too. I learned it two decades ago from my friend and teacher Maurice Dennis, as he stood behind his house in the Adirondack village of Old Forge, carving into a cedar pole the shapes of Bear and Turtle, the two main clan animals of our Abenaki people.

Maurice's parents had come down from Odanak, the Abenaki reserve in Quebec, when he was a small child. Like my great-grandparents, they were basket makers. A number of Abenaki families made their way from that town of refuge in the far north to return to upstate New York or Vermont or New Hampshire—new European names grafted onto the land their ancestors once called simply Ndakinna, "Our Land." They came now as either "French-Canadian" loggers or as "Canadian" Indians, playing the role of fishing and hunting guides and makers of souvenirs for tourists. They were no longer people who belonged to this land, not in the eyes of those who held pieces of paper that proved ownership. But their stories still remembered a long connection with an earth that would never forget those who loved it. Maurice Dennis was telling me such stories that day, stories of canoes that could cross the sky, stories of the meaning of the thirteen plates on the back of Turtle, stories of how some things came to be.

Long ago, he said, the Abenaki people had no knowledge of corn. They gathered plants from the forest, hunted, and fished. But one year the game grew scarce and the fish were few, and when they went to gather berries and roots and nuts, those too were hard to find. The people made it through the winter, but when the spring came they worried that they would not survive.

One man went out hunting and this happened to him. He saw no game, but when he entered a clearing in the forest, he saw a woman there. One moment there was no one, and then there was this woman. Her long hair was a strange yellow color.

That woman with hair as yellow as the sunrise stood there, looking at the hunter. Her clothing was all green and her thin blonde hair blew in the wind. The hunter came closer to her, and though she swayed back and forth, dancing in the wind, she still did not move from the place where she stood. It was as if she had grown up out of the earth there in front of him. As he looked at her, feelings of great love swept over him—not the kind of love a man feels for a woman, but more like that grateful love a child feels for a caring grandparent.

"I have come to help your people," she said. "I am going to die. When I die, you must loosen the earth all around this clearing. Then drag my body over that earth and bury me. Keep my grave clean and protect it from the birds and animals. If you do this, you will see me again and I will feed your people. Care for me well and I will never leave you."

Having spoken those words, the beautiful maiden fell to the earth. The hunter tried to wake her, but he soon saw that she no longer breathed. So he did as she had told him to do. He took his spear and used it to loosen the earth all around the clearing, and he dragged her body around and around. As he did so, she became smaller. When he was done, all that was left of the maiden were her green clothes, which had begun to turn brown.

Day after day he returned to the clearing to keep her grave clean and drive away the birds and animals. Now small plants were growing. When he saw they were as green as the clothing the maiden had worn, he understood they were her children. They grew taller and taller until they were as tall as a man. Late summer came and silky strands like hair, hair as yellow as the sunrise, grew from the tops of those plants and from the ears of corn that formed on their sides. That corn was the gift which helped the people survive. So it was that the Corn Maiden gave herself to the Abenaki people a thousand years ago.

• • •

I picture my grandfather when I think of this story, picture him in the one place where he always mentioned Indians. He spoke of them in a way both reverent and bemused, almost the way a person might say the name of a parent he had been separated from not long after birth. *My mother? My father?* Always with a hint of uncertainty. That one place where my grandfather always mentioned Indians was in his garden.

My grandfather's name was Jesse Bowman. Jesse E. Bowman. The E was for Elmer, though no one outside the family was allowed to say that middle name to him. He and my grandmother ran their little gas station and general store on the corner of Middle Grove Road and State Route 9N. The road rose up the hill so steeply from Saratoga Springs, three miles to the southeast, that the iron-shod hooves of the horses straining to pull wagons up the hill would splinter the wood of the plank road that had once been there. So the hill where the store was located was called Splinterville Hill. Fifty yards behind their store was another road, named for the mill that used to be located on it, a mill and a now-vanished pond that had belonged to my grandmother's parents, the Dunhams. Bell Brook, the stream that had powered that mill and filled the pond, still rippled down over the stones.

Sometimes, in my dreams, I am walking again down Mill Road with my grandfather. He carries in his arms the black-and-white fox terrier that he named Pudgie, a wiry little dog that never growled at me. The closest that she came was an indignant yip one day when I was two years old and she was eight—getting on to be an elder in dog years. My grandparents turned to look and saw that I had just bitten off one of her whiskers. My grandfather liked fox terriers. Though they were little, bigger dogs stepped aside from them. They lived a long time—for a dog. They were compact and tough.

"They be almost as smart as a mongrel," my grandfather said.

When I was a very small child, as soon as I could walk, I was following my grandfather. In addition to running the gas station and store, he was still doing other work. He worked on the road crews, especially in the winter when he drove a snowplow. He had done that since the days when the plows were pulled by horses, and there were times when he would whisper "Gee" and "Haw" as he drove one of those big vehicles, smiling to himself as he felt the truck answer his commands to turn, just as teams of horses had done three decades before.

He worked too at the butter plant down the road. His job there was a good one. I was old enough to know that. Without him that plant would not have been able to run, for he was the man who shoveled the coal into the boilers. Grama had taken me to see him working there. I was proud of the way he looked, his brown arms glistening with sweat and with gleaming dust from the hard coal that flew into the open maw of the great boiler, as he bent and dug the blade in, lifted it up, and tossed it with no more effort than another man would expend to take a deep breath. And the fire breathed back its thanks to him with each shovelful it swallowed.

He had a strong relationship with fire, my grandfather did. So many memories of him are around the fire. Around the woodstove in the kitchen, where our lives centered in the cold seasons. My grandfather and I kept the wood box, with its hinged lid, filled with split ash and maple. Since my grandmother cooked on that stove, it was warm most of the day; and as soon as the leaves began to turn colors, it was kept burning day and night.

It was behind that stove that the cats had their kittens. There was just enough space for me to crawl back in there with them to feel their little claws hooking into my shirt and my pants as they crawled over me, mewing in their tiny, insistent voices. And it was there behind that woodstove that Grampa placed the chilled calf which had strayed from its mother, warming it back to life wrapped up in his red flannel shirt.

Each spring he would burn the grass in the field—the way his father had taught him to do it. Clearing the way for new green growth, burning back the dry tangles of berry bushes at the edge of the field so that fresh, strong canes would rise up to be covered with blackcaps in late summer. I followed behind him, helping him make a circle of fire that would feed on itself, the circle growing smaller and smaller until it became a single ember at the blackened heart of the field. Our feet would be black with the soot of burned grass, and it would be on our faces and in our hair.

There were times, though, when the wind would change. Then the fire would turn and run ahead of us in directions that we did not expect. We had rakes and shovels in our hands, and we would beat the burning grass, making sparks fly up so high that I was certain they became stars. But we could not stop that burning grass, and more and more smoke filled the air.

Then my grandfather would stop and lean on his rake. I would do the same.

"Guess the fire department'll get here soon," he would say.

"I guess," I would answer.

And we would listen for the familiar sound of their siren, coming down from Greenfield after the fire spotter in his tower on Spruce Mountain, eight miles to our north, had seen the rising smoke and called it in to them. We knew what he probably said: "Them Bowmans is burning that field again."

Distant and then closer the sound of the siren would come, a sound that was exciting to me not just because I knew I'd soon see the red truck of the Greenfield Volunteer Fire Department and the men dressed in boots and slickers and hats. It was exciting because I knew, even as a small boy, that open burning like this was illegal without a permit. My grandfather never went to get one and I wondered if this would be the time that they would come with guns and handcuffs, and—just the way they did to the criminals I saw in the movie serials at the Congress Theatre—take my grandfather away. If they did, they would have to take me, too. I would show them the pack of matches in my hand and tell them I was the one who started the fire.

But, while the time would come when I would see my grandfather handcuffed and taken away in a police car, it never happened when he burned his field and the fire truck arrived.

Instead, big smiling men would climb off the pumper truck and begin to wet down the edges of the fire.

"Jess, you old firebug!" one of them might yell.

My grandfather would not answer. Sometimes, though, he might lean over to me and say in a soft voice, "This here is one way to keep them firemen in business."

I would nod, understanding his words. You couldn't have firemen if you didn't have fires.

Just as I remember those fires every spring, so, too, I remember my grandfather's garden. It was around back, between my grandparents' house and the small two-room building we called "the Little House" and used for storing things. It was in the Little House that my grandmother's parents spent their last impoverished years, cared for by my grandmother and the husband they'd looked down on when he was their hired help.

Another of my earliest memories is walking through the furrows of that newly plowed garden with my grandfather—who seemed taller than the biggest trees then—holding my hand. I could barely walk, even on level ground, but he wouldn't let me fall. I wore the same kind of overalls that he did, and people were already calling me "Jess's Shadow."

That was how Lawrence Older put it one day when he was buying gasoline at my grandparents' filling station. I was following behind my grandfather, my tiny hand holding onto his overalls because his hands were too busy to hold mine.

"Jess," Larry said, with a twinkle in his eye, "that grandson of yours stays so close to you he don't hardly leave room enough for your shadow."

Jess's Shadow? I didn't quite understand that name. My name was Sonny. I knew that for sure. That was the name my grandparents called me by. I never heard either of them speak to me or about me by any other name.

I remember the day—I could not have been more than two and a half years old—when my grandfather said to me, "Sonny, cup out yer hands." I held them out together, trying to make a really good cup. Carefully, taking the seeds out from the cloth sack he had slung over his shoulder, he filled my hands with kernels of golden corn. I stood there holding those seeds for him, watching as he took them, four at a time, to plant them.

"Yer turn now," he said when those seeds were gone, and he held out one leathery hand filled with corn. I'd watched really carefully, so I knew what to do. I did it so well that my grandfather allowed that I was already better at it than he was. Then, as I planted my first hills of corn, he talked to me about things. He always talked more when he was in his garden.

There in his garden, as he spaded or began to hoe, he would talk about the different plants, about the birds we heard singing, about how we had to watch for the woodchucks or the rabbits or the raccoons. Sometimes he would talk about the old way of plowing with a team of horses, and he would tell me the names of the horses he'd loved—the last of them dead and gone a decade before I was born. He told me how, as their plows cut their way down into the rich earth that was the same color as his face, he and his father used to turn up arrowheads.

"Indian arrowheads," he would say.

He had a name for that work of preparing his garden for the sweet corn and green beans and butternut squash we always put in. I never heard anyone else say it just the way he did until I met Grampa's younger brother Jack, many years later, when I was a grown man. "Fitting the ground to plant." That is what Grampa called it. That is what Jack called it. That is what their father, Lewis Bowman, had called it. Fitting the ground to plant.

Another spring day, perhaps a year later, I was following my grandfather while he worked in the garden. He had made a small hoe for me that year, and I was, as always, trying to do exactly what he did. Then he stopped hoeing. I stopped too and waited. I remember that I heard a bird sing just then, a long ululating song.

"Oriole," my grandfather said. Then he bent over and picked something up. He brushed soil from it and went down on one knee next to me.

"Sonny," he said, "looky here."

I leaned close to look at the dark, blocky piece of flint that filled my grandfather's broad hand.

"Indian," my grandfather said. "Axhead."

He hefted it first in one hand and then the other. He did it with the same care that my grandmother used when she was gathering eggs in the henhouse and putting them into the basket hung over her arm. Then he placed that axhead into my hands.

Thirty years after that day when my grandfather put the stone axhead in my hands, I understood at last why, as I held that stone, my mind had filled with images of tall corn swaying in the wind, images of slender women dancing as they held the season's harvest in their hands. Hearing Maurice Dennis tell the story of the coming of corn was the last stroke of the hoe that fit my own mind to the earth my grandfather had given to me. And I knew that as long as my hands had the strength to hold a hoe, I would work that garden where corn had been cared for by my grandparents and by my great-grandparents before them. I would listen to that land just as it had once been listened to by other men and women, generations of Abenaki people and Mohawk people whose stories were told in a tongue as old as the soil. Spring would find me preparing the earth for the Corn Maiden, find me fitting the ground of my grandfather's garden to plant.

Charles Brumley

How fitting for the region to have a working Adirondack guide who not only has the itch to canoe, hike, and fish, but also to write. And write well. How fitting indeed, after more than a century of writing by travel writers who helped make the Adirondack guide a figure of legend, both romantic and notorious. (For starters, see W. H. H. Murray's Adventures in the Wilderness, first published in 1869, and jointly reprinted by the Adirondack Museum and Syracuse University Press in 1989.)

Chuck Brumley's essays and features have appeared widely, in regional newspapers and in Adirondack Life. In addition, his radio essays are heard on the National Public Radio affiliate that serves the Adirondacks, North Country Public Radio. His first book, Guides of the Adirondacks: A History—A Short Season, Hard Work, Low Pay (North Country Books, 1994), surprisingly, is the first book-length study of the Adirondack guide. How comprehensive is it? The lives of more than two hundred guides are discussed, detailing a tradition that goes back more than 150 years.

The essays included below, "The Future of Adirondack Guiding" and "Cyber Woods and Virtual Mountains," first appeared in 1999 in, respectively, the Adirondack Journal of Environmental Studies, edited by Gary Chilson, a professor of environmental studies at Paul Smith's College, and The Sequel, a quarterly publication for the alumni and community of Paul Smith's College.

The Future of Adirondack Guiding

My folly in trying to predict the future of Adirondack guiding may be rendered harmless to me by the fact that if I project far enough ahead, I'll be gone from this mortal coil when none of it comes true.

But if you look at the history of guiding and try to stretch the direction ahead, certain trends look as if they might hold true. Among the trends is the fact that Adirondack guiding has been mostly reactive rather than pro-active. We shouldn't confuse the idea that guides did, indeed, actively go out into the woods and waters with the fact that they did it only in response to a need they hadn't created.

The earliest guides were market hunters and trappers, a number of them extremely antisocial Revolutionary War veterans who were better left alone. But they knew their own area, which usually was on the periphery of the Adirondacks, quite well. The early tourists pressed them into service; if we posit for the tourists an adventurous and accepting nature, they were perhaps the very best that fate could have sent the quarrelsome hunters. It was the literal or metaphorical sons or grandsons of these hunters who began to develop a bona fide profession as guide.

On paper there was not much to it. A stream of hikers, would-be developers, writers, artists, scientists, theologians, poets, and others came to the Adirondacks beginning in the first half of the nineteenth century. Lacking decent maps, guidebooks, woods skills, and trails, they needed someone to show them the way. Most any native teenage boy in the Adirondacks was thought to have the requisite skills to lead tourists— he might have lacked the ability to keep up his end of a metaphysical conversation around the evening campfire, but at least he knew the way back.

But the guides received the brunt of the results caused by more and more people putting greater pressure on less and less fish and game. Their livelihood was snatched away from them, and they formed a private association in the 1890s to deal with the problems. In addition to the diminishing of the fish and game, the whole nature of recreation in the Adirondacks changed a hundred years ago. Big hotels meant more people could come and not have to rough it outdoors with guides; Mom and the kids could come and enjoy croquet, leisurely hikes on better trails with better maps, golf, speed boats, and a host of other activities. By the turn of the century the guide and their beloved guideboats had lost their raison d'être.

The early associations in the 1890s, along with some early guide books, and the later state licensing of guides—voluntary in 1919, mandatory in 1924—gave guides a first chance at actively marketing their services. Pamphlets, with lists of guides, were prepared that could be sent to tourists. The guides didn't have to depend as much on word of mouth or the vagaries of being a low-on-the-totem-pole hotel guide. In the twentieth century, a very few guides created a niche for themselves almost by default: Dan and Bill Frayne, for example, became fishing guides in Lake Placid for affluent tourists, many of whom stayed at the Lake Placid Club. They were on a retainer; that is, Tuesdays might be judge so-and-so's day. If he wanted to go fishing with Bill, Bill was on stand-by ready to go. If he didn't, Bill got paid anyway. Thus, the two brothers were paid for every day of the season. They had been discovered by word of mouth, aided by their father being a guide before them.

But such an arrangement was the exception, not the rule. Probably not until the 1970s and 1980s did a shift occur in the general makeup of the guide population, from wood-wise local boys to transplanted college graduates. The transplants, even though they may have gone to college to study something such as wilderness recreation, still had plenty to learn when they got here—where to hunt and fish, the secret and best spots, the routes out and back, the fact that the locals didn't think much of them as interlopers.

But the newcomers also brought other interests and skills that the locals never thought of: specialties in skills such as photography, all-women consciousness-raising outings, corporate team-building trips, the adrenaline sports such as rock and ice climbing, white-water rafting and canoeing, and others. Many skills that could be adapted to the outdoors were now marketed to mostly urban populations that at some level in their souls cried out for them. The new breed of guide could talk the talk as well as walk the walk; they were up on the news, they understood the pressures of urban living and could make allowances for them, and they could serve as meaningful sounding boards for the clients for the myriad problems they came to hear around the campfire.

They began to market these services to their perceived clientele. But it was and has been a tough sell, not so much because the services are not good, but because some of those audiences are hard to reach, or don't know exactly what they lack, or companies won't spend the money, or the same services can be provided in a warm hotel. Additionally, the total number of guides may be dropping as new guides discover they haven't even recouped their initial licensing fee, increased to more than a hundred dollars in the mid-eighties, or the enthusiasm of youth has given way to the reality of making a living. (The true full-time year-round Adirondack guides can probably be counted on one hand.) In 1998 the state listed approximately 1,840 guides statewide; a Great Lakes fishing guide based in, say, Pulaski, New York, would be included in this number.

Thus we see that the guides have become more formally educated and somewhat better and more diversified at marketing their services. But once again, as in the last quarter of the nineteenth century, we have to look at what the greater pressures from the outside world hold. On one hand the increasing aloofness of life from the land has created in many a fervid desire to experience the land, and to test themselves in rigorous ways: triathlons, adventure courses, "extreme" sports of all kinds that push the limits of what has traditionally been thought of as sane. These people will need leaders, even if it is merely to shepherd them through their trials.

But this gap between what it means to live day in and day out with the outdoors, in at least a kind of push-pull harmony, and a life most of the year in a removed state from the outdoors grows. The gap throws an outdoor experience into the realm of adventure, almost fantasy, an experience foreign to what is for the denizen of the electronic world "real," because it takes up such a short period of time and is so different.

How will the guides cope with that? What will increasing population pressures on the outdoors mean? Project the situation out a few hundred years and try to imagine a worst-case scenario. While I can all but guarantee it won't be the one I think of (I'll be gone, remember?), picture one where all at once the supply of fossil fuels runs out, solar and nuclear energy have fallen onto some sort of bad or ill-managed times, and a burgeoning population needs, for fuel . . . trees. How long do you think that Adirondack forests would last? Weeks? The "Forever Wild" amendment would be gone in an eye blink. What about water needs? If there is one thing we don't lack, it's water. But suppose the water here had to be piped away? Or, if discretionary money continues for recreational wants, what will follow in the figurative destructive wake of the jet-ski? Any of these could throw the guides for a tail spin.

I believe the gap between what most people do with most of their lives and their outdoor experiences will grow. The outdoors will attain a sense of precocity, the down-staters will continue to vote to protect the Adirondack Park, while the residents will vote to sell it down the river in the interests of short-term economic gain. The guides will need to couple New Age touchy-feely therapy with woods skills. Unisex thinking will negate the old notions of manliness, with a concomitant wish to preserve all wild animals. Hunters and trappers will be beleaguered as smokers are now. The outdoors will become a laboratory for metaphysics and poesy. Greater restrictions in the form of party size and camping rules will be put in place; the guides themselves may have to lobby to be given preference for hiking permits in restricted areas. Running a guiding business will have all the growing attendant headaches of any small business, the"sign-your-life-away" forms will provide less and less protection, and many guides will say the heck with it.

The old days will grow increasingly older, and not just from the passage of time. The whole gestalt of life will drive guiding more than ever. The Adirondacks, now a mostly safe version of the end of the road for some, will lose that quality; the true misfits will still push on for a while to Montana and Alaska and then have nowhere to go. They will then be with us everywhere. I pray they will learn to give thanks for what we have left, and, as guides, see the wisdom of taking the clients' money, and preaching the poetry of the outdoors.

Cyber Woods and Virtual Mountains

The river, the brooks, the ponds, the mountains, and the trees, the
fleet deer, the rushing trout, the wild cat and the bear ruled
supreme. It was their land and there was no Sunday there.
—Charles Leete, 1925, writing on the Adirondacks

From the top of Bloody Mountain, reached by a modest bushwhack by way of Hammond Pond, near North Hudson, you can look in every direction and see no obvious signs of humankind.

From Bloody Mountain you're gazing into identifiable High Peaks to the west, but the mountains in the southwest are tough to call. Boreas? Blue? Their very distance, even if you've been to them before, coupled with some haze gives them the attraction of the far away. "Something lost behind the Ranges," as Kipling said.

But it's hard to wax too poetic about the view when you're sweaty and thirsty—two tramps in black fly time. My pal, the Jackrabbit, and I fell into an inevitable, what-will-this-place-come-to discourse at the same time we were in tempered reverie at the view.

Our worldly-wise chatter circled around what it meant that millions of people were within a day's drive of where we were that summer day, but none of them were there. Even with all the perfectly good reasons for not being there, surely a few other lay-about hike-abouts might be expected to be somewhere in sight. In about six hours of hiking—almost a mile to Hammond Pond on a dirt road, the bushwack to Pine Pond, carrying our little canoes, then finally hiking up Bloody Mountain—we hadn't seen anybody.

But maybe they weren't coming. Maybe one of those insidious bell-shaped curves could tell the tale, and we were on the downward slope of it, ahead of it, the past as prologue. Maybe zillions of people had already been here—virtually. Because if the hordes were amassing in Manhattan, they were being damn discreet about it.

I know the lemming forays of Memorial Day, Labor Day, and Columbus Day bring great numbers of hikers and others into the Park. But it's as if their forays are ritualistic ones, partly based on when they can come, partly a function of that's when you do that. Only a few who need their regular fixes of outdoor experiences, seemingly, come any old time, higgledy-piggledy, rain or shine. What the rest do the rest of the time is what has me worried.

And it's because of the current bugbear: cyberspace. Because if virtual pictures (cyber optics?) become good enough, I think the dream— the real dream, based in sweat, and the scent of pine trees, and dragon flies, and lily pads lifting their naïve little faces in a stiff wind—may fade away. People won't come because they don't think they have to.

They can be voyage voyeurs without leaving home. If that happens, perhaps a good news/bad news scenario develops.

Having grown up with a healthy dose of Calvinism, let me start with the bad news. And let me stop picking on Manhattanites for a moment and sing their praises. When the chips—the old fashioned poker kind—are down on a crucial state-wide vote on the Forest Preserve, they come through to protect it, or support efforts to buy more. If they cease to come, maybe next they will cease to dream about the Park, and the joy of knowing this place is up here may no longer have any inspiration. The crucial votes to counter the short-sighted economic dealings of some of the residents may fade away. Not to mention what they're missing by not coming.

The good news is my friends in some aspect of the tourist game tell me the web has increased their business many fold—the web helps bring people here. A lot of them indeed come from Manhattan; I know from years of guiding. When there is a phone number on my answering machine (yes, Virginia, guides have come to that) that begins with the 212 area code, there is a Manhattanite on the other end.

Bless them. If I can get them up here and work my wiles, they will vote my way next time for sure. But when they do come, all the cyber stuff and gizmos will get in the way if they can't shuck them easily. Goodbye nature, hello computer chip. Case: From the top of Mt. Marcy a man whips out his cell phone and calls the Forest Rangers. He reports a broken leg—this is serious. The Rangers arrive in a helicopter. The man *runs over* to the chopper and gets in. There was, indeed, some minor injury to the man's leg. But, perhaps, in their confusion and maybe despondency, and the fact they were already there, the Rangers fly him away. Free. With your tax dollars. (The same year in the Swiss Alps, an American skier with a real broken leg takes another chopper flight. His bill: $3,000.)

Such a shenanigan by a hiker is the worst sort of irresponsibility. But this cluelessness goes deeper. Case again: Two hikers set off on that self-same Mt. Marcy, but in winter, abandon their equipment at treeline, get lost, damn near die, and sue their outfitters because their rescue wasn't started soon enough. As the editor Clint Willis said, quoted in the *New York Times*, "To enter into danger ignorantly has become a civil right in the latter half of the 20th century."

What's lost in the litigation and the abdication of responsibility is the mysticism of it all. Try to tell me there's no mysticism: I've seen it in people's eyes. I've seen them stand there at the far end of the carry ready to cry—both exclaim, and shed tears—"we're here, we're finally here."

What's lost is the sentiment expressed by Mildred Phelps Stokes Hooker, of Upper St. Regis Lake, writing in later life in *Camp Chronicles* in 1952: "As a child when anything went wrong, I would say to myself, 'Never mind, we're going to the Adirondacks,' and just the thought of this place would make me happy again."

How to gain back what's lost? Take what you need and leave the rest. A hundred pounds of lightweight camping gear on your back, with maybe a cell phone thrown in, is too much. Pare down. Take responsibility. As Paul Fussell noted in *Doing Battle*, "Fitzgerald and Hemingway agreed that if you're any good, you understand that everything that happens to you is your own damn fault and you embrace that knowledge and go from there."

Still, the worst of the weight, the stress, the hardship, comes not from the gear and the elements. It comes from what we bring with us when we come to get away from it all. Much of it is between our ears. As for the cyber age, once you have some idea how it works, all the self-hype notwithstanding, there's not much mysticism to it.

But the top of Bloody Mountain, now that's something.

Neal Burdick

Neal Burdick's deft touch as an editor has been appreciated for years by readers of Adirondac, *the magazine of the Adirondack Mountain Club. In his editorials and occasional features, Burdick betrays a sensitivity to the land and an understanding of the region's issues matched by few. In addition to his work with* Adirondac, *Burdick writes poetry, essays, and features, and he is a regular contributor to* Adirondack Life.

Burdick has also edited a raft of books, including the Adirondack Mountain Club's best-selling series of guidebooks. Burdick resides in Canton, New York, with his wife, Barbara, and their two children.

The essay reprinted here is the title essay in the collection, A Century Wild: Essays Commemorating the Centennial of the Adirondack Forest Preserve *(The Chauncy Press, 1985).*

A Century Wild

In the northwest quadrant of the Adirondacks, off a dirt road that parallels the St. Regis River between Paul Smiths and Santa Clara, stands Azure Mountain. Although its summit is only 2,518 feet above sea level, it offers a sweeping view that is unmatched by that from many higher peaks. To the north and northwest, the St. Lawrence River is a silver line cordoned by numerous towns, rich farmland, and the telltale smoke of heavy industry. To the south and southeast can be seen many of the High Peaks of the Adirondacks: Whiteface, Marcy, Giant, Algonquin, the Sewards. More toward the east, it's possible to see all the way to the last ridges before the land drops quickly to the Champlain Valley. Nearer at hand is a mosaic of forest, bog, and pond that is interrupted but rarely by logging roads that emerge momentarily from the woods, only to be swallowed up again.

On top of Azure Mountain, precariously near the brink of its precipitous southwest face, sits an immense boulder. I suppose it is a glacial erratic, transported from who knows where by incomprehensible tons of ice and left behind like refuse when the ice retreated north 10,000 years ago. It has always fascinated me, mysterious monolith perched there like a gargoyle high on a Gothic spire.

Within sight of the rock, nearly upon the true summit of the mountain, stands a fire observer's tower. It has been abandoned for some years now, but I can remember, when I climbed this mountain as a child, winding my way up the spindly stairs—my heart nearer my throat with every step—and being shown by the observer how to pinpoint on his map a suspicious plume of smoke. It stands now like an erector set deserted by a young boy grown up. But it, too, fascinates me. Who built it—and how? What manner of men passed hours at a time in its crow's nest of a cabin, scanning hundreds of miles of forest for signs of a fire that might destroy everything in sight? What fires never raged thanks to the use of this decaying hulk?

A tower and a rock. Man and nature. Most of Adirondack history over the past two centuries or more can be condensed in these two ideas. To trace Adirondack history is to trace man's relationship with nature.

Often when I am on the top of Azure Mountain (or any other Adirondack peak, for that matter) I imagine myself in a time machine. I travel back through Adirondack history.

It is 1903, and vast areas of the Adirondacks are burning. The fire tower isn't here, but the rock is. It is 1892, and most of the land I can see has just been designated the Adirondack State Park. The rock is here; it looks the same, whether it is suddenly part of a park or not. It is 1885, and the land has been stripped of its trees, by lumbermen who have left behind acre upon acre of stumps and mud. But in Albany, somewhere over the ridges fading to the south, the legislature has created the Adirondack Forest Preserve, and said the lumbering must stop, the public lands in the Preserve remain forever wild. They don't look very wild now; man has conquered nature and claimed the spoils. But the rock is here.

It is 1792, and Alexander Macomb has purchased from the state most of the land I can see, for the purpose of speculation. It is 1535, and out of sight to the northeast, Jacques Cartier, standing on high ground that will later be surrounded by the city of Montreal, is the first white man to see the Adirondacks. It is 1300, and a single aborigine appears momentarily in a clearing below me, perhaps stalking a deer, and the rock is here. It is 5,000 B.C., and the rock is here.

The difference between the rock and the tower, of course, is that the rock has been on top of Azure Mountain a lot longer than the tower has, and it will be there long after the last remnants of the tower have vanished. Over the centuries, man, with his purchases and his lumbering and his fires and his roads, has come and gone, but the rock has stayed. It measures time in millennia. I will not say it is permanent—a future Ice Age could move it just as surely as a previous one did—but I must concede that it is a lot more permanent than any of man's devices. The tower is a moment in the march of time, but the rock remains. And that is one of the lessons wilderness teaches.

I said Azure Mountain is part of the Forest Preserve, but not much of the Adirondack Park that I can see from its summit shares that distinction. Most of the northern and western parts of the Adirondacks are owned by individuals or companies, although from my perch on the mountaintop it all looks the same to me. That is because, for one reason or another, most of the private owners choose to keep their land in a relatively forested condition. Oh, logging does go on, but from a third of a mile up it is hardly visible.

But even though it may look the same, it is not likely that I would have the freedom to climb Azure Mountain whenever I feel like it were it not part of the Forest Preserve. I doubt whether a private owner would want just anybody walking up and down "his" mountain, picking his blueberries when they cover the summit every August, enjoying his view, and so on. When the solons of a century ago created the Forest Preserve, they may have intended to do no more than satisfy the shipping interests of this state that the Erie Canal would always have water in it, but they also gave the rest of us a certain measure of freedom. The

Erie Canal no longer plays the lead role in New York's economy, but we still have the freedom to hike the trails of the Forest Preserve.

I have known this Forest Preserve in many moods, many moments. I have stood on the tops of the tallest mountains in New York State and known what it is like, to paraphrase the guide John Cheney, "to have all creation placed beneath my feet." I have stepped above timberline on more than one of the highest peaks and been devoured by a vicious wind. I have seen lightning blow an eighty-year-old tree into slivers in a second. I have looked in awe at trees that were seedlings before the Forest Preserve was conceived, before the lumbermen arrived, perhaps even before the first great purchases were made. I have heard waterfalls roar with the accumulated power of five months of winter storms. I have listened to the haunting song of the loon, and I have watched a pair of golden eagles soar on summer thermals. I have seen a deer drink calmly from a beaver pond, a coyote dart across a lonely road, and a snake swallow a frog.

To each of these I was an observer, one who happened to intercept eternity. Over eons yet to be, the mountains will continue to rise and fall and the wind to blow. The shattered tree will nourish its successors, and they will nourish theirs.

Water will continue to flow down to the valleys, shouting in spring and whispering in early fall. The deer will return to the pond, the coyote to hunt, and the snake to swallow frogs. I feel privileged to have witnessed these moments, but I feel more privileged knowing they will continue to occur long after I have passed by. There is that dimension of timelessness to the wilderness; it is greater by far than I.

One of my favorite sections of the Forest Preserve is the Five Ponds Wilderness Area south of Cranberry Lake. From its high spots, I can look in every direction and see nothing but forest, undulating like the sea, and imagine I am Daniel Boone beholding an unknown continent for the first time. Here, if I work at it, I can find true wilderness—not places that have been allowed to return to a wilderness condition, but places that have never been anything but wilderness. They have been spared settlement, fire, even the long tentacles of the logging railroads. Not even a purist can deny that these places are wilderness. There are few such places left, at least within easy reach of millions of people; without enlightened legislation it is likely there would be none.

Late one summer night a few years ago, at a lean-to by one of the Five Ponds, seven college students and I watched with mingled amusement and distress while a very determined bear made off with some of our food. We, with all of our powers of reason, had cached the food from a tree limb high off the ground; he, with all of his powers of instinct, sensed we had not suspended it far enough out from the trunk of the tree. He was right, naturally, and so we lost a small amount of our food.

There was an undeniable simplicity in our situation that night. It came down to a matter of survival, for which we needed food (as did the bear, of course). Each of us, human and bear, wanted to obtain it as effortlessly as possible; each of us, bear and human, could have foraged for it had it not been available in a nylon bag at the end of a rope.

We later learned that at that very hour, halfway around the world, a jetliner was destroyed by a missile. That event helped us put our situation in perspective. Those doomed airplane passengers were not in control of their destinies, but we were. They, in one of the marvels of modern technology, could do nothing to save themselves, but we, in the virtually complete absence of civilization, had choices. There is that simplicity about the wilderness. I have heard it said that wilderness holds answers to questions we have not yet learned to ask; perhaps it also holds answers that we have not yet learned to see. And that is a good reason for preserving it.

But are abstract notions like permanence and simplicity reasons enough to preserve a wilderness? What matter if we have places that look the same as they did before our ancestors were born? Why should they be unchanged when we are ancestors? Is it not extravagant to set aside two and a half million acres of forest and say they should always be wild?

Less than one percent of the land in the forty-eight contiguous states of this nation is classified as wilderness, and much of that is of questionable quality because it is too close to a major highway, or has been lumbered too recently, or is subject to noise from an air route (parts of the Adirondack Forest Preserve suffer from these and other compromises, arguments about the distinction between "wilderness" and "wild land" notwithstanding). Given that a majority of the population regularly indicates that it wants wilderness, this does not seem extravagant. We could as easily ask if we have too many symphonies, or too many libraries, or too many books. The presence of wilderness is an indication not that civilization has failed to advance, but indeed that it has advanced so far that wilderness can once again be allowed to exist.

I would like to think we have progressed far enough that we no longer need fear the wilderness, no longer must have every ounce of its resources, no longer find it an impediment to our continued development. I would like to think we can afford to leave places for the deer to drink, the snake to swallow a frog, and a bear to outwit eight backpackers—and for their descendants to do the same things in the same places. I would like to think we can leave a huge, inscrutable rock near the edge of a cliff in the northern Adirondacks until some power other than our own decides to move it. I would like to think the wilderness will be allowed to outlive all of us.

Thurston Clarke

In the last decade, Thurston Clarke relocated with his wife and three daughters to Willsboro in New York's Champlain Valley, or what he likes to call the "Banana Belt of the Adirondacks." Clarke is the author of eight book-length works of fiction and nonfiction, including Equator *(Morrow, 1988) and* California Fault *(Ballantine Books, 1996). A recipient of a Guggenheim Fellowship and the Lowell Thomas Award for Travel Literature, Clarke is a frequent contributor to the* New York Times Book Review *and* Conde Nast Traveler.

His most recent work, Searching for Crusoe *(Ballantine Books, 2000), is about the universal fascination with islands. It was inspired by the view from his home of Lake Champlain's Four Brother Islands.*

"The 1812 Homestead" first appeared in Adirondack Life, *in 1997.*

The 1812 Homestead

My three daughters dragged me to the Apple Fest at the 1812 Homestead, in Willsboro, last October, assuring me this collection of simple early-nineteenth-century structures, and *not* New York's Metropolitan or Montreal's Musée des Beaux Arts, was the "coolest" and "most awesome" museum in the world.

They had visited the homestead on Willsboro Central School field trips and in the summer as campers at nearby Pok-O-MacCready, so I had already admired the twisty candles they hand-dipped in the candle cabin and the shingles they split in the wood shop. I had heard stories about Wilma, the recently deceased pig, and the one-room schoolhouse where they had to write their lessons on chalkboards, and the teacher who was so strict she made bad kids stand with their noses to the blackboard. I liked the sound of the place, and that they always returned from it carrying something they had made, instead of something they had purchased. But because of the homestead's limited hours, I had so far enjoyed only brief glimpses of its brown-shingled Federal house as I drove north on Route 22.

The Apple Fest had drawn more than a hundred people, but far from overwhelming the homestead's attractions, they made it seem even more like a flourishing frontier community. The twentieth century was not simply artfully concealed, it was invisible. The small clearing girded by dense woods, split-rail fences, and rocky pastures resembled an illustration from *The Last of the Mohicans*. The barns and cabins were authentically ramshackle and weathered, cars had been parked out of sight, and there were none of the food concessions and modern lavatories that mar the authenticity of other period villages. Even the sounds—a school bell tolling, turkeys gobbling, and axes whacking into logs—encouraged the illusion.

The girls led me around like little aristocrats showing off an ancestral estate. I had to admire the goats, drink a cup of freshly pressed cider, and sit behind a school desk while they took turns playing the strict schoolmistress, making me look straight ahead and balance a book in each hand to improve my appalling posture. They demanded that I name the president of the United States, and hooted with laughter when I said Bill Clinton instead of James Madison (1809–17).

Other Apple Fest visitors were equally busy chopping apples, cuddling rabbits, and admiring Wilma's replacement. They gathered like witches around a kettle of bubbling glycerin, threw hatchets at a target and peppered costumed staff members with questions. They trooped through the house and tavern, sitting on the beds and chairs, fingering the simple wooden toys, and cooking apple cobbler in an open hearth. There was nothing in the schoolhouse, barn, tavern, sugar shack, smokehouse, or garden that couldn't be touched, manipulated or held. And perhaps this was why here, in the ultimate hands-on museum, I saw none of the impatience, frustration, or whining that is part of taking children to most museums—even those with a concessionary back room filled with "please touch" artifacts.

The homestead is the brainchild of Jack Swan, director of Camp Pok-O-MacCready, who opened it as a living-history museum in 1973 and twenty years later created the nonprofit 1812 Educational Foundation. The relationship between Pok-O and the homestead has always been close, and every summer many of its campers come here to learn blacksmithing, weaving, and other crafts.

On the afternoon of the Apple Fest, Swan took time off from greeting visitors to explain that his grandmother acquired the property in 1910. It has stayed in the family ever since, and he had the idea of turning it into a museum after visiting New Salem, New York, a recreation of an 1832 village.

"I believe in the Frederick Jackson Turner thesis that the frontier made America the kind of country it is," Swan said. "And when I saw kids splitting rails at New Salem I decided to do the same thing here on a smaller scale and create a place where kids could experience the hardships of living on the frontier, where they could be encouraged to participate, to look *and* touch."

Over the years Swan added various structures to the original building, which had been a tavern. He moved the corn crib and barn from Camp MacCready and brought the one-room nineteenth-century schoolhouse from Essex, where it had served students until the 1950s. Now there is a wooden cabin for candle-making, a blacksmith's forge, a sugar-house, and plenty of room for more additions. He seemed to relish the idea that, as he said, "The homestead is *never* going to be really finished."

Kristen Bronander, who manages the daily operation of the museum, was bewitched by the homestead while a camper at Pok-O-MacCready. She had promised herself then to return and help it flourish. Bronander invited me to come witness a visit from one of the many school groups that came throughout the year, and so several weeks later I watched sixty eighth-graders from North Warren Central School, in Chestertown, pour from two school buses, jazzed up with sugary breakfast treats and teenage hormones. Staff members from the Pok-O-MacCready Outdoor Education Center divided them into groups and handed out schedules rotating them among six activities.

Bronander's tour of the 1812 house highlighted some offbeat features guaranteed to appeal to thirteen-year-olds. She spun stories about a resident ghost and pointed out a commode built into a bedroom chair, a wrench used for tightening the rope mattress, the fleur-de-lis stenciled onto the ceiling to make Quebecois feel at home in the tavern, the hook embedded in a ceiling that was used to hoist the corpse of a three-hundred-pound woman who expired here in 1908. She recounted how, during the restoration of the house, an 1813 penny had tumbled from inside a wall, perhaps placed there to indicate when the structure was completed.

There were murmurs of "cool" and "awesome"—but what thirteen-year-old wouldn't prefer hearing spooky stories or learning how Indians threw sticks to kill small animals for the stewpot to a day bent over their textbooks? More impressive was how, as they moved between activities, they became less jumpy. Perhaps it was the simple surroundings, the rough wooden planks and barnyard animals, or the aroma of a wood fire and baking apples, but the homestead had soothed even these rambunctious adolescents. Whether they knew it or not, their six hours here had been a subtle counterattack on their Nikes, flimsy mall fashions, and the cellophane-wrapped snacks they devoured at lunch. Before they left, Bronander distributed complimentary membership cards allowing them to return for a weekend visit with their parents. "You'd be surprised how many come back," she told me. The cards were part of a calculated strategy of giving the homestead's young visitors a feeling of place and ownership. If they were like my daughters, they would return again and again.

Michael Coffey

Michael Coffey was born at St. Vincent's Hospital in Greenwich Village, New York City, in 1954 and was adopted at birth by John and Eleanor Coffey of Saranac—the hamlet in Clinton County along the Saranac River, not Saranac Lake. He was raised there, graduating from Saranac Central High School in 1972.

He is a graduate of the University of Notre Dame and Leeds University in England, where he received an M.A. in Anglo-Irish Literature in 1977.

He currently resides in Greenwich Village with his wife and two children, and gets back to the Adirondacks as often as possible for many reasons—his parents are buried in the Independence Cemetery on the back street in Saranac, the fishing is better, and, he says, try finding a pickled egg in Manhattan.

Coffey has been the managing editor of **Publishers Weekly** since 1988. In 1996, Sun and Moon Press published a book of his poems, Elemenopy. He served as editor on **The Irish in America** (Hyperion, 1997) and is author of **Days of Infamy: Great Military Blunders of the 20th Century** (Hyperion, 1999). His work has appeared in the **Village Voice,** the **Los Angeles Times Book Review,** the **New York Observer** and **Adirondack Life.**

The following selections are from his second book of poems, 87 North, published in 1998 by Coffee House Press.

The Saranac River

I look so much better
in the mirror of home

since I left—
a kind of sumac grows at its edges.

Light like a liquid
or a wind streams
over me—a father's word
yields a red berry in the fall.

Their tumbling shapes,
a mother's graces rippling past
burnishing my face—
notions bouldering down the gorge.

I stand in the current
my eyes have opened,
and when they close
the Algonkians walk down from Canada.

I remember
a poem by Theodore Roethke
but vaguely—it is far upstream—
they crushed the red berries for war paint.

Mouthing a torrent of images
a mentor read it to us aloud:
Where the mind can go in poetry, he said.
The river isn't moving, I am.

I'll see them when they come,
dark bent bodies intent in the dawn.
And there's no hurry—
they are chanting the unknown French.

Miles from home like them,
ranked against a warm building,
a poem wades in riverlight,
guessing how a river got its name.

Adirondack Sounds

I put the words in his mouth—
this image of myself,
my son at three years of age.
I say to him

Cadyville, Saranac, Schuyler Falls.
Dannemora, Redford, Beekmantown,
Chazy Lake, pronounced *chez Zee.*
And he says them back to me,

eyes big, his tongue clumsy and sweet,
saying the names of towns of my youth.

I'm far from them now,
these syllables holding mysteries
of places people came to,
of how things were then.

I knew my own—Saranac—
without curiosity.
It was like my name.
But Cadyville was where pretty girls lived.

Schuyler Falls a forest cleared for playing ball,
Dannemora a prison town with tall, tough Irish,
Chazy just a cold, deep lake.

The places are on a map
I never need to study,
just hamlets to drive through.
The people that built them,

the sites there, now gone,
yielded to spells of indifferent offspring,

to places fallen down.
Still, Beekmantown

in my boy's mouth
is a clear parcel of fields
farmed for stone and apples,
Redford the soft fold of our church.

He repeats them to me
as I ask, happy at the drill,
expecting something for his effort.
I give him my confused joy.

I say to him *"Paradise,"*
and hear the pure word.

Shadow Limb

It was a Dr. Murphy
who cut my mother's leg off
below the knee
on December 14th.

It wasn't diabetes, exactly,
but the cumulative effects
of poor circulation, of
not caring to move too much,
of having given up.

I mean of missing Dad.

I signed a "Limb Disposal Agreement,"
allowing the hospital to do
whatever it does
with body parts, even though

there was another option—
assignment to a mortician.

But that seemed too grim.

For an evening, and ever since,
I thought of the "shadow limb"
amputees are said to imagine,
that sensation of itching or of pain, of
heat, of cold, the dear, unweighted density
of living flesh extended into space
where an arm once was or,
in this case, a lower leg.

I wondered in the waiting room
if Mom would have me scratch it
with a straw, something she'd come to like
in her old days.

She loved Pond's Cold Cream slathered
on the coming-away flesh, and then
a good raking after, nails getting down
to the vasculature, if she could stand it.

But Mom didn't last long enough
to miss the left leg, not long enough to swear
to me, by god,
that it's still there.

Perhaps I *should* have sent
my mother's left leg
to the funeral home
to keep her whole in her grave.

But maybe then I wouldn't hear her voice
or see the shadow of her shoulders
move from room to room,

as if we were in a house we loved,
and the shadows were mine.

Adirondacks, Easter Sunday

Experience, in linguistic terms,
is all but shot: the trees
are simply bare, the dead
stand in no relation even
to a distant will. Maybe
it's spirit I'm after and not

the words. The scribble
of the roadside bramble a cold,
soaked soot giving no light.

The lake doesn't shimmer either
in the fading afternoon as much as
shiver, the light fleeing
across its surface like a chill wind.

Where are these things
inherited from, images
of death-in-life in a soul-less vocabulary?
But then you catch the rock cut
at Pokamoonshine, sunwarm sluicing
down the icy face of a god.

Later, to the south, yellow rays and rain.
There's a rainbow coming if the light just holds.

Cassie Pickett's Molasses Cookies

One half-cup sugar,
one teaspoon cinnamon,
half teaspoons ginger, salt. Mix together.

One half-cup shortening,
one egg (not necessary to beat);
half-cup molasses, quarter-cup
cold coffee.

Teaspoon soda,
two cups flour.

Mix all together and bake
at 375 degrees, 12 minutes, as Florence wrote.
Anything with molasses is likely to burn
quicker than without, so I use 350
and watch them.

Jon Dallas

Raised on a farm in northern Ohio, Jon Dallas moved to the North Country fifteen years ago. Dallas is a product of two esteemed writing programs—the Iowa Writers Workshop, begun in part by Robert Frost, and the graduate writing program at Bennington College, where he was the Jane Kenyon Scholar. Despite his elite training, Dallas's poetry is filled with the detritus of well-grounded experience. His résumé includes stints as an air traffic controller, a car mechanic, a big band trombonist, and a computer technician.

He teaches writing and music at Paul Smith's College, and is the founding editor of Barkeater, the only literary journal based in the Adirondack Park. His poems have appeared in several journals, including Green Mountain Review, Riverrun, Trestle Creek Review, and Riverwind.

"She Starts From Sleep in Winter" first appeared in Windless Orchard, Summer 1994; "When the Weather Turned Around" first appeared in New Orleans Review, Fall 1999; "Night Skiing" is forthcoming in The Antigonish Review. The other two poems are published here for the first time.

In and Out

The fog, a maw at the top of the hill
in mist so fine you have to look up
to feel it: winter trees like spiked hair let
the light drop, even though there's nothing
alive under anymore—you go further in,
and late snow stings your eyes like doubt, gathers

on your brows and lashes until, despite good
intentions, you've gone blind, dreaming like
any animal of water for the fires inside.

The woods has told itself about you, so
you'll find nothing hidden here—the fish dig
their nests, foxes worry their kits—and I'll
bet the murder of crows, sleeping: you
couldn't get lost here if you wanted to.

When the Weather Turned Around

He only ate things that flew—woodcock, pheasant,
quail, (never crow), partridge, dove, rail, mallard, pigeon—

And he always stewed them through, tarring the meat
with rose petals. He would chew slowly through the tiny

sinews and only leave the bones for the wind
to take from a windowsill high above his house.

He would feel himself losing the edges of his ribs,
as if he were stepping into a body that the birds had made

for him, with a light crate for a skeleton and muscles
thin as wires. The small meat would eat slowly through him:

pin-feathers sprouting from behind his eyes before his sight
was zipped shut in the soft barbs. The woman

he lived with was already a bird, with not a straight
hollow bone in her body, and she took the wind

with the shape rather than tempo of wings. And when
it snowed, he felt the earth swag away from beneath him

and the house above his head became their home. At night,
she dreamed of where they were; he still had much to learn.

She Starts from Sleep in Winter

Around here, the end of the world would be
less disturbing than watching a dog keel
through four feet of new snow: you wipe away
disaster casually as rain takes
stray chalk for hopscotch on sidewalks in green
and red pastels—a home you could go, not
far from here, if you were to jump just right:
from honeymoon past one-two-three, toes first.

Gables stare at you around here, and there
is a tamarack growing on a three-
story roof. Of course, the roots leached into
the bedroom's hot water where their son died
and they slept. It took years for the tendrils
to touch them, but the Mister and Missus
Hoyle liked the effect when they took ahold
in their bed. She conceived at fifty-five.

And such a girl as you never saw—hair
like willows' beards and eyes color of rain.
Though no one could place her name and she'd six
fingers and remnant toes, not a soul could
watch her call bright weather from her stoop (she'd
missed only once, on a trip to aunts in
Arkansas), but stop and check itself.

                                    She
falls off again, mumbles about the light.

Night Skiing

The wild children take the dark run down
the mountain snow, dogs silent fire-eyed
at their heels. A few gray men and women
used to try and confound their speed with pine
and balsam boughs, but they died off
and the children tucked, barefoot on boards
run smooth as driftwood, their bright jackets
chuting and heads so low that for all
anyone knew, they were only color.

Standing in a Canoe

The dock is not far wherever you
are on the water, and if you've lost
anything on the bottom the odds
are best looking for it when the sun's
high—at dusk the light makes dark mirrors
on the surface that you can't see through,
unless you've brought a wooden pole bright
and steady to sweep underneath, but
even that you might lose in searching.

If what is lost was large, and your eyes
are clear and keen, strip down and dive,
but it's colder the deeper, and your arms
just keep up, so you're forced to swim then
become the water, where clues move quick
and balance is never a question.

Michael G. DiNunzio

Mike DiNunzio writes natural history with the grace of a poet and the accessibility of a journalist. With graduate degrees in botany and forestry, DiNunzio has lived in the Adirondacks for more than two decades, employed as a state biologist, educator, and free-lance consultant to various governmental and conservation organizations. He is currently on the staff of the Adirondack Council, an advocacy group based in Elizabethtown, New York.

Written in 1984, DiNunzio's Adirondack Wildguide: A Natural History of the Adirondack Park *(The Adirondack Conservancy Committee and the Adirondack Council, 1984) is simply the best of its kind. A chapter describing the region's rare alpine summits is excerpted below.*

Islands in the Sky

At the end of the Ice Age the Adirondacks were colonized by communities of plants and animals similar to those now found in the arctic tundra far to the north. Ground-hugging shrubs, herbs, mosses, and grass-like plants dominated the landscape. For a short time tundra-like vegetation held sway, but as the climate moderated and soils developed, forests invaded the region. Nevertheless, small areas of arctic habitat are still found atop some of our highest mountain summits in what is called the alpine zone.

In all, about 85 acres of land on 11 major peaks are covered by alpine vegetation. Each site is an isolated outpost along the southernmost border of the community's range in the eastern United States. Most plants

67

that try to establish a foothold here cannot stand the rigors of being alternately baked by the sun, moistened by fog, and lashed by sand, ice, and rain driven before a howling gale. Alpine species, survivors from the frigid Pleistocene Epoch, are therefore at an advantage since their unique adaptations help them in the struggle for existence under the severe conditions of their mountaintop environment.

The microclimate of alpine peaks is much more harsh than that found at the base of the mountains. For example, the mean annual temperature at the peak of Whiteface Mountain is about 10° colder than seven miles away in Lake Placid, which is 3,000 feet lower. This is exactly the difference in mean annual temperature between Lake Placid and Poughkeepsie, New York, about 200 miles farther south. The frost-free season on the summits is limited to approximately two months as compared to around 100 days in Lake Placid. Precipitation averages 25 percent more than in surrounding lowlands.

Nearly one-half of the total area above timberline consists of exposed rock, most of which is covered by lichens and mosses. These hardy pioneers are able to colonize bare mineral surfaces by gathering nutrients from rain, dust, and decayed fragments of their own tissues. Lichens also secrete acids that help dissolve substances from the rocks on which they live. Each different organism is adapted to a slightly different set of environmental conditions. Rock mosses live in the moist micro-valleys whereas lichens cover the drier, more exposed micro-ridges on bedrock and boulders. Life for these organisms is so demanding that they grow very slowly but may live an astonishingly long time. Some individual alpine lichens are perhaps several thousand years old.

Alpine pioneers modify their environment in many ways. They provide a source of nutrients, shade from sun, protection from wind, and a supply of moisture that enables other plants to grow in their place. Gradually a carpet of different mosses, lichens, and herbs spreads over the rock. Sphagnum moss soon infiltrates this carpet and becomes dominant. The thirsty sphagnum adds a great deal of living and dead material to the community which then acts like a blotter in the sky, drinking moisture from rain, dew, and clouds. Soil composed largely of organic duff thickens, acidifies, and forms the matrix in which woody-stemmed heath plants and dwarf trees become established. In many ways alpine summits are like inverted bogs, covering a lofty dome rather than a lowland depression.

Wind is perhaps the most important factor in determining which plants will eventually live on a particular site. Sharply-angled rocks that jut above their surroundings into the full blast of the wind may pass thousands of years with little more than a scant covering of lichens and tiny mosses. Close to the surface of the ground, wind, temperature, and moisture extremes are less severe. In these areas compact colonies of shrubby "cushion plants" such as Lapland rose-bay and *Diapensia* add a delicate splash of color to alpine gardens. On bare soil and in pockets of muck and gravelly sand, clumps of mountain sandwort seem to defy the elements with their long-lasting white blooms. Relatively level, exposed sites are likely to accumulate enough soil and moisture to foster development of a grassy meadow composed of Bigelow sedge, deer's hair, and the sweet-smelling alpine holygrass.

Depressions in the bedrock and sites in the lee of ridges and boulders usually have a dependable snowpack, and it is here that sphagnum helps create a true heath community. Winter protection under a blanket of snow is essential for the growth of shrubs that have perennial stems more than a few inches high. If this covering is blown away, buds and twigs are dried beyond recovery at a time when the frozen ground prevents replacement of precious moisture. Alpine bilberry, a relative of lowland blueberries, prefers this habitat which it shares with such familiar bog-dwellers as leatherleaf, Labrador tea, and bog laurel. Many alpine specialties are found here too, including black crowberry, a diminutive variety of cotton grass called hare's-tail, dwarf birch, and bearberry willow that has fuzzy catkins like its lowland pussy willow cousins but only grows a few inches high.

Plants from the boreal community are able to penetrate the alpine zone within deep bedrock fissures and under the shelter of ledges and boulders. Balsam fir, mountain paper birch, and mountain alder are common. Bunchberry, bluebead lily, twinflower, bristly clubmoss, false hellebore, and a variety of mosses crowd beneath the shrubby over-story. Far from its lowland haunts, black spruce is at home here, where conditions are suitable to its sun-loving, acid-tolerant, low-nutrient lifestyle. Since these plants are unable to thrive when exposed to winter winds, their branches seldom extend much beyond the confines of protected microhabitats. Wherever terminal shoots of trees poke above the snow they are dried to death. Ground-hugging lateral branches survive, however, and mats of foliage extend from gnarled, twisted, bonsai-like trunks, a form called "krummholz," from the German words meaning crooked wood.

Even though alpine plants have adapted to harsh microclimatic conditions, they live within a fragile community that is easily damaged by natural or manmade forces. Wildfires have eliminated many species. Air pollution now threatens delicate lichens. Hiking boots cause great harm to the shallow, peaty turf, and once this mat is cut, water erodes it quickly. Organic matter that has taken perhaps thousands of years to accumulate is then washed away, leaving a naked scar that widens at a frightening rate. But this situation is changing. Work is under way to stabilize damaged areas by fertilizing, planting grasses, and by confining visitors to marked pathways.

The only birds you are likely to see near the ground on barren mountaintops are dark-eyed juncos and perhaps a white-throated sparrow or two. Neither bird breeds above timberline, but they feed here on seeds, berries, and scraps of food left by visitors. White-throats whistle a loud, clear song, whereas the juncos limit their vocalizing to a soft, bell-like, tinkling trill or a metallic "tink-tink-tink." The white outer tail feathers of the junco can be seen at a distance, but you must be closer to see the sparrow's white throat.

Common ravens are returning to the Adirondacks from which they were nearly extirpated early in the century, and you may be fortunate enough to spot one. Like crows, these black scavengers of the high country usually travel in family groups but are much larger than their lowland cousins. Size may be difficult to judge at a distance, so listen carefully for the guttural croaks and loud squawks that distinguish the raven's calls from the familiar "caw" of the crow. If you have binoculars look closely at the tail. It is fan-shaped on crows but narrows slightly at both ends on ravens to give a wedged appearance. Ravens are superb acrobats and seldom fly for long without twisting and tumbling in aerial maneuvers over these fog-shrouded islands in the sky.

Elizabeth Folwell

Betsy Folwell joined Adirondack Life *as a contributing editor in 1984, and is currently senior editor. Which is to say that she, along with two or three others, has earned a bear's share of the credit for the flourishing of Adirondack letters in the last two decades. The writing in* Adirondack Life, *both that edited and authored by Folwell, has been some of the best seen in a regional magazine anywhere in the United States. Not surprisingly, during those years* Adirondack Life *has been the recipient of several prestigious magazine awards for general excellence.*

Her book-length works include two specialty guides to the Adirondacks, The Adirondack Book, A Complete Guide *(Berkshire House, 1992) written with Neal Burdick, and* Adirondack Odysseys: Exploring Museums and Historic Places from the Mohawk to the St. Lawrence *(Adirondack Museum, Berkshire House, 1997), a guide to places of history and culture in the region. Folwell and her husband reside in Blue Mountain Lake, New York.*

"Why We Bagged It" appeared most recently in Adirondack Life's *Silver Anniversary issue (October, 1994).*

Why We Bagged It

We moved to the Adirondacks in March 1976 and became gradually cemented in place by the accumulation of certain worldly goods: wood stove, chain saw, snowshoes, canoe. Collecting experiences helped us put down roots as well. We learned how to make maple syrup (don't tap cherry trees, for starters), how to execute a proper do-si-do, how to swim in frigid waters (the first lesson coming after sinking a friend's sailboat because we forgot to check the drain plugs, and the second after demonstrating white-water canoe strokes without informing our dog what we planned to do). We joined the fire department and the ambulance squad. But nothing was quite so declarative of our notions to become part of the community as going into business in downtown Blue Mountain Lake.

It was spring 1980, and my partner and I were both on unemployment following the end of the Olympics and the demise of CETA, a federal workforce training program. Once a week we had gone to a church basement in Tupper Lake to correctly answer the Three Big Questions: Were you able to work? Did you look for work? Did you refuse any work? Next!

Clearly there was no future in that activity, and few full-time jobs loomed on the horizon. There was a tantalizing prospect, though, since the old general store in town was for sale at a reasonable price. We attempted to buy the place, but someone else moved more quickly. They desired the property as an investment and had no intention of running a business, so we ended up as tenants.

Our strongest asset was ignorant enthusiasm. What could be so difficult about running a grocery store? Why, we had spent countless hours buying and eating food! Our combined experience in retail sales had been limited to part-time jobs at a ski shop and a discount department store, which didn't exactly prepare us for being owners, managers, cashiers, butcher, and book-keeper, but we had ideas about the possibilities of being merchants.

We had about six weeks to get the place washed, painted, refurbished, and stocked. We had to find suppliers for groceries, produce, meat, soda, beer, dairy products, ice cream, newspapers, candy, crackers, chips, bread, ice, bags, and sundries; it turned out there were two or three companies we had to buy from in each category, because, for example, Coke doesn't sell Pepsi. The bills began to pile up, what with orders and repairs to things like compressors for walk-in coolers. Then there were permits to get, paperwork to file, and deposits to pay.

We connected with a huge wholesaler for our main grocery supply, and the Syracuse office sent a salesman to walk us through our first order, which was utterly mind boggling: imagine every item you could possibly expect to find in a compact but well-stocked grocery store, then order a couple cases of it. Then think of all the things you don't like and would never in a zillion years waste your money on, and order some of those too.

Then pay for it all. Because we were new customers, our first order—thousands of dollars worth of ketchup, tooth-picks, dish soap, onions, soup, baby food, dog biscuits, paper towels, TV dinners—was cash. Not a check or money order, but actual dollar bills exchanged for a tractor-trailer load of stuff. The salesman helped us arrange the shelves according to the protocol that dictates the olives go next to pickles go next to vinegar and so forth. Within hours, the place looked like we were in business, and we had totally blown years of savings. Even if we failed miserably and no one came to our store, we wouldn't starve, we rationalized, and if necessary, we'd learn to make wholesome meals out of condiments.

We opened on May 15, offering free coffee and cookies. Folks came, drank coffee, said nice things and left. We got some good advice—"Eat your mistakes at home," "Don't let anybody talk you into charge accounts," "Take orders over the phone, but don't do it for free"—and hired a couple of strong, tireless teenagers and a savvy neighbor so that the store could be open seventy hours a week. My partner and I took Sunday afternoons off, but that was all.

The building itself was what drew us into commerce. A solid, three-story structure, for more than half a century it had anchored the community, providing all the necessities and more than a few luxuries. A small room had served as the post office for several years, and the upstairs, a vast open space about thirty by sixty feet, once sold hardware and dry goods. The nail bins were still there along the wall, and a wire rack for lantern chimneys hung above a display table.

Under the eaves were the records for M. Callahan and Company, boxes of bills with ornate engraved letterheads, and the odd, charming mementos of town life from long ago: a poster for the House of David basketball team playing in North Creek and miniature slates for ordering staples like blacking, bluing, codfish, currants, sago, sal soda, and saleratus. The place hinted at a tradition that we hoped we might recapture, and perhaps even profit from.

We got to know our suppliers, who provided a human link to that past. As you'd expect, they were older men, independent guys who worked long hours. There was Milton, who went to the Syracuse farm market at four a.m. each day, then drove north to sell produce to restaurants, lodges, camps, and stores. He marveled when we bought watercress and sold it out in a day. "You've got the trade here," he said, and proceeded to educate us by bringing up ambrosial white peaches, succulent yellow cherries, and tiny salt potatoes. There was John, who'd arrive with his dual-axle truck brimming with plump old-fashioned tomatoes he grew on his farm, and Freddy, who was a pirate at heart but always made deals on lightly bruised bananas, slightly limp spinach, and other bargains. Ralph the iceman was a gentle soul who refinished barroom shuffleboard rigs and transported them to tournaments in a cut-off school bus during cold weather; he timed his deliveries to our place so he'd arrive just as we were closing up and we could sit in the back office next to the roll-top desk, sipping root beer and listening to him talk of selling block ice from a horse-drawn wagon throughout Black River valley towns.

The meat purveyors weren't a link with the past but a feeble connection to the future. Our main supplier, in Utica, was in the throes of computerizing its operations, which meant unfathomable bills, mixed-up orders and deliveries that invariably came between midnight and dawn. There's nothing quite as rude as being awakened from a sound slumber to unload cold, dripping boxes of beef, pork, and chicken.

Our first big weekend was Memorial Day. It was exhilarating to ring up orders and help customers depart with bulging brown bags. Everything seemed to work; nobody seemed to notice that we were clueless. June was slow, but it offered a chance to practice making hamburger, trimming lettuce, and keeping track of inventory.

All hell broke loose in July. Our customers wanted things (rolling papers, condoms, racy magazines) that we never dreamed of selling, and sometimes bought far more off the shelves than what we had anticipated. I spent a sleepless night before Independence Day wondering where I'd find a case of butter to go with the thirty dozen ears of corn we had to sell. My partner gallantly turned huge ungainly hunks of meat into symmetrical roasts and chops (we ate the wedge-shaped nubbins that defied categorization). I vowed we'd never run out of toilet paper or disposable diapers. We became snack-food connoisseurs.

We learned a lot about provisions, planning, and human behavior. Since most of our daily customers were on vacation, we were witness to subtle social dynamics. For example, no one grocery shops for fun. People have certain expectations of how food stores should work and tend not to be open-minded when things are a little bit different. Dads shop while on vacation, but from our sample it seems that they do not participate much in the activity during the rest of the year. We base our finding on the oft-repeated episode of the man of the house ordering a custom-cut steak the size of Delaware and responding with hysterical disbelief to the cost.

Some people also clearly leave their good manners at home. I spent twenty minutes sobbing in the meat locker after a customer called me a bad name because I had ordered caraway-rye bread rather than dill. Another customer threw lamb chops at my partner, shrieking they were spoiled. (She was wrong. They were delicious.) A frail-looking, determined woman wrenched the lock out of our door when she forced her way in to get a Sunday *New York Times*; apparently she missed the large poster that said CLOSED and couldn't hear us yelling, "Wait! Stop!!"

The newspapers truly were our worst nightmare. We likened summer folks' need for news of the outside world to an addictive drug that blinded them to their immediate environment. On brilliant sunny mornings, when any right-thinking individual would be hiking or canoeing or at least enjoying the fresh air from an Adirondack chair, people would line up outside to get a paper, watching through the window with pathetic hope etched on their faces as we bustled to assemble hundreds of papers from all the different sections. There was a newsprint shortage that summer, so we never quite got our requested allotment. Papers were highly sought after and occasionally caused ugly incidents, such as the infamous *New York Times* tug-of-war.

One summer morning, a female visitor muttered that the twenty-five-cent profit we eked out of a six-pound Sunday paper was despicable and accused us of ripping her off. "Don't buy it," said my partner, gently removing it from her hands. "But I want it," she said, as she yanked back. "Then pay for it," he said, holding firmly onto his end of the bundle. "You're impossible," she shouted as she tried to wrest the paper from his grasp. "So are you, lady!" he said. The other customers cheered as she exited.

That day marked a subtle yet profound change in our attitude. No more tears in the cooler, no more apologies for ground round that cost two bucks a pound. We realized most of our customers didn't want to have a relationship with us, they just wanted to buy things and get out of the store. We began to understand what our neighbors had probably known all along, that no matter how much we wanted it to, the store couldn't sustain us through the winter. The days when the place was the life-support system of town were long gone. We couldn't compete with the bright lights of Long Lake and Indian Lake, and folks had become habituated to going ten miles down the road to the bank, the hairdresser, the lumberyard, and, yes, the supermart.

We put a last, best effort into stocking the store for big-game season with the kinds of things we imagined hunters would crave after a long day in the woods: hot dogs, Canadian bacon, pork rinds, doughnuts. We were about twenty years too late, though, since most hunters had long ago gotten in the habit of picking up the essentials before they left home. Business dwindled to a trickle, then stopped altogether, which was a good thing because it was awfully hard to keep the building from freezing with one lonely kerosene heater. On November 1, we gave it up for good.

What we gained from those frenzied weeks was all the wieners the hunters eschewed (two full cases, or close to five hundred; to this day, the sight of a hot dog fills me with a curious mixture of nostalgia and loathing), several cases of cheap beer and soda, lots of canned goods (butter beans, creamed corn, and sardines), boxes of Jell-O in assorted perky colors, jars of generic jam, crates of industrial-strength paper products, and enough breakfast cereal to last a year. We made about as much money as we would have had we both found minimum-wage jobs.

Beyond that, though, the store was an education, a graduate semester in small-townology with a minor in micro-economics. We're not in business anymore, but once in a while we imagine what it might be like to stand again behind the counter on a sultry evening, washed in the wan neon glow of a Genesee sign and counting out change.

Phil Gallos

Born in New York City, Phil Gallos moved to Saranac Lake in 1957, where he has lived, more or less, ever since. A graduate of Towson State University in Maryland, Phil worked for several years as a reporter and photographer for the Adirondack Daily Enterprise, through which he immersed himself into the local landscape. He combined his love of the outdoors—canoeing, hiking, cross-country skiing—with a fascination for social and natural history.

The result was his first book, By Foot in the Adirondacks (Adirondack Publishing, 1972). He also was among a few local writers who assisted author Barbara McMartin with Discover the Adirondack High Peaks (Backcountry Publications, 1989), perhaps the best backcountry hiking guide for the popular high mountain region.

Gallos's most enduring work to date, no doubt, is Cure Cottages of Saranac Lake: Architecture and History of a Pioneer Health Resort (Historic Saranac Lake, 1985). More than a simple record of local history, the exhaustively researched and beautifully written and illustrated book captures a poignant moment in the history of America, when tuberculosis befell thousands without regard for class and ethnic lines, and many victims relocated to Saranac Lake in hope of a cure. Gallos tells a story that reveals the remarkable relationship between a community's natural and built landscapes.

The first selection below, "The Vanishing Cure Cottage," is the closing chapter to Cure Cottages of Saranac Lake. The second work, "Tyson's," is a personal memoir of change in a small Adirondack town, and is published here for the first time.

The Vanishing Cure Cottage

One by one they go, and they cannot be replaced. Since Trudeau Sanatorium closed and Saranac Lake's days as Pioneer Health Resort ended thirty-one years ago, the village's built environment has changed drastically. Most of this change has come as a loss of buildings. Very little new has been built since World War II. A great deal has been destroyed.

The attrition of Saranac Lake's stock of structures has been a phenomenon that has gained momentum in the past three decades. At first, the primary culling force was fire. Some buildings were demolished through acts of private enterprise, and some were lost to municipal or state projects, but it was not until the mid-1970s that fire took a back seat. In the five years from 1975 to 1980, probably more of Saranac Lake became landfill than in all the preceding twenty years. Fire was certainly responsible for much of this, but the single most potent agent of destruction was the bureaucrat wielding public funds for such things as road building and "urban renewal." This spasm of demolition ended with the advent of the 1980s, but the face of the village has continued to change—often for the better, often not. One doesn't have to knock a building down to destroy it.

The irony is that what is one person's destruction is another person's improvement. Since the oil crisis of 1973, more and more people have been "improving" their buildings to make them more "energy efficient." Here, though, unadorned reality collides with unfortunate fact.

The unadorned reality is that, regardless of our own feelings about it, Saranac Lake's place of significance in global history is due solely to its role as a center for the treatment and investigation of tuberculosis; and, the Great Camps notwithstanding (they are a regional rather than a local development), its one contribution to the architectural heritage of the nation is the cure cottage. The unfortunate fact is that much of what has been done in the name of energy efficiency strikes at the heart of what remains of that contribution.

From an historical point of view, any structure can be called a cure cottage as long as someone cured in it; but, architecturally, a cure cottage is only a cure cottage if it is equipped with some sheltered space for the patient to take the air. As stated in our discussion of the evolution of the cure cottage, the glass-walled room called the "cure porch" became the hallmark of the cure cottage as a distinct and unique building type.

Externally, visually, a cure porch depends on its fenestration. To alter its sliding glass panels or ranks of double-hung sash or casement windows is to alter the very essence of its character—and thereby compromise the character of the house to which it belongs. Put simply, a cure porch with its windows covered over or reduced to a few patches of thermopane is not a cure porch; its parent structure can no longer be called a cure cottage; and the architectural wealth of the village, and the nation, is diminished.

In a climate where "winter" lasts six months, the passive solar potential of Saranac Lake's hundreds of cure porches has too often (and quite sadly) been overlooked. The disturbing trend, as has been noted already in this book, has been to reduce or remove windows, especially on porches—thereby destroying the sole features that make the majority of Saranac Lake's houses architecturally and historically unique and important. The harsh truth is—because of the way many cure porches were added onto buildings by whatever means would work, regardless of compatibility or balance—that when these porches are insensitively "modernized" they become merely peculiar warts on so many very ordinary houses. The result on the visual balance sheet, between Saranac Lake as the nation's Pioneer Health Resort for the treatment of tuberculosis and Saranac Lake as anywhere U.S.A., is yet another shift toward architectural anonymity and the obliteration of identity that has befallen so many other small American communities in this century of cultural homogenization.

What is crucially needed to prevent these shifts is a change of perspective. Cure porches must be viewed as an asset rather than as a liability. Instead of being mutilated or destroyed to prevent heat loss, they should be creatively insulated, ventilated, and equipped with thermal drapes or shades to exploit their potential for heat gain. Then, cure cottages may stop vanishing.

But there must also be an appreciation of the worth of history, the value of a heritage, as well as of the price of a BTU. The saying goes—summing up the story of thousands of small towns—that we don't know what we've got till it's gone.

If this book has accomplished anything, it is hoped that it has helped us to know a little better what we have *before* it is gone, so that the maxim may remain a lesson to remember instead of becoming a lament for what is lost.

Saranac Lake is a village with a rich, unique, and inspiring history; and its history lives in its architecture—particularly that of the cure cottages. Without denying the importance and contribution of lumbering, farming, and the sporting and tourism industries, it must be said that the seven decades of the fresh-air cure made Saranac Lake perhaps the most cosmopolitan, most vibrant, and most oddly extraordinary community of its size in the United States. Farm boys and factory workers, bankers and baronesses, Americans and Cubans, Norwegians and Filipinos, and so many others of every social and cultural origin, of every talent and temperament, came here because of one inescapable fact: they had tuberculosis. Wherever they were, they had to leave. Whatever their lives had been, they had to change them. Before the advent of the "wonder drugs," there was no alternative save certain death.

They came to Saranac Lake, and Saranac Lake gave them hope— and, often, it gave them back their health. The whole town revolved around the cure, existed for the cure, was geared to the cure. The needs of the health seekers and the seriousness of their situation were reflected in everything from the motto, "Sanitary Saranac" ("you wouldn't dare spit on the street"), to the "Rest Hour" from two to four p.m., so sacred that the local radio station even went off the air for those 120 minutes.

This was a place where the pariahs of an ignorant and fearful society, shunned as carriers of the White Plague, were welcomed to live together under a law of hygiene as part of a human family—while those who had rejected them rode down the streets in their closed cars on their way through to other places, their handkerchiefs held to their faces.

This was a time when grief and compassion, struggle and joy were so pervasive, so intense, that the base and the petty in people was hardly noticeable.

This was a world unto itself, where the fleeting moment was finally grasped and lived to the fullest because one always knew that moment might be the last.

This was the final sanctuary at the center of an emerald citadel of forest enfolded mountains, where the medically condemned came to breathe the blessed air that was their last reprieve.

From every place they came and from every circumstance, with every misconception about their disease but all with the same hope. They filled the hotels and the institutions. They filled the tents and tenanted the spare rooms of the citizenry; and by the force of their need and numbers, they founded and filled the cottages of cure.

Some stayed, some moved on, some left in the arms of death. Victorious or vanquished, always valorous, they were warriors battling an invisible enemy—as were all who cared for them or housed them or who worked with the weaponry of test tube and microscope or delivered vegetables door to door or who stoked the furnaces or stocked the pharmacies or who met the newcomers at the train under the bright blue winter sky or who rode back with them when the blue finally yielded to black.

Each of them had a story—all the stories being the history making the memory of this community. Some are spoken every day; others have slipped beyond recall; but all are embodied in the buildings wherein the stories were lived. When the last breathing witness of the Pioneer Health Resort has passed from our midst, only the buildings will remain to remind us of what happened here. They are the silent, lasting pages of a history book written in stone and wood and glass, in the language of architecture, in the dialect of the Outdoor Life. They are ours to read if only we can learn not to burn them or crumple them or obscure their words with our own senseless scribble.

This is a belief, a basic conviction about the meaning and quality of community, which we may sometimes feel is doomed to be always spinning in the wake of current fashion and economic expediency; but there are those who share it and who show it by the way they have respected and cared for the inherent character of their buildings. They have preserved the integrity of the cottages they own, maintaining original features, restoring what has been removed or covered over, and, most importantly, honoring the porches and verandas by using them: sleeping on them, working in them, resting or playing or loving within those sheltered realms of air and light. We should praise these people and encourage them; we should encourage others to join them, and we should join them ourselves. We must take the cure cottages with us, beyond vanishing, into the future.

Tyson's

I'm not going to tell you a story.

I thought I'd deliver a dissertation on the difference between memory and recall, but I'm not going to do that, either. It's just that memory seems to have a life of its own. Recall records facts and is tied to them. Memory isn't tied to anything. It manipulates facts—turns them into experience.

What's there now, across the street from St. Bernard's School, in Saranac Lake? No, don't stand down on the sidewalk. Get up a little higher where you can see something. Walk up the driveway till you're almost in the parking lot. Now turn around. What's down there beyond the end of the old pavement that runs away from under the toes of your shoes?

There's a new highway that's still called River Street even though it's four lanes wide. And there are guardrails of Corfam steel, formulated to rust a rustic brown—heavy industry's gift to the Adirondack Council. There's a thin strip of eroding soil and piles of rip-rap blasted out of Brewster Mountain and finally the lake, the one the village elders named for Governor Flower. If you don't look any farther outward, you won't see the big houses on Riverside Drive, or the red-brick senior-citizens' high-rise, or the steep, creased, hardwood slope where Captain Pliny Miller built his homestead in 1821. But now is not 1821, nor is it even 1957.

In 1821, when there wasn't a lake or a four lane highway or Corfam, you'd have seen trees, and a free-running river, and more trees, and perhaps a cabin and a man with dam-building on his mind; but I don't remember any of that.

I *do* remember 1957. In 1957, you'd have seen Tyson's smack-slam up against the pavement of the real River Street, a truck thoroughfare so chock full of chuck-holes that local journalists called it the Burma Road or, later, the Ho Chi Minh Trail. Behind and around Tyson's was Thomas's Boat Landing, where the *Miss Saranac* was moored.

Tyson's was a shoebox with stuccoed sides and a red tile roof. The stucco was supposed to be white, but it never had a chance. At each end there was a door, and facing the street were three plate-glass picture windows.

Tyson's was off-limits. We weren't allowed to go there; and we probably wouldn't have, regardless of how alluring a place so odd looking might have been to boys our age; but it was the inside of Tyson's that was irresistible.

Essentially, Tyson's was a diner; but, on the inside, it was a backwards diner. When you go into a normal diner and you sit at the counter, you sit with your back to the windows, and you face a wall with all kinds of short order machinery lined up along it. At Tyson's, the counter didn't face a wall. It faced those three big windows. All the equipment was arranged in front of them, including a donut maker—something usually not found out front, something usually hidden in a back room, probably out of fear that if you saw the process you might not want to eat the product.

Have you ever seen a donut maker in operation? Have you ever watched one when you were nine or ten years old? There's a hopper on a swivelling arm, and there's a crank on the hopper or on the arm or somewhere, and there's a big vat under the hopper, and the hopper is full of donut batter, and the vat is full of grease or lard or something, and somebody turns the crank, and fat rings of batter fall from the snout of the hopper into the vat with a satisfying, sizzling splat; and the crank turns and turns, and the fat rings fall and fall and float and bump and cook and crowd together until there's no more room for sizzling. They just sit and soak awhile.

But that's not all! It's Spring! Outside, the layered glacier of sand and ice that's covered the street for four months is melting. All the chuckholes are brimful with soupy brown slush, and the heavy trucks that made those chuckholes are rumbling by no more than a foot beyond the windows, the big tires slapping the slush out of the holes and sending it up and out in graceful brown fountains that hit the glass with a gritty splash. All the while the crank turning, the batter falling and sizzling as curtains of pebble-peppered road slop cascade down the windows. We would sit there transfixed, more attentive than we ever were in school or church. This was a spectacle. This was a symphony!

When the donuts were ready, they were layered between blottings of paper towel and then served up to us with the waitresses' unfailing warning: "Be careful. Let 'em cool a little more before you eat 'em."

Who knows what kind of junk they were? Who cared! Nothing could quite compare to a fresh, hot Tyson's donut: forbidden fruit eaten in a forbidden place.

We were fortunate, my friends and I, to attend River Street School. That put us close enough to Tyson's to get there quickly, far enough away to go undetected. The poor kids across the street at St. Bernard's could never have gotten through the door without the nuns spotting them.

Aside from the symphony of slush and donuts, there were other things about Tyson's that fascinated us. Here are some images that memory has cultivated for me: thick fingers holding short cigarettes; the big, stainless steel coffee urns with glass tubes on the sides to show what was left within; the ham-handed men loudly wondering what had been used for a coffee filter that morning—newspapers, an old dish rag, the head of a mop. The banter between waitress and customer was endlessly entertaining. Though I don't believe most of us understood the implications of much of what was said, the whole adult world as it unfolded in that small space entranced us.

Certainly it was not an ideal world. Certainly it was a bit tattered and tawdry. It was what it was pretty much without pretense; and we, we boys, were still young enough to be unpretentious. As Tyson's was what it was, we were who we were. Our parents, it seemed, wanted it and us to be something else; and, since there was nothing they could do about the character of the place, they did what they thought best for our futures—they forbade us enter Tyson's, as though this would keep us out of harm's way and free from the forces of evil.

We were refused Tyson's, but we were allowed Bernie Wilson's. Bernie Wilson's was where Alice's is today, right on Berkeley Square. You could go there and get your hair pomaded for free by standing a moment below the big exhaust fan that filled the alleyway with the aroma of infinite French fries; but Bernie's wasn't simply a greasy spoon. It was also a malt shop, and that made it very different from Tyson's. Tyson's was full of adults. Bernie Wilson's was full of teenagers, older kids from the high school. Intoxicated on their own hormones, self-infatuated and amok with strange ideas about sex and status and dominance, they were almost like another species. If you're a boy of nine or ten or eleven, there are few critters as unpredictable and dangerous as a sixteen-year-old sub-dominant male. I don't believe any of us ever felt menaced in Tyson's the way we were sometimes truly menaced in Bernie Wilson's; and we came a lot closer to sin and violence there than we ever did in the forbidden establishment on River Street.

Nineteen-sixty-two: an era is about to end. Eldred Gauthier and Ronnie Fina are going way too fast on that still novel speed strip called LaPan Highway. They're headed toward town. They fly across the big new bridge and under the Main Street traffic light, but there is not yet a four-lane, New York State Department of Transportation engineering marvel on the other side. There is the real River Street, the Burma Road with sudden kinks and ragged holes instead of smooth, banked curves.

Tyson's stood hard by the first kink. Eldred wasn't driving a sports car. He was driving a pick-up truck, and he didn't make it turn where he should have. The next morning, the truck was still there where he'd left it—parked inside Tyson's. He'd gone right into the west end, where there had been a door; but the door was too small to admit a pick-up truck, so he'd taken out a good piece of the wall, as well.

It's hard now to remember whether the truck was all the way in the restaurant or whether there was still a bit of the rear sticking out. That's memory doing battle with recall, and it really doesn't matter anymore—nor did it matter then. What mattered was that Tyson's as we knew it was gone: that legendary, grease-coated interior demolished; the long counter splintered; squat stools overturned; the great coffee urns flattened. I don't remember, either, whether anyone was seriously injured; but I do remember that I never saw the hallowed donut machine again.

After that, everything gets kind of fuzzy for awhile, as though the trauma of it all had broken my will to remember—or maybe it was because I moved to Baltimore. Anyway, eventually Tyson's was renamed Joy's. Eventually, I made it out of high school and into college; and, in the summer between my freshman and sophomore years, I came back to Saranac Lake to work as a milk man for Crystal Spring Dairy and to have some freedom.

It was 1967. In San Francisco, they were calling it the Summer of

Love. That's what it was just about everywhere, though some places and some people were slow to understand it, and some refused to accept it; but, all over the United States you could hear the Beatles singing "Sergeant Pepper" and the Doors "Light My Fire" and Jefferson Airplane and Jimi Hendrix and Janis Joplin—even in Saranac Lake, where the most-played song on the jukebox in Chuck's Bar on Broadway was "White Rabbit."

It would be a few more years, though, for the full impact of psychedelia to be felt here. Not many of us smoked marijuana (let alone dropped acid), but an awful lot of us drank beer. Some nights seemed an endless series of green and brown bottles coming to hand, fingers ritually scraping the labels away as the cold glass perspired in the warm summer air.

Almost every evening, a group of us would gather at Chuck's to decide what to do with the night. More often than not, we would go to Lake Placid to drink and dance at Freddie's Inn; and, later, if we had found the right person there, or if we'd brought the right person with us, we would walk when the band was done to Happy Jack's Sun & Ski Lodge on the Wilmington Road to sit in the basement bar-room where the walls were lined with books and weird paintings. We would sit against a pile of pillows with a fireplace in front of us and a parachute hanging from the ceiling above us, and we would drink more beer and listen to more of our music, so potent with meaning for us that we could not leave until Jack Wikoff turned down the stereo and told us it was time to close.

But in Saranac Lake, Joy's was not closed. Like Tyson's, it never closed. The three picture windows still shed light out onto River Street as they had in nights long past when we saw them go by from the back seats of our parents' cars; but the counter faced away from them now, and it zig-zagged like a yellow Formica serpent so that the little place could accommodate more customers. There were still entrances at either end of the building, and the stucco still failed to be white, and inside there were still coffee urns and wisecracks about what they contained, and, of course, there was still grease; but there was no donut maker. In many ways it was the same place it had always been, but in some crucial ways it had changed—just as we ourselves had changed.

This, though, had not changed. After last call in the bars, Joy's would fill as quickly as the bladders of its patrons had, till we empty-bellied awaiting-a-seat were pressed against the windows, and it seemed the building would burst. We had staggered or sauntered or shuffled in according to the rhythm of the byproducts of the beer in our blood; and when we finally were sitting, we ate without thought of the cost or caring whether we could pay. For one mouth, two hamburgers, an order of French fries, a cup of coffee, another cup of coffee, another hamburger: a mob of inebriated teenagers ordering and eating and sometimes barfing, and the waitresses working so fast they didn't have time to keep track of the cash. We often left Joy's without paying, though some of us were still calling it Tyson's.

Nearly nine years later, I stood where I have told you to stand, and I photographed at night the small building, stuccoed and unwhite, that was by then called B.J.'s. It stood all but empty amid the slush piles of early April. Behind and around it, the rotting ramps and sheds of old Thomas's marina were dark and silent and nearly useless, ruin approaching where once the proud *Miss Saranac* had docked.

East of Tyson's and Thomas's was Prescott Park. It was separated from River Street by a chain link fence and a line of tall pines. There was grass and sand and the rim of the lake, a bathhouse and a swimmers' dock and, out on the water, a raft with a divers' tower. Miss Mary Prescott had purchased the land for public use early in the century. She had come from Massachusetts with money in her purse and tuberculosis in her lungs. She took Dr. Trudeau's cure: air and rest, food for the body, peace for the mind. She regained her health and made Saranac Lake her home. She built a hospital on Helen Hill, and on River Street she gave the people a place to play. At least that is what folks who've preceded me have recalled and written down. When we were children, Mary was well into her eighties. By the time we were teens, her bones were already under the ground; and I don't think there was a single one of us who had known her in the flesh. Nor did any of us when we were boys or even young men know her gift to us as Prescott Park. We all just called it "the beach."

West of Tyson's was a small and nameless patch of park in which three birch trees stood, day and night, through all seasons, constant and serene: mature and lovely ladies who in summer were sometimes visited by a wayward park bench. In May of 1975, I photographed this grassy bit of land. At the time, the bench was elsewhere, but in its place were two boys—one reclining, one sitting on the green—and the scene was one of timeless repose, as though a spell had been cast that nothing would ever change.

The *Miss Saranac* had found repose also, though of a different kind. It lay in the lake at the parklet's edge, its hull stuck in the mud, its decks awash and full of holes, its long, window-walled cabin totally demolished. It was an ignoble end for the vessel that bore our collective name. Less than a year later, it was gone, as were the birch trees and the patch of grass they had inhabited; as were Tyson's and Thomas's; as were Brewster's Gulf and Dave's Sunoco and the Lake View Restaurant, an automobile dealership and an armory and half a dozen residential buildings. The Main Line Garage and Keough Marine Sales moved without too much pain to Lake Flower Avenue; but Prescott Park was dismembered, its pines cut down, the municipal beach banished to Lake Colby on the far fringe of town. River Street was shedding the skin it had worn so long to become a sleeker if fatter snake sashaying along a lake shore stripped of human artifact; but this is not a plaint for what has past.

Another dozen years slid over the Lake Flower Dam. By 1987, the park was triple its original size, though still no one seemed to know its proper name. The pines had been replaced by ashes and maples, the private buildings by a public boat launch, and a new *Miss Saranac* made excursions up the river. For the first time in thirty years, the people were skating that winter on Pontiac Bay; and they had never let go of their beach, regardless of "no swimming" signs and threats of arrest. After a decade of protest and unauthorized use, the village government gave the people a lifeguard and reopened Lake Flower to public swimming.

Now, it is 1997. The Village Board giveth and the Village Board taketh away. The Lake Flower lifeguard lasted but a single summer. Yet still the people swim. Near the spot where I made my portrait of the boys under the birches twenty-two years ago, boys the same age now do cannonball dives off that Corfam guardrail. The new *Miss Saranac* had a short run, as well; and the last time I saw her she was stranded on blocks in somebody's back yard off Colony Court. But a freshening current is flowing through the Saranac River corridor. People of all ages, shapes, sizes, and sexes are giving time and money and sweat to build a river walk to link the Lake Flower shore with Denny Park at the foot of Pine Street rapids. A plan that was planted by the Olmstead Brothers back in 1907 is finally coming to fruition.

I hope Mary Prescott's bones are happy.

Alice Wolf Gilborn

Alice Gilborn began writing in the Adirondacks when the region's community of writers could probably have fit in her living room. In 1979, she was the founding editor of the region's first literary review, Blueline, *which is now published at Potsdam State University. And for many years, she has acted as the Adirondack Museum's books and publications editor. The museum's aggressive publications strategy, led by Gilborn's keen editorial insight, has resulted in a long line of quality books that has, aside from providing readers with bookshelves of pleasure and satisfaction, helped articulate a regional identity for the Adirondacks.*

In addition to editing several important and seminal works related to the region, Gilborn writes essays and poems. Her work has appeared in numerous publications, including Adirondack Life. *"The Proving Grounds," an essay first published in* Blueline, *and "Birds" and "Transit," two poems, appeared originally in* The Woman in the Mountain *(State University of New York Press, 1989) a collection edited by Kate Winter. "The Night Rockwell Kent Showed Me His Etchings" has been simultaneously published in the June 2001 issue of* Blueline.

Alice and her husband, Craig, former director of the Adirondack Museum and author of three books on Adirondack subjects, lived for twenty-eight years in the central Adirondacks.

The Proving Grounds

Not long ago my young daughter selected me to read her a bedtime story about the solar system in her new children's encyclopedia. I pointed out the earth, which occupied front page center, and its important orbit around a huge and fiery sun. On the next page, however, the sun was reduced to the status of a star no larger than a white dot in a great swath of stars called the Milky Way Galaxy. The galaxy itself had shrunk to an indistinct white whorl on the following page, one among millions, the book cheerfully informed me.

I pondered the implications of this for about ten seconds. If the sun was just a pinprick of light in the scheme of things, then the earth was microscopic and I was infinitesimal. Zero, in fact. The few cubic feet of space my body filled counted as nothing. I continued staring at the bouquet of galaxies until my daughter poked me. I sighed. This sort of thinking could lead to insomnia. But then again, it had possibilities. What if I didn't exist?

If I didn't, I wouldn't have to read bedtime stories. I wouldn't have to have a nice day. There'd be no need to take charge of myself or take a course in assertiveness training or behave like Jane Fonda. Best of all, I could sit serenely in my living room and gaze at Blue Mountain without a twinge of guilt because I hadn't climbed it in ten years. If I didn't exist, I could live happily in the Adirondacks without ever having to challenge nature in order to prove myself.

I have nothing but admiration, on the other hand, for those who come here each year to do just that. They congregate at the trailheads, their worldly possessions roped to a frame on their backs so that from the rear they look like ladders wearing boots. Sometimes one overturns and lies stranded in the road. You know they have hiked a long way or are preparing to hike a long way, but you don't ask them why because part of proving yourself is to do it and not talk about it except to yourself. That you can do endlessly. Stories I read are full of interior monologues on the how-to's of proving yourself. It seems you first get in touch with nature, then you overcome it, then you get in touch with yourself, and at last you find your roots. Unfortunately, my roots extend only as far as the first comfortable chair.

Once I asked a backpacker why he wanted to snowshoe up a mountain in the dead of winter with a windchill of minus 30° and risk a broken neck skiing down. I received a look of utter contempt. Now I hold my tongue when muscular young men and athletic gray haired ladies tell me they've been to the top of all forty-nine of the Adirondacks' highest peaks or paddled 100 miles through rain, sleet, wind, and clouds of biting insects. They've tested themselves against the elements and I have not, even though I live smack in the middle of the proving grounds. Because I'm a woman, I feel especially guilty; my duty is to prove myself so I can tell all the men about it. For instance, I could build a log cabin in the woods, live in it a winter, then write a book about my experience in the wilderness. Or I could build a lot of log cabins and sell them. But I suppose that would be sacrificing character for quantity.

Every summer joggers and bikers labor up Blue Mountain Hill, and by their knotted muscles and grimacing faces, I know they are quietly proving themselves. Every fall early bear hunters loudly prove themselves at the town dump and at the Bear Trap Bar. Once I rafted through the Hudson River Gorge when the waves looked like the broad side of a bus, but that only proved my luck was good and I was eligible to survive that day. When we first moved to the Adirondacks, we bought a canoe in anticipation of conquering numerous large lakes, including Raquette, but the canoe had all the hydrodynamics of a bathtub, and despite our efforts stalled in the slightest headwind. So we bought a motor for it. I should have realized then that there was small hope of my ever rising to nature's challenge when I could so willingly trade a paddle for a three-horsepower engine.

After a few moments of heavy silence my daughter instructed me to forget the universe and move on to insects. Once more my perspective went into shock. From an ant's point of view, I not only existed, I was an immense mound of flesh capable of creating a colossal disturbance. With my every step a shudder passed through the anthill. Being a giant, I was well equipped to confront whatever nature had to offer, even ants. Being human, I'd have to prove myself after all. I sighed. I could ease into it slowly by taking a walk in the woods during hunting season. But I'd rather do something more appropriate to my size, something gigantically human, like digging through the rubble of an earthquake for eight days straight and bringing forth, alive, a newborn baby. That would be proof to last a lifetime.

Birds

They struck with brief beating wings
against the fender; something
shuddered. I kept going not
daring to brake. In these mountains
winter roads are packed with snow,
on top, sand, and birds flock down
to glut their craws with grit.
Grosbeaks, sparrows, crows,
grounded, slow to sense
the tremor in the frost,
wheels dense looming,
rise with effort,
too late.

There was a jet that sucked into
its engines wild swans passing
south, a fatal confluence.
In that glacial brilliance
all flight stopped, struck
earthwards, blazing steel
and feathers. Accident.
Justice. Death by any
name. I keep going
certain of it. Behind
me the road, the snow,
the corpses on
the sand.

Transit

Today he brings me wildflowers
with tenderness erratic as the first

red that flags the August maples.
His gift recalls an old gesture,
youth to parent, man to woman,
yet he bears the flowers like a child,
some uprooted, petals dropped
in transit, the whole unedited
bouquet plunged in a screw top jar.

I gaze through the glass at aquatic
undergrowth, hope for a fish
to part the leaves but think again
of trees laden in the torpid air
their hard green cargo dragging
at the branch. My son swims out
to shake them of apples like last
winter's snow; all spring skywards.
How much weather it will take
for them to redden, drop and die.

The Night Rockwell Kent Showed Me His Etchings

He called this painting "Adirondacks" but it could be
anywhere, weathered buildings, wireless posts
against a fallow field, mountains rising darkly—
Empty homesteads strewn across the plains, hosts
to owls and spiders—these shells of former
lives ghosted my childhood. Landlocked then
I pondered more exotic scenes.

Raw turbulence of mighty oceans is what I dreamed
at fourteen reading that black book, the whale's huge snout
streaming from the cover's depths. Every night I sailed
a restless sea aboard the *Pequod*, Ishmael, witness to it all
Captain Ahab's mad pursuit of Moby Dick, the great whale
breached, transcendent, snapping boats in his jaws

smashing ships with his tail, diving finally as the sea
swept over, his tormentor lashed forever to his white
leviathan side. The book is gone but not the whale. Kent's
apotheosis leaps from the spray of Melville's wild
imaginings, etched a lifetime on my mind.

Later on a Massachusetts shore I watched the flat deceptive
sea and dug my heels into the sand, dwarfed and ignorant,
as when I met the man himself, Kent at Asgaard, images
of Moby Dick maneuvering his walls. From a drawer he
pulled proofs, spread them for inspection, larger than
the drawings I remembered. Freed from their
wordy element, they lay profoundly still
beached at last on Adirondack soil.

The hand that drew the ocean drew the land. I see it
in the mountains heaving toward the sky, motion
arrested, clouds roiling to a storm. Into this bleak
scenario slides light, washes mountain, house
barn, seeps into fields, into the earth itself
where underneath the ocean lies in wait
and all the great beasts swim.

Amy Godine

Readers of Adirondack Life *may be familiar with Amy Godine's features on the region's ethnic and social history, ranging from antebellum African-American homesteaders to Chinese illegal aliens. She has single-handedly refreshed the Adirondack community's collective memory about its immigrant roots, an accomplishment perhaps equal to preserving large tracts of wild land in the region.*

An independent scholar who resides in Saratoga Springs, New York, Godine teaches at University Without Walls at Skidmore College. Additionally, she has curated several museum exhibitions on ethnic history in New York's North Country, as well as researched ethnic history for the Adirondack Museum exhibition, "Peopling the Adirondacks." With Elizabeth Folwell, Godine co-authored Adirondack Odysseys, *a guide to historic sites in northern New York. She is currently writing a book on 300 years of ethnic history in the Adirondack region. The article reprinted here first appeared in 1999 in* Moment, *the most widely circulated independent Jewish magazine in the United States.*

Jewish Peddlers

The village of Tupper Lake in northern New York's Adirondack Park is not an easy one to love. No bustling Main Street beguiles you with picturesque good looks. The former boomtown that once rang with the robust French of Canadian lumberjacks looks bone-weary and all buttoned up. But swing off the main drag onto Lake, one block to the west, and prepare to reconsider. See the austere clapboard building delicately crowned with three wood-framed Stars of David? Eastern European immigrants founded Congregation Beth Joseph in 1899, whence comes its *other* moniker, "The Peddlers' Synagogue," after the Yiddish-speaking immigrants who came and prospered a century ago. And *now* say, no surprises here!

In the course of researching ethnic history in the Adirondack region, I've had the chance to meet *not* peddlers—the peddlers are long gone—but the next generation, men and women mostly in their eighties and possessed of vivid passed-down stories about their fathers' first years in the Adirondack woods. The ambitious routes of northern New York's peddlers crosshatched this region as finely as a web. Peddlers ventured into mining camps, logging hamlets, river towns, and isolated farmhouses. They came on foot, forced into an arthritic hunch by unwieldy, duffel-like packs, and in dusty, many-chambered wagons. Each had his specialty: the "junkie" sold tools and tinware, and reclaimed scrap metal for the rail-side junkyards in the towns. The ragman sold gingham, calico, denim, and wool workshirts and gathered sacks of rags for mills. Chair bottoms, rosaries, harmonicas, flea powder, waffle irons, drawing pads, and sheet music—all this passed from peddlers' wagons to the kitchen tables of Adirondack homes.

Peddlers had been tramping the back roads of rural America since colonial times. As early as the Civil War, the New England-born Yankee peddler was a cultural cliché. Shrewd, hard-bargaining, a lanky, lean-jawed, slicker kind of Uncle Sam, the Yankee peddler was immortalized in James Fenimore Cooper's *The Spy*, lampooned in penny joke books for his broad, folksy A's, denounced for his characteristic "coarse impudence" and "cunning" by Yale College president Timothy Dwight in 1832. If not himself a pioneer, he followed hard in the wake of the Indian trader and the frontier trapper, and was first to lay a scrim of routes from Maine to Georgia that mapped the territory of generations of distinctly *non*-Yankee "hawkers and walkers" to follow.

And follow they would, the German Jewish immigrants who thronged American port cities in the great migrations of the 1830s and 1840s. By 1844, almost half of the eighty-five "pedlers" who registered in Albany to sell foreign goods in New York State bore Jewish names. And just as these immigrant newcomers would assume and expand the Yankees' routes, they also came to bear the hoary stereotypes and clichés that have always dogged the peddlers' path—compounded, naturally, by the reflexive anti-Semitism of the age. Of the forty-three Jews who opened accounts in the Utica Savings Bank from 1847 to 1855, nearly all the men were peddlers, identified in bank records in terms like these: "Moses Holstein . . . Jew pedler, dark jew face . . . Harris Zacharias, a Jew Pedler, writes only Hebrew, 46, 5'4¾", dark."

How many of these Utica peddlers stayed in the city, and how many used Utica as a springboard for forays into the Adirondack interior, is hard to ascertain. Water-driven milltowns like Utica, Amstersdam, Gloversville, Glens Falls, Plattsburgh, Massena, Malone, and Canton ring the Adirondack region like the fence posts of an irregular corral. These were the rough-edged, industrial boomtowns that launched the livelihoods of Jewish (as well as Italian, Greek, and Syrian-Lebanese) peddlers-turned-backcountry storekeepers, the base camps for merchandise and supplies. Then, after markets were established and a clientele assured, came the fledgling storefronts, the gleaming cash register, the first anxious sales. Follow the newspaper ads for these frontier outposts, and you can track the changing demographic profile of the Adirondack peddler from the colonial era to the first half of this century as names like Webster and Cosgrove are supplanted by Merkel, Loeb, and Wurtenburg, and these, in turn, are overtaken by Goldbergs, Fiores, and Marouns.

This last group, the one that rode into the region on the crest of the Great Migration from the 1870s to the 1920s, discovered the Adirondack region at the same time that it was coming into its own as a resort Mecca, a prospective "Central Park for the World." How many Jewish peddlers operated in the Adirondack region in this era? When I match up odds and ends from archival sources, oral histories, and conversations with peddlers' descendants, I come up with about fifty Jewish peddlers who plied at least a portion of their trade inside "the Blue Line," as the border of the present-day Adirondack Park is known. But peddlers came and peddlers went, here settling down but for the most part moving on. Factor in the ones who didn't settle in or near the Park, numbers probably quadruple.

There were the nameless peddlers of town histories, here homely, risible, a little bit pathetic with their fumbled English and plodding nags, there mysterious and even sinister, the stuff of murder mysteries, ghost stories, and many folkloric exegeses on the role of "The Other" in the American small town. There were the holy men, the keepers of the flame, who founded the region's first four Jewish congregations in Plattsburgh (1862), Ogdensburg (1875), Lake Placid (1879), and Tupper Lake (1899), originally peddlers' shuls every one. Legendary, tough-knuckled "junkies" like Kirk Douglas's fight-prone father, Harry Demsky from Amsterdam. Bad luck peddlers like William Sheffer (slumbering beside his horse in a Chestertown stable, he dreamed he was being robbed and in his delirium stabbed his horse to death), or Joe Galinsky (the sheriff's daughters locked him in the Lake Pleasant town jail for a lark, then took his horse and wagon for a ride), or Edward Cohen (he let a gang of North River garnet miners buy goods on credit, then had to prevail on their paymaster to make them pay back $43 for razor blades and soap). Horatio Alger-style boy peddlers remain the most familiar and beloved type—outsiders-turned-local heroes like Lithuanian-born Mose Ginsberg, brave enough to elude the Czar's Cossacks at age twelve and make his way to New York City, but so unnerved by the witchy shadows of a tree on an Adirondack road he froze for hours, certain it was a ghost. (Mose got over it. The store he opened up in rough-and-tumble Tupper Lake became the biggest department store in the Adirondack region, and Mose himself was named Tupper Lake Citizen of the Year, and featured in an exhibition at the Adirondack Museum, "Peopling the Adirondacks.")

Some peddlers specialized in eggs and dairy; others traded furs, tramping in and out of backwoods homesteads on snowshoes, washing down decidedly nonkosher stewed fox meat with moonshine, bargaining hard with their French Canadian hosts and trappers for prized hides of muskrat, mink, coon, and deer. For a peddler like Glens Falls' Schmuel "Big Sam" Shapiro, merchandise changed with the fashions. Shapiro went from chair seats to tinware to ladies' dress goods. Farmwives were particularly partial to his sample fabric swatches for how nice they looked stitched into quilts, and immigrant eastern European mill workers and quarry laborers responded gratefully to his pidgin Polish and Lithuanian (for that matter, many of them knew some Yiddish, too.)

Why peddling? What was the appeal? For one thing, peddling was a job Jews knew: poor Jews in central and eastern Europe were peddling for a century before they bore their tradecraft to the States. Second, peddling required access to suppliers, and this the immigrants had in spades, thanks largely to the German Jewish domination of the "rag trade" in New York. Finally, peddling was a career that let the devout immigrant plot his route so he could make it home for Friday Sabbath when other Jewish men were counting on him for a minyan, and that let him honor a religious diet on the road as working with a pork-and-beans-eating railroad gang or logging crew could not.

But no one peddled for the love of it. Company was a farm dog nipping at your heels, bed a hay mound in a barn or a rope bed in a frigid attic that raised mean welts. Even if the stick-ups, Indian ambushes, and duststorms that beleaguered the intrepid Jewish peddlers who went west weren't a problem for the peddlers of the Adirondacks, the road was slow and the frontier just as wild. For most Adirondack peddlers, indeed, for peddlers all across the nation, the point of peddling was nearly always to get *out* of peddling, and into a store or business of your own. Even before the century's turn, at least a dozen one-time peddlers' emporia lined the business district of Tupper Lake. "Jew stores" they were called, once as key a fixture of the American smalltown frontier as the tavern, boardinghouse, grange or church.

There are no peddlers anymore. The commercial heyday of the smalltown Main Street, and the competitively anti-peddling ordinances that often followed, all saw to peddling's regional demise. No landmarks or plaques mark their influence or tenure. And the same goes for the immigrant-founded storefronts—almost all of them long vanished, and the loyal small town minions, too.

But if you're in the Adirondacks, you might find your way to the synagogue in Tupper Lake, a living house of worship from early summer into the High Holy Days, and open the year round as a community center and small museum. The one building in this village on the national historic register, Beth Joseph alone stands proud to bear witness to an age when the reach of Jewish life was as wide as the rural American frontier, and to a time when peddlers cut as thick and bold a swath across the nation as the Milky Way on a moonless Adirondack night.

Jim Gould

Born in Buffalo, New York, Jim Gould has lived most of his adult life in the
northern Adirondacks. For more than sixteen years, he taught writing and
literature in the Environmental Studies program at Paul Smith's, the College of the Adirondacks. A graduate of Columbia University's M.F.A. Writing Program, Gould lectures and writes frequently on Adirondack topics
and issues, and his essays and feature stories have appeared in the New
York Times, New York Magazine, Outside Magazine Online, Backpacker,
Adirondack Life, Washington Post, and other publications. An avid hiker,
cross-country skier, and flatwater paddler, Gould and his wife and two
daughters have a home near Lake Placid, New York.

"The Wolf at the Door" originally appeared in the Albany Times
Union in 1999, and the personal essay included here, "Great Blue," won a
1992 Roberts Writing Award, as judged by noted editor Gordon Lish. "A
Letter to My Father in Winter" is published here for the first time.

The Wolf at the Door

Tonight I'm standing outside the door of my home in the Adirondacks,
on an open-air deck reaching out into a parcel of woods that stretches
several miles to the horizon. I think I can see animal shapes in the
grainy half-light, but I'm more likely suffering from a bad case of wish-
ful seeing.

My eyes are straining for something to focus on because my ears are
filled with the shrill chorus of a pack of coyotes. The pack must be just
a few hundred yards away. Or a few miles. It's hard to tell with coyotes.

Their song, if it can be called that, is less howl and more keening than anything I've ever heard. Try to imagine these sounds: dozens of tires in a long sustained screech on wet pavement. Or the peels of silly, excited laughter from a schoolyard of caffeinated boys and girls. Or maybe a violin factory in a hurricane. Of course, it's none of them at all. It's exactly like what it is: the sound of coyotes, talking, singing, calling out, entirely filling the near-black with their living, breathing, noise-making lives. It's the insistent sound of wildness out there, spilling across the domesticated boundaries of my yard.

More than a century earlier, wolves were out there, too. But Adirondack settlers, like most other early Americans, considered the wolf all but the anti-Christ. An established breeding population was decimated, literally hounded and hunted into extirpation.

You and I probably would have done the same if we were scratching out a homestead in the Adirondacks, where the topsoil is rarely more than a few inches deep, and the already-brief 100-day growing season sometimes sees killing frosts even in July. And, more to the point, you and I would have done the same if our chickens, a good percentage of our liquid assets, were being liquidated by a wild canine that, with one rifle shot, could be turned in to the town clerk for a generous bounty. The last wolf in these mountains was reportedly shot in the western Adirondacks, in St. Lawrence County, in 1901.

Now they want to bring them back. Of all pronouns, "they" is the most loaded in the Adirondacks. It usually means outsiders, environmentalists, city-folk, summer residents, tourists, or agents of the state or federal government. In this case, it's a multiple hit. "They" are Defenders of Wildlife, a Washington, D.C.-based environmental group that announced in Albany in November, 1996, that they were seeking the reintroduction of the eastern timber wolf to some of its original habitat: the vast, forever-wild Adirondacks.

Ever since, a din has filled the pages of our local newspapers and local government meetings. Even with an abundance of competent field biologists, woodsmen, hunters, and wildlife managers in this neck of the woods, there was a real dearth of accurate information. Even the smartest among us were saying things we had probably better not have said. Like a county pol who was quoted by a local reporter: "I don't know much about it, but I'm sure we're against it."

The recent history of the Adirondacks is checkered with this kind of stimulus-response to park-wide, top-down policy-making. For many, the resentment towards outsiders is probably based on generations of underemployment and unemployment. The disenfranchised and dis-empowered—they're as common across this landscape as blackflies in June, and they make the community vulnerable to all sorts of political whipsawing.

The intensity of the wolf controversy is reminiscent of the furor surrounding the establishment of the Adirondack Park Agency in 1971, or more recently, then-Governor Cuomo's Commission on the Adiron-dacks in the 21st Century. Both episodes were marked by high emo-tions and little respectful, informed dialogue. In 1990, as the Cuomo Commission was carrying out their work, violence was threatened, gunshots were fired, and a commissioner's barn was burned. Now, with the wolf poised at the Park's door, our community, once again, was hun-kering down for another hard season of hard words.

To the surprise of many, through a series of events—some planned, some accidental—this latest installment of the Adirondack story is de-cidedly different.

Working with Defenders of Wildlife and other groups, Paul Smith's College was asked to bring together a group of people representing con-stituencies throughout the Park to see if they could help design a study that would answer three very basic questions about wolf reintroduc-tion: is it biologically, economically, and socially feasible in the Adiron-dacks? A citizen's advisory committee was formed that includes representatives of hunting and sportsmen's groups, timber interests, environmental advocates, recreational groups, land rights organiza-tions, and state and federal agencies.

At first, I was simply a neutral observer to the process. Then, per-haps because I was perceived to have no axe to grind, or because I had unlimited access to a copying machine, I was pressed into service as the non-voting chairman. More accurately, I was a witness to a new kind of local history in the making.

In the course of the informal meetings, twenty-plus stake holders, mostly residents, began talking emphatically, yet reasonably, and the inflammatory rhetoric found in front-page stories was nearly absent. Hard-core hunters and greens, trappers and recreation reps, all discussed the concerns of their neighbors, sharing a vision for their community and landscape. Don't get me wrong—we weren't holding hands and singing "We Are the World," but it was a big step forward for the Adirondack community.

A key to our progress was, surprisingly, food. We began each evening meeting by all sitting at one big table and sharing dinner. Time to catch up on the news, kids, work, the weather. ("I haven't seen ice like that since, well, never.") Another key, perhaps, was that folks generally were fed up with fighting, especially getting caught up in barroom brawls begun by others—the dreaded "they."

After working together for more than six months, the Adirondack Citizens Advisory Committee on Wolf Reintroduction put together the specifications for a preliminary feasibility study that included the concerns of nearly all Adirondack residents. The committee then interviewed several independent research groups from around the United States, and after much deliberation, awarded a $114,000 grant, underwritten by a special fund-raising effort by Defenders of Wildlife, to a team that has successfully carried out similar research in other wild areas of the world—the Human Dimensions Research Unit of Cornell University and the Conservation Biology Institute of Corvallis, Oregon. The research is expected to be completed any day now. In fact, a report of their findings will likely be released before January, 2000.

When our neighbors now ask if this study will bring wolves back, we have learned to politely correct the questioners. This preliminary feasibility study is not a proposal to bring wolves back. It's a study to see if Adirondack residents should proceed in a very long process that may or may not mean the reintroduction of the eastern timber wolf in the Adirondacks. As a group, we are not pro-wolf or anti-wolf. We are pro-community, the Adirondack community.

At home, in the dark, listening to coyotes, it's not hard to remember where I really live. My home stands at the edge of the High Peaks Wilderness Area, just a small part of the much larger Adirondack Park. At six million acres, it's the largest park, state or national, in the continental United States. Yellowstone, Glacier, and Yosemite would fit easily within its boundaries, with room for a Shenandoah or a Great Smoky national park thrown in.

But we're not a park like Yellowstone (where, in fact, they have recently reintroduced wolves) or the others. First, it's a wilderness mosaic of private and public lands. Second, people live here. More than 130,000 spread over an area larger than the state of Massachusetts. The largest village (there are no cities) is Saranac Lake, population 5,000. The result: the Adirondack Park is the largest and oldest example in the world of an area where people live and work alongside wilderness.

I guess that's easy for some to forget in Albany, Manhattan, or Washington. Still, "they" are inadvertently teaching us some lessons about our own home. The question of wolf reintroduction—through perhaps the first truly community-based problem-solving approach in this landscape's history—has in one small, yet important way, brought the Adirondack community together.

Before the end of my life, maybe the din I hear outside my door will include the howl of wolves. Maybe not. At the very least, for many of my neighbors, we'll be better prepared to listen to each other. Perhaps all those who don't live here, but care as much about these wild lands and their human and natural communities, will be better prepared to listen, too.

A Letter to My Father in Winter

At 5 A.M. I wake to sugar maples cracking like rifle shots. During the night a stiff breeze must have tossed away that blanket of clouds. The stars prove it. I let the dog out, remembering to put on gloves first. The night before last, my moist hand stuck to the frozen doorknob. Outside the kitchen window, the thermometer reads minus 18 degrees F.

The early-morning man on our local radio station tells me—I must be the only listener this Sunday morning—there's a storm warning in effect later in the day for the northern Adirondacks. Temperatures will rise, probably into the low teens, and another foot of snow is coming.

I remember your stories, Dad, about when you were a young boy on your aunt and uncle's farm up in northern Ontario. Tough winters there, too. Plowing snow with the horses, stoking the stoves every hour, keeping the chicken coop warm enough so the chickens would lay, and praying, during each evening's Bible reading, that the money and food would hold out until spring. When the wind blew, you said you could see your breath in that small wood-frame house. When you went down the road to school—a one-roomer where one year you were the whole sixth grade—every child brought a helping of coal or hardwood for that day's heat.

I feed my wood stove with some maple and beech that has seasoned all year. The wood acts as if it's been soaked in kerosene, immediately blossoming into yellow, red, and blue flames. I look at another piece of stove wood; I think I recognize it. Since this wood splitting business isn't a very efficient affair, I know I've probably touched this piece several times. I cut sixteen-inch sections from a log, throw those in the back of my truck, then unload them in the yard near where I split and stack, and then finally, months later, haul them into the house for burning. Some pieces I do recognize, especially if they have a knot or twist that took some sweat to split around. I am not sure I recall this piece, but it's a beauty. The grain is straight and golden and red, a bit like a salmon fillet. The draft roars like a jet engine when the stove door is open, and it sucks this piece in whole.

Dad, you said that up in Canada on that rock farm—that's what your uncle called it when he was tired of dulling plow points in the rocky soil of the Canadian Shield—you never went hungry. The family had a big vegetable garden, of course, and a root cellar, and chickens and pigs for eggs and meat. They even had a little stream where you fished for trout—just little ones, you said, careful not to exaggerate—and Aunt Effie would clean up enough to fill a skillet.

When you told me these stories, even the one about your skinny boy's body shivering under the covers all night, you had a warm, tender look on your face. Even a smile.

I know you wouldn't be smiling here with me now, even though the woodlot near the house is layered with champagne powder, even though the sky is glowing blue-black and the sun will fill up this clearing as soon as it clears that hill. When I turn the key in my old truck, it turns over in the sluggish, caramel-like oil but does not catch. I try it again and again, feeling the lifeblood of the battery turn the starter and light the cold plugs. But the plugs aren't firing.

This has happened before. That's why I keep an extra set of new plugs under the seat. They'll fire up hot and clean, creating a fire in each cylinder that even these freezing temperatures cannot quell.

My fingers burn to the touch of bare metal. I must start each new plug without wearing a glove to avoid cross-threading. I try not to get cross myself. When you worked at a stubborn chore like this, Dad, you would go into a slow burn sometimes. I've learned to ignore that tightness in my jaw, in my chest. Ignore it, relax it, and go through the motions. The plugs go in methodically, one by one, as if I'm watching a slow-motion replay. There are eight plugs in my light, four-wheel drive truck. Two on a cylinder. Ingenious design. It maximizes the burn, the combustion, in each chamber. A set of four go on the intake side, another set on the exhaust side. The first set goes in easily, but I'm starting to lose feeling in my hands, even though I'm warming them after I ratchet in each plug.

I cannot hurry. But I do, or maybe it is some snow that causes the ratchet to slip, bang into the hard plastic distributor cap and crack it. This half-hour project is now extended another twenty-four hours, when I can hitch a ride tomorrow to the auto parts store in town for a new cap.

Dad, you told me about an older cousin on the farm whom you often helped at chore time. One day while milking the farm's only milk cow, after taking too many kicks from the cranky animal, your cousin took his milking stool and smacked that cow flat in the forehead, full-force. The cow dropped to the floor and soon stopped breathing, making for one of the saddest days you could recall on the farm. Your cousin didn't mean it, you said. His temper just got the best of him.

I'm trying real hard to not let my temper get the best of me today. After I shovel out a path to the woodshed, I hear the dog crying the way she does when she wants to go for a walk. I take her and a pair of snowshoes and tramp through the backyard towards Jenkins Mountain.

The first mountain I ever climbed was here in the Adirondacks, and it was Cascade Mountain, only about thirty miles from here. After years of working and living in different places in the Northeast, I took a job up here on a friend's recommendation. I was guided up to the top of Cascade, following a stream and then a rock slide, and then bushwhacking through heavy cripple brush to the bare rock dome of the summit. It was so clear that day we could see Lake Champlain and Vermont fifty and more miles to the east, and endless wooded mountains and hills in every other direction. I didn't know it then, right there, cutting up chunks of hard cheese and bread and oranges for lunch, that I had found a new home. My bones must have known though, because I settled in quickly like a coyote, scavenging up new skills and adapting new ways to flourish in these woods.

Dad, after you left your aunt and uncle's Ontario farm, you returned to gritty Buffalo. You and your mother, brothers, and sisters got through the Depression without a father by taking in laundry, candling eggs, and working the grain elevators down in the First Ward, Buffalo's Irish ghetto. And after nearly forty years of working two jobs every day, of humping it in steel mills and on the docks and in the rail yards to raise six kids, you never forgot about your real home. You always wanted to get back to the farm, to the woods, to the land.

On the occasional day off, we would drive into the rolling hills of western and central New York, away from the smoke stacks and gray right angles of Buffalo. You were looking for that place, your true home. Just twenty acres or so, half-wooded and half-pasture, a house and a small barn, maybe a stream with some trout swimming in it. Something simple, nothing grand. No Ponderosa, you would say. Just a little place in the country.

On my way up Jenkins Mountain, the powder is a full three feet deep. The dog gracefully dolphins forward, cutting a trail for me. I wonder how long she can maintain this pace, and I wonder about me, too, as the sweat comes down my face and freezes in my beard. We won't make it to the top today, but that's not why we keep going. The sunlight sparkles through the airborne ice crystals, deer and snowshoe hare have left trenches perpendicular to ours, and I can see deep into empty woods that are dense with foliage the rest of the year. It feels good to just go. So I go, like the dog, just lapping it up.

Dad, you're retired now, and you still haven't found your place. Those places never turn out to be like they're described in the real estate ads, nor do they happen to fit the picture in your head. But when you visit in the summer and see what I have here in the Adirondacks—the gardens, the woods, the ponds, the mountains—I know what you're thinking. This is your Someday Farm, your place with the wild blueberries and big trees. And it seems so easy and so happy. And mostly it is all of that.

Except, though, on some days, when you're a long-distance phone call away, the truck doesn't start, the pipes freeze, the sun cannot break through a month's worth of clouds, the snow drifts up to the window sills in March, and the pay checks are half of what they ought to be. Or you lose your temper and kill the family cow. Or crack a distributor cap.

Find that new home fast, Dad, so you will see that you can taste and hear and smell and touch it all without the thin gauze of memory dulling the immediacy and joy and pain of the whole show.

Like when you break onto the shoulder of a snowy mountain with your dog and catch your breath and spit and watch it freeze on a tree's bark. And you have to squint with the sweat and glare from the snow and blue sky but you can see down into the valley and maybe catch a glimpse of the place where you live, there in a clearing surrounded by tall white pines. My place. And yours, Dad, until you can find your own.

Great Blue

My walks through the woods near my home take me by lots of water—creeks draining ponds, streams feeding lakes, all crowded to their edges with alder, reed, and balsam. There I see the great blue herons.

They are the best indicators of time and space here deep in the mountains. In the fall, when every other sun-seeking bird has abandoned me, the great blue sticks around well after those mornings when ice fringes the bays and banks of the ponds and streams. After a frigid, monochromatic winter, a season that most years stretches almost six months here in the Adirondacks, I am ready for something else, something new. Just before the grasses and ferns and trees green up, the heron returns to break the loneliness like the ringing of your phone on a solitary Saturday night.

Today, the first day of June, I notice the heron there, loitering in the shallow green water. Tall and gangly, he plays a coy game, pretending to be a sapling or a cotton tail or some blowdown. He's waiting on a small frog, and he doesn't see me. A few minutes pass. He moves his head to one side. A few more minutes pass. Then, with his quick forceps-like beak, he plucks the meaty amphibian and flips it up into his gullet. No astonishment or accomplishment registers. Except for the lump sliding down inside his boa-like neck, the heron remains still.

Ten minutes later, the heron lifts out of the water, in an act that must defy the laws of gravity, the laws of common sense. But he's in the air, suddenly streamlined and graceful, his clumsiness tucked under that six-foot wingspan, a straight head on a crooked neck, focused and flying ahead.

One day a friend suggests that maybe I feel a strong connection with the heron because we share the same body and personality type— knobby knees, lanky limbs, exaggerated gait, solitary temperament. I remind my friend that it's just a bird, for goodness sake. Let's not get carried away.

What I could say is that I admire the brilliance of an animal who adds adjectives to his surname and makes them stick. Smart move. When you're the Ichabod Crane of birds and you've got to compete with the formally attired loon, the darling of the masses, you'd better think of something fast. Simply "heron" doesn't quite cut it. Great blue heron, on the other hand, is a stroke of genius.

I am becoming familiar with the three or four great blues that live in the local woods. I would even go as far as to say that I assume some relationship with them, that we are simpatico. So I wonder when it might be appropriate to make a visit to their home. Although they fly miles to feed and return to their young, their rookery must be around here somewhere.

My friend says her Aunt Jane probably knows where the rookery is. Aunt Jane is in her late seventies and has lived in the Adirondacks all of her life. Unlike me, she considers herself a birder. In fact, Aunt Jane used to go birding often before her youngest son, Harry died last year. Yes, she knows where there's a rookery. But she says she's pretty busy with affairs in town, and rain is forecast this week, and isn't it too late in the year to visit a rookery? I've got topographical maps of the area— will she at least show me the rookery's location on a map? No, she says, but I can sense Aunt Jane weakening. She wants to help, though some- thing is holding her back. The rookery's a secret she can't share. I ask again. Aren't we both due for a walk in the woods? Okay, she says, we'll meet this week, at a turnoff on a wooded road about fifteen miles from home.

After I hang up, I know it's only a matter of time until I am with the big blue birds. I feel lucky and privileged, as though I am being allowed into a coveted clique of friends.

It's a humid day, and as we step into the woods, those dark clouds crowding the treetops open up. The rain pops on the beech, birch, and maple leaves above us. This is now a problem. Not the downpour, not the soaking of our clothes. The problem is this: Aunt Jane and I were going to wander into these dense woods a mile or so, zeroing in on the squawking sounds of a rookery of nesting herons. But now all we hear around us is the steady rush of a heavy rain.

Although it's been a while since her last pilgrimage here, Aunt Jane says she can find it just by eyeballing some landmarks. She's looking for a downed white pine, a massive one, that has fallen almost perpendicular to the shore of the pond. She says when we hit that, we just walk southwest away from the pond and then cut into the woods to the left and then walk some more. Maybe an hour of walking, maybe less.

Following her directions, we both walk deliberately, slowly, since her legs, she says, don't bound over blowdown like they used to. I am anxious to see my friends, the great blues, but this slow pace forces me to look around, to take a moment or two to really take it all in.

I am in a stand of mature hemlock now, and I feel as if I've walked under a green circus tent. The seventy- or eighty-foot hemlock masts hold up a lush canvas of short needled branches. A sparse understory of witch hobble, fern, and striped maple saplings tangles at my shins. I am already soaked, yet the shower is warm, enveloping, reassuring.

After a time, too long a time, I think maybe Aunt Jane is lost. She's looking around more than climbing through brush. She hasn't been here for seven years, not since she bushwhacked out here to show the rookery to Harry. When Aunt Jane agreed to escort me out here, I wondered a bit about her grief. There seems to be some emotion crossing her face now, although with the rain and bugs and hard hiking, it could just as well be something else.

The rain still pops, drips, hisses. We come to a clearing, with a half-dozen dead trees clustered in the middle. She says this is the place. But when I look up into the rain, I see that there are no big stick nests up in the tops of those snags, no adult blue herons feeding their young.

She says that she recalls counting twenty-six or twenty-seven nesting pairs here the last time she visited. I am quiet. I don't see any evidence of nests above or any broken down ones below. I feel like a jerk for thinking it, but I begin to doubt Aunt Jane's memory. Out of respect, I say nothing.

But this seems only to make her anxious. She talks about maybe walking more to the east. Is that a clearing over there? she asks me. Or maybe we should go west. Maybe we didn't walk far enough beyond the pond, she says.

The rain wins. We can't hear much of anything, let alone distant heron squawking, so we decide to come back another day.

Aunt Jane walks out of the clearing. I am at the edge of it when I just happen to look up. Directly overhead, silhouetted against the sky, is a rough collection of sticks. A heron stick nest, clearly, unmistakably. Aunt Jane smiles and hurries back into the clearing.

I back out from under the tree for a better look and there, sixty or so feet up, in the thinning crown of a large white pine, hide two adults and a fledgling. All three are sitting upright, eyes on me, beaks curiously angled up, apparently trying to imitate the sticks and bare branches surrounding them. They don't move. Five minutes pass. The same stiff pose, still as can be. I wonder about this. I look through Aunt Jane's binoculars to be sure, in fact, they are herons. One adult sits up on the edge of the nest, the other adult back just a bit with the fledgling wedged between. Three pairs of eyes focus down intently. They are not happy to see me. Clearly. Like I've shown up uninvited at a neighbor's home—they've turned off the lights, pulled the drapes, and are hiding behind the door while I ring the bell. Take a hint, go away, they are quietly intimating.

Back at the side of the road, we wonder why the large rookery is down to only one nest. Is this natural? Is the life of a rookery cyclical? Have they just moved to another site?

I see the animation that was in Aunt Jane's face is replaced now by lines. Lines that crease her forehead, lines around her eyes, lines that mark the outline of her mouth. They're lines of distress. She doesn't know why the rest of the birds aren't there. But she doesn't know where they've gone either. I don't know what to say. I want to help by suggesting we'll come back soon, that when it's not raining so goddamned hard we'll find all twenty-some pairs. The necklace of ponds and small lakes surrounding this wooded site will always provide a full menu for these birds. They're out there somewhere. I am sure of it.

Aunt Jane keeps looking off, still tracing and retracing her memory for clues to these woods, to these great blue and green birds.

I now remember her look: it was after Harry's burial, when she thanked me for being a pall bearer. When I wanted to say something besides, You're welcome. When her eyes wanted something else. When I first saw those lines on her face.

Later I tell my friend that I was just happy to see that one nesting pair. No big deal not seeing the whole bunch of them squawking and preening and mock fighting and putting up the usual din. Those big guys are out there somewhere, I say. When my friend asks about Aunt Jane, I tell her that, except for the blowdown slowing her down, she is still quite a hiker for her age.

The next day, when I go back to the neighborhood stream, I catch a glimpse of a heron. This guy could be the same one from the rookery, so I want to have a little talk with him. I admit that maybe I've overstepped some boundary. Pushed too hard, asked too much. Okay, I get the message. I wonder how to ask for forgiveness. I will ask for forgiveness. The rookery didn't need another visitor. Aunt Jane didn't need another line on her face. I'm sorry. Sorry.

Sue Halpern

Eleven years ago, Sue Halpern traded in a Manhattan apartment for a farmhouse in a small, quiet hamlet of two hundred people in the southern Adirondacks.

Inevitably, Halpern has been intrigued by a person's need for solitude. Her first book, Migrations to Solitude, *(Pantheon Books, 1992) chronicles her search for both extreme and everyday examples of people who have voluntarily or involuntarily found themselves alone a lot of the time. The Adirondacks are the setting for a good part of the book. Although Halpern and her husband live in a remote, wood-frame house with a mountain and state forest in the backyard, she says they have no desire to remove themselves from society like the elderly Ned and Mae, who are the subject of one of the following essays and part of* Migrations to Solitude. *"Solo," the second essay included here, is also from* Migrations to Solitude.

The third essay, about the creation of a small town library, explores the connections to community the writer feels are so important in a landscape marked by isolation. It appeared in Orion: People and Nature *in 1998. Halpern's newest book is* Four Wings and a Prayer: Caught in the Mystery of the Monarch Butterfly *(Pantheon, 2001), an exploration of the migratory riddle of a remarkable flying insect.*

The Place of the Solitaries

To get there you drive past the village of Severance and through the town of Paradox, names that make sense when you are going to visit hermits. Then you go five miles one way and nine and a quarter another, look for a stump between two blue spruces, walk half a mile through an open pine forest, turn at the forked birch, cross a stream on a slatted bridge, walk uphill another quarter mile, and listen for her ax or his shovel. Actually, this is not how you get there at all. They asked me not to tell. "Otherwise we wouldn't be hermits, would we?" the one I call Ned says. The other one, Mae, nods in agreement. She is just over five feet, and tough, like beef jerky. She wears blue jeans and a striped man-tailored shirt. Her hair is clipped short and shaped like a helmet. It is white. She is sixty-eight. She has been a hermit for forty years.

The same with Ned. He has merry blue eyes and a gap-toothed grin, and he's tall and as thin as a split rail. He is so thin, in fact, that his green cotton pants, which are held up by suspenders, look like waders. He's got on a plaid flannel shirt and work boots. He is seventy years old. He wears his clothes sincerely.

"[W]e readily attribute some extra virtue to those persons who voluntarily embrace solitude, who live alone in the country or in the woods or in the mountains and find life sweet," the aspiring recluse John Burroughs wrote in a volume called *Indoor Studies.* "We know they cannot live without converse, without society of some sort, and we credit them with the power of invoking it from themselves, or else of finding more companionship with dumb things than ordinary mortals." But with Ned and Mae it is not this way for they have each other. They are solitaries together, but solitaries nonetheless. They live deep in the forest in a house of their own construction. They are self-sufficient. They would prefer not to know you.

Ned and Mae were not born to this life. They had conventional upbringings—as conventional as upbringings were during the Depression. After high school in Herkimer, New York, where they were sweethearts, Mae worked as a clerk in a five-and-ten-cent store and Ned strung lines for the telephone company. His health was bad, he had kidney disease, and a doctor suggested that a month or two in the woods would be restorative. If two months might help, the newlyweds reasoned, what about two years, or twenty-two? They quit their jobs and moved to the southwestern end of the Adirondack Park, where Ned's father, a lawyer, had been given a parcel of lakefront in exchange for legal work. There was a summer camp on the lake, and the two of them found work there as carpenters and caretakers. They started an egg and chicken route. Ned tied flies and sold them through the mail. But after a while the lake got "too busy," Ned says, and they decided to move.

"We took out a map of the Adirondacks and circled the places that interested us," he recalls. In their spare time they visited each one, camping out or sleeping in their car in order to see it through varied grades of light. It took three years before they found the land they wanted. "B'gosh, we liked it over here," Ned says. They sold their house on the water and bought 175 acres of ridge and hill.

"He shouldn't be here," Mae says of Ned. "The doctor told his father he wouldn't see forty. That was fifty years ago. See what the Adirondack woods can do for you."

But it's not just Ned. The Adirondack woods have long been hospitable to hermits. In *Tales of Hamilton County,* local historians Ted Abner and Stella King devote page after page to the likes of Noah John Rondeau, Ezra Bowen, Laramie Harney, and Adirondack French Louie— men who lived in the interior by their wits and the good graces of the land, eighteenth-century men born a century too late, men who would have been born a century too late no matter when they were born. Once, according to Abner and King, a consumptive city dweller came to spend the winter in French Louie's cabin in the hope of regaining his strength. As soon as he arrived he tacked a calendar to the wall near his bed. "It was the first thing that met the hermit's eyes when he reached the door. Instantly he snatched the offensive decoration from the wall and shoved it into the stove. 'If you stay with me, tomorrow will be just like today, and today just like yesterday—no different,' he pronounced."

It is time, as much as distance, that distinguishes the hermit's life. It is Thoreau sitting in his doorway from sunrise till noon. It is Rousseau, self-exiled on the island of Saint-Pierre, trading philosophy for flowers. ("Botany is the ideal study for the idle, unoccupied solitary," he writes; "a blade and a magnifying glass are all the equipment he needs for his observations. . . . This ideal occupation has a charm which can only be felt when the passions are entirely at rest.") It is Ned and Mae spending two years laying nine hundred feet of pipe by hand from a stream to their house. It is Ned and Mae spending an entire winter peeling the bark of the balsams, oaks, maples, and pines they felled in the warm seasons before. They brought these logs down without benefit of a chain saw or a skidder or horses. And they raised them up again to build their house without using a crane. Six years—that's how long it took them.

It is a playful corduroy house on a rise, with windows that open to every point of the compass, to tree and bird and sky and hill. Inside there is a root cellar and a mud room, a bathroom, a bunk room, a kitchen and hearth on the first floor, and a bedroom, study, and sitting room on the second. The house has running water—hence the nine-hundred-foot pipe—some of which is left to bake in a holding tank off the kitchen, and an indoor toilet, a concession, they say, to their advancing ages, though Mae still prefers the outhouse. They built this hermitage when they were in their sixties.

Before this they lived in a similar two-story home-made dwelling, but without plumbing. It is downwind from this one, overlooking a pond. They built the pond, too, clearing the half acre with picks and shovels, digging down six feet, prising the stones with their hands, using the stones to make a dam and a retaining wall and a walkway. They have built other things as well: a log garage, a summer kitchen, three garden plots, two wood-fired hothouses, a storage shed, a carpentry workshop, a composter, and three pavilions filled with enough split wood to keep them going for a year if need be.

Ned and Mae are off the power grid. They don't have electric lights, telephones, a toaster, or a washing machine. If they did, they wouldn't have anything to plug them into. "I guess most people would go crazy," Mae says. For them it is the other way around. The absence of electricity doesn't simplify things; it keeps them simple. Day begins at sunrise and ends with darkness. What do they do then? "We make popcorn every night in the winter," Ned says. "Well, that takes a lot of the evening. I guess it's what you'd call kind of a slow lifestyle."

When Emerson writes in "Self-Reliance," "The civilized man has built a coach but has lost the use of his feet," he suggests that people like Ned and Mae, who are fleet, are uncivilized, and this is true. Before everything else, civilized man (and woman) is a consumer. He lives in a market economy, he feels bound to do his part. Not Ned and Mae. They have taken a lien on nature's capital. They have a three-season refrigerator a few yards from their door—a galvanized tub sunk in a swift, cold stream—and a winter refrigerator indoors, which captures the frigid air of outdoors. They can't afford a "real" refrigerator; their income is three or four thousand dollars a year, about half the amount the state welfare office pays to individuals on home relief. In conventional, civilized terms they are dirt-poor. But poverty is a matter of desires as well as of means. Ned and Mae *would be* poor if they wanted a sixteen-cubic-foot white enamel frost-free refrigerator or a ten-cycle washing machine. What they want instead is to spend the afternoon in the sun, kneading their dirty clothes in a metal basin. What they want is to have as few clothes to wash as possible. And so they are not poor. Wood that you chop for fuel is said to warm you twice, first in the splitting, then in the burning. In the same way, Ned and Mae say that they are enriched by their wants.

A few years ago, on December 25, a neighbor hiked in on snowshoes to wish the hermits Merry Christmas and was treated to a sermon denouncing the holiday. Every day is a celebration, they grumbled. No day a holiday if you have to work so hard at it, and so on. Chastened, the neighbor retreated. A few days later walking in the woods, Ned and Mae found a small package, a gift, hanging from a tree. "I guess she was too scared to hand it to us," Ned says, laughing.

He can laugh. He takes himself seriously, but not grimly. He doesn't confuse their way of life with religion and make it an orthodoxy or a mission. (He doesn't tell you their way is the true way because he probably doesn't think you are up to many of its truths.) Nor does he confuse religion with God. Religion is the creation of people—to Ned it is as artificial as electric light. God is the creator of the world he holds dear and *is* the light. In the poems Ned writes, this theme plays like a fugue. "High up in the mountains a fir tree stands / By a lakelet beneath a bright star—/ The icy wind shivers its snow-laden hands, / Sparkling and glittering in light from afar. . . . / Other fir trees glory in tinsel and gold / For 'tis Christmastime all over the land, / But none are more loved in heaven above / Than this wildling cared for by God's own hand." The title of the poem is "God's Christmas Tree."

Most of Ned's poems and essays exalting the natural world and lamenting its destruction, as well as his gardening tips, and Mae's too, can be found in a little index-card-sized magazine they put out on a hand-cranked mimeograph machine in the sixties and seventies called *Backwoods Journal.* ("We thought other people might be interested in doing what we were doing," Ned says. Or at least daydreaming about it.) It cost two dollars a year for six issues, and at its peak there were a few hundred readers across the country whose letters found their way to the hermits' post-office box to request a subscription. A typical issue had thirty-five articles spread over sixty pages, most of which were written by Ned and Mae, using six or seven pseudonyms. (Their real names never appeared in the publication.) Rhubarb, the dangers of lead shot, winter camping, and migrating geese were popular subjects. There were no ads, but there was a Personals column. (From a man in Greeley, Pennsylvania: "I'm looking for a Birthday Twin to correspond with and compare notes on our trail through life, a person who was born October 10, 1911, the same day as I. I was an only child as my Mother passed on shortly after my birth. I'm married to a wonderful wife.") Ned did all the artwork in the magazine—pen-and-ink portraits of pine martens and coyotes, sketches of waterfalls and mountains—and though he was not trained as an artist, it is clear that he has a gift for this, too. In another life he might have been able to parlay it into a career and consider himself blessed to be able to work at what he loved.

After they turned over *Backwoods Journal* to a couple of homesteaders who had been regular contributors, and the homesteaders found it harder to put out a magazine than to live in a tent in the mountains in winter and gave it up, Ned and Mae began to sing. Putting their poems to music, they recorded "Songs of the Wildwood" on a battery-operated, dual-head boom box, from which they then made a bunch of copies, one at a time. The album is dedicated to "those folks everywhere who find inspiration in unspoiled wild lands." On it, Ned sings melody in a wobbly baritone and Mae joins in with a thin soprano, and the overall effect, which is to make you want to turn off the tape player and go for a strenuous hike, is probably what they wanted to accomplish anyway.

But why shouldn't they sing, and even sing badly, especially when they have something to say? ("When life becomes a weary thing, and each new day is hard to bear, take your burdens to the hills, and you will find them lighter there," begins one song.) And why shouldn't they write poems? It is symptomatic of how civilized we have become that poetry must now be written by poets. But if poetry is left to the poets, it means that something else, picking apples, say, is left to the apple pickers, and not only don't we get good poems about harvesting apples, we get a society that believes that apple pickers can't write poetry—which is what we have. But not Ned and Mae. They have the society of each other, and they have poems, and they have fresh apples, and no one to tell them they can't.

When Thoreau went to Walden Pond to live for two years, it was a young man's experiment. When the time was up, he quit his cabin and moved back to Concord and got on with his life. Ned and Mae were about thirty when they settled on their land, and it was no more an experiment than tilling the soil is an experiment for a farmer. It's like the difference between dating and marriage, Thoreau's retreat and Ned and Mae's. The hermits are wedded to their life in the woods. It's a marriage that's not about what they don't have (central heat, newspapers, ice cream) but what they do (buffleheads on their pond, a pond), and it's not about what they have given up (children, light bulbs), but how to use what they have to make what they need.

Ned shows off his tomato plants, which are still bearing fruit in the late fall, and his cucumbers and lettuce. He mentions the filtration system he rigged up to collect leaves from the pond and points out a ground-floor skylight he built to illuminate trips to the root cellar. He seems genuinely surprised that the things he knows are not common knowledge. Maybe five or six people visit a year, mostly family. "My sister comes and wants to go shopping," Mae says. It's as if she had heard of the practice but can't quite picture it. They don't get out of the woods much. When they do, encounters with their own kind send them back to seek the fellowship of the wind and the whippoor-will. They are happy there. Not gleeful, get-out-the-noisemakers happy, but happy as larks, or buntings.

"We felt kind of funny at first, living this way," Mae says, "but not anymore." Forty years in the woods earning a life, not a living. "A lot of people, I think, wished they would have done it."

Solo

What I really want to do is take the dog. We will head off into the woods by the lake; she will be my scout, my guide. She will chase rabbits and flush grouse. I will wade out into the water at noon and float on my back, shielding my eyes to look at her treading water like an otter, barking like a seal. Just after dusk we will sit in the lee of the fire, listening to the bullfrogs grumble, and the owls. When it gets cold I will let her into the tent. I will sleep in *her* lee.

If only I weren't as weak as a new convert, unable to bend the rules. Taking a dog along on a solo camping expedition, isn't that like a hermitage with a telephone? John Burroughs's brief essay on solitude is not yet known to me. "If Thoreau had made friends with a dog to share his bed and board in his retreat by Walden Pond, one would have had more faith in his sincerity," says Burroughs. "The dog would have been the seal and authentication of his retreat. Worried myself about authentication, I take a copy of *Walden* and leave the dog at home.

My husband sees me off. We are a mile down the eastern shore of a lake where our friends' Adirondack guideboat is beached. Hybrid canoe or hybrid rowboat depending on your orientation, a guideboat sits low to the water on a narrow keel. This one is no more than six feet bow to stern, with a wingspan, fully extended, that's maybe twice as long as that. I take yawning, rangy strokes, going south. In a minute I turn a bend and lose sight of the landing. I hear the cough and rattle of our old car as it heads out, and then I hear it no longer. It is an exquisite summer day. It's about 78 windless degrees. I am not the only one out on the lake in a boat, but I am the only one rowing. I glide past a tree stump, two hundred yards out, before I see atop it the harbormaster, a great blue heron, who nods my way with a shiver of feathers.

It is a dogleg lake, three and a half miles top to bottom, and I am rowing to the spur, where there is a spit of land shielded by an arc of pines whose soft brown needles cover the ground. It takes twenty minutes plowing through the water to reach it, and another twenty to set up the tent. Afterward I open up my raccoon-and-bear-proof cooler and scrounge around for lunch. Everything I packed not more than two hours ago now looks remarkably dull, or worse. Sardines in tomato sauce? Hard-boiled eggs? What was I thinking? I settle for apples and cheese and the opportunity to wield my Swiss army knife like an authentic camper. I look at my watch. It's 12:17. The day stretches out before me.

"Sometimes, in a summer morning, having taken my accustomed

bath, I sat in my sunny doorway from sunrise till noon, rapt in a revery, amidst the pines and hickories and sumachs, in undisturbed solitude and stillness, while the birds sang around or flitted noiseless through the house, until by the sun falling in at my west window, or the noise of some traveller's wagon on the distant highway, I was reminded of the lapse of time," I read in *Walden*. I look at my watch. It is 12:19.

Two fishermen in a Boston whaler make the turn into this part of the lake, cut the motor, and drift. I have chosen this spot to be alone, but not so alone that someone would not eventually hear me if I yelled for help. The edge of the wilderness is not the wilderness, though, and here come my fellow nature lovers to prove it. Propped against a tree, I am not visible, but my tent is, and so is my boat. They know I am here, so I *feel* they can see me, that they are watching. I don't want to be part of their consciousness, part of what they carry away from this scene. I don't want them to know I am here by myself.

All week I have been following the trial of three teenagers who are part of a gang accused of beating and raping a woman who had been jogging through Central Park at night. What was she doing there, people asked each other—didn't she know better? This peculiar distaff knowledge—of the danger of untraveled roads, unpeopled train compartments, empty houses, open fields, and dark streets—stalks women into the woods. Once, 11,000 feet up the side of a mountain, my husband and I stopped to catch our breath at a Park Service hut and read in the visitor's log an entry from a woman who had to stay overnight in bad weather with four men, all strangers. "Spent a fitful night worrying about the one-eyed trouser snake," she wrote the next morning.

In the broad daylight I am not afraid of the fishermen, just annoyed. They have every right to be here, of course, but my annoyance is extrajudicial. "I have my horizon bounded by woods all to myself; a distant view of the railroad where it touches the pond on the one hand, and of the fence which skirts the woodland road on the other. But for the most part it is as solitary where I live as on the prairies," Thoreau writes. I look up and see two men in an outboard, their lines slack, reeling in. I see them cast, port and starboard. Their lures charge toward the water like meteors. I see the men reel in again, snagging a patch of water lilies. I am annoyed because I expected to see something else, some kind of nothing.

Another boat chugs into the bay. I pull myself up and walk deeper into the forest, bushwhacking in as straight a line as possible so as not to get lost, until the water is no longer visible, not even the glint of it. The outboards fade until they're smudges, not fingerprints. I share a log with a colony of termites and a red squirrel that clucks like a bird. "Why does a virtuous man take delight in landscapes?" asks Kuo Hsi, an eleventh-century Chinese watercolor artist in his *Essay on Landscape Painting*. Because "the din of the dusty world and the locked-in-ness of human habitations are what human nature habitually abhors; while, on the contrary, haze, mist, and the haunting spirits of the mountains are what human nature seeks, and yet can rarely find." A plane grinds overhead. It is true that affluence brings solitude and privacy in the form of, for instance, country cottages, cars, and personal aircraft. But only for a minute. Then rural property values increase, houses are built on smaller parcels more closely together, and the highways and airports clog with commuters heading for the hills together. No matter how far I go into the forest today, that plane will still be grinding overhead.

The fishermen retreat a little before five. I follow the throttle and whine of their engines, moving back toward camp as they dim. A wind comes up and passes through the trees on the opposite shore, which rustle in succession like baseball fans doing a wave cheer. The trees are teeming with thrushes. Their voices fill the basin, yet the birds themselves are nowhere seen. So many of our perceptions are learned, not intuitive. I mean, why don't I think the trees are singing?

I shed my shoes and walk into the water, pulling the boat behind me. I know this lake better than I know any other body of water, better than I know the pool of land surrounding my house. I have taken its temperature and measured its pH and acidity; I have swum it side to side, skied its circumference, paddled and rowed it end to end. I have climbed the mountains that grow a few thousand feet above its shore. I have done these things in the gray of winter and at the start of June when the hardwoods hang their damp new leaves out to dry. I have been here at midnight with the beavers, and at dawn with the perch. It is easy to get carried away. "A lake is the landscape's most beautiful and expressive feature. It is earth's eye; looking into which the beholder measures the depth of his own nature. The fluviatile trees next to the shore are the slender eyelashes which fringe it, and the wooded hills and cliffs around are its overhanging brows," Thoreau tells us. So easy to get carried away.

Rowing forward, I nose between the remains of what was once the beavers' dinner, many nights running, and is now their leftovers. The lake is so shallow here I can palm the bottom. The warm water rings my wrist like a bracelet. Red-winged blackbirds spy on me and tell the other birds what they see. I am happy—relieved—to be out in the open again. I feel, I think, like a deer at dusk on the last day of hunting season.

People talk about the silence of nature, but of course there is no such thing. What they mean is that *our* voices are still, *our* noises absent. Tonight when my fire failed, I sat on a rock and followed the course of a cloud that looked like a trillium, watching as its whorl broke apart. The frogs were honking like ducks; the ducks were laughing like women. I could barely make them out, those loons, but just before the light faded they rose from the lake, and for a moment their white breasts hung above the water like moons.

In the dark, in the tent, every sound is amplified. Individual mosquitoes demand to be let in. Pine needles fall one by one. A beaver sharpens his teeth on an aspen nearby. Bears on either side of the lake hoot lustily; it is time to mate. I feel safe inside this thin nylon skin, for no apparent reason. So safe, in fact, that once I have drawn in my world between its walls, I grow fearful of what's on the other side. A porcupine screams in the distance. Coyotes bray. The world of night is primal. I am frightened because fear is the only instinct that has not been bred out of me. But the world of night is vast, too. It ignores me. After a few restless hours I fall asleep.

A man wakes me up. He is standing forty feet from my bed in an aluminum boat, baiting a hook. The sun is aloft, barely. He waves to me when I emerge from the tent with the bonhomie of one who has been awake since before dawn. If he wants to chat, I give him no opportunity, abandoning camp for the shore due west where the beavers have carved a rogue obstacle course. Sitting on one of their benches, I notice millions of cobwebs strung from the trees to the water. When the sun shines on them they look like lines of fish wire being pulled in at once. The man in the aluminum boat leaves the neighborhood pursued by a cloud of greasy blue smoke, and I am alone again, and not sure what to do.

If the forest were a room with a door, I'd probably be inside, reading. But the open wood demands something else. A hike up the ridge, an hour with the chickadees—something like that. Solitude would appear to be defined by place as well as dependent upon it. What passes for being alone at home, say, wouldn't pass here. You don't pitch a tent to curl up with a novel.

But this is just an aesthetic. Place is of consequence only to the extent that it encourages or demands the confrontation of the self by the self, which is solitude's true vocation. There is the solitude of experience and the solitude of despair, which can happen anywhere. There is the solitude of the jail cell and of the sickbed and of the hermitage, which differ by degrees of isolation. And there is the solitude of darkness, my grandfather's solitude, which was absolute.

He was fifty-nine when he went blind. Actually, he didn't lose his sight so much as his sight left him, the way a lover might, first in spirit, then in fact. When it was gone for good, friends encouraged him to go to a social service agency, to learn how to be blind. He resisted, memorized the number of footsteps from his apartment to the elevator, from the elevator to the courtyard, from the courtyard to the bus stop. Then, having nowhere to go, he gave in. He was told to report to the Lighthouse for the Blind in Manhattan for aptitude testing.

"My first day there, my wife brought me down from the Bronx, packing a two-sandwich lunch as the cafeteria was under construction," he wrote later, in an essay titled "I Hate Institutions." "After inquiring, we were told where to report, and I found myself in a large noisy room that contained a carpenter's shop, noisy with power machines and noisier semiblind adolescents, and a basket-weaving shop with blind men and women speaking in many different tongues, that to a neophyte like me sounded like the Tower of Babel. The instructor sat me at a bench between a retarded five-year-old blind boy and a man of about twenty-five who did not speak English, while I did not speak his language, so our conversations were held to a minimum. Now my twisting begins, making leather belts, rubber doormats, etc. This method must be all right, but did not appeal to me. When I remonstrated with the supervisor, I was told to be patient and cooperative.

"Then it was time for lunch. I gathered up my sandwiches, which were lying on the bench all morning, and was ushered down to the cafeteria and was left on my own, stumbling, ailing, until I found an empty seat, unwrapped my lunch, and ate the sandwiches in silence, all the time feeling tears welling up in my eyes. I recall having seen such scenes in the movies, and now I was the leading actor and I did not relish the part. Since it only took me fifteen minutes to finish lunch, and having no one to talk to, I wandered out into the vestibule and asked someone to direct me to a phone booth. I called my wife, and as she was asking me about my activities, I broke down and cried. To think that at fifty-nine years of age, having worked all my life, now to face a most difficult future at best. My wife, sensing my disappointment, wanted to come down and take me home, but I warned her off and told her it was a challenge and I was determined to go through with it. This testing went on for five weeks. I kept protesting until I was sent to typing class."

The essay, which was sent to me by a relative who found it when she was cleaning out her desk, is typed.

I return to what I have begun to think of as my front yard and defiantly open Thoreau. "We need the tonic of wildness," I read, "to wade sometimes in marshes where the bittern and meadow hen lurk, and hear the booming of the snipe." Chastised, I put down the book and survey the great outdoors. An ample, flat-bottomed boat with a blue-and-white-striped awning is steaming into view. Three people lounge on its deck chairs, one wearing a hot pink sweat suit, one in orange-and-blue shorts, the other wrapped head to toe in lemon knit sportswear. This is wildness of a different order. Shortly, a motorized canoe rasps into the inlet behind them, and then come two more canoes, powered by five actual canoeists, who look to be in their sixties. The three women wear fluted bathing suits and have zinc oxide on their noses and shoulders. One of the men wears a Red Sox cap.

My grandfather hated the Red Sox, like any loyal Yankees fan. He adored the Yankees. Even when he couldn't see a thing, he would go to Yankee Stadium and sit there with a transistor radio plugged into his ear, just to cheer. During baseball season, when he came to visit us in Connecticut, he would lie outside in the hot sun, hatless and shirtless, listening to that radio from the first pitch to the last. His scalp would redden, and the sweat would dam on his eyebrows and run into his ears. My mother, his daughter, would try to get him to come inside, or to move under a tree, as if he didn't know exactly what he was doing or where he was. But he knew. Sometimes he would ask me— I was about six— to hold a newspaper in front of his face, and then to take it away, so he could see the light.

"Are you going to Denver and then to San Francisco or are you going through Sacramento?" a woman in one of the canoes asks a man in the other. I don't wait to find out. Vowing to return in a different season, I collapse the tent and stow my gear in the hull of the guideboat, which I pilot past all canoes, paddled and powered, and the floating porch too, rowing home.

Civic Literacy: The Johnsburg Library

Imagine you have been asked to draw with two colors, green and gray, a small town tucked high in a piney forest. The background is white: snow. There is a main street, and along it a school, a hardware store, a supermarket, a garage, two churches, and a number of abandoned two-story wood-framed buildings. Add to these a town hall, also made of wood, trimmed in faux chalet style, and a handful of people walking between one end of the main street and the other. Do not draw more than five people. This is a remote, sparsely inhabited place. This is where I live—Johnsburg, New York, in the Adirondack Mountains. If, a year ago, I would have described it as relatively poor, I am unable to do so now. A few months ago we got a library.

When I say "got" I don't mean that somehow we went out and bought ourselves a library, or that one was given as a gift. Rather, the town board allocated $15,000 and appointed nine citizens to figure out how to make that into books, furniture, supplies, and a librarian's salary. Seven months later the Town of Johnsburg Library opened in a cozy room at the back of town hall with 3,000 books, most of them on loan from the regional library consortium, and a librarian who seemed to have materialized from nowhere.

It is rare these days to be able to create public institutions. Our country is old enough, and our municipalities financially strapped enough, that for the most part we inherit what we have, that which others have made before us. So it is also rare to be able to watch what happens when a new public institution is introduced into a community—how it is received, how quickly its absence becomes unthinkable. Last Thursday, people took out 126 books from the Johnsburg library; the day before, 113 items went out the door. Seven thousand books were circulated in the first four months, and not long after that, the 800th library card was issued. Eight hundred library cards and we're now approaching 900, which means that nearly half the people who live here are library users. It's as if the local newspaper were running a banner headline that said "New Portable Interactive Technology Available for Free at the Back of Town Hall." But there is no such headline. Instead there are announcements for a preschool story hour, a free classic film series, a local history lecture series, and a weekly list of new (which is to say new to us) books.

Of course, people in Johnsburg had seen books before, but they had never had access to them in the abundant, organized, diverse way a library provides, and that has made all the difference. I have watched my elderly neighbor Jean in the library learning how to use the computerized card catalogue so she can order large-type books for her homebound husband and quilting books for herself. I have seen a group of three year olds clustered around the board book edition of *The Very Hungry Caterpillar*. I have noticed teenagers poring over *Rolling Stone* and heard them requesting Roald Dahl. I have listened to a discussion of Virginia Woolf—should it be *To the Lighthouse* this week or *Mrs. Dalloway?*—between men who work with their hands. I have watched as the dozen or so volumes that constitute our art book collection have been passed around with such excitement and care it's as if they were originals and not bound reproductions. And I have seen how people come into the library and prowl the shelves looking hungrily and plaintively for authors and subjects and titles that might not have been there a week before—and certainly were not there six months ago. (But who can remember when we didn't have a library? How could that have been possible?)

This is the way we become literate, both as individuals and as a society. It is not simply a matter of being able to read, though that is essential, of course, and the Johnsburg library is working with Literacy Volunteers to teach adults who can't, to read. But it is also a matter of community. A library starts with one book passed from hand to hand. The book is the cable, the fiber optic, that connects the first hand to the next and that one to another. Invisibly, the book binds them. It establishes, then maintains, civic literacy. Which is to say that living in proximity is not the only thing that makes us neighbors.

It is erroneous to think that people read in isolation, for while it is true that for the most part people read silently by themselves, books give us a set of images and experiences and emotions that become part of our common language. "You've got to read this," I heard one nine-year-old boy tell another, pointing to C. S. Lewis, *The Lion, the Witch and the Wardrobe*. "It's awesome." "Thank you for showing me the Narnia series," that same nine year old said to me. And so the two of us share a language and a landscape. We are able to talk, to be neighbors and friends. We are not isolated.

Recently, a group of people met at the Johnsburg library to listen to a public radio book show. All of them had read the book that was to be discussed, and they were planning on using the radio show to guide their own conversation. But no one had counted on the mountain behind town hall blocking reception, so when they tuned into the station, all they heard was static. Undeterred, the group piled into someone's four-by-four and drove around town until they could pick up the show. And there they sat for two hours, shoulder-to-shoulder, people who hardly knew each other, talking about books. No—about books and kids and work and retirement and the price of chicken and health insurance and health care and everything else. It is no longer accurate to say they hardly know each other.

Mary Hotaling

As a community, Adirondackers historically have had their eyes set on the horizon, upon a magnificent view of river and lake, field and mountain. On the other hand, the built landscape in the Adirondacks has always been an afterthought.

That has begun to change in recent decades. As the founding executive director of Historic Saranac Lake, Mary Hotaling has been an articulate voice and organizing force in the movement to uncover, understand, and preserve the region's architecture and its compelling social history. She is equally accomplished as a writer. Her work has appeared widely in regional publications, including Adirondack Life.

Hotaling resides in Saranac Lake, New York, in a historic Cure Cottage-era home, with her husband, Jim.

The features included here, "All Aboard" and "A Bacillus Grows in the Adirondacks," first appeared in, respectively, the Franklin County Historical Review (1994) and The Sequel, a quarterly publication for the alumni and community of Paul Smith's College (1998).

A Bacillus Grows in the Adirondacks

Until February 1873, Dr. Edward Livingston Trudeau's future had seemed promising, with his new medical practice in Manhattan and a happy family life. But all his prospects were shattered by his doctor's diagnosis that the upper two-thirds of Trudeau's left lung was involved in "an active tuberculous process," at that time a death sentence. Following the then-current climatic treatment, Trudeau and family trav-

130

eled to Aiken, South Carolina, returning early in April with his health unimproved. The Trudeaus' second child Ned was born on May 18, and a week later his father, accompanied by a friend, left for Paul Smith's Hotel, a backwoods haunt on Lower St. Regis Lake in the northern Adirondacks which was frequented in summer by the wealthy and prominent from the major Eastern cities.

Trudeau expected to die, and he chose the Adirondacks, which he had visited before on a hunting trip, only because he loved the wildlife and the woods. Unexpectedly, his health improved.

At the end of September, Trudeau returned to New York, but his fever recurred and his physicians sent him to St. Paul, Minnesota, for the winter. His stay there produced no improvement in his health, and he returned to Paul Smith's in June of 1874, this time with his young family.

At Paul Smith's, he met Dr. Alfred Loomis, a New York physician in camp with a hunting party. Loomis had tuberculosis himself and was particularly interested in the effects of climate on health. He advised Trudeau to spend the winter. At this time conditions were very primitive; few people could bear the harsh Adirondack weather and the isolation, forty-two miles over unbroken roads from the nearest doctor or railroad. With the hotel closed, the Trudeaus boarded with a reluctant Paul and Lydia Smith and their children through the long winter of 1874–75.

In his *Autobiography*, Trudeau described how far removed from science he had become:

> Up to this time I had almost forgotten I was a doctor. I neither read medical literature nor practiced my profession, except on the rare occasions when some of the guides were injured or sick and could get no other medical aid.

The next winter the Trudeaus rented a house on Main Street in Saranac Lake. By this time the doctor was also treating a few winter tuberculosis cases sent by Dr. Loomis. In the fall there was no question of going back to New York; the family returned to Saranac Lake to board with Mrs. Nellie Evans at her cottage on Main Street. Winters in the village and summers at Paul Smith's became the pattern of the rest of their lives.

With more patients, Trudeau's interest in medicine was renewed. In his *Autobiography*, he described his sources of medical information at that time:

> I subscribed to *The American Journal of the Medical Sciences*, the *Medical News*, the *Medical Record* and Dr. (Luis) Walton sent me, after he had read them, his copies of the *English Practitioner*, edited by Anstie.

Still, Trudeau wrote, "Up to 1880 I did little but hunt and fish."

This convalescent life began to change in 1882, when Trudeau read in his second-hand copy of Anstie's *English Practitioner* about two developments in Germany. Dr. Gustav Herrmann Brehmer had opened a sanatorium for pulmonary tuberculosis in 1859 in Silesia, on the theory that high altitude exercise would build up his patients' hearts, strengthening them "to pump away poisonous accumulations from the lungs." Brehmer's student Peter Dettweiler had founded his own establishment in the Taunus Mountains in 1876, where he developed a contrary regimen of rest. Though Trudeau saw "no reference to either Brehmer's or Dettweiler's work in my American journals," he thought their ideas were worth testing. That summer he suggested the plan of a semicharitable sanatorium in Saranac Lake to Dr. Loomis, who immediately agreed to examine and refer prospective patients in New York at no charge. Trudeau began to gather donations to build the Adirondack Cottage Sanitarium.

On March 24, 1882, in Germany, Dr. Robert Koch read his paper, "The Etiology of Tuberculosis," before the Berlin Physiological Society with its startling conclusion that the disease was caused by an identifiable organism, the tubercle bacillus. Trudeau read abstracts of the paper in his journals, and it excited his imagination. He inquired of his friend C. M. Lea, a medical publisher from Philadelphia whose wife was a patient, what the doctors there thought about it. Though Lea found the American medical establishment almost uniformly indifferent, he gave Trudeau a Christmas present of "a very full translation" hand-written in a copy book. Wrote Trudeau, "I read every word of it over and over again."

Convinced by Koch's logic and enchanted by the possibility of a cure, Trudeau determined to learn how to stain and recognize the tubercle bacillus under a microscope in order to try Koch's experiments for himself. On his next trip to New York, he applied to Dr. T. Mitchell Prudden, who taught pathology at the College of Physicians and Surgeons, and who directed its first laboratory, a new addition since Trudeau's student days there. Located in a narrow store-front at the corner of Twenty-third Street and Fourth Avenue between an ice-cream store and a harness shop, the laboratory struck Trudeau as "a large, dark room, with a high ceiling . . . gloomy, ill-smelling." Vibrations from passing brewery wagons frequently interrupted work at the microscopes.

> Prudden partitioned off for bacteriology a small corner of his dark and crowded laboratory with second-hand glass sashes, the wreckage of a livery stable. The worker standing at his table with its twilight illumination could touch the walls in all directions, while at frequent intervals he must beat a hasty retreat for a breath of fresh air. This was one of the earliest bacteriological laboratories in this country.

By luck, Trudeau had found a like-minded mentor: Prudden published two articles in 1883 demonstrating the presence of the bacillus in tuberculous lesions. With some simple instructions from Dr. Eugene Hodenpyl, Trudeau spent several days in Prudden's lab struggling through the staining and decolorizing process, particularly difficult with the tubercle bacillus, until he was confident that he had become proficient enough to work alone. In 1899 Prudden remembered those days: "Just as soon as Koch's announcement of the tubercle bacillus came, Trudeau was down in my laboratory and was at work at it, as he is today."

Prudden and Trudeau were among the first in the United States to be convinced by Koch's results. Anticontagionism, the doctrine that disease arises spontaneously out of filth, was the dominant philosophy of the time. Even Dr. Loomis "didn't believe much in 'germs,' " and many years passed before he changed his mind. The infectious nature of tuberculosis would not be officially accepted in New York City until as late as 1907.

Trudeau's new sanatorium, grounded as it was in the traditional concept of climatic treatment, was a far more acceptable idea than the radical germ theory, and Trudeau received immediate support for it. The first building was built and occupied by the fall of 1884.

"In the fall of 1885, as soon as I had equipped my little laboratory-room," wrote Trudeau, "I began to work." At first the room was his own eight-by-twelve-foot office in the family house he had built two years before on the corner of Church and Main Streets. Coal and electricity were not yet available in Saranac Lake; the house was lighted by kerosene and heated with wood. "On very cold nights the doctor often had to get up and replenish the fuel," noted historian Alfred Donaldson.

> These quarters were so cramped, however, that I soon built a little addition off my office, and this became the laboratory in which I worked until 1893. One side of this room was occupied by a long, high, stationary shelf-table . . . with shelves underneath the table for glassware, a dry and a steam sterilizer, an oil stove, etc. At the other window was a small table with my microscope on it, some bottles of stains, and slides in boxes. By the side of this stood a shelf of books, on top of which was always Mr. Lea's precious translation of Koch's paper.

The extraordinarily cold mountain environment in which Trudeau was working demanded that he improvise special equipment "in which the high temperature needed for the growth of the germs could be constantly maintained." He described this equipment in his *Autobiography*.

> I had the tinsmith at the hardware store send for some sheets of copper and make a thermostat, which consisted merely of a small copper box about eight inches square inside of a larger copper box, the space between the two being filled with water heated from beneath by a minute kerosene lamp. A tube allowed a large thermometer to be placed in the inner box, and its readings to be taken outside as it emerged through a perforated cork at the top of the apparatus.

I soon found this answered fairly well in the daytime, when the temperature of the room varied little, but at night, when the fire in the wood stove went out, the violent loss of heat in the room soon caused a corresponding fall in the little apparatus. To obviate this I put the thermostat in three or four wooden boxes, each a little larger than the other, and packed the space between these with wool and sawdust. These boxes all had doors, and by opening and shutting these, according to the temperature outside of the house, I could maintain a fairly regular heat in the inner thermostat. After some practice I grew quite expert in keeping my thermostat near the right heat, and indeed, it was with this little home-made apparatus that I first succeeded in growing the germ in pure cultures outside of the body.

Not only was it unusually difficult to maintain a steady temperature in which the bacillus would grow in the extremes of a Saranac Lake winter, but it had to be maintained for an extraordinarily long time compared to "any of the disease-producing organisms discovered before it." *Mycobacterium tuberculosis humanis* "reproduces slowly, doubling its numbers only once within fifteen to twenty-four hours." Koch had had to wait nearly three weeks before his medium first showed any sign of culture growth. After many failures, Trudeau became "the second experimenter in the country" to grow a pure culture of the tubercle bacillus.

The first was apparently Dr. George M. Sternberg, an Army physician and pioneer American bacteriologist who later became Surgeon-General. Writing in 1901, Trudeau admitted that Sternberg, "located on the frontier, in a far distant military post . . . succeeded in accomplishing this nearly a year *before* I did." This "frontier" was apparently outside of the United States, however; in the *Autobiography* he wrote just prior to his death in 1915, Trudeau allowed that he was the first in this country to cultivate the tubercle bacillus and confirm Koch's discovery. "With these cultures I repeated all of Koch's inoculation experiments," wrote Trudeau, and then "began making original ones."

It is remarkable that this pioneering achievement of American medical science, the growth of tubercle bacilli in artificial culture, was accomplished by a lone experimenter, without funds, equipment, or associates. It was a lucky coincidence that E. L. Trudeau was a trained physician with a personal interest in tuberculosis, with access to European medical journals and the time to perform experiments. It is a measure of his faith that he believed in the science he was studying when others did not, a measure of his tenacity that he could keep a wood fire at a steady temperature for three weeks, day and night, in the harsh weather conditions of the Adirondacks, never knowing if the experiment had been spoiled from day to day, until at last he saw that the bacilli had grown. That this breakthrough occurred, not in a metropolitan center of science, but in a doctor's house in the backwoods crossroads of Saranac Lake, seems like a near miracle even today.

All Aboard

Try to imagine the six-million-acre Adirondack Park without paved roads, without railroads or airports. Early pioneers and explorers—Ebenezer Emmons, Verplanck Colvin, Archibald McIntyre, E. L. Trudeau, and Paul Smith, to name a few—were confronted every day with the riddle of how to get people and goods in and out and around the Adirondacks. It took as much as a week by land and water in the best of conditions, more if you were up to your knees in mud or snow. Railroads were the solution in the late 1800s, followed by the paved road and airstrip.

Rail service for the Adirondacks is an idea whose time has come again, although in a somewhat different form. In March 1998, the New York State Department of Transportation selected the Adirondack Railroad Preservation Society to develop as an active rail line the 118 miles of track between Remsen, in the southern Adirondacks, and Lake Placid.

Some history: The first rail line here—the narrow-gauge Chateaugay from Plattsburgh—was finished in 1887 during the winter that author Robert Louis Stevenson spent in Saranac Lake for his health, and the suddenly easy access—plus the publicity which Stevenson's visit generated—set the stage for an explosion of growth in the following years. The depots at Lake Placid and Saranac Lake, built by 1904, were now serving the New York Central.

In those early days Saranac Lake saw twenty trains a day, half originating in Lake Placid. The depot's long 600-foot platform graphically illustrates the many passenger cars that once unloaded at this relatively remote spot.

In addition to helping create a tourism boom, rail access facilitated the growth of major institutions in the area: the Trudeau, Gabriels, and Ray Brook sanatoria, and the Lake Placid Club.

When passenger service ended in 1965, the depots were closed. Freight service ended in 1972. The tracks from Lake Clear north to Canada were torn up, and the remains of the main line plus the spur are what we call the Adirondack Railroad today. The Department of Transportation acquired the line as receiver for the state as part of the Penn Central bankruptcy proceedings. After brief operation during the 1980 Olympic Winter Games, the tracks were abandoned until the Preservation Society successfully re-established a short line for tourists out of Thendara, near Old Forge. The railroad right-of-way, including all engineering features and associated buildings between Remsen and Lake Placid, was listed on the National Register of Historic Places in 1993.

Early last autumn, at the Hotel Saranac, Governor George Pataki announced a grant of $5 million to the Preservation Society, especially for the development and resumption of tourist service between Lake Placid and Saranac Lake. Henry Parnass, president of the group, said part of the money will be used to repair wash-outs between Thendara and Saranac Lake—repairs that railroad operators see as essential to move rolling stock up from Thendara. With its historic connection to Utica re-established just this year, the Preservation Society envisions anchoring the project with Saranac Lake-Lake Placid service, and then developing the entire length of the line.

Reactivated rail service is intended to co-exist with the current uses of the right-of-way by hikers, mountain bikers, cross-country skiers, and snowmobilers—uses which have developed in the seventeen years that the tracks have been out of service, a sort of "Rails to Trails" —though accommodations will need to be negotiated where these uses are in conflict. A light locomotive was trailered into Lake Placid in spring, 1999, to begin brush cutting and track maintenance.

Saranac Lake's Union Depot—the only depot along with the right-of-way in New York State ownership— will be ready when activity is expected to begin here in the summer of 2000. The Union Depot has recently been restored with grants of more than $500,000 (ten times what it cost to build in 1904), chiefly through federal funding sources.

Leased by New York State to the Village of Saranac Lake, the depot will be operated as a tourist, transportation, recreation, and community center on behalf of the village by Historic Saranac Lake, a not-for-profit historic preservation organization which previously sold salvaged historic preservation building materials there. Several spaces in the depot will be sublet to businesses serving travelers and recreationalists.

The waiting room will house an historic exhibit based on three important local activities: tuberculosis treatment, sporting recreation, and the railroad. Of course, space is being reserved for railroad operations, including ticket sales.

Most times I've worked at the depot in Saranac Lake in *any* capacity, visitors have come by unbidden to look at the building. It's a thrill to be able to show them, almost twenty years after the first community clean-up day, that the rehabilitation is complete.

The Adirondack community has recaptured some of its past, and it has re-embraced that most elemental economic truth—moving people and goods efficiently and cheaply is critical to the long-term health of our communities and the Adirondack wilderness. I like to think our forebears would be proud that we are again learning the lessons of the region's past.

Tom Hughes

Tom Hughes is not to be taken seriously. An outsized man with an outsized wit, he is a refugee from the suburbs of New Jersey who, after several successful years in publishing in New York City, relocated to Jay, New York, to write screenplays and invent excuses to avoid hiking and skiing. His work has appeared in several publications, including Sports Illustrated, Antioch Review, *and* The New Yorker.

He has been on the staff of Adirondack Life *since 1989; and he has been the magazine's publisher since 1995. He is an abundant source of the occasional doses of irreverence and wit so necessary in a landscape that too often verges on the gray, grave, and grim (see also Fred G. Sullivan's essay, "What's So Funny?").*

"Seven Months of Winter" first appeared in 1997 in The Sequel, *a quarterly publication for the alumni and community of Paul Smith's College.*

The Seven Months of Winter

My brother, recently split from the Adirondacks for more suburban climes, claimed, until the day his smoke-belching U-Haul crossed the Blue Line heading south, that the North Country was a land of winter—exactly seven months of it each year. Case closed.

But I opened the case every time he slammed it shut (he's my little brother, after all). I cited, for example, the lovely weather of early November (not too cold, actually nicely crisp, and with few people—and no bugs—around), the inevitable, teasing January thaw that could give the most hard-bitten Adirondacker hope, the odd April that was nearly tolerable. He wouldn't listen.

But the more I thought about his complaint, the more wisdom I saw in it, not so much in the observation (largely based on a shallow well of serotonin and a nutrient-poor diet similar to mine), but in the wisdom of having seven months of winter. Think about it: who among us could tolerate any less?

When we're not having winter, we're having people. People all over the place. I think old Paul Smith himself—king of Adirondack tourism, hospitality dude of the first rank—would agree that you just can't be hospitable all the time. Can't be done. Seven months of winter is the minimum required if you live in an area to which tourists flock. (And, yes, it is true that we get our fair share of winter tourists, but they're skiers mostly. They move faster. They slalom to get out of our way. They use the ridiculous word "mogul" in intriguing and suggestive contexts.)

Let's take a look, then, at what the seven months of winter have to offer. (The musically inclined among you may sing the following paragraphs to the tune of "The Twelve Days of Christmas." But, please, not anywhere near me.)

In the first month of winter, the Adirondacks gave to me—November. Leaves off the trees so you can really see the mountains. Quiescent downtown Lake Placid. Movie theater, restaurants, Main Street itself, returned to the general Adirondack public for thirty days. Enjoy it while you can. There was once a time when local folks would complain that you could shoot a cannon down the middle of Main Street during any winter month and not hit anyone. Now that's only true during this glorious month and the penultimate month of winter, April, though right-thinking individuals might be tempted to shoot a cannon down the street during every month but those two.

In the second month of winter, the Adirondacks gave to me—December. The first real snowfalls that stick to the ground, the first real cold snaps that can stick a dog's tongue to a parking meter. The first real opportunity to clean the mouse nests and their stores of dry dog food out of my guideboat-sized Sorel's. And Christmas in the Adirondacks, one of the great things the world has to offer that the world doesn't know much about.

In the third month of winter, the Adirondacks gave to me—January. The Scrooge McDuckish displeasure of paying my plowman every other day. Days cold enough to give me an excuse not to do anything I don't want to. The joy of standing outside in jeans and T-shirt and just letting the cold seep in. (Note: don't try this unless you're sporting a healthy 50 to 60 percent body-fat content.) And the thaw, the lovely thaw, that always leaves me wondering bitterly why I ever paid the plowman in the first place when the snow was all going to melt anyway.

In the fourth month of winter, the Adirondacks gave to me—February. The opportunity to apologize to my plowman for ever thinking of not paying him for his absolutely, positively necessary services, okay? Only two more months of having to convince people that I'll be out cross-country skiing any day now. Sunsets at two in the afternoon. Five inches of beautifully patterned ice on my windshield, my scraper frozen to the carpet.

In the fifth month of winter, the Adirondacks gave to me—March. See February. Modify sunsets to two-thirty. Add cabin fever and inevitable jokes about same. Midwinter Adirondack terseness.

In the sixth month of winter, the Adirondacks gave to me—April. Faux spring. Everything melting, the ground beginning to yield. Hey, is that a crocus? Maybe things are . . . Then the annual Easter storm. Everything frozen, the ground buried. Much troubled shaking of the head. Dogs again belly deep in snow, seeming to hold the whole thing against their masters. Eyes and ears peeled for possible revolt.

In the seventh month of winter, the Adirondacks gave to me— May. Yes, according to my brother's definition, this counts as a winter month. And in many ways May is the best winter month. Viewing the havoc an Adirondack winter can play on home and property. Taking it all in. Raking it all up. Plenty of opportunity for rationalization, to wit: if it stays cold enough through Mother's Day the blackflies will never hatch. Or, if it stays warm enough through Memorial Day we'll be able to enjoy the mountains for ourselves. The first line of cars badged with out-of-state plates moving thirty miles below the speed limit, and officially marking the end of the season.

Cherish the seven months of winter, I say to you and my absent brother, when inhospitality in weather and works makes this the most wonderful place to live.

Paul Jamieson

It is hard to believe that a thorough guide to Adirondack rivers, ponds, and lakes was missing from Adirondack bookshelves until Paul Jamieson wrote one in 1975, after three years of enviable field work. Adirondack Canoe Waters: North Flow (Adirondack Mountain Club) with multiple editions and thousands of copies sold has made Jamieson the bard of Adirondack canoeing.

The author didn't stop there. Consumed with a passion for the landscape as well as literature, he culled through literally centuries of Adirondack writings, many considered ephemera, to assemble The Adirondack Reader (Adirondack Mountain Club, 1982; second edition, 1983), the definitive collection of Adirondack thought, reporting, memoir, and literature from Samuel de Champlain's first sighting of the Adirondacks in 1609 to literary works from the first part of the 1980s. That works out to nearly four centuries of coverage, with more than one hundred individual writers and works. Needless to say, like the canoe guide, The Adirondack Reader has been considered a regional classic since it hit booksellers' shelves.

Jamieson accomplished all this while a professor of English at St. Lawrence University in Canton, New York, from 1929 to 1965. He played hooky as often as possible to visit the south and to explore the storied past and present of the Adirondacks.

"American Adam," reprinted below, first appeared in Adirondac magazine in 1960 and was collected in Adirondack Pilgrimage (Adirondack Mountain Club, 1986), which contains the many essays and features Jamieson authored throughout the years. "Pen and Paddle," also reprinted below, is an excerpt from Uneven Ground (1992), a memoir published by the St. Lawrence University Library, to which Jamieson had donated his significant personal library.

142

American Adam

Steve's first act, after sinking down on the deacon seat and throwing off his pack, was to light his pipe. I knew this gesture well, from twenty years of hiking and canoeing with him in the Adirondacks. It might be late in the day. We might be hungry. A thunder cloud might warn of the need to get dry wood in. All these are secondary things. For Steve a night in a lean-to after a long day's tramp is a peak of existence and must be savored with deliberation. The pipe on the deacon seat is his ceremony of house-warming.

Steve is that national type known as the American Adam. The frontier is in his blood. His ancestors landed on a continent of virgin forest and prairie and then, after an interval of wonder, began with reckless energy to exploit and destroy the wilderness. The memory of a lost paradise passed on to their descendants, and in each generation for nearly three centuries the dreamers of the family moved west to look for a new Eden and repeat the cycle. Pioneering became a way of life, the means by which the nation renewed its vigor.

Now that historians are writing about the closing of the frontier, politicians have invented the winning slogan "the New Frontier." But a slogan, however potent in a presidential race, will not take the place of a wilderness. Once a year at least the American Adam will suddenly begin to feel a prisoner in city streets and covet the freedom of the wilds. Then he will begin to talk crazily, like the pilgrim to Walden: "I went to the woods because I wished . . . to front only the essential facts of life."

Luckily the westward migration bypassed a large wilderness in populous New York State. When the loggers and miners began to enter the interior of the Adirondacks in the middle decades of the last century, tourists and sportsmen came with them. Many of the latter were exploiters like the former. But some had learned how foolish it is to destroy what one loves. Joel T. Headley, for example. In the 1840s he joined issue with the Reverend John Todd, who had proposed cutting down the trees in the Adirondacks and settling one million good Christians on prosperous farms in mountain valleys. Headley won this debate by pointing out a few facts about climate, soil, and topography and then adding that he liked the trees as they were, and all that goes with them. "I love the freedom of the wilderness . . . I believe that every man degenerates without frequent communion with nature."

Ten years later S. H. Hammond, an Albany newspaper editor, echoed the same thought ("It is natural as well as necessary for every man to be a vagabond occasionally") and went on to propose that the Adirondacks be sealed up by the state constitution as a place where the forest grows, dies, and renews itself unmolested. Verplanck Colvin and others applied themselves to this end, and since 1885, when the Forest Preserve was created, and 1894, when the "forever-wild" amendment was adopted, the state land in the Adirondacks has been better protected than the national parks against the whims of office holders. The Forest Preserve is a perpetual frontier where the American Adam can return to his beginnings and renew his zest for life.

Steve is no Leatherstocking or Daniel Boone. City and suburban living and the passing of years have softened him since the days when he worked his way to Europe on a cattle boat, ran the mile in college, and earlier still, as a husky eight-year-old, worked in the harvest field of his father's farm near Independence, Missouri, alongside an interesting young man named Harry Truman, who had come over from the adjoining farm to lend a hand. Each year now Steve is a bit more gingerly at the start of his vacation. The question is, will he be fit? He shuns bushwhacking as a rule, saying that an Adirondack trail is rugged enough to satisfy reasonable demands for wildness. He would like to camp and tramp for a week, but he considers the weight of his pack. He goes in for a period of conditioning. First come the short hikes to some pond. Then the fire-tower peaks in the two- or three-thousand-foot range. But all the while he has his sights fixed on the big events of the last week or two—the high peaks, the two- and three-day hikes, and nights in the lean-tos.

The Adirondack lean-to is to Steve what the hut at Walden was to Thoreau. It strikes a neat balance between primitive instincts and civilized habits. Protected against the worst that wind, rain, cold, and damp ground can do, Steve is free to revel in all the minor inconveniences and discomforts of camp life. At his age the bare plank floor takes some getting used to. But the sleeplessness of the woods is not fretful like that of the city. It may even elevate one into that state of "spiritual alertness" that William James experienced on a moonlit night in a lean-to under the dome of Mount Marcy. The open front invites big thoughts. It is the key feature of the design, putting one in touch with chaos and eternity.

The mysterious night sounds, the crowded dark shapes against the sky, hint at a strange inhuman world that probably doesn't share the solicitude of two exposed campers for their own precious security. In a bivouac such thoughts could be oppressive, but in the lean-to they stir only an exhilarating half-fear. Where the roof sets limits to the sky and predators are balked at least on the rear and flanks, one can front the wilderness and the night with some spirit. His situation is like that of Robinson Crusoe after completing the shelter on the desert island. Risk is still there, but it is limited by human resourcefulness. Steve is as self-satisfied as if he had built the lean-to with his own hands.

There is a limit to how much Steve can regress during a three-day camping trip. He never gets back to the heroic age of the early guides, trappers, and surveyors in their makeshift shelters. The hollow log, even when not shared by a bear, has no charm for him. He lacks the hardiness of the guide John Cheney, who, during a miserable night in an improvised lean-to in Indian Pass, remarked to his patrons how lucky they were: "Now, many's the time I have been in the woods on a worse night than this, and, having no axe, nor nothing to make a fire with, have crept into a hollow log, and lay shivering till morning." After reading some of Colvin's reports, Steve concluded that the surveyor was half mad, using up all the daylight hours on a mountaintop with theodolite and barometer, starting down the trailless slopes after dark, and getting hung up on the edge of a precipice till dawn.

The surveyor's jaunty way of bedding down wherever accident and obsession placed him wakens no response in Steve. A Colvinesque yarn like the following leaves him cold: "Here, in clambering and crawling amidst the dead forest, which, crumbling and decayed, was a perfect *chevaux-de-frise*, after an hour or more of exhausting labor (the fog rising thick around us), we were compelled to acknowledge that we were lost. About dark, after crossing numerous hills and ridges, we succeeded in extricating ourselves from the slash. Below us was an almost precipitate steep of dark spruce woods. Seeing that we should have to camp, we descended and hastily searched for water. A rill was at length found, and the guide casting off his pack hurriedly proceeded to cut

wood for the night. Our food all disappeared at supper, and we slept—
one on either side of the fire—on spruce boughs cast on the wet ground.
Some wild creatures came around us at night, but we were too tired to
pay attention to them."

Steve avoids all such casual bedding. He sees to it that there is a
lean-to at the end of the day's tramp. He is willing to take the chance of
its being occupied, he will go that far. But to pick a goal on the map
where the familiar symbol of a Department of Environmental Conservation housing project is missing seems foolhardy to him. He is suspicious about so-called natural shelters. Once on the Phelps Trail he
examined Slant Rock with distaste. A gusty rain would make it unten-
able, he decided. He is equally skeptical of the poncho shelter.

He admits that the lean-to circuit restricts his range, and that it
might be exciting to explore the mysterious realm of the trackless
woods. I have suggested packing a tent, but so far he has resisted. His
reasons for preferring the lean-to to all other shelter are aesthetic as
well as functional. A tent may keep one dry, but it has no style to speak
of. A lean-to on the other hand, looks like an emanation of the forest
floor. Opening on a bouldered brook with a wall of forest behind it, it is
a thing of beauty.

Its fitness to place and purpose is no accident but the result of long
experiment in which guides like John Cheney had a hand. Though a
hollow log might serve for John, his patrons were finical. Given a
stormy night near Summit Rock in Indian Pass in September of 1837
and two "cits" on his hands, one of them sick, Cheney set to work with
characteristic resourcefulness, as told by C. F. Hoffman:

" 'It ain't so bad a place for camping out,' said John Cheney, 'if it
didn't rain so like all nature. I wouldn't mind the rain much nother, if
we had a good shantee; but you see the birch bark won't run at this season, and it's pretty hard to make a water-proof thatch unless you have
hemlock boughs—hows'ever, gentlemen, I'll do the best by ye.

"And so he did! Honest John Cheney! The frame of a wigwam used
by some former party was still standing, and Cheney went to work in-
dustriously tying poles across it with withes of yellow birch and thatch-
ing the roof and sides with boughs of balsam fir. Having but one axe
with us, my friend and myself were, in the meantime, unemployed, and
nothing could be more disconsolate than our situation as we stood drip-

ping in the cold rain and thrashing our arms, like hackney-coachmen, to keep the blood in circulation. My hardy friend, indeed, was in much worse condition than myself. . . . We both shivered as if in an ague, but he suffered under a fever which was soon superadded. . . . John began to look exceedingly anxious.

" 'Now, if we had a little daylight left, I would make some shackle-berry tea for you; but it will never do to get sick here, for if this storm prove a northeaster, God only knows whether all of us may ever get away from this notch again. I guess I had better leave the camp as it is and first make a fire for you.

"Saying this, Cheney shouldered his axe, and striding off a few yards, he felled a dead tree, split it open, and took some dry chips from the heart. He soon kindled a blaze, which we employed ourselves in feeding until the 'camp' was completed. And now came the task of lay-ing in a supply of fuel for the night. This the woodsman effected by him-self with an expedition that was marvelous. Measuring three or four trees with his eye, to see that they would fall near the fire without touching our wigwam, he attacked them with his axe, felled, and chopped them into logs, and made his woodpile in less time than could a city sawyer, who had all the timber carted to hand. . . . Matters . . . seemed to assume a comfortable aspect as we now sat under the shade of boughs, drying our clothes by the fire, while John busied himself in broiling some bacon, which we had brought with us. But our troubles had only yet begun. . . .

"Our camp, which was nothing more than a shed of boughs open on the side toward the fire, promised a sufficient protection against the rain so long as the wind should blow from the right quarter. . . . A sud-den puff of wind drove the smoke from the green and wet timber full into our faces and filled the shantee to a degree so stifling that we all rushed out into the rain that blew in blinding torrents against us.

" 'Tormented lightning!' cried John, aghast at this new annoyance. 'This is too pesky bad; but I can manage that smoke if the wind doesn't blow from more than three quarters at a time.' Seizing his axe upon the instant, he plunged into the darkness beyond the fire, and in a moment or two a large tree came crashing with all its leaf, honors, bearing with it two or three saplings to our feet. With the green boughs of these he made a wall around the fire to shut out the wind, leaving it open only on the side toward the shantee. The supper was now cooked without further interruption. . . . I did full justice to the culinary skill of our guide and began to find some enjoyment amid all the discomfort of our situation. . . .

"Just as the curtain of brush on the windward side of the fire was consumed, the cold rain changed into a flurry of snow, and the quickly melted flakes were driven into the innermost parts of our wigwam. . . . My sick friend must have passed a horrible night, as he woke me once or twice with his coughing; but I wrapped myself in my cloak, and placing my mouth upon the ground to avoid choking from the smoke, I was soon dreaming as quietly as if in a curtained chamber at home. The last words I heard John utter, as he coiled himself in a blanket, were 'Well, it's one comfort, since it's taken on to blow so, I've cut down most of the trees around us that would be likely to fall and crush us during the night.' "

Honest John Cheney! He was the quintessential American Adam, akin to his fictional prototype, Leatherstocking. Hoffman himself saw the likeness. "If it did not involve an anachronism," he said, "I could swear that Cooper took the character Natty Bumppo from my mountaineer friend, John Cheney."

John was even a conservationist in his way. He discouraged his patrons from taking more trout and deer than they could eat, and when in need of a tree for himself, he crept into a hollow log. But for his patrons' comfort a quarter acre of timber was not too much to despoil, and that in a vital scenic spot.

Under conditions like these the Adirondack lean-to came into being. The guides eventually hit on a design that protected their parties against most kinds of trouble. A skilled guide could build such a camp in two hours. Opinions differ on its reliability. One enthusiast calls the structure "impervious" to rain. Another camper remarks that the bough or bark roof is "perfectly water-tight, except when it rains." He must have picked the wrong guide.

After Adirondack Murray had declared the woods safe for "delicate ladies" and the Murray Rush was on, the bark shanty, as it was called through most of the last century, raised a social problem that our easygoing generation finds hard to appreciate. In the age of prudery the problem was acute, adding moral suffering to the physical discomforts of camp life. This is dramatized in a scene from a novel by Gertrude Atherton, *The Aristocrats.* When Miss Page, a Southern girl visiting a luxury camp in the Adirondacks, sees her first lean-to at the end of a hard day's tramp, she says: "I cannot believe it is possible that we are all going to sleep in there. Why, it is shocking! I begged Mr. Van Worden to put in a partition, but he says it is quite impossible, that there won't be room for us to turn over, as it is. I wish I hadn't come. Suppose it should get out? Why, people would be horrified.'

" 'Really,' I said. 'I think you take an exaggerated view. We are all going to bed with our clothes on, the camp is open, there are nine of us, and our chaperones will sleep in the middle. We may not be comfortable, but I think the proprieties will take care of themselves.'

" 'I think it is shocking,' she said, 'perfectly shocking. It seems so coarse and horrid. I'll remember it as long as I live.' . . .

"About ten the men all marched up the hill in single file, singing, and we had the camp to ourselves for a half hour. We took off our boots, corsets and blouses, put on dressing sacks, tied our heads in silk handkerchiefs, and, our night toilet was complete. Miss Page had evidently made up her mind to accept the situation, but she was so manifestly uncomfortable that I tied nearly all of her face up in her handkerchief and tucked her away in the corner with the blanket up to her nose. She turned her back upon us and regarded the chinks of the bark wall in silent misery."

Manners have changed in the last sixty years more than the design of lean-tos. There are still no partitions, but there are no Miss Pages to fret over the proprieties. In social evolution a new national character has emerged —the American Eve.

The bark shanty of the last century embarrassed nice consciences in another way. It became an eyesore the moment it was abandoned. The semi-permanent lean-tos of today correct this situation. Sites are chosen with care and the surroundings are as little disturbed as possible. Most campers have accepted a measure of self-discipline.

The modern Adirondack lean-to, exported now to many parts of the nation, is nevertheless the outgrowth of the bark shanty of a century ago and has the same basic design. The earlier model was easier to heat because it was lower. But the higher gabled roof of today permits standing, and the plank floor lessens ground dampness. Perhaps the most notable improvement is the deacon seat. Seated on this throne, the American Adam is monarch of all he surveys.

It doesn't matter to Steve that he hasn't built this shelter with his own hands, like the guides of old. His do-it-yourself urge is satisfied by building the fire. If the wood is wet, he will spend half an hour collecting spruce gum for tinder. This having failed to work, he ransacks a spruce stand for droppings of birch bark. Finally a thin flame creeps up through wet twigs, and Steve nurses it till in another half hour his fire is fit to boil water. John Cheney would have constructed a bark shanty and had trout in the frying pan in less time. But he wouldn't have enjoyed himself as much.

What Steve lacks in knack he makes up in manners. He is hospitable to all comers, human and animal. He is careful to leave a camp cleaner than he found it. After cutting and arranging a neat pile of the best firewood available for the next occupants, he polices the area as if a top sergeant were hanging over him. When he strikes camp, the forest is not ashamed to take the lean-to back.

Steve has certain favorite lean-tos. His partiality for one of them, Bradley Pond, comes from its association with Santanoni, the peak that means most to him because it dominates the country east of Long Lake, where he has summered for many years. The lean-to itself is an old one not in good repair. But when Steve cleaned it after the previous occupants, whose leftover food had made a field day for the animals, the place looked less like a marginal piece of housing. It kept, though, the easy social familiarity of the slum. We had open house most of the night to a stream of curious, hungry neighbors. Paper rustled, firewood was knocked about. Sleeping bags became runways, and our legs twitched under the pressure of small feet. Claws scraped over tin cans and aluminum pots. A jam jar tumbled off the shelf and rolled against Steve's foot. A loud protest from him was followed by rumors of mass evacuation. But the poltergeists were soon back. A heavy falling body crashed on the roof, shaking the rafters. Then the sound of scampering feet, not so small, across the shingles and a thud on the ground. After all hope of forage must have expired, the game went on, more in sport now than in earnest. Steve decided to make a night of it too, contributing to the crude humor of the game with flashlight and umpire harangue. Bradley

Pond gives plenty of scope to the primitive in Steve. It is the gamiest of lean-tos.

Other favorites are the Cold River lean-tos for their remoteness, Scott Clearing for its whitethroat serenades, and Bushnell Falls for its tame fawn. But the one that appeals most to him is Feldspar. The rushing of its twin brooks, the steep slopes around, and the dense spruce forest give him the sense of being in a true wilderness. Besides, no lean-to fits its surroundings with more inevitability and grace. We sheltered there once during a heavy rain that lasted the better part of two nights and a day. Steve didn't mind this setback to climbing plans. He applied himself earnestly to reducing life to its lowest terms. He dawdled over chopping wood, nursing fires, savoring meals, drying clothes, and, during lulls in the storm, searching the woods for spruce gum, loose birch bark, and firewood. Or he sat on the deacon seat and smoked his pipe, with an occasional remark about the satisfaction of remaining snug in our shadow of a shelter with only the fire and the dripping eaves as defense against the weather and the wilderness out there. The last morning dawned clear and sparkling. Swollen by the recent rains, the Opalescent rushed by as if liberated. With no restraints on our activities either, we felt "free of mountain solitudes." But the confinement of yesterday had its value too. The open front of the lean-to, on the fine edge between security and risk, the civilized and the primitive—we had been out of the rain, but just barely—had again served the needs of the twentieth-century American Adam.

Note: Because of the scarcity of dead-and-down timber at lean-tos, most campers now carry stoves and a fuel supply.

Pen and Paddle

Early in 1972 Grant Cole, executive director of the Adirondack Mountain Club, asked me to prepare a canoeing guide to the Adirondacks. Three of my articles on canoeing in the Park had appeared in the club's periodical, *Adirondac*. After considering the proposal for some time, I agreed in a letter of July, 1972. My first intention was to deal with all five major watersheds, but this was too ambitious for the time frame proposed. I decided to limit coverage to the two north-flow watersheds, the Lake Champlain basin and the St. Lawrence River basin, the latter being the largest of the five. My book would then be followed by another on the Hudson, Mohawk, and Black River basins. (Alec Proskine later prepared a guide to those watersheds.)

During the next three years I devoted most of my time to this congenial work-play. From ice-out to ice-in I scouted, sometimes by solo canoe, more often in tandem, the rivers, other navigable streams, lakes, and chain ponds in the central and northern Adirondacks. I was often on the waters three days a week and utilized the other days to write descriptions from the notes I had taken.

Coincidentally the Adirondack Park Agency was engaged in scouting Adirondack rivers under a legislative mandate adopting the recommendation of the Temporary Study Commission for a state Wild, Scenic and Recreational Rivers System. I knew two of the men on the APA survey team, Clarence Petty and Gary Randorf. As we proceeded simultaneously with field studies, we exchanged findings. I submitted to Clarence a copy of my preliminary manuscript. Clarence in turn corrected some errors of mine in measuring distances. The APA field summaries in pamphlet form have a continuing value in supplementing my own study of each river.

Adirondack Canoe Waters: North Flow was ready for publication by the Adirondack Mountain Club in 1975. It was favorably received, not only as a guidebook but a celebration of the Adirondack landscape. Sales through 1991 have reached thirty-five thousand. Revisions appeared in 1977, 1981, 1984, 1986, 1988, and most recently in 1991. In the third edition of 1988, a co-author, Donald Morris, joined me, enabling me to retire from most active scouting. His advanced whitewater skills neatly compensate for my deficiency in this regard. Don and I project a major overhaul in a fourth edition, probably for 1993, taking into account recent developments that open several river segments long closed to the public by private owners in the Park.

The situation just alluded to has occupied much of my attention for the last twenty years. It is surely an anomaly that in a park dedicated at the founding in 1892 "for the free use of all the people for their health and pleasure" twenty-five navigable rivers (1972) were closed, in part or in whole, to public navigation because they flowed through the sixty percent of the Adirondack Park that was privately owned. This closure contravened common law, under which a public easement exists on all rivers navigable in fact. In the New England states and in New Jersey common law has prevailed to keep all rivers open to navigation. Indeed, this is true in most of New York State outside the Adirondack Park. Why not in the Park itself? This situation seemed to me intolerable. The wonder was its passive acceptance by the public for nearly one hundred years. I believe I was the first to document this injustice in a series of letters-to-the-editor, letters to Department of Environmental Conservation officials and the Governor, and articles in *Adirondac* and *Adirondack Life* magazines. The opener, a rather fumbling treatment before I was fully informed through work on my canoeing guidebook, was in the form of an open letter to the magazine *Conservationist*, July 7, 1969.

The foot traveler in the Adirondacks has God's plenty at his disposal. If the thousands of miles of trails in the Forest Preserve and easements over private land are not enough, he can bushwhack in a dozen wilderness areas. It is the small-boat traveler that is underprivileged today. There were more open waterways before the creation of the Forest Preserve in 1885 and the Adirondack Park in 1892 than there are now.

Most of the four hundred pages of E. R. Wallace's *Descriptive Guide to the Adirondacks* (1872–1899) trace boat tours open to everyone in the last century. In the 1860s and 1870s "Adirondack" Murray ranged everywhere among the lakes and ponds, rivers, and navigable creeks of the central and western regions. "For weeks I have paddled my cedar shell in all directions," he wrote, "an easy and romantic" mode of travel that made the Adirondacks a paradise, "above all its rivals, east or west." Unfortunately, hundreds of miles of the waterways described so winningly by Murray, Wallace, Headley, Hammond, Stillman, Emerson, Street, and other travelers of the last century are no longer accessible.

For a canoeist nothing is more inviting than chain lakes or winding rivers in hill, forest, and whitetail country. But he is due for a frustrating experience if he tries to match Wallace's boat tours with present realities. Many of the most attractive routes are now closed. This is true, for instance, of the greater part of the Bog River, including all of its system of lakes. A chain of lakes and carries from Raquette

Lake to Big Tupper which used to make possible a popular circular trip when combined with the Raquette River is no longer open. One must go both ways on the Raquette.

The most interesting stretch of the St. Regis River, the thirty miles below Keese Mill, was once open to navigation. Wallace recommends especially the "Sixteen-Mile Level, this grand secluded reach of boatable stillwater." On a recent trip over the Blue Mountain-Brandon Road with canoe on my cartop, I found this section of the river, like others downstream, blocked at both ends and at a bridge crossing in between by posters and other means. Likewise with a fifteen-mile stretch of stillwater on the East Branch of the St. Regis beginning a mile and a half below Meacham Lake.

Here at the top of the state, outside the Blue Line, where nearly all land is private, we boat freely on our rivers with access and exit at any highway bridge. It puzzles many of us that this free access is denied in many parts of the Adirondack Park. There is a widespread belief that the rivers of the state are public highways.

The closing paragraph posed three questions, the answers to which by a Conservation Department official amounted to an admission without a resolution. I was better informed when I wrote the first of a series of articles on this subject for the May-June *Adirondac*, 1971. "Lapsed Paradise" was a carefully documented survey of how this situation evolved and of the great extent of the restricted waterways in the Park.

The Adirondack Park is unique in the nation in combining a mountainous terrain with a vast network of waters, as if Venice were stretched out over Switzerland. The latest count is over three thousand lakes and ponds of a half acre or more. Thirty river systems flow from interior elevations to the perimeters of the dome-shaped uplift. Those main-branch rivers have numerous tributaries, also navigable, some of which form cross-grained interconnections so that geography makes possible cruises of a hundred miles or more in all directions, as W. H. H. Murray pointed out in 1869. All of this network was open to the public in the nineteenth century until about 1890, when posting began in earnest in private parks and corporate timberlands.

"Lapsed Paradise," reprinted in *Adirondack Pilgrimage*, lists some of the lost opportunities for the public of today in Murray's paradise of waters. It brought several responses in letters I received from readers.

The most interesting was from Hector Prud'homme, mentioned earlier as a guest I met at the Hochschilds' some months after our exchange of letters. He argued that, strictly from the standpoint of preserving the natural environment, it may be fortunate that much of the Adirondacks is in private hands. If all the waterways were open to the public, you would encourage the invasion and trashing of streams and stream banks. The public would leave refuse and spoil places once scenic and wild. These, I felt, were the typical arguments of large landowners bent on preserving privacy in their twenty- to fifty-thousand-acre estates. They were good reasons, not the real one.

Here is my response to Mr. Prud'homme:

Thank you for your interesting, pertinent letter in response to my article in *Adirondac*. I agree that preservation of the natural environment is the most desirable goal, even if public use is to be restricted. But I don't think that private ownership is the best way of preserving wild forests and streams.

Private owners come and go, and each has whims that may or may not accord with true preservation. One owner may clear thirty acres or so to build a gaudy tourist trap such as Storytown. Another is just now beginning to sell a hundred lots for a colony of summer cottages on Thirteenth Lake, at the edge of one of the prime wilderness areas of the Park. Septic tanks will drain into the lake and motorboats will swarm over it. Another type of owner, representative of the largest of privately owned tracts in the Adirondacks, practices "managed" forestry. The Whitney and Litchfield Parks are honeycombed with logging roads, as well as the holdings of International Paper, St. Regis Paper, and Finch, Pruyn. Lumbering operations are not pretty while they are going on or for some years after. Bulldozers are the worst litterbugs.

It is true that some private owners have preserved beautiful tracts of forest, mountain, and lake. Mr. Hochschild is one of them. The Ausable Club is another. In these two instances public use is permitted on a limited basis. Eagle Lake is part of the chain that is kept open for the enjoyment of canoeists, and the public is freely admitted to the mountain trails of the Ausable Club. But these cases are exceptional. By and large, the state, bound by one of the most effective preservation laws in the country, the "forever wild" amendment to the constitution, is a more trustworthy custodian than private owners.

In spite of much evidence to the contrary, I still believe it possible to educate the public. The conservation movement is beginning to make an impact across the country. Outdoor clubs are publishing leaflets on manners in the woods, holding briefings for camp counselors, and organizing clean-up crews. This summer, it seems to me, the trails and camp sites I have observed are a little cleaner than in recent years, in spite of ever-increasing use.

Another answer to the littering problem is zoning, as recommended in the recent report of the Temporary Study Commission that Mr. Hochschild chaired. The classification "wilderness" for fifteen areas of ten thousand acres or more would automatically limit access to those willing to expend some energy in getting there, afoot or by canoe or rowboat. Such people are more scrupulous about leaving things as they found them than the casual tourist. They know the value and the fragility of the thing they are seeking.

The trash problem is far worse, I am told by my traveling friends, in third-world countries than here at home. Maybe we have come a little up the scale of decency and are capable of further progress. Few canoeists, at any rate, descend into Cockneyism. They are disciples of Thoreau.

To return to restricted waterways, I have felt for the last twenty years that this is an issue worth a persistent crusade. Some of my friends might disagree. Bernie Lammers would say that I should join him in opposing a bloated defense budget or in holding peace rallies on the village green rather than squandering the finite wisdom and energy of old age on a secondary issue. But opening Adirondack canoe waters is the crusade nature and experience have designed me for. A legacy of untrammeled forest recreation, it seems to me, is about the best thing one can pass on to future generations. As Americans inheriting a once virgin continent, we have a little of Francis Parkman in our nature: "haunted with wilderness images day and night" to such an extent that his monumental history of the French and English in America became for him, essentially, a history of the American forest.

Henry James went abroad to be humanized. His brother William stayed at home and went to the Adirondacks for the same purpose. Spending a sleepless moonlight night in a lean-to above Panther Gorge, William experienced "a state of spiritual alertness . . . as if the Gods of all the nature-mythologies were holding an indescribable meeting in my breast with the moral Gods of the inner life. . . . The intense signif- icance of some sort, of the whole scene . . . its utter Americanism . . . was indeed worth coming for, and worth repeating year after year." In my youth I was a follower of Henry's way for a brief period, but after set- tling in northern New York at a corner of the Adirondacks, I turned to William's way. To an American the forest is humanizing. Personal rela- tions flourish there. No matter how divisive our interests are in civilian life, in the forest we have our heritage of wilderness in common. We connect.

Christine Jerome

Chris Jerome, as evidenced by the preface of her book, An Adirondack Passage, *is an Adirondacker at heart, if not by birth. Born and raised on the Canadian Shield in Ontario, Jerome knew more than a decade ago when she first saw the Adirondacks—a sort of geological peninsula of the Shield—that she was in familiar territory.*

A former editor of Car and Driver *and* New England Monthly *magazines, Jerome has written for several publications, including the* Boston Globe Magazine, Outside, Countryside, *and* Adirondack Life. *Jerome and her husband, John, who is also a writer, live in western Massachusetts, which for many is really Adirondack foothill country.*

Both selections below are excerpts from An Adirondack Passage: The Cruise of the Canoe "Sairy Gamp" *(HarperCollins, 1994). The first is from the preface, and the second is from the second chapter.*

Preface

From *An Adirondack Passage*

I had never seen the Adirondacks before September 1988, when on a friend's recommendation John and I drove over from western Massachusetts to spend a couple of days rubber-necking. As often happens in that upland region, however, the weather closed in and we ended up in a cabin in the village of Blue Mountain Lake, visibility nil, a chill rain battering the windows. Like hundreds of other rainbound tourists, we opted for history over hypothermia and visited the Adirondack Museum, just up the road.

158

Among the canoes in the boat building, one in particular seemed to beguile the crowds. Her cedar hull had aged to a mahogany glow and her size, at nine feet, was positively lilliputian. *Sairy Gamp,* the card read. Among the details of her provenance was this brief story: In the summer of 1883 a sixty-one-year-old writer named George Washington Sears, pen name Nessmuk, had paddled and portaged her 266 miles, from Boonville to Paul Smith's hotel and back again. I had no idea where these places were, but the distance was appalling. How could anyone have gone so far in such a toy? And who was Sears? When I realized I was creating an eddy of tourists I moved on, but later that day I ducked back for another look.

For weeks afterward the *Sairy Gamp* and George Sears kept elbowing their way into my consciousness. What had he written? How long had his journey lasted, and where, exactly, had it taken him? Could you follow his route today? Finally, in something like exasperation, I went back to the museum for some answers. It was mid-October, and Blue Mountain Lake was again cold and gray. The leaves were mostly down, and waves of Canada geese were passing over, their calls bringing a lump to my throat. The *Sairy* reposed just where I'd left her, and I hadn't imagined it: she really was beautiful. I bought a shopping bag full of Adirondack books, rented a cabin, and shivering beside an anemic space heater, began to tease out the story. I learned that the cruise of the *Sairy Gamp* ran almost the length of the Adirondacks, from the southwest to the north-central part of the region, and returned by a slightly different route. Once under way, the trip took Sears about a month. And yes, you could still do almost all of it; the longest leg, from Old Forge to Upper Saranac Lake, is one of the region's most popular canoeing excursions.

Another discovery awaited me in that frigid knotty pine room: I was, it seemed, inordinately happy to be back in the Adirondacks, although I wasn't sure why. Perhaps it was the mountains. I'd lived for twelve years in northern New Hampshire, and now I realized I missed having wilderness outside my door, missed a way of life dominated by natural forces. I also missed the people, whose code of mutual assistance, capacity for hard work, and impatience with pretension are increasingly attractive the older I get. It occurred to me that in many ways, north country men and women—especially the women—taught me how to be an adult.

Yet it wasn't simply mountains that moved me. This place was special. In his memoir *Upstate*, Edmund Wilson described traveling to the western Adirondacks as a boy and discovering "a foreign country but a country to which I belonged." That was it. From the outset I had felt a powerful tug of belonging. In an act that puzzled me at the time, I had cut short our first visit because I couldn't bear to be treated as a tourist in a place that was so patently home. There was an eerie familiarity to the landscape, but it was months before I understood that the lakes and forests of the Adirondacks reminded me of my childhood, when we escaped our cramped Toronto apartment for brief visits to northern Ontario and Quebec. (I would later discover that my instincts were right: the Adirondacks are an extension of the Canadian Shield, a relic of my native geology adrift in upper New York State.)

At six million acres the Adirondack Park is roughly the size of Vermont, but its character is quite different from that of its neighbor just across Lake Champlain. There is in the Adirondacks an odd, brooding beauty that writers from Dreiser to Doctorow have struggled to capture. It can be a lonely place: only a handful of roads penetrate the densely forested interior, and the hamlets strung along them are small and spaced far apart. Climb one of its mountains and you'll see chains of peaks rolling away in all directions, ridge after ridge growing paler toward the horizon. Deep valleys cup thousands of lakes and rivers. In the Adirondacks the woods run right down to the shore, a constantly reiterated theme of dark trees, granite, and black water. It is spruce and pine and hemlock country, deerfly and punkie and blackfly country, wool and four-wheel-drive country, loon and osprey and raven country. My kind of country.

The more I learned about the cruise of the *Sairy Gamp*, the stronger my urge to retrace it. This would be no wilderness expedition, no two-thousand-mile, woman-against-the-elements feat of derring-do. Most of the larger Adirondack lakes are lined with cottages, and for long stretches a state highway parallels the route. By any standard this would be a modest undertaking, a couple of hundred miles through vacation country. Still, I wavered. I had never attempted anything like an extended canoe trip. My paddling experience consisted of a few tandem runs down an unchallenging local river. Although I was strong and had once been an athlete, years at a desk had left me seriously out of shape.

I had done enough day-hikes in the White Mountains to know I liked being in the woods, but I hadn't a clue about how to live there: I had never spent a night outdoors.

On the other hand, when I felt bullish I decided I could find out what I needed to know; this was not, after all, neurosurgery. I was healthy, I was thirteen years younger than Sears had been, and I had had my share of physical adventure. When I was in my teens, a pilot friend often took me along while he practiced stalls and spins. As a journalist in my twenties, I had gone 168 miles an hour in the passenger seat of a race car. I'd also spent a week learning to race a Shelby Ford Mustang, a trick assignment, since I'd never driven a car before. Surely, I thought, I could paddle a canoe a couple of hundred miles. So I decided to follow George Sears. The trip would be great exercise, and besides, it was a way to spend time in a place that would not, it seemed, let me go.

For a year I shuttled back and forth to the Adirondacks, haunting libraries, scouting the route, soliciting advice. Although Sears started out in early July, I decided to wait until late August; this would give me a week of typically crowded waters and then, after Labor Day, an experience more like the one he'd had in 1883. I wanted very much to go solo, but I was persuaded that with my lack of paddling experience this would be a bad idea; if I got into trouble on one of the bigger lakes, no one would know what had become of me.

There was another consideration: since I planned to approximate Sears's experience as closely as possible, I would be traveling in a very small boat with almost no space for gear. To my relief, John, who had been intrigued by the project from the beginning, volunteered to come along in a second, larger canoe. A slim, six-foot-two-inch Texan who won my heart with an ability to fix anything and a modest but polished repertoire of clown-diving stunts, he is the best of company. He is also an accomplished writer of nonfiction and a storyteller in the great southern tradition. He has another talent I envy: he can fall asleep so fast it makes him dizzy, and once under is impervious to any kind of mayhem, except my gentle snoring.

The critical piece of equipment was my canoe. I wanted something exceptionally light and sturdy, but I was disappointed by what I saw advertised. Eventually Sears settled on a design by J. Henry Rushton, and in the end, so did I.

Hearing that an Adirondack resident named Peter Hornbeck built Kevlar *Sairy Gamps*, I called him at home in Olmstedville. "I'm not trying to make a replica of the *Sairy Gamp*," he told me. "I build working boats. I use Rushton designs because they're still the best." Many of his canoes, he explained, were used by wildlife biologists because they were easy to carry into the backcountry. At ten pounds, his smallest model weighed eight ounces less than the *Sairy* and almost exactly duplicated her dimensions. Best of all, Lost Pond boats, as he called them, could be bolted to a pack frame, which freed the hands for other gear and eliminated the drudgery of "doubling the carries"—making separate trips to haul canoes and equipment over each portage. Hornbeck also made double-bladed paddles because nothing on the market had the resiliency he liked.

I hadn't dreamed I could come this close to the *Sairy Gamp*. Hornbeck himself was a bonus. An elementary school teacher, he had a gentle, self-deprecating sense of humor and a passion for hiking and canoeing. Besides, how could I resist someone who'd named his cat Velcro? We ordered a nine-foot boat for me and a ten-and-a-half-footer for John, and in February 1990 I drove over to pick them up. Hornbeck turned out to be taller than I'd imagined, over six feet, with a puckish face framed by curly white hair. After showing me around his small operation, he introduced me to my boat.

I don't know what Sears thought when he saw the *Sairy Gamp* for the first time, but when I saw my nine-footer I laughed out loud. She was tiny. *Tiny.* Her manila-colored hull was translucent in the sunlight, and when I lifted her, the Kevlar under my fingers flexed. Could material this thin really be strong? Absolutely, Hornbeck assured me; more of his boats were damaged by blowing off cartops than by hitting rocks, and in those cases it was usually the mahogany gunwales that needed fixing.

He showed me how to attach the canoe to my pack frame and how to stoop underneath, slide into the straps, and shrug the whole affair onto my back. It was peculiar to see the bow looming over my head, but the harness was comfortable, the weight nicely balanced. He insisted on checking John's rig himself, adjusting several of the buckles and then striding off down his snowy driveway, a tan banana on legs. When he came back, he was beaming and shaking his head. "You know, for the Adirondacks," he said to no one in particular, "this is really the cat's ass."

Seven weeks later the ice went out of our pond and we could finally haul our boats out for their baptism. Mine was trickier to get into than John's, but once under way, both canoes felt so maneuverable they might have been part of our bodies. They were fast too, flying the length of the pond with a couple of strokes. We paddled around in delirious circles while our Lab and our golden retriever watched in utter disbelief from the shallows.

That summer we assembled our equipment and made two shake-down cruises with experienced canoeists. By the last week of August, John had mailed off his book manuscript and I'd finished the stories I was editing for *New England Monthly*. The cars were loaded, the house sitter was ready to move in, and at last there was nothing more to do.

When Sears told his friends he was taking a nine-foot canoe through the wilderness, they were so skeptical about his chances they took out five thousand dollars of insurance on him. He himself had no qualms. "I am as sure to make that cruise as you are to turn in when you start for your berth," he wrote in *Forest and Stream* magazine. "It wouldn't take a strong rope to hang me, but a bear trap on one leg and a grindstone on the other wouldn't drown me in ten fathoms." In a matter of weeks he was boarding a train for his rendezvous with the *Sairy Gamp*.

Old Forge to Inlet

Excerpt

Peering up at the hillside where the Forge House used to be, I imagined a bruised and exhausted Sears stumbling up to the door after his trek from Moose River Settlement. The hotel was decidedly homespun then, but it didn't stay that way long. Eleven years after Sears's visit the railroad laid a spur from its main line, to the west, to the waterfront. As the trains brought more people, the hotel accreted stories, ells, dormers, and verandahs. By the July afternoon in 1924 when someone noticed smoke curling out of a gable, the Forge House had become a five-story behemoth. In a few hours it was glowing rubble. The hilltop has remained empty; a squat motel now sits at its foot. The railbed lies buried beneath an asphalt street.

We turned our backs and headed for the mile-and-a-half channel that leads to First Lake, a small contingent of mallards escorting us. The forty-five miles from Old Forge to Long Lake would take us four or five days and represented our longest stretch on the water (our limited carrying capacity meant we had to stop often to reprovision and leapfrog cars). This first leg would harden us off physically and, in a way, psychologically: the scenery we'd encounter was typical of the alternating wild and developed country we'd find along our route.

As we made our way down the channel I was swept with the sensuous pleasure of paddling, the soft plash of each stroke, the rocking of my boat, the sweet tang of fresh water. Because my polyfoam seat was placed right on the bottom of the boat, I was not only on the water, I was in it, my outstretched legs actually below surface level. The low vantage point made me feel I was skimming along at inordinate speed—getting over the water, Sears put it, "like a scared loon." The sensation of speed was sheer illusion, but it was an illusion Sears shared, and it was right here that he had his comeuppance. In 1880, paddling his first Rushton canoe, he challenged a guide named Fred Hess to a race. They started from the Forge House landing, Sears with his double blade and Hess rowing a much larger guideboat. By the time they reached the finish, less than two-thirds of a mile away, Sears was lagging. He ascribed his loss to age and lack of conditioning, but his defeat so rankled him that he directed Rushton to build him a faster canoe. Rushton demurred, explaining that a double blade is by nature slow, and instead built him the ten-and-a-half-foot *Susan Nipper.*

Although I had never kayaked I found the double-bladed paddle easy to get on to and a sensible solution for a boat this size. A canoe wants to veer away from the side you're paddling on; the smaller the canoe, the sharper the veer. With a single blade you have to switch sides every few strokes or constantly twist the shaft (the venerable J-stroke is one way to do this) to compensate for this tendency. With a double blade stroking on both sides, you're automatically correcting all the time. The only problem I had in the beginning, and it soon became second nature, was learning to keep a quiet lower body while my arms did the work. Leaning too hard into the stroke tipped the canoe radically and threatened a capsize. This preternatural responsiveness, in which a wiggle of the hips translated into a substantial wobble of the canoe, would come in handy later, when rough water called for maximum maneuverability.

The channel, uninhabited in Sears's time, is now lined with homes, docks, boathouses, cottages, and waterside patios. A light rain began, tracing Escher patterns on the water, delicate rings growing, merging, and dissolving. With visibility limited by the fog, the landscape seemed oddly intimate. In the orange glow of a table lamp a man sat by a kitchen window with coffee and his morning paper. The sight gave me a swift pang; it would be a long time before I sat in my kitchen again. Paddling side by side, John and I chatted desultorily as we slid past yards decorated with whirligigs, plaster elves, ducks, flamingos, deer, and one three-foot-tall reclining black figure holding a fishing pole, its line trailing in the water. The Museum of American Lawn Art.

At the entrance to First Lake a dozen herring gulls were perched on the rocks at Indian Point, a peninsula that stood well out of the water until the dam was rebuilt. This spot became notorious in September 1833, when a marksman and trapper named Nat Foster secreted himself in the woods and picked off a Saint Regis Indian named Drid as the latter paddled up the channel. Foster, who had installed his family in the abandoned Herreshoff Manor, had been feuding with Drid for a year, but on this day the two had quarreled bitterly near the dam. Foster stomped off ostensibly in the direction of the Manor but doubled back through the woods to ambush his enemy. The dead man was roundly disliked and Foster was eventually acquitted, but, fearing reprisal, he left the area. (Oddly enough, for a time he lived in Tioga County, Pennsylvania, where Sears settled.) Drid, whose English name was Peter Waters, was buried beside the dam, his grave marked by a boulder inside a low railing. In the early 1940s the town decided to move his remains because a building was planned for the site. Photographs of the dig show four men in shirtsleeves, suspenders, and fedoras leaning on shovels and squinting at the camera. They never found their man. Some said he had long ago been exhumed and buried nearby in an Indian ceremony; others claimed his family had taken his remains to a reservation up north. I like to think he still rests beside the dam, his spirit heaving up the asphalt in a corner of the Chamber of Commerce parking lot.

As we passed Indian Point, the gulls flapped into the air, their gray-and-white bodies swallowed by the fog. Although First Lake is small, we could make out no shoreline. The entrance to Second Lake lay somewhere ahead and to our right, between a long point and an island. We struck out blindly and were startled when a drifting boat materialized nearby, two ghostly fisherman huddled over their poles. The rain had stopped.

The point was right where it was supposed to be, and we quickly passed through the strait into Second Lake, which is even smaller than First. In Sears's time there was, on the north shore, a sandy bluff covered with poplars. "Passing this," he reported, "you come in sight of the Eagle's Nest, the most-noted landmark on the Fulton Chain. The oldest guides could not tell me how long the nest had been there. For several years the birds deserted it, owing to the fusillade kept up by the cockneys of the Muggins tribe, who usually considered it the correct thing to empty guns and revolvers at the eagle's nest, occasionally hitting a young eaglet. The thing is better ordered now. With one exception, no one has fired at them this summer. . ."

The sandy bluff is still there, but the eagles departed many years ago, victims of harassment, loss of habitat, pollution, and the effects of DDT. Of New York State's once-healthy population of bald eagles, only one nesting pair remained in 1976, and they could produce no viable eggs. Now the state Department of Environmental Conservation has undertaken a vigorous effort to restore the species, releasing eaglets in remote areas of the Catskills, the Saint Lawrence River valley, and the Adirondacks. As of 1990, the DEC's work had paid off in ten nesting pairs, three of them in the northern section of the Park.

By the time we reached Third Lake, the fog was beginning to lift, but Rondaxe Mountain (formerly Bald Mountain) was still veiled. We could make out a row of cottages on the north shore where in Sears's day there had been only one building, a place owned by Charlie Grant, who one April day overestimated his strength and froze to death on the Brown's Tract Road. On both previous trips Sears had stayed at this camp, and it may have been here that he contracted tuberculosis. In

1881 he found the place jammed, but he could not get away. For days a cold rain slanted out of the northeast. "In less than forty-eight hours after landing," he reported, "I had joined the little band of coughers, coughing oftener and louder than any of them. As I had made the trip to the woods for health mainly, this was most provoking. I thought it was only a surface cough, so to speak, but it was constant, hard and irritating." The cough would remain with him for the rest of his life.

In 1883 Sears found new camps everywhere, evidence of a building boom that continued for years. At the turn of the century a politician named Martin Van Buren Ives remarked, "The shores of these lakes are ornamented by innumerable private camps or cottages, which serve to give the locality a sort of camp-meeting appearance." By the First World War the region was hopelessly civilized: "The Fulton Chain," journalist T. Morris Longstreth observed, "is a navigable string of lakes dedicated to the summerer. He lines their banks. His victrolas fill in the natural vacancies of an evening in the woods. His womenfolk enjoy themselves shrilly. . . . Stores are not so far apart that you will suffer if you've left the ax at home. Steamers are at hand to pick you up if blistered. The carries are supplied with carriers if your pride goeth before a haul."

In the short channel that leads from Third to Fourth Lake, a cramped trailer park extends for much of the distance along the left bank. Those who live here, in units separated by inches, must be as gregarious as the mallards that dodge among the patio boats and outboards tethered by the shore. This has always been a friendly place. At the turn of the century three community rowboats used to be kept at the far end of the channel for people headed to the other side of Fourth Lake. If you took the last boat you were expected to tow one of the others for the next traveler.

When the channel broadened into Fourth Lake, we followed the south shore to a state picnic area where we could stop for breakfast. No sooner had we claimed a table than a ranger appeared to collect three dollars. He nodded when I asked if he'd heard a weather forecast; there was a chance of a thunderstorm, so if we headed out we should stick close to shore. We could camp just across the way, on Alger Island, but it would cost us extra. This news we digested along with coffee and cold cereal.

"What do you think?" I asked John.

"Well, we've already come, what?—four miles?"

"Four and a half. But the next campsites are nine miles from here. If things get hairy . . ."

"Yeah, but it's only quarter after nine. I can't see stopping this early. We'd have to kill the rest of the day. Let's keep going. We'll stay right by shore."

"I guess we could get a motel room at Inlet if we had to. That's only five miles or so. Okay, let's go for it."

I had shipped a bootful of water when we landed at the log breakwater and reembarking there in knee-deep swells provided a refresher course in such principles as displacement, volume and gravity—physical laws I would test, with precisely the same result, throughout the trip. I had chosen boots that were too low, which meant that at any depth greater than six inches, water poured over the tops to engulf my feet and ankles. This was unpleasant but not a disaster: my mother did not raise me to be a sissy. No, the difficulty occurred at the crux of my slow-motion fall into my canoe, as my left leg cleared the gunwale and the accumulated liquid cascaded down the back of my calf and thigh to pool—I cannot say this delicately—in my crotch. The sensation, which would intensify as autumn advanced, often caused me to utter strange sounds and to curse Leon Leonwood Bean, whose fault it was not. Wet underpants smack of childhood, but at least in childhood there was a moment (oh, too fleeting!) of suffusing warmth.

Off we went down the largest and most populated lake in the chain. The fog had dissolved into lowering clouds that hid everything above a few hundred feet, and the water was gunmetal gray and restless. Fourth Lake—"the Stormy Fourth" to Sears—has long had a reputation for treachery; in 1881 Sears barely outran disaster here. "I have been in a white squall in the tropics, in a *pampero* off the Argentine coast, and have seen the terrific electric storms of the West," he recalled. "But I never saw so heavy a sea kicked up on an inland lake at such short notice. In two minutes the water was dashing up the sloping landing to the door of the boat-house; sharp, steep, white-crested waves were chasing each other like racehorses; the gale tore their spumy tops off and sent them whirling to leeward in a white mist of blinding spray; tall trees a century old were seized by the hair of the head and dashed to earth, while the zig-zagging of lightning and the heavy bellowing of thunder were just the adjuncts to make the scene perfect. . . . In twenty minutes the storm had howled and whirled itself away to the northeast, the sun came out warm and mellow, the air was a delight, and the lake subsided to a placid, sleepy roll as quickly as it had risen."

A gusty west wind had come up while we ate, and I felt increasingly apprehensive. We crossed over to Alger Island and paddled along its pro-tected south shore, then cut back to the mainland as a moderate rain began. Once we left the island's lee the water became rougher, tossing our boats around and spraying over the gunwales. Hugging the shore wasn't nearly as reassuring as I'd hoped: where the land ran straight, waves bounced off the breakwaters and collided with incoming rollers to create extra turbulence; where headlands thrust out, all hell broke loose and the chop became deep and disorganized. (I later asked my old-est brother, a former naval officer, about this phenomenon: "What's the nautical term for that condition around a headland where the seas are, you know, confused?" He put on his most owlish face and said, "Well, for a couple of hundred years we've called it confused seas.") Beyond each headland we found a patch of calm water that allowed us to re-group. We were learning a lot in a hurry about the physics of wind and water.

It soon occurred to me that instead of using my life vest to pad my backrest, I ought to be wearing it. In twisting around retrieve it, how-ever, I leaned too far and shipped several quarts of water, which pro-ceeded to slosh back and forth around my outstretched legs. It was not possible to be wetter, but the extra weight was deadening the canoe's handling, so we headed for a private beach where I could unload and swab out. I half expected someone to bolt out of the boxy brown house nearby and run us off, but apparently only idiots were abroad in such weather. It took no more than a minute to toss my gear on the sand, raise the canoe over my head to drain it, and then reload.

Within half an hour the rain had stopped and the sun was making brief appearances through racing clouds. Now I could lower my hood and look around. The north shore was nearly a mile away, our destina-tion somewhere on the hazy green horizon. We passed a house with a luncheon party in progress, nicely dressed people lounging on steps with drinks in hand, clinks and tinkles and laughter floating over the water. Farther along a monarch butterfly hovered over a coppery hydrangea, perhaps as amazed as I at the sight of these great blowzy flowers at the edge of the forest. As the sun strengthened we shucked off jackets and let the warmth soak into our skin. Suddenly the world seemed altogether fresh and fine.

Edward Kanze

Edward Kanze, a recent transplant to Bloomingdale, New York, descends from Adirondack settlers who farmed near Hope before the Revolutionary War. A syndicated columnist and nonfiction writer whose subject material more often than not is the natural world, Kanze is the author of four books: Notes from New Zealand *(Henry Holt, 1992),* The World of John Burroughs *(Sierra Club Books, 1999),* Wild Life *(Crown, 1995), and* Kangaroo Dreaming: An Australian Wildlife Odyssey *(Sierra Club Books, 2000).*

Born in White Plains in 1956, Kanze has been a frequent visitor to the Adirondacks all his life. He is currently working on a book about the relations between homo sapiens and wildlife, focusing on eighteen acres he and his wife, Debbie, have purchased along the Saranac River.

The first selection included here appeared in Adirondack Life *in 2000, the second in 1995.*

Rite of Passage: Why the Salamanders Cross the Road

When the first spring rains shower down on Adirondack forests, spotted salamanders make ready to move. The leaf debris is soggy then, and on it a few clumps of snow, stubbornly refusing to melt, lie scattered on north-facing slopes. As cool rainwater filters into the soil, hordes of *Ambystoma maculatum*, the spotted salamander, set out for ancestral breeding pools.

The amphibians often move in substantial numbers, although there is little coordination among individuals. But forward they go, on the same wet night, not so much slithering or crawling as plodding on short chubby legs.

In the Adirondacks, spotted salamanders generally emerge in late April or early May, says Ted Mack, director of the library at Paul Smith's College by day and salamander enthusiast on rainy spring nights. "Where I usually see them along the Keese's Mills Road near Paul Smiths," Mack says, "they appear around the time of ice-out." The soft-spoken librarian lights up with interest as he addresses this favorite subject. "I pick them up and move them off the road. It's a spring ritual."

Mack usually rounds up some students and friends and heads out when the conditions are right. Because the salamanders are easily flattened by cars, Mack and company appoint themselves crossing guards, helping the wanderers over the asphalt.

Most of the year, these spotted amphibians live in the soil, crawling through mole and mouse tunnels in search of prey like insects, insect larvae and other salamanders. They belong to a group known as the "mole salamanders" because they spend nearly their entire lives underground. Few of us see them. The salamanders pass the winter in the earth, insulated by leaf litter until the early soaking rains of spring summon them to romance.

The males often move first. Awakened by the rain (scientists aren't sure if it's the moisture or patter that rouses them), they burst from the leaf mold, orient in the direction of the shallow, generally fishless ponds in which they breed, and wriggle into motion. The trip to the pond from the point of emergence may take several hours. Along the way the salamanders encounter obstacles. The most troubling are those erected by humans—roads (on which hundreds of salamanders and frogs may be squished on a rainy night), walls, and houses. Since the Ice Age, the salamanders have been living on and under the hillsides where we harvest timber, build our homes, and play. They inherit breeding pools used by their parents, grandparents, and distant forbears. Salamanders do not readily change their ways. They are simple creatures of habit. One bent on reaching its breeding pond is a diminutive, sloweddown version of a charging rhinoceros; it is not easily deterred. The waters that call salamanders so strongly are scattered through the Adirondack woods. Naturalists call these small, shallow depressions "vernal ponds," because in spring they fill with snowmelt, then typically dry up in summer. Because such ponds are short-lived, they rarely support extensive populations of fish, turtles, newts, and other predators of spotted salamander eggs and larvae. Into such basins, after navigating obstacles such as Keese Mill Road, the polka-dotted creatures descend.

There is no getting around the fact that a spotted salamander is comical to see. Perhaps six inches long from permanently smiling face to graceful, pointed tail, it is covered by thin jet-black skin creased at regular intervals along the flanks and daubed with pea-sized yellow spots. Seeing my first spotted salamander years ago, I thought it looked like a creature invented by Dr. Seuss.

Upon reaching the ponds, the male salamanders slip quietly into the water. Their silence often contrasts sharply with the clamor of wood frogs and spring peepers that use the same pools for breeding. Spotted salamanders swim expertly and remain submerged for long periods. Once in the water, males stake out patches of pond bottom and on them deposit as many as eighty peculiar structures called spermatophores. Each consists of a tapering, gelatinous cone, about a quarter inch in height, four-pronged and concave at the top. In the concavity the male leaves a dollop of seminal fluid. Rather than copulate directly with females, male spotted salamanders do their best to lure them toward their own field of spermatophores.

In the water, male and female spotted salamanders move gracefully. When a male is courting a particular female, the two often swim together in synchrony. (The person standing on the bank watching with a flashlight is sure to be enthralled.) If a male is successful, the female dilates her cloaca (an all-purpose urogenital opening) like a cargo plane opening its hold. She collects the package atop one or more of his gelatinous constructions and swims away. It's a strange sort of fertilization, internal yet not involving sexual activity, at least as we think of it.

Among male spotted salamanders, scientists find that the competition for females is intense. Studies show that males outnumber females in most ponds, and the gender ratio may reach or exceed three to one. It's the reverse of a prom at an all-girls school. Here it's more like Alaska: a mob of men hunting for dancing partners among a small cadre of women. When all is said and done, a female spotted salamander may collect contributions from fifteen or twenty males. The sperm she gathers fertilizes eggs carried in her swollen belly. Two or three days later, the expectant mother starts to deposit tapioca-like egg masses, generally attaching them in cylindrical globs to submerged sticks and stems. Females usually lay between two and four of these masses, and altogether they may hold about two hundred eggs.

In any pond used by spotted salamanders, you can often find two kinds of its egg masses, one clear, the other milky. A study in the southern Appalachians suggests that milky egg masses may have an advantage over clear ones. In the milky masses, the developing embryos are apparently better hidden and less likely to be preyed on by eastern newts and insect larvae. Both kinds of egg masses are invaded by a green algae that lives in the jelly and supplies the developing embryos with oxygen.

Between four weeks and two months after the eggs are deposited in the ponds, they begin to open. Out wriggle tiny, dark, tadpole-like larvae the length of a little fingernail. While adult salamanders are probably toxic to most animals who would otherwise eat them, the larvae seem to be tasty. In fact, so many insects, fish, birds, and fellow amphibians feed on them that only a few from each egg mass survive to adulthood.

Acid precipitation—rain, fog and snow—may pose serious trouble for spotted salamanders in the Adirondacks, especially in the embryo and larval stages. Studies show that water with a low pH—or a higher acidity—may harbor abnormal numbers of the caddisfly *Ptilostomis*. This predatory insect thrives in acidic waters and may reduce young salamander numbers by as much as ninety percent.

The larvae generally remain in the pond until summer. Those that survive grow swiftly on a diet that consists chiefly of tiny aquatic copepods and cladocerans. Eventually the larvae lose their feathery external gills, develop four nimble legs and march onto land.

It may take a female seven years or more to reach breeding age. Males mature more quickly. Once grown, spotted salamanders tend to lead long lives if cars don't kill them. One study reported found a salamander that had reached the ripe old age of thirty-two. After the spring breeding, male and female spotted salamanders leave the ponds, plod back to home ground and go their separate ways. Somewhere, somehow, they choose places to disappear into the soil. There the salamanders roam through rodent burrows, fattening themselves on earthworms, spiders, land snails, centipedes, millipedes, and insects. Occasionally one is found under a rock or log, but normally these amphibians operate well beneath the surface.

With the help of Ted Mack, his friends, and others like them, Adirondack spotted salamanders may one day gain the respect they deserve. How can the rest of us get involved? Mack advises us to avoid driving on the first rainy spring nights, or better yet, to don waterproof boots and raincoats, grab flashlights, and meet the amphibians face to face. Some dark wet night, the salamanders may go marchin' into a pond near you.

An Adirondack Wilderness: The West Canada Lakes

Through a vast tract of Adirondack woods, streams, and ponds that may qualify as the wildest place east of the Mississippi, my friend Jim Alsina and I march a rutted trail toward Spruce Lake. Our knees wobble. Our feet throb. Laboring under the first backpacks either of us has carried in years, we have advanced nearly sixteen miles since morning.

We awoke in a lean-to south of Piseco after being sung to sleep by barred owls. Now every step pushes us deeper and deeper into the West Canada Lakes Wilderness Area, a 156,735-acre reservoir of wildness that stretches south and west across Hamilton County from Route 30 near Indian Lake until it spills twice over the Herkimer County line.

The terrain has been easy, but the trail, like so many in these mountains, has proven rough, an obstacle course of exposed roots and hollows. We have one mile to go.

"How are you?" I shout over my shoulder.

"All right." Jim's footfalls echo mine.

"Is it worth the pain?"

"Ask me later."

Later, Jim and I sprawl on the threshold of a lean-to, nursing sore shoulders, aching legs, and blisters. Clear blue water spreads before us and beyond, low mountains wooded in balsam fir, beech, and maple rise in the west. Just out of sight, a loon calls. The demented laughter of the bird brings smiles to our grim faces. Jim finally answers my question. "This is heaven," he says.

Heaven still seems like heaven as several thousand stars blink on one by one, and the lake sinks into darkness. For an hour we do nothing more than sit on rocks at the water's edge, enjoying the contrast between the warmth of the stone and the cool night air, and gaping at the immensity of it all. Then serenity turns to shock. Two military jets appear over the western hills and race toward us. Flying just above the spruce spires, they scream and thunder over our heads and batter us with flashing lights. Silence returns, but the spell is broken beyond mending.

Look at the West Canada Lakes Wilderness Area on a map, and you see a shape like that of a headless, narrow-waisted man hurling a javelin. Spruce Lake lies at the man's belly. The next morning, fueled by powdered orange juice and lumps of instant oatmeal, we hurry toward his heart, the cluster of clear, cold lakes known as the West Canadas.

I scowl and complain of blisters that are fast becoming wounds; Jim curses muscle cramps. Mile after merciless mile, ignoring glorious forests painted by fall colors, we advance.

We have failed to heed a cardinal rule of backpacking: If out of shape, begin a journey with a few days of easy walking so muscles can stretch and feet can toughen. Instead—with cheerless determination—we pursue our aim to hike the Northville-Lake Placid Trail from Benson to Averyville in ten days.

At midday we break loose of dark forest and find ourselves on the sunny shore of a lake. This is 250-acre West Lake, largest of the West Canadas. The hermit known as French Louie lived here from about 1875 until 1918; born Louis Seymour, he was renowned for his prowess as a trapper and woodsman as well as for a love of solitude and whiskey. My mother's father, Burdett Brownell, of Northville, met Louie when the hermit was old and my grandfather was young. Having heard my grandfather's stories of Louie, I have long wanted to visit this place to see the site of his cabin.

But we can't linger. With only a glance at a long, striped garter snake we find in the ruin of Louie's fireplace, we abandon the lake and stagger onward. I wonder, when my mind gets off my blisters, if the serpent is a great-grand-snake of the reptiles Louie put in his vegetable garden to eat pestiferous insects.

Late in the afternoon, we reach the Cedar Lakes, a collection of ponds and swamps that sprawl north and east of the West Canadas. We collapse on a footbridge; it's time for a talk.

We concede that we're pushing ourselves too hard too fast. And we agree that we've underestimated the appeal of the West Canada Lakes wilderness. Among Adirondack lands designated as wilderness, this place is second in size to the High Peaks, but it receives only a fraction of the visitors. We have seen no other hikers in four days, save for two brawny Minnesotans we met at the Piseco post office. Access is limited to a few trunk trails, black bear and beaver are plentiful, and the woods—logged earlier than most in the Adirondacks and well healed now—are largely dense and trackless. Jim and I are won over by some of the finest hills, valleys, forests, and lakes either of us has ever seen.

Soon we reach a momentous decision: To hell with our itinerary! Feeling as joyously free as liberated prisoners, we shake off our packs, peel off our boots, and slow down and smell the balsam.

In an instant the entire character of our journey through the West Canada country changes. It's like the moment in *The Wizard of Oz* when the film shifts from black-and-white to color. We find ourselves in a wonderland surrounded by beauty, the path ahead no longer a trail of tears but a shining, enticing, yellow-brick road.

We set up camp in a lean-to beside the foundation of a ranger's cabin destroyed by New York State Department of Environmental Conservation officials after the region was declared a wilderness. On the lean-to's log walls we find graffiti, including farewells ("J. R. was here") and political commentary ("The Sierra Club sucks"). The afternoon basks in an Elysian glow that projects from my gladdening soul and from the sun that hangs soft and puffy in the sky. We rest. We eat. We laugh. We watch loons and mergansers cruise the lake, listen to the cry of an osprey that circles in the sky, and rejoice in the fact that the world, for all its faults, still harbors places of such wildness and beauty. The only sour note is the fact that our supply of moleskin is exhausted. We dare not swim, despite the lure of the water; if the padding that covers our deepest blisters peels, hiking out of these remote lakes might prove impossible.

After dark, loons deliver a concert of trills and wails. I walk to water's edge to get an earful and nearly step on a frog. It's five or six inches long, green and spotted, and as I bend for a closer look, my nose wrinkles. The frog smells unpleasant. It is, I realize, a mink frog, an amphibian of northern forests that gives off the sour, urine-like bouquet of a mink. Back at the lean-to, listening to loons and the distant hooting of barred owls, I float into a deep, easy sleep.

Jim and I limp out of the West Canada Lakes wilderness the next morning, hiking by way of the Cedar River. Along the trail we stop to identify trees—red spruce, white spruce, red pine, white pine, sugar maple, American beech, white birch, and hobblebush—and to talk with an old man who greets us with a loud "Halloo." He is red-faced and white-haired, perhaps nearing eighty, and dressed in a uniform of dark-green shirt and trousers. On his back perches an Adirondack pack basket, worn and stained by age. He tells us about the big blowdown of 1950, waving his hand at the rotting evidence that still makes bushwhacking difficult here, and about the group of Boy Scouts he is leading to the lean-to we just vacated. We part, and a few minutes later two men and a group of boys appear, drenched in sweat, struggling to keep up.

A year has passed, a year in which I scheme and conspire to get back to the West Canadas. This time I will give the wilderness the homage it deserves. I will stay a while and let something of the woods creep into my soul.

I return by way of the Cedar River. Another friend, Jeff Main, and I drive in from Indian Lake to the Moose River Plains. We paddle a borrowed canoe up the Cedar River Flow and as far as we can go into the narrow river, then hide the boat in a tangle of high grass and blackberry. The sky is blue and bright, the air cool. We throw on backpacks, plunge into a wet, mossy forest of maple and birch, and cross the border into the wilderness.

That afternoon, a Saturday, we arrive at the Cedar Lakes. To our dismay the lean-tos are occupied, the lakes and trees echo with conversation, and the woods abound with tents and people. We respond by deciding to rough it and sleep under the stars. At first this proves a good idea, and we lie awake for hours hypnotized by the stars. But halfway through the night rain begins to fall.

Neither of us wants to pitch a tent, so I fish a tarp from my pack and pull it over our sleeping bags. By morning the rain has stopped and everything is damp—the woods, the ground, our gear, our spirits. We struggle to our feet, light a stove, and soon have breakfast cooking.

By evening the woods have emptied and the lakes are ours alone. For two days we lounge, swim, lounge some more, sleep, explore the woods around the lakes, catch mink frogs, study the stars at night, and botanize. Among the trees here are white and red spruce, white and yellow birch, balsam fir, and an array of prospective heirs—sugar-maple seedlings and beech saplings. On the forest floor we see wood ferns, great patches of hay-scented fern and mosses. Wet places bristle with carnivorous plants such as sundews and pitcher plants; sunny areas glow brightly with tall clumps of fireweed.

The woods teem with birds. Juncos rattle in every bush. Near our shelter a great blue heron, tall as a fourth grader and just as single-minded, stalks frogs. Song sparrows belt out snatches of Beethoven, waxwings and swallows dart for flies over the water, a raven chortles from the crown of a balsam, and loons fly, paddle, and submerge.

In the end the loons gain the greatest share of my interest. The other birds I can see nearly anywhere, but loons thrive only in wilderness, and nowhere have I seen them more sumptuously at home than here in the West Canadas. By day they float regally in the waters near our shelter, turning with the breezes like weathervanes, singing when the mood strikes, diving after fish and launching themselves on reconnaissance flights. By night they cry and wail as if the world were ending.

On the morning we pack to leave I watch a loon land. As it rockets in at an acute angle, its feet rake the smooth water into furrows. The belly makes contact, friction overcomes momentum, and the great northern diver plows slowly to a halt. The loon shakes its head, rearing out of the water to stretch its wings, and settles down to drift.

The loon stays but we must go. I shoulder my pack, making silent MacArthurian resolutions about returning, and follow Jeff into the woods. One day, I vow, I will make long visits here every month or two through an entire year and deepen my acquaintance.

Ralph Waldo Emerson, a one-time Adirondack visitor, celebrated what he called "the true harmony of the unshorn landscape with horrid thickets and bold mountains and the balance of the land." Leaving the West Canadas, I see the harmony Emerson saw in wild places and feel its tonic, restorative effect on me. I arrived harried and divided but leave serene and whole. Inside my psyche, after long happy days of stretching muscles, exercising senses, and living the kind of life for which nature itself designed me, I enjoy a balance between the wild animal nature that brought me here and the civilized social nature that drives me home.

Maurice Kenny

Maurice Kenny is native North Country in the truest sense of the term. The author grew up in Watertown, New York, where his father, of Mohawk and Irish descent, worked for the Water Department, and his mother, of English and Seneca descent, raised Maurice and a sister. The Faddens of Onchiota, New York, and his Aunt Jennie Sanford, among other influential Native American family and friends, instilled in Kenny an understanding of his distinctive roots.

That has led to a prolific career as poet, fiction writer, and playwright, with more than a dozen books of poems, essays, memoir, and reviews published. His titles include Blackrobe: Isaac Jogues *(Chauncy Press, 1982);* Between Two Rivers: Selected Poems *(White Pine Press, 1987); and* Tekonwatonti: Molly Brant, Poems of War *(White Pine Press, 1992). His most recent works include* Tortured Skins and Other Fictions *(Michigan State University Press, 1999) and* In the Time of the Present: New Poems *(Michigan State University Press, 2000).*

Kenny is known primarily for his success as a poet, winning the prestigious American Book Award in 1984 for The Mama Poems *(White Pine Press, 1984). A member of several organizations' boards and advisory groups, the writer plays a leadership role in the Native American literary community across the United States, as well as in the community of writers at large here in the Adirondacks. In 1995, St. Lawrence University awarded Kenny an honorary doctorate in literature. For a good part of the last two decades, Kenny has lived in Saranac Lake, New York.*

The selections included here appeared originally in a variety of works. "Garden" is from On Second Thought: A Selection of Poems, Essays, Memoir and Fictions *(University of Oklahoma Press, 1995); "Walking Woods with Dogs" is from* The Short and Long of It *(American Native Press*

Archives, University of Arkansas at Little Rock, 1990), and "Listening for the Elders" and "Archeologist" first appeared in Is Summer This Bear (The Chauncy Press, 1985). The first selection is excerpted from the preface to Is Summer This Bear.

Preface

From *Is Summer This Bear*

I have never recognized humankind's supremacy. I have never granted humankind that boastful ego. Humans forget there was a time before them, and perhaps shall be a time after them. Perhaps. And though I have never had a particular fondness for the Norwegian rat nor the Brooklyn cockroach, I find it difficult to deny them breath. Someplace, somewhere, somehow they join the family of all creatures and have a purpose in the Creator's perfect design. I would suppose that rat has as much right in city sewers as hawk a perch upon an elm, or wild strawberry in a spring meadow. It has its own set of rules, its own needs for survival, and undoubtedly its own niche in the balance of things.

There is no fear in my heart, however, that either the Norwegian rat or the Brooklyn cockroach will not survive whatever nuclear blast. They accommodate themselves so much more easily than the wild strawberry dependent upon clean sun and new spring. I fear more for the survival of hawk, rainbow trout in the Adirondack lakes, pike in the St. Lawrence, iris in the marsh, and bear of the forest; yes, yes, of course, even humankind in its human beauty and human stupidity, creativity and destructive foolishness. I bed nightly in trembles that its foolishness, its blindness will overpower good sense, and that all creatures, little and large, will die. And, yet, is not humankind beautiful, as handsome as wolf or turtle, though perhaps not as courageous as muskrat nor quite as bountiful as corn, or beans, or squash, the three sisters? But humankind has spirit, as much spirit as eagle's good sight, blackberry's sweetness, honey bee's flight. And because of this spirit, perhaps humankind will survive, modesty prevail, and common sense allow all other creatures the justful right to survival as well.

Should they listen to the elders, humankind will be guided to the right path; should humankind respect hornet or fisher or willow, they will come to understand the nature of things and the design the Creator wove into the tapestry of life, all life. And humankind will thank stars and rivers, birds and animals, winds and dreams: turtle who has so long carried them on his shell, and those who shall surely follow. Adowe.

Herein are songs and stories to remind humankind of their beauty and that around them, and to suggest their obligation. Here is the drum reverberating within woods and meadows, across great bodies of water and sky, and in spirit of all kind.

Listening for the Elders

is summer this bear
    home this tamarack
are these wild berries song
is this hill
    where my grandmother sleeps
    this river where
    my father fishes
does this winter-house
    light its window for me
    burn oak for my chill
does this woman sing my pain
does this drum beat
    sounding waters
or does this crow caw
does this hickory nut fall
    this corn ripen
    this field yellow
    this prayer-feather hang
    this mother worry
    this ghost walk
does this fire glow
    this bat swoop
    this night fall

does this star shine
  over mountains
  for this cousin who has
  no aunt picking sweetgrass
  for a pillow

is summer this wolf
  this elm leaf
  this pipe smoke
is summer this turtle
  home this sumac
  home this black-ash
is summer this story
is summer home
is twilight home
is summer this tongue
  home this cedar
  these snakes in my hair

reflection on this sky
  this summer day
  this bear

Archeologist

Out of a sandy field
of wild strawberries
he kicked up
an arrowhead,
and his foot
bled.

Walking Woods with Dogs

After a Snow Fall

green pristine only a miracle could devise
green color of lake water
billowed in foam
    foam of snow
And, odd, high on a naked tamarack
a banana peel dangles in forest light
some bird will supper

English setters pounce through the banks
noses rutting the fluff
    tails snapping
against a sapling birch
    barks echoing

Spruce sags and white pine under snow
        your
shoulders deep in mystery of thought
end of the year soon to replace holiday

You cannot see the mountains, Marcy or Whiteface
through the green needles, yet they are collecting
winter on shoulders, too
You cannot hear loons
    lakes and ponds frozen to flight
Yet they are there with bear snoring into spring
raccoon plotting the dangling banana peel
deer quietly waiting the setters
        leave
and the crunch of your heavy boots
skunks trailing the scent of dog meat on your hands

Have you dropped bread on the snow for swallows
      or
your own return

Setters, too, can lose the way in blizzards
as snow covers track and scent while conifers bend
disfiguring the scene you remember these years
of challenging wood and mountain

You have known your way
   always through winter
whatever corridor you stalked
but now in the broad light of this green afternoon
among these green trees, snow covering thin creeks
which yapped like puppies in summer, covering
the dead housecat fox took down months ago
        there
there, hear it, do you hear it?
the howl? is it wind in the trees, pine
or some spirit of the woods attempting
      seeking
or is it merely wolf searching its den and young
You shake your head in total disbelief
shake snow off your shoulders
stomp your boots, whistle for the dogs
      time
time to go home in the green light
as it darkens on your face
     green
wind bites your green cheek and smile as you stop
listen to the silence now that the dogs
      stand
erect tails to the wind as if frozen in frost

You look up
   the banana skin still hangs too high
for raccoon

a bluejay wings off knocking
snow puffs to a fallen log crumbling in age
you must go back to the house
wood to chop for the stove, reports to make
your wife has a plate of cold chicken for a snack
and wild grape jam for a slice of hot toast
        coffee
so black it will stand your hair on end
You start the return
        think a moment before calling
the dogs, your stance perfectly still
and realize the setters have already reached the backyard
You listen
        the howling has faded into the approaching
                gloom
pause to catch the scratching of raccoon on bark
fox crunching bones of a bird
or the late flight of summer mallards

Smiles break open
        you drop a glove on the purple snow
sniff, rub the back of your hand against your cold nose
and know there is time
again tomorrow you will walk woods
        with dogs
touch snowflakes with a warm tongue
        listen
fall of light and the hush of darkness
swallowing these green woods
        green
as new spring fermenting in the earth

Garden

Turtlehead

bloodroot   ginseng
touch-me-not   gentian
arrowhead   pitcher plant
fireweed   toothwart
meadow rue   strawberry

Smartweed

indian paint brush   indian pipe
meadow sweet   heal all
              EVERLASTING

James Howard Kunstler

Jim Kunstler, a novelist and formerly an editor of Rolling Stone, *is the author of* The Geography of Nowhere *(Simon and Schuster, 1993), a book-length study of American communities that has become required reading at schools of planning and architecture across the United States. At the core of the work is his passion for the small Adirondack towns and villages that are home to most of the region's 130,000 year-round residents.*

A sequel, titled Home From Nowhere, *was published in 1996. Kunstler, who lives in Saratoga Springs, writes frequently on issues of land-use and community planning. His work has appeared regularly in the* New York Times, Harper's, Adirondack Life, *and other publications.*

The first essay appeared originally in 1996 in The Sequel, *a publication of Paul Smith's College. The second work, a profile of hot dog millionaire Roger Jakubowski, appeared originally in* Adirondack Life *in September/October, 1987.*

A New Blueprint for Adirondack Towns

It is a mistake to suppose that all we cherish about the Adirondacks is the region's wildness. Certainly the human imprint also matters to us. That imprint is embodied both by the rugged sporting life of the woods, and by the region's towns, resorts, and legendary great camps.

The disease of suburban sprawl that threatens the Adirondack way of life is the same condition that afflicts the rest of the United States. The symptoms just seem worse here because the suburban sprawl mentality erases the distinction between the town and the country. What could be more ruinous to the character of the Adirondacks and the people who live here?

Americans now consider suburban sprawl the "normal" living arrangement, and Adirondackers are no different. Proof of this can be seen in villages like Lake Placid and Saranac Lake where the new commercial strips compete with traditional downtowns, and all development decisions are subordinated to the issues of parking and traffic control. There's a reason for this. These towns use conventional zoning laws that are no different from those used in New Jersey or Florida. Naturally the results are terrible.

Think of conventional zoning laws as the manual of instructions for building sprawl. Zoning mandates the separation of everyday activities and thus mandates dependency on the automobiles. Zoning is abstract, not particular. Zoning has never been concerned with the question of beauty. It treats the public realm as meaningless. It produces a cartoon of a human settlement.

Under the regime of zoning, "growth" and "development" have become dirty words. People don't want anymore of the cartoon architecture and parking lot wastelands that are all you can build under zoning. So, they become political NIMBYs ("Not In My Back Yard").

Ironically, under conventional zoning it is literally against the law to replicate the kinds of places that Americans consider worthy of their affection, or can afford to live in, or recognize as consistent with their historical traditions. Under zoning, Main Street and Elm Street are illegal. And, by the way, there is a reason that Main Street and Elm Street resonate so deeply in our cultural memory: because the development pattern they represent produced places that worked wonderfully and which people loved.

The antidote to zoning is traditional town planning based on the principles of civic art. The chief difference is that traditional town planning seeks to physically integrate the various activities of our everyday world, not separate them. It is concerned with details and particulars, not abstractions. It values beauty as necessary to the human spirit. It declares that the public realm must be honored and embellished in order to make civic life possible.

Have you noticed that practically all modern strip malls, including those in the Adirondacks, are one-story high? That's because zoning has declared shopping to be an obnoxious industrial activity that people shouldn't be allowed to live near. The consequences of this are severe. By forbidding people to live in apartments over the store, we have eliminated the most common form of market rental housing ever known. It now exists everywhere in the world except the United States. This is one of the reasons we have an affordable housing crisis in this country, and it is a crisis entirely of our own making.

A region as ecologically sensitive as the Adirondacks desperately needs to replace conventional zoning laws with traditional town planning ordinances. Otherwise, you are left in the ridiculous predicament of only being allowed to develop precisely the kind of suburban fabric that is inconsistent with the way of life here. The result will be exactly the kind of political paralysis that makes any growth or economic development impossible.

Unfortunately, most planning officials receive virtually no education in traditional planning. There's a reason for this, too: a generation ago, the planning departments at many universities, including Harvard, were moved out of the architecture schools and into the schools of public administration. In other words, since the end of World War II, planners have been taught how to shuffle papers, not how to draw. They've been taught how to be bureaucrats, not designers. The tragic incompetence of today's planning officials is the result.

Developing new college curricula—with a focus on regional issues, sustainable development, and interdisciplinary problem-solving skills—goes a long way toward positive change in the education of our civic planners. But courses like "Land Use Planning," which normally deal with macro-land management problems, should also seriously consider the micro challenges of town planning, while reestablishing the traditional principles of civic art.

Both the region and the nation are desperately in need of such professional training. The towns of the Adirondack region are small enough and still retain enough traditional physical fabric to serve as excellent models for the twenty-first century. Adirondackers deserve a new blueprint for future development, and it ought to be home-grown. Most of all, it must preserve the distinction between town and wilderness.

Human settlements are like living organisms. They must grow, they will change. But we can decide on the nature of that growth, particularly on the quality and the character of it, and where it ought to go.

We don't have to scatter the contents of our civic life all over the map, impoverishing our towns and ruining the countryside at a single stroke. We can put the shopping and the offices and the movie theaters and the library all within walking distance of each other. And we can live within walking distance of all these things. We can build our schools close to where the children live, and the school buildings don't have to look like insecticide factories. We can insist that commercial buildings be more than one-story high, and allow people to live in decent apartments over the stores. We can build Main Street and Elm Street and still park our cars. And we can start right here in the Adirondacks.

The Man Who Would Be King

ROGER JAKUBOWSKI: *I decided that I can't work for nobody. They're liable to find out how dumb I really am. Never educated or nothin'. What can I do? A guy'll tell me to take out the trash, I won't even do that right. I have to be the boss.*

JK: Why do you think you're so dumb if you've done so well?

RJ: Because I should have a hundred times more, I should own the entire Adirondack Park, that's what I think. I don't own it. The whole Park, including upstate, the 1000 Islands. Yeah, that's what I think.

The story of Roger Jakubowski's preternatural arrival in the North Country two years ago has already entered the annals of Adirondack legend, but for those of you who have been out of state or in a coma since 1985, or don't get the New York papers, here's the recap in a nutshell:

New Jersey hot dog millionaire Jakubowski comes to the Adirondacks to inspect an old spring water bottling operation that's for sale and is so charmed by these mountains that he at once starts buying up everything in sight. His foremost purchase is Camp Topridge, the old Marjorie Merriweather Post estate on Upper St. Regis Lake, north of

Saranac Lake. The shopping list also includes Crab Island in Lake Champlain, the Big Tupper Ski Center, most of pristine Lake Ozonia, radio stations in Plattsburgh and Tupper Lake, and more. A flamboyant fellow, his appetite for publicity is bottomless. He courts the press and his droll utterances make great copy.

I'd gone on the state tour of Topridge back in '84—long before Roger Jakubowski took the property and everything it contained off Governor Cuomo's hands—so I knew which stuff was Marjorie's and which was his. What few people understand about Camp Topridge and its creator Mrs. Post is that her taste in home furnishings ran along the lines of Elvis Presley's. Then, of course, Roger moved in some stuff of his own.

There were, for instance, the skunk pelt table mats (hers), and the four-foot-tall brass candlesticks (his), which looked like a gift to the College of Cardinals from the President-for-Life of a third world republic. There was the polyester leopard-skin sofa (hers)—as though nobody would notice it among the dozens of real fur couches, settees, chaises, divans, chairs, and ottomans—and the chess set (his) with pawns the size of pepper mills and kings on the order of Wade Boggs' baseball bat. There was the clunky, cheap-looking, sludge-colored dinner service (hers), including demitasse cups, and the unusual tapestry made of stitched-together shearling sheepskin patches depicting Simon Bolivar astride a charger (his) tacked to the lofty ceiling. And of course there were all the motheaten stuffed animals, the beaver, porcupine, fox, marten, flying squirrels, elk, bison, caribou, moose, pronghorn, bighorn, cape buffalo, gnu, eland, ibex, zebra—a veritable Mutual of Omaha Wild Kingdom of dead critters (not to mention whole schools of stuffed fish)—all Marjorie's. And there was Roger's 100-watt-per-channel McIntosh stereo with the six gigantic Klipsch horn speakers, disguised in "rustic" cabinets as big as port-a-johns, blasting out the late and great Marvin Gaye singing "Heard It Through The Grapevine" at a volume loud enough to raise all the aforementioned slain beasts from their sleep of death and send them thundering for the doors.

I'd arrived early one morning in mid-spring to find the main gate open and unattended—a situation, I learned later, which had made Jakubowski furious on numerous occasions, according to former em-

ployees. But much as he harangued the staff about the gate, the damn
thing had a way of staying open, so that any boob, including a nosy reporter, could gain entry to the estate.

The Topridge compound of sixty-odd buildings bristles along a narrow spine of rock and conifer that forms a kind of wall between Upper
Saint Regis Lake and Upper and Lower Spectacle Ponds. Begun in the
1930s by the daughter of cereal tycoon C.W. Post, the hodgepodge of
little guest cottages and assorted party shacks, along with the main
lodge, is a maintenance crew's nightmare. In fact, the staggering cost
of upkeep, amounting to several hundreds of thousands of dollars a
year, was the chief reason behind the State's eagerness to unload the
place (possibly illegally, since Marjorie had willed it to the people of
New York). In any case, Roger Jakubowski was already up before nine
on the morning of my visit, a little bleery perhaps, his long silver hair
tousled as though from sleep, trying to instruct his somewhat overwhelmed three-man maintenance crew on their chores for the day. He
had one of them in person and issued orders to the others over a crack-
ling walkie-talkie.

Finally, satisfied that his minions would proceed faithfully as ordered, Roger ushered me gruffly up the ridge, past the drabber buildings
formerly occupied by Mrs. Post's army of guides, gardeners, and house-
keepers, to the gargantuan main lodge. Then, he vanished.

In his place there soon appeared a man of impressive girth, late for-
ties perhaps, who somehow managed to look dignified despite his out-
fit—a kind of blue-denim smock suit. The man introduced himself as
Roger Jakubowski's "art advisor," Victor Bacon. In fact, Victor served
Roger in a wide variety of roles, usually as cook, but he was also family—well, in a way—having once been married to Roger Jakubowski's
sister. Roger referred to Victor as the "proctor" of Topridge. (Oddly, two
weeks before my visit Victor Bacon had left Topridge entirely according
to a former employee who chanced to meet Victor at the airport. That
day Victor had been full of gall and resentment at the Lord of Topridge,
and it was astounding, the former employee said, to hear that Victor
was back again. Later, Victor attributed his leave to health reasons. "I
needed a little vacation, actually," he said.)

In any case, Victor offered to show me Roger's art collection while
his boss washed up before breakfast. In the center of Marjorie's thirty

foot long dining room table—between the giant brass candlesticks—stood an imposing silvered bronze statue of a sword-wielding Viking by a sculptor named La Port. One had to admire the droll effect of placing such a pugnacious figure amid the salad plates and soup bowls, his broadsword ready should some dinner guest utter an incorrect remark.

At the head of the main stairway, built out of colossal tree trunks, stood a Japanese bronze urn the size of a stockpot full of old rose petals that had lost their scent. "Late Meiji period," Victor said—meaning the early 1900s, around the time of the Taft administration. Across the vast main room, before a fireplace as big as a walk-in closet, lay another bronze sculpture about four feet around of two bulls fighting. At one-tenth the size it would have made a nice paperweight, or perhaps a doorstop. I asked Victor what his prior experience had been in this line of work.

"I used to be in the gift and art-ware business," he replied. Art-ware? I wondered. Anyway, he too made to disappear now, saying he had to prepare Roger's breakfast, and I was left alone again with the music of *The Big Chill* blaring from the Klipsches.

Just then I happened to notice what seemed to be a rummage sale going on in one of the sun porches off the main lodge. There was some-one—a young woman—searching through a lot of clothes on one of those portable metal racks. Plus, there was an array of miscellaneous bric-a-brac spread out on tables all around the sun porch. You could tell it was Marjorie's old stuff. For example, there were two outsized ceramic candelabra the same sludge color as her tableware. I ventured in.

Now, the idea of a rummage sale here was fairly preposterous—not just because we were more than a mile away from any public road—and indeed that's not what proved to be going on. In fact, it was an advertising company doing a shoot for one of its clients: the K-Mart clothing division. The clothes on the racks, then, were K-Mart fashions. The photo crew was down below somewhere, near the old boathouse. I barely had a minute to chat up the wardrobe girl before Victor Bacon summoned me to the breakfast table.

Roger Jakubowski is hardly the first rich outsider to try to carve a personal empire out of these mountains. Adirondack lore is filled with case histories of megalomania.

Consider Robert Schroeder, the nineteenth-century beer baron who built Debar Park in the Town of Duane, Franklin County. The estate included what was reputed to be the world's largest hops farm—the flowering herb used to give beer its characteristic flavor. The centerpiece was a sixty-room mansion with adjoining Thoroughbred stables and a private racetrack. By and by, however, Schroeder's business went bust, he lost everything, and committed suicide in a Brooklyn rooming house.

Or take Litchfield Park, a failed attempt to create a European-style shooting preserve filled with walking hunting trophies. Around the turn of the century, Edward H. Litchfield fenced in 9,100 acres in the Town of Altamont and tried to stock it with elk and moose—long extirpated by the white man—and also wild boar. For years he and his son kept at it, but the animals all dropped dead sooner or later, and in 1905 the experiment was abandoned. It wasn't until seventy-five years later that scientists discovered a brain-rotting parasite carried by slugs and spread by white-tailed deer (who are immune to it) which devastated the moose and elk.

Roger Jakubowski's plans are, well, perhaps less elegant than these strange examples. But in two years he has unquestionably become the most conspicuous citizen in these parts. Meanwhile, much of the North Country establishment—that is, the powers-that-be, the old money sports, the WASPy-snobby club folk, the Adirondack Council members, the civic leaders—are scared to death of this Jersey parvenu who makes no bones about wanting to buy up the entire gosh-darn Adirondacks like some kind of devouring forest demon out of Algonquin mythology.

"The things he says are more worrisome than the things he's done," said Dick Beamish, spokesman for the Adirondack Council, the Park's chief watchdog organization. "His statements that the only future for the Adirondack Park is development, and that real estate is scandalously underpriced, trouble us. The fact is that despite the Agency's zoning plan, the law has weaknesses, and there is room for a lot of potential development. Someone like Roger Jakubowski can be a threat to permanently preserving the natural character of the Park—but so far he's only made a lot of boasts."

Breakfast was served to Roger on another sun porch opposite the one where the K-Mart thing was happening. It was a simple repast, a buttered English muffin to be exact. Roger—who often refers to himself as Roger, in the third person form of address—was a little slow to warm up for our interview. But having a keen sense of his own outrageousness, he soon reached full stride. His discourse is often punctuated by the phrase "you know what I mean?," but spoken rapidly so as to come out more like, "you know whimean." Anyway, here are some highlights from the dialogue that ensued:

JK: Did Roger Jakubowski have any dreams of the North Woods when he was a kid?

RJ: Didn't even know what the North Woods is. It took me two months to say the word Adirondacks.

JK: Do you have a grand plan for developing the Adirondacks?

RJ: Yes, I do. As different things are collected, it's my plan as a businessman to enhance, which enhances me personally and enhances the area. I think the first initial step—which has only been better for my business—is awareness of the Adirondacks for people such as myself who never heard of it. Don't forget, this is not the Canadian wilderness or Rhodesia. An hour and a half, you're in New York City. I can understand why people kept this place a secret. It's a wonderful place. Take a look at the people on the lake. You can't even get to their home by boat. If they want people to visit, they don't put in a road, they put in a helipad.

JK: You must be aware that a lot of people are nervous about you and all your money.

RJ: They're nervous anyway. I can't really think of anybody in the Adirondacks, anybody, who would be against progress in a controlled way, which is how I want it. There are guidelines, laws. I've lived up to every law. I'm not changing anything. If anything, I haven't done anything.

JK: What actual opportunities are there here for business, other than Big Tupper (the ski center).

RJ: Plenty of opportunities. The place is crawlin' with 'em.

JK: Like what?

RJ: The manufacturin' industry. Some people up here, they seem to want to work, you know whimean?

JK: Doesn't the Adirondack Park Agency have pretty stringent restrictions on that?

RJ: For people wanting to work?

JK: No. For manufacturing, industrial uses.

RJ: This is my home. When you come home your wife will tell you please, don't manufacture in the living room, go manufacture in the garage. That's the same thing. So, we got a bigger house in the Adirondack Park.

JK: Is there anything in particular you're thinking of manufacturing here? Any particular sort of products?

RJ: Yeah, probably water-related. It could be shampoo, you know whimean? Look at all the ingredients of everything in the supermarket. Everything: the major addition is water.

At this point, Roger was having trouble opening one of the miniature jam jars that Victor had brought to the table. Roger had injured his hand tinkering with a motorboat engine the day before. Sensing his boss's distress, Victor quickly seized the jar, opened it, and spooned the jam out onto Roger's plate. There was something touching about his helplessness and Victor's eagerness to please. Then our interview continued.

JK: You spent the first forty odd years of your life not knowing about this area, and now you're enchanted by it,

RJ: Enchanted, in love, mesmerized, and I believe I have no reason to go anywhere else in the world. Do you know what a place like this would cost in Lake Tahoe? I was offered 4.5 million for this place ninety days after I bought it (for $911,000).

JK: Do you stay in Marjorie Merriweather Post's cottage?

RJ: There are living quarters throughout the camp. But I do not stay in her home. I would like to keep it as a memento to the prior owner who no doubt will go down in history as one of the finest most intelligent women there ever was. The reason I know that is you see what she created throughout the country. It has to be that way. Who else done something like what she have done singlehandedly? Without benefits—she had benefits of husbands, but they were only temporarily. She withstood them all.

We talked at great length about the history of Roger's business exploits in New Jersey, what has become a standard résumé in the newspaper stories about him—his lowly beginnings selling meat off a truck in

Camden, his retirement to California to promote arm wrestling tournaments, his return to the east at age thirty-one, and his subsequent conquest of the hot dog business at the Jersey seashore. This all led, naturally, to his 1986 arrival in the Adirondacks, to the subject of his real estate buying binge since then, and his oft-made boast that he would like to buy the entire Adirondack Park, if it was possible.

JK: What would you do with it all?

RJ: Who cares? What would I do? First get it! You know, I'm not an "if" man.

JK: I'm kind of curious where your burning desire comes from to have all this.

RJ: It's not a burning desire. It's a regret, and the sympathy I give myself for not having it.

JK: Does it cause you any pain that other people have it and you don't?

RJ: Positively.

JK: Like Joe Blow across the lake has a camp, do you want to have his camp?

RJ: I'd like to have it all.

JK: So the question of what to do with it isn't important at all?

RJ: First get it. We'll worry about that next. One day at a time. See, if I owned it all, there'd be no beaver dams because I'd take care of the beavers. We have a crew who goes out and takes care of the beavers. We don't have to worry about going out and killing them because we're gonna take him and we're gonna have a beaver.

JK: Do you want the Adirondack Park to be your private amusement park?

RJ: No, I don't want the Adirondack Park. No, I want Roger's Park to be for my own amusement.

JK: When is the next load of your friends coming up here to Topridge?

RJ: Next week. People who help me make money, that's a friend.

JK: Marjorie had people coming here all the time.

RJ: Making her billions. When she had her army here, all the generals were here. I guarantee you if you went to an outpost in Outer Mongolia where the United States Army was, they were drinkin' nothing but Maxwell House coffee and eatin' nothin' but jello, and havin' nothing but Post for breakfast. You know what it is to have five billion customers all at once? That's how she done it.

JK: So, this isn't enough here?

RJ: Never enough! Never enough!

JK: You have this general philosophy that just about everything is undervalued.

RJ: That's correct.

JK: Why do you suppose that is?

RJ: It's like the state buying land, you know, for $75, $100 an acre. Anybody's got them kind of prices, call me. Call up the State and see what they're paying.

JK: Do you consider yourself lucky?

RJ: Story of my life. Everything I touch turns to gold. Automatic. Wherever it is. Jeez. Go turn on the radio station I just bought in Tupper Lake. You couldn't hear it outside the city limits. Go turn it on now. You can't get it off the station. What, did the airwaves change? What happened that all of a sudden you can hear the radio that's been around for a hundred years?

JK: I dunno. What?

RJ: Roger owns it.

JK: Did you put up a bigger transmitter or something?

RJ: Yeah, we got a couple—yeah.

JK: Well, that helps, doesn't it?

RJ: Yeah, but you're not supposed to know that.

JK: Aside from the stuff around here (Camp Topridge), how are you keeping busy?

RJ: Jeez, a number of things. We got Big Tupper which was a pretty big business. We kept this place going all winter. I like to see the twenty-foot icicles coming off the side.

JK: Did you feel like you were in fantasyland?

RJ: I just felt so special. Like I was in Christmasland, Santa Clausland. Rogerland.

Our interview concluded, Roger sent me off on a tour of other buildings with Victor Bacon. Among our stops, the hallowed personal cottage of Marjorie Merriweather Post, all the original decor in place, the enormous boudoir still painted the nightmarish livid pinks I remembered so well from my first tour, years before Roger came along. Shortly, Victor too excused himself in order to go and prepare lunch for the K-Mart advertising crew. He, in turn, snagged a young maintenance man, whom we shall call "Bob" in order to protect his job, and told him to show me around the putting greens and tennis courts.

To get to these we had to cross a little slough down by the lake where, evidently, beavers had done a considerable amount of feasting in recent months. The characteristic pointed stumps of their cuisine could be seen all around. I mentioned this to Bob.

"Oh yeah," he agreed avidly. "But we got rid of them last week."

"Got rid of them? I said. "What? Moved them somewhere else?"

"Naw," he said. "We offed them."

Anne LaBastille

Anne LaBastille, an ecologist and free-lance writer, is best known for her series of books about life in a cabin on Black Bear Lake. Enormously popular with readers inside and outside the Adirondacks, LaBastille's writings seem to touch a nerve in the American reader's psyche that stretches back to Thoreau's two-year sojourn alongside Walden Pond. It's a powerful American myth, and for the most part, LaBastille mines silver in a romantic vein that recalls Emerson, Wordsworth and Coleridge. For LaBastille and her literary forebears, nature is a place for retreat and restoration, a leafy cathedral for spirit and soul.

However, certain residents and readers—both male and female— question the authenticity of a self-proclaimed "woodswoman." Their complaint, as it were, is that many Adirondack men and woman have been making their lives on the land year-round in the region for generations. (LaBastille is a seasonal resident on a real Adirondack lake, although renamed "Black Bear" Lake by the author for reasons of privacy.)

Perhaps in the manner of the stoics, LaBastille's critics feel little need for what they might see as some degree of self-promotion on the part of the author. Still, while the author's style and approach are open to question by some readers, her passion for all things Adirondack is unparalleled. Her years of service to the region in the name of preservation have had an effect, especially in bringing attention to a vast resource that had been receiving relatively little until that time.

LaBastille's titles include Mama Poc *(W. W. Norton Co., 1990),* Women and Wilderness *(Sierra Club Books, 1980), and* Jaguar Totem *(West of the Wind Publications, 1999). Her free-lance work has appeared in* The Conservationist, *the* Boston Globe, National Geographic, Sierra, Natural History, Adirondack Life *and numerous other magazines and newspapers. The selections here are from* Woodswoman III. *(West of the Wind Publications, 1997).*

Opening Camp

The call comes through late on April 30. "Ice is out," drawls Andy, my laconic best friend in the Adirondacks. "At noon today. Road seems okay." A pause.

"I'll help with repairs and hauling boxes up to your cabin." On that note he hangs up. Andy hates phones.

My heart starts racing like that of a caged bird which suddenly finds its door swung open. One of the worst winters of the century is over, and I'm heading for camp! No telling what havoc the high winds of November, the four-foot drifts of January, or the Siberian super-cold of February have wreaked upon my log cabin.

Next morning I'm up at 5:30, worrying about the "what ifs." A comealong and tow chain for what if I veer off the dirt road and bury my truck in a soft shoulder. A propane torch and pry bar for what if the padlock is frozen or my boat is iced onto shore. An ax for what if ice lingers around my dock and I must chop a channel to land. A life vest for what if I fall into the frigid water.

Finally my two German shepherds and I are in the vehicle. We arrow off the Northway and into the Adirondack Park. Fog as white as polyester fluff drifts above lakes black as onyx. That's hot spring sun heating up ice-cold water. This is the year's third and final death. First comes the death of summer's greenery; second, of fall's vibrant colors; and last, of winter's rock-hard ice and packed snow.

We reach Black Bear Lake, jump out and skip to shore. Tears and euphoria engulf me. A pair of loons floats two hundred yards away as if they'd been anchored there since September. It's Nina and Verplanck, our lake's resident couple. I yodel. They answer—my first welcome home.

How lucky I am to feel this way about homecoming in a world where millions return to elevators and nondescript apartments that offer no sense of belonging. Where no loons greet and confirm one's harmony with nature.

Eager to be on the water, I easily unlock my boat, flip it over and slide it into the lake. Wrassling the motor onto the transom, I give three cranks. Eco! Chekika and Condor leap in and point like bowsprits as we take off. It seems I'm the first one on the lake this spring—a point of enormous pride. Only one good neighbor is back, deeply tanned from a Florida winter. He lives on the dirt road, so he really doesn't count, does he?

Halfway up the lake I notice many broken treetops along the shore. The woods streaking by are winter worn, beaten, bleak. Not a trace of green shows at this elevation. A canoe has been smashed. A dock tilted. A neighbor's camp has actually exploded outward from the snow load. I dock the boat and walk apprehensively up my trail. The cabin stands intact!

My min-max thermometer registers -38° and 93°F, with present air temperature at 62. Gingerly I unlock the door. The aroma of wool Navajo rugs, balsam pillows, and cold ashes in the wood stove wafts out. I draw in the smells hungrily. At once I light the fire that's been waiting to glow since last fall. After opening windows to help warm the icebox interior, I fly back outdoors to look for damages. The dogs race ahead of me, going from outbuilding to outbuilding, sniffing wildly.

The north wind has ripped off the plastic that swathed my lean-to. Its floor is still wet from melted snow. Squirrels have gnawed a new hole in the mattress. No big deal. At the outhouse, a huge pine limb lies alongside, having gouged a nick in the roof. Inside the hole is filled with ice. Under the cabin roof lies a three-foot snow pile.

No need to light the gas refrigerator—I'll keep groceries in a snow hollow. I check my long-departed Pitzi's grave. Still shrouded in snow. Come Memorial Day I'll carpet my beloved dog with wildflowers. The woodshed top is atangle with branches. Easy to sweep clean. I carry yellow birch logs indoors, then stoke the fire. The cabin is mellowing. Those cheery flames remind me to fetch water.

On the dock I stand still and soak in the silence. I fill two pails and kneel for my first drink of wild water in six months. It's probably the cleanest water this side of Montana. I scoop up several swallows. The pH be damned. *Giardia* be damned. In over two decades here I've never gotten sick. That ritual over, I lug the pails up to the cabin. Beside the trail, in the same thicket where I saw him last spring, a winter wren is belting out his melody—my second welcome home.

Time to think of tranquil time as sunset nears. And dinner. I slide a precooked casserole into my small gas oven and step outside to turn on the propane tanks. Praying that no lines have cracked in the severe cold, I sniff along the system until I'm sure all's safe. While supper is warming Chekika and Condor eye me expectantly. I feed them extra, knowing how hungry the mountain air and exercise has made them. Then I plug in my phone, hoping it works, and call Andy. He promises to come in the morning to help unload my truck and ferry the gear to camp.

Late light dancing off the lake turns my log room golden. I sweep up some mouse droppings and pick up two books toppled by a trespassing squirrel. In the sleeping loft, I discover old birdseed hidden in my wool blankets. Such is the extent of interior damages. No real repairs are needed.

I head down to the dock carrying an Adirondack chair and snuggle into it. A winter down jacket and the steaming dinner on my lap warm me inside and out. The sun sets behind bare trees. Two white gulls wheel overhead. Not a sound. I contemplate my good fortune after this horrific winter. Seems to me that Nature tempered her fury predictably with protective snows, strong trees, thick ice. She's brought the earth full circle to feel the caress of a warm sun again. All the forest refuse and litter will slowly turn into rich duff. Green plants and bright birds shall soon return.

Yet it also seems to me that Nature deals out as much chaos as predictability. Why was my neighbor's camp flattened—but not mine? Why was another neighbor's woodshed canted cockeyed? Why was someone else's canoe smashed—but not my three? This wild winter treated my property and cabin kindly. The next may not.

A barred owl hoots across the lake so chill—my third welcome home.

Like a Kestrel

Dawn, adazzle, conifers sparkling in the early sun with raindrop lights. Clinging to needle tips like tiny Christmas bulbs, they flash ruby, gold, chartreuse, silver, aquamarine, and emerald. The morning is fresh, clean, and fragrant. It has an innocence and timelessness that I remember from my first years here at the cabin. Years when I was innocent and timeless as well. I breathe deeply. My skin tingles in the cool August air.

Rusty blackbirds are chattering to their young in the spruce tops. They were doing the exact same thing when I was newly arrived at Black Bear Lake. Often they kept me company, flying here and there along the shoreline as I worked or read on my dock. Purple finches are warbling, too, on the balsam spires. They sound and look as winsome as ever.

One of the loons calls sweetly from out on the misty lake. Wondering where your mate is this morning? No loons lived on this lake when I moved in, and I didn't hear any for several years. Suddenly, they appeared: Nina and Verplanck. Could this still be the same pair? I think so. Loons are long-lived. They know me and my motor well, and acknowledge my presence by their trust. They approach when I call in tremolo, often fish close to my dock, and float nearby during my dawn dip. They never shriek at *my* boat when I cruise up and down the lake.

Back behind my small office two hermit thrushes are hymning, and a winter wren's song cascades out of a balsam thicket. Any day now they'll migrate. Years ago, a veery lived here. That solemn, shy songster, related to thrushes, poured out flute-like notes down the scale like a musical waterfall. Two ravens fly over, *crauk-ing* to each other. They've swooped down from the cliff near Thoreau II with their youngsters and are out on a training flight. The adults probably are the ones I've know for three decades, for ravens also live a long time. Nothing much has changed in nature, or so it seems.

Thirty years! Can it be? I moved into my cabin at Black Bear Lake on July 4, 1965 (by coincidence), just like Henry David Thoreau did at Walden Pond on July 4, 1845. Unlike Thoreau, I was afraid of many things at first. I was scared to live alone after my divorce. I was concerned because so few people came to the lake (only one older couple lived here full-time). Who could I turn to in time of trouble? Fear of assault and rape troubled my thoughts. Yet none of these worries lasted more than three weeks. They were replaced by the joy and challenge of living at the edge of wilderness. How satisfying it was to be self-reliant. I reveled in being alone and able to write or watch wildlife as long as I wished. Within the month I grew more confident that violent men would not attack me in this peaceful place, if at all. Men may question such fear, but women all over the world will recognize and relate to it.

Today? Everything's changed. I'm afraid of a whole new set of problems. I'm concerned because so many more people are coming to Black Bear Lake. Next year, summer 1997, our narrow dirt road will be paved right to the public landing and that will entice more outsiders to visit this small remote lake. Last winter the first burglary ever occurred here when two young men from outside the Park entered several vacant camps and stole guns and tools. It was rumored they did it to support a drug habit. Luckily for me, the cabins at the upper, wilder, hard-to-reach end of the lake weren't touched. What about next time?

I'm also troubled by the hostility of the big boat group. How can we convince them to act like caring members of our community and less like adolescents indulging their own whims? What if I get hit by a large powerboat or swamped by its wake while I'm in my canoe with the dogs or a guest? What if the water's dangerously cold? As the situation stands now, I fear our lake is just waiting for an accident or drowning to happen.

I worry a lot about the continued decrease in trout, frogs, deer, songbirds, and spruce trees in the Adirondacks. Big native brookies no longer rise to the lake's surface. Most have been replaced by an acid-resistant strain of hatchery-reared trout stocked every fall. Frogs, spring peepers, and salamanders at higher elevations in the Park are being wiped out by acid rain.

My dearest neighbors, who came here forty years ago, tell me that deer often used to play and splash along the shoreline on summer evenings. I've hardly ever seen them do that, and their numbers seem low these days. Barn swallows, too, used to swoop and circle over the lake by the dozens. There are only a handful now. The tracts of large red spruce growing around our lake and other bodies of water are 30 percent to 40 percent dead. I proved this by counting them on many lakes while I researched my article for *National Geographic*, "Acid Rain—How Great A Menace?"

Not all the changes have been bad. When I started living here, very few motorboats traveled up and down the lake. Most were old clunkers that spewed a lot of gas and oil into the water. Today there are seventy-five runabouts with small motors and twelve large powerboats. The

208 | Rooted in Rock

newer motors are more efficient and thus somewhat less polluting. However, there is still no such thing as a two-cycle marine engine with catalytic controls or devices to keep hydrocarbons from being discharged directly into the water. The U.S. Coast Guard reports 16 million motorboats and almost one million personal water craft are afloat in the United States today. Imagine all this pollution for pleasure!

Thirty years ago phone service, electricity, and TV didn't exist on the lake. Today they are available and most camp owners enjoy them. More affluent and professional people live here than before. There are a few new camps, and the same familiar old ones have additions, guest cottages, and sleeping shelters built to accommodate the second generation. This was bound to occur. The big change is that many owners make use of their camps from almost ice-out to almost ice-in. Formerly, folks vacationed primarily on summer weekends and during big game season. People really love this place and use it more and more. As visitor numbers and uses rise, we all need to do more to protect the environment, especially the lake, from harm. Property owners must care about clean water, healthy wildlife, silence, and ecology. *A good lake is hard to find.* It's why we're here. This should be our number one concern: keeping Black Bear unpolluted, preventing erosion and turbidity, and limiting excessive noise.

These thirty years have also brought many external changes to West of the Wind and this "ol' woodswoman." The cabin's just the same, except I added a very low basement for files and storage. The outhouse has moved 100 feet farther from the back door as I keep digging new pits. Builds character! I've also added the tiny office, a shed for my log splitter, and a new woodstove. That's about it.

Physically I'm in good shape, slim, with silvery-blond hair and plenty of energy. I notice a small loss of muscle power and an increase in achy old injuries. But these changes are compensated by knowing how to move, pace myself, and persevere. I make use of good tools and safe machinery, like a safety-feature-laden chain saw, heavy padded pants, ear muffs and helmet for sawing, a battery-operated drill, and automatic shifting and four-wheel drive in the truck. This technology has extended my ability to survive in the woods and also extended my life span, rather than being burned out like an old lumberjack at thirty-five. It also allows me more time for watching wildlife and guiding. It lets me harness and direct my energies to write, rather than let my life force seep away on chores. Heaven knows I've wasted enough hours doing jobs the slow, hard way, and had enough accidents and pain to last this lifetime.

Now let this ol' woodswoman pound the pulpit for a few pages. Retirement, in my mind, is a fantasy for many Americans. It's not good for you. I believe that working hard your whole life, even though you may change jobs and activities often, is the way to stay fit, youthful, and tough. If you work and play outdoors as much as possible, it may help prevent cancer and heart disease. I intend to continue sawing up tornado damage, repairing buildings, stacking wood, playing with my dogs, hauling buckets of water, writing, and guiding right into my nineties—just like Albert.

There's an excitement to aging. I wouldn't go back a day. I like where I live, what I do, how I look, and what I know. The obsession with youth in our culture is sick. Over fifty and you're ready for the ash heap. Baloney! Older women should tell people forthrightly, "This is what it looks like to be fifty-seven." (Or whatever your age is.) Let your hair go grey. Remember the full moon, which I marveled at, at my baby cabin? Let your head be haloed with "silvery veils and white chiffon." It's beautiful.

Older women have the experience and maturity to offer the greatest service and skills to society of any segment of our population. They are at the peak of their promise. Look at the facts. Older women command 60 percent of the wealth in this country. They've learned much and are free to study, travel, teach, and participate in anything they wish. Child-rearing is no longer a responsibility. Women live longer. Since we're the natural care-takers in this world, I feel the greatest good that women can do is help the environmental movement. Women can save Earth's creatures and the planet.

To be effective, we must keep calm, be flexible, stay persistent in our environmental concerns. We need to feminize ecology and bring on more grass-roots activism. We should use our female powers of keen observation, extra-sensory perception, diplomacy, and persuasion.

What about men in my life? I know and work with many. I have many close male friends. Yet the few I've truly loved are gone. I'm not the only woman in this situation. I scarcely know a woman over fifty

210 | Rooted in Rock

who still has a man in her life. Indeed, half of all women in America over forty live alone. Some keep looking for the right one; others don't even want a relationship. "Life's a lot easier when you don't have to pick up after someone," a divorced friend says jokingly (except she's serious).

Women are the strong, enduring sex. As I see it, older women can't depend on older men much anymore. We can't hope that they will stay alive as long as we do, that they will always help us, be chivalrous and courteous, or even excite and pleasure us. Too much has happened. We've experienced women's liberation, equality of the sexes, harassment in the job market, loss of good manners, and much more. These phenomena have eroded relationships between women and men.

I still recall my astonishment right after the tornado when I realized that not one man had come by my camp or the camps of any other lone women at the lake to see if we were dead, alive, pinned under a tree, or needed a helping hand to clean up. Thirty years ago men would have rushed to assist women after an emergency—not just because we were women, but also because of their commitment to old, traditional, fine Adirondack values of helping out the community.

Today, some men are angry at women and their independence. How else can we explain women being battered, gang-raped, victims of sexual harassment in the armed forces, the workplace, everywhere? Some men are bullies. In their minds a woman with no man taking care of her, with only modest means, and with no power position is fair game to be bullied. My feeling is that every woman should have a position of power in her later years. She should get involved with a community activity that gives her exposure and prestige: set up a scholarship fund, get on a board of directors, help the poor and disabled, write and publish, volunteer at the library, go for a Master's degree, or guide nature walks for kids. Every woman should do something that makes her important in her eyes and her neighbors'. And if a woman spends much time alone and outdoors, I guarantee the best assets she can have today are a dog, a firearm, and an assertive attitude, posture, and walk. Be prepared. As we know, there are a few bad men out there.

Some women I know still dream about finding the "right man." Sure, he's out there. Must be at least one among the five billion people on earth. The hard part is finding him. So meanwhile we should cultivate independence and our women friends. One of the most wonderful parts of being an "ol' woodswoman" is my circle of friends—the ones who click and stick over the years. Of course it takes nurturing and patience to keep a friend. Kindness, courtesy, and correctness help and go a long way. Nothing is more comforting and enduring than friendship with a good woman.

All my friends over fifty delight me by having great things to look forward to. My oldest chum from high school just got her first dog, an elegant collie. After years in an abusive marriage, a divorce, and bouts of anxiety, now she can't wait to wake up and take her dog for a walk. Then she rushes home from work to go out with him together again. A colleague from The Explorers Club, Dr. Sylvia Earle, an oceanographer, says, "I hope to reach bottom by the year 2000." She means she plans to explore the bottom of the Pacific Ocean—in a seven-mile-deep dive. She'll be sixty-four and probably going deeper than any human in history. Another pal in her seventies plans three unusual trips a year, some with Elderhostel, some alone. She is a walking encyclopedia of curious geography facts. Her scrapbooks are gems of photos, maps, menus, and interesting quotes heard abroad. My colleague Dr. Eugenie Clark, about whom I wrote in *Women and Wilderness*, predicts, "I plan to keep on diving and researching sharks and conserving reefs until I'm at least ninety years old." Margaret Murie, author, conservationist, and great-grandmother, who is in her nineties, is a guru to young people all over the United States. She loves to help them plan careers in conservation and sort out their problems. In her late seventies she was made an honorary park ranger by the National Park Service.

Here's my last bit of advice. To anyone who dares say, "My, you're getting older," you retort, "No, I'm getting *better!*" Age? Defy it! Stay slim, strong, defiant—like a kestrel—flying into the wind.

Brian Mann

Brian Mann is the Adirondack correspondent for North Country Public Radio. His radio features on topics and issues relating to the Adirondacks are often heard across the United States on National Public Radio. Raised in the Tongass National Forest of Southeast Alaska, Mann worked as the bush reporter for Alaska Public Radio for years where he often reported on natural resource and environment issues, including the Exxon Valdez Oil Spill. His articles and commentaries have appeared in Alaska *magazine and the* Adirondack Explorer.*

When North Country Public Radio opened its Adirondack Bureau at Paul Smith's College in 1999, Mann jumped at the chance to be involved. "In the Adirondacks, people and wilderness are co-existing in a way that's creative and clumsy and wonderfully intimate," he said. "The stories that bubble up out of that chemistry are unique." This recounting of the Adirondack Canoe Classic first appeared on North Country Public Radio in September 1999.*

Ninety Miles into the Adirondacks

Everybody has these moments. Things are moving very fast and there's lots going on, a kind of happy, muddled chaos. Then comes this little parenthetical moment of quiet and you think, "How did I get myself into this? What am I doing here?"

It's a cool, overcast Friday morning. I'm sitting in my canoe looking out from the public beach at Old Forge. There's a crowd of several hundred people, but I keep looking at the long stretch of water, a shade of blue-gray just slightly colder than the sky. Ahead of me lies the Fulton Chain of lakes and portages that once served as a sort of highway into the Adirondacks. The Chain will take me thirty-five miles, past the town of Inlet, across Raquette Lake. And that's just the first day.

The Adirondack Canoe Classic, known as the Ninety Miler, is one of the premier flat water boating events in the country. People come from all over the world for the race. Over its seventeen year history, the three-day marathon has become a world unto itself, a community of paddlers that winds its way from Old Forge to Saranac Lake.

To say that I'm woefully unprepared for this odyssey would be an understatement. The course we'll follow punches through some of the most rugged country on the East Coast. There are huge bogs, steep portages, wide and windswept lakes. I'm out of shape, inexperienced, not so much a paddler as a dabbler. But it's too late now for any of that to matter. The starting gun cracks, echoing dully from the low hills.

I've started. We've started. Two hundred fifty boats leave in waves, streaming up First Lake. Most move swiftly, easily. Even the war canoes, manned each by eight or ten people, have a kind of grace to them as they blow past. Their chanted cadence fades into the morning as they pull away.

In some cultures, slowness is revered. Things are valued because they take time. In such a culture, my canoe-craft would be legendary. I am, in a word, glacial. Through that first morning, I creep from lake to lake, meandering clumsily over the portage paths. It's a painful, meditative crawl, but by early afternoon I reach Brown's Tract Inlet. The long, low, sinuous marsh is golden and gray with autumn. A great blue heron flushes before me.

Abruptly, the wetland opens into Raquette Lake. It's late now. The sky has a dusky quality and I can see lights starting to flicker on along the shore. The view is open, expansive, but the lake itself is an ocean to be measured one stroke at a time. Meanwhile, I'm passed by everyone, by senior citizens and little kids, by people who seem to be drifting along without paddling at all.

Finally, after ten hours, we stragglers slip into Forked Lake and make a final push for the campground at the north end. It's a respite, a chance to pause, unhinge aching backs and shoulders. A chance, also, to take comfort in the fact that I'm not alone.

Fellow first-timer Dominic Watowski, from Albany, laughs and shakes his head: "Wow. It was good. The finish line was a heck of a feeling of accomplishment, put it that way. The portages actually broke it up nice for us. Came just at the right times so we could stretch and get out a bit. Wasn't easy."

"It was a little rough," echoes Kimberly Reed, another novice paddler from Dallas, Texas. "Actually, thoughts crossed my mind of not finishing it, but we've decided to go on and I think we can do it so I'm pretty excited."

"What got you to do this?"

"My twenty-first birthday," Kimberly says ruefully. "I wanted to do something with my father and I chose this. My sister chose to go to a dude ranch and I chose to . . . do this."

"I guess you wish you were riding a horse right now?"

"Yeah."

It's day two of the Canoe Classic and things are looking up. I paddled solo from Old Forge, but today, I'm partnered with Phil Brown, managing editor of the *Adirondack Explorer*. Now we're both looking at the water: at Long Lake, which stretches fourteen miles to the north and east.

"We'll paddle the length of Long Lake," says race organizer, Brian McDonnell. He talks through a bullhorn, outlining the day's course. "Then head into the Raquette River. Please be aware that there are very shallow spots, where you'll probably need to pull your boats."

The real obstacle today is Purgatory Portage, around the Raquette River Falls. By all accounts, it's half a mile straight up, then half a mile straight down. Everything must go overland—boats, paddles, gear. My own canoe, an Adirondack St. Regis, was built for day trips with the family. It carries like a coffin, hunkering down on my shoulders like old guilt.

Long Lake is a breeze, literally. A following wind pushes us through and it's early afternoon when we slip into the first length of the river. It's glorious country, narrow and intimate, threaded with oxbows. Then we reach the portage and it's like something out of an old World War II film. Racers are literally bent double under their loads as they pick a way up the rocky path.

"It's been hell at times, but at other times it's been really great." Ruby LeVesque, from New York City, is making the race in a solo kayak. "But it's been hell two thirds of the time. Our boats are too heavy to carry, so we need a set of wheels and these wheels are useless. I mean, they're okay on flat ground, but some of these portages, where it goes up and down with rocks and roots ugh! I mean, it's embarrassing."

It's lucky, I guess, that I don't embarrass easily. As Phil and I pick our way down the last miles of the river, we're the very last boat. Not almost last, but finally and absolutely last. A woman on the flat waves a checkered flag as we limp in. And you know, as we head to Tupper Lake for a steak and a beer, I realize that it's been glorious. It's been—a perfect day.

"All the turns and twists in the Raquette were splendid, with the silver maples on the shore," Phil shakes his head, worn out but satisfied. "We saw an otter. We saw two common mergansers. We saw a turtle on a log. Those were all good things."

It's day three now. The final day. I'll spare you my inventory of bodily dysfunction, but thank God for ibuprofen and caffeine. I've got a new partner today. Bill Burris is a retired math teacher from Maryland and a skilled paddler. With his dog Sam as ballast, we get ready to head for home, for Saranac Lake, still twenty-five miles away.

For those racing to win the Ninety Miler, this is a day for sacrifice. The true athletes eat on the run. To save time, they piss in their boats or on the jog while crossing the portages. They paddle until their hands bleed, until they can't stand up. I watch this ritual with a feeling of— what? Awe, I suppose. Envy at times.

But then, on the far side of Bartlett Carry, there's a canoe waiting for us. It turns out that Bill's wife Khaki and his sister-in-law Jacky are also in the race. They're middle-aged women, strong and patient and laughing. Through the morning, they've been making up haiku, poems about wind and porcupines and the ubiquitous Power Bars that racers chew between strokes:

"A swimming chipmunk crosses the Raquette then shakes," Jackie recites, "then blends into the fall."

"Beast sleeping in tree. Too early to wake up yet, but she shows us quills."

"Appropriate for the paddling experience," Jessica says, "Adirondack wind, roars or whispers, but blows the boat. Sometimes foe, oft friend."

There at Bartlett Carry, miles yet from the finish line, the point of all this starts to come half-way clear. It's not only the place—the demandingly beautiful Adirondacks; or the satisfaction of saying you did it, you paddled ninety miles in three days. It's not even the camaraderie of the race, though that's beautiful too, in its way.

What I find, looking out at the caravan of boats trailing up the Saranac River, is that the journey itself has assumed its own meaning. There's a sort of gypsy, nomadic connectedness, tying together all the accidental parts and pieces. I'd love to be stronger, of course, in perfect control of my boat, up there in the lead. But now I find myself wishing I'd gone slower, lingered longer in any of a thousand places, talked a bit more with the people who made the trip with me.

As we turn into Lake Flower and see the crowd on the shore, I ask Bill what he liked best about the day. He thinks a minute and says, "Rocks and outcroppings and water lilies. But then you come out into the lakes and see the mountains off in the distance. It was all great. Wonderful. I'd be glad to do it again."

Sore and weary and humbled, I say, "Exactly."

Bill McKibben

Bill McKibben was fresh out of Harvard in 1982 when he was the hand-picked prodigy of the late William Shawn, editor of the New Yorker. After writing almost exclusively for the "Talk of the Town" from 1982 to 1987, McKibben left New York for a small farmhouse in the Adirondacks near North Creek and dedicated himself to writing about environmental issues.

His move to the mountains has been fruitful. The End of Nature (Random House, 1989), which has been translated into seventeen languages, examined from the Adirondacks the long-term threats of global warming, ozone depletion, and other man-made forms of pollution.

Through the research and writing of The End of Nature, McKibben became intrigued by the world's apparent unwillingness to change its behaviors in the face of probable environmental catastrophe. This led directly to his second book, The Age of Missing Information (Random House, 1992). It blends the personal and cultural while revealing the connection between our television-driven consumer society and environmental degradation.

In 1993, McKibben received a Guggenheim Fellowship to travel and write in the Adirondacks, Brazil, and India. This research formed the core of his third book, Hope, Human and Wild (Little, Brown, 1995), which documents three stories of, as the author puts it, people living lightly on the earth. The book's first story focuses on the Adirondacks, which the author describes as the world's largest experiment in ecological restoration.

McKibben's essays and features on the Adirondacks have been published in Outside, Natural History, Esquire, and Rolling Stone. His most recent book-length works are Maybe One: A Personal and Environmental Argument for Single-Child Families, (Little, Brown, 1998), and Long Distance: A Year of Living Strenuously (Simon and Schuster, 2000).

"Deeper Twilight Still" is an excerpt from The Age of Missing Information. *"Save the Black Flies, Sort Of," appears here for the first time. And the third and fourth selections are excerpts from* Hope, Human and Wild. *The author's attempt at Adirondack doggerel—"Forty-Six, But Who's Counting!"—appeared originally in the 75th anniversary issue of* Adirondac *(1997).*

Deeper Twilight Still

I've been sitting on a flat rock next to the pond for many minutes, watching the sun go down and seeing the stars come up. When I got out of the water, I drip-dried in the last sun—the stored soft heat in the rock warmed my back. I sat there without a shirt on, for the breeze kept down the few mosquitoes. The air grew cooler and cooler—the breeze felt great, and then right on the line between great and chilly, and then just plain cool till it raised gooseflesh, but I was too happy with the stars to move. Finally I got up, and wandered back to the tent, dug out a clean T-shirt, and pulled it over my head—and thought about how great it felt. How dry against the back of my neck where my wet hair still dripped, how warm against the breeze, how soft compared with the rock I'd been lying on. It occurs to me that I may have cast myself as a killjoy in this book, an antimaterialist, the unsensual man, but it isn't true. The mountain is filled with deep animal satisfaction—far better stocked with physical pleasure than any fancy home or leather-lined car. That's because the mountain also exposes you to cold, damp, wind, heat—when you finish with these and move on to warm, dry, still, cool, you feel not just comfort. You feel *pleasure, joy.*

The difference between comfort and pleasure is enormous, though hard to set down in words. Albert Borgmann says "comfort is the feeling of well-being that derives from an optimally high and steady level of arousal of positive stimulation, whereas pleasure arises from an upward change of the arousal level. Since there is a best or highest level of pleasure that constitutes comfort, one cannot indefinitely obtain pleasure by rising from comfort to more comfort. . . . Hence pleasure can only be had at the price of discomfort." What he means, I think, is, if you walk out of the bitter cold into a seventy degree room, it will feel *marvelous, toasty, cheerful, a haven, a nest.* But if you spend all your time in a room where the temperature is seventy degrees it will feel neutral. I can remember my father talking about taking a long hiking trip around Mount Rainier. At the end of the trek, after days of water and the kind of food you carry with you on a trail, he emerged, went to a restaurant, and ordered a milk shake. And I think he can taste that milk shake still—whereas, of course, if you have a milk shake every day you hardly notice it. This is the most obvious thing on earth, and yet it is the easiest to forget. When you are sitting inside on a cold and windy night it is nearly impossible to make yourself get up and walk the dog, even though when you do, the fresh air feels bracing, and the home you return to is a magic place.

The great virtue of the mountain is that once you're up there away from the car, there's no way to escape those kinds of swings—the information about what actually feels good is forced on you relentlessly. The second day I was up there it rained like crazy—little rivers finding the stitching holes in my old tent. It stopped for a while in the morning and I went out for a short hike—ten minutes from the tent the clouds opened up again, and by the time I was back you could have wrung me out. Nothing to do but crawl into my damp sleeping bag and read. It was too hot inside the sleeping bag and my legs sweated. Outside was too cool—clammy. And then, in the afternoon, the sun broke through, the rain fled, the world warmed up. I stretched out my gear and myself on a rock and warmed up—and that sun felt ten times as glorious because of the rain that came before it.

We are stubbornly unwilling to acknowledge this kind of pleasure—either that, or we habitually overstate the discomfort that precedes it. On the *Today* show, Bryant Gumbel announced that in a few weeks the whole cast was going on a camping trip so they could broadcast from the great outdoors. Co-host Deborah Norville shrieked girlishly: "We're not sleeping in tents, are we?" When Bryant said yes, she said, "The heck we are. There's nothing in my contract that says I have to sleep in tents. I feel an illness coming on. Exactly what date is that? Oooooh, crawly things," and so on.

If this were simply a physical phenomenon, it would be bad enough—a loss of information about our bodies that has enriched the lives of most members of every previous generation, and a loss of understanding about what it is like for others to be cold and hungry and dirty. But it's more than that. We have developed a series of emotional thermostats as well, by far the most potent of which is television itself. Instead of really experiencing the highs and lows, pain and joys, that make up a life, many of us use TV just as we use central heating—to flatten our variations, to maintain a constant "optimal" temperature. A pair of academics, Robert Kubey and Mihaly Cziksentmihalyi, recently published a massive and novel study of why people watch TV. Instead of assembling their subjects in a college classroom somewhere, showing them a program, and passing out questionnaires, Kubey and Cziksentmihalyi tried to find out what TV meant to people in the ordinary course of life. Each subject was given a beeper, which went off eight or nine times a day at random intervals between 8:00 A.M. and 10:00 P.M. When the pager sounded, the subjects were supposed to instantly fill out a form that showed what they were doing at the time and how they were feeling—whether they were concentrating, what kind of mood they were in, if their head was aching, whether they really wished they were doing something else.

Some of the findings were obvious: "Television is used by some singles in lieu of company when dining." But much of their research broke new ground. Their data showed quite convincingly that people watch television when they felt depressed—that the strongest variable predicting that people would watch TV in the evening was that in the afternoon they felt the day was going badly. Only a minority, described as "rare" in one study, watch television "selectively," in order to see a few favorite shows—only about half of Americans report even using a television guide. Instead, we use the set like a drug. Not an addictive drug exactly—the idea that people are addicted to TV has a long history, and surely all of us have sometimes felt it to be true. But the new research indicates that it's not a drug like crack—that watching it actually makes us feel more passive, bored, irritable, sad, and lonely. There was certainly no euphoria, not even much active pleasure. TV didn't dominate people's thoughts all day—when they were beeped at work, in only five of three thousand cases were people thinking about programs. If our lives are going pleasantly, if there's something else to do that's attractive, even if it's as undramatic as chatting on the phone with friends, then we're much less likely to watch TV. We use TV as we use tranquilizers—to even things out, to blot out unpleasantness, to dilute confusion, distress, unhappiness, loneliness. The reason that television can be counted on to work this way—the way that television most nearly resembles a drug—is its predictability. It is *not* a drug like LSD; you don't take it to see where you'll be transported to today. You take it because you *know* where you'll be transported. *General Hospital* can be counted on to rouse the same emotions at the same time each day, as can *Jeopardy* or *Nightline* or *Letterman*. In an uncertain world, TV restores an old familiar pattern. The Corporation for Public Broadcasting once commissioned a study to discover why people weren't flocking to its "innovative" programming. It found people preferred commercial TV precisely *because* on the networks they were "more likely see familiar actors and episodes of programs they had viewed previously." When Rhoda separated from her TV husband the ratings dropped; when *M*A*S*H* killed off McLean Stevenson, it drew bagloads of angry mail.

That's one reason the *Playhouse 90*-type programs that originally dominated TV have fallen by the wayside—you wouldn't know, from one night to the next, if you were going to be scared or shocked or amused. It's why all those people who called Walter Cronkite the most influential man in America were wrong. He held our affection because he was utterly predictable, right down to his inflection, and had he suddenly urged us to rise up and break our chains he would instantly have gone from soothing to alarming—he would have broken the trance we turn on television to create.

This tranquilization has its advantages—anyone who ever checked into a hotel room knows that TV masks the loneliness. And if it really made us happy, who could argue? Loneliness, stress, fear—these aren't to be desired, exactly. But television doesn't leave us happy; it only presses our boredom and alienation a little to the back. "Obviously," wrote Kubey and Cziksentmihalyi, "if they possibly could, TV producers would regularly broadcast programs that would make people feel significantly happier than they do normally. They would do so because of the obvious commercial gains that would accrue. That television viewing helps us feel more relaxed than usual but generally does not help us feel substantially happier says something about human nature and what makes for happiness. Happiness is a more complex state than relaxation. It requires a more elusive set of conditions, and is therefore more difficult to obtain. Others can successfully attract and hold our attention and help us relax, but perhaps only we can provide for ourselves the psychological rewards and meaning that make for happiness." In the same way that traveling by airline assures your comfort but rarely allows you any adventure along the way, watching TV insulates you from anything real. We all know this—when researchers ask what activity best fits the description 'I should have been doing something else,' television is the hands-down winner. But that something else might be unpleasant—it might mean dealing with a spouse you'd rather not deal with, or thinking about a job that leaves you empty and unfulfilled. Or that something else might be risky—television never even thinks about rejecting you. Under the pressure of your thumb it comes instantly to life, cooing and making eyes.

That's why TV makes us feel so guilty sometimes. It's a time-out from life. Which is okay if you're really winded—TV as white-noise therapy has its occasional value. But the time-outs soon last longer than the game, which at some level you realize is passing you by. TV makes it so easy to postpone living for another half hour. I can remember hundreds of Saturday afternoons as a boy spent staring at *Wide World of Sports*. I wasn't much of an athlete then—a deep fear of embarrassment kept me out of Pop Warner and Little League. So I lay on the sofa and watched cliff diving in Acapulco and learned to mildly loathe myself.

I've taken friends up the mountain to the pond many times, and at the top suggested a swim. Invariably some of them hang back—it's too cold, or they don't want anyone to think they're fat, or they'd be soggy on the hike down, or all the other inhibitions we feel in such situations. But you can tell, when everyone else is whooping and hollering in the frigid water, *that they wish they'd come in.*

Save the Black Flies, Sort Of

To be under siege from a cloud of black flies is to feel your sanity threatened. In and out of your ears they crawl, biting as they go; in and out of your nose, your mouth, the corners of your eyes. If you've covered up everything but your hands, they will start there and crawl to your wrists, leaving welts wherever they feed. I went out to the garden one spring evening without my shirt tucked in tight enough, and when I came in five minutes later my wife described the perfect row of bites, twenty or thirty of them, that ran along the narrow gap of skin that had winked open when I stooped to weed.

Black flies hover in a cloud about your face, moving with you for miles, so great is their need for your warmth and company and blood. Every writer of the mountain north has tried to describe their omnivorousness—"winged assassins," "lynch mobs," "jaws on wings." Here in the Adirondacks of upstate New York they constitute their own season, one that lasts as long as spring or high summer or fall color (though not as long as winter). For six or seven weeks, from before Memorial Day to after the Glorious Fourth, the paradise of a town where I live, an enormous expanse of mountain and river and stream and lake and pond, is a paradise flawed. Most of the land here is protected by the state constitution as "forever wild," but the legislature has never managed to resolve away the black flies.

It's not that no one's tried. As early as 1948, local towns seeking to extend the tourist season were spraying DDT from helicopters and tossing chunks of it in the streams. Rachel Carson put an end to that by 1965 (and by the early years of this decade the first eagles were finally returning to the Adirondacks to nest, the shells of their eggs thick enough again to hatch.) In subsequent years, some towns used Malathion, Methoxychlor, and Dibron-14, usually sprayed from the air, but always in the face of opposition. Then, about a decade ago, some scientists began experimenting with a more natural method of control, a naturally occurring bacteria called *Bacillus thuringiensis* that has been used for many years for organic control of garden pests. The *israelensis* strain, isolated in the deserts of the Middle East, is highly specific for mosquitoes and black flies. And so there was soon a small Adirondack industry of private contractors who would bid for the right to treat streams each spring, killing off the black fly larvae in ways that appealed both to environmentalists and to tourist-seeking local businesses.

But our town had never gone in for Bti, in large part because it is a frugal place, with the lowest property taxes in the region. No one had ever brought it up, and so spring after spring we had black fly season, hard on the heels of mud season. Then, last year, that changed. Suddenly a petition was circulating demanding that Johnsburg join the list of towns that treat their streams. The movement may have started one morning at a Rotary Club meeting in Smith's Restaurant, where a local realtor got up to complain that she'd lost a sale when she couldn't even get a couple from car to house, the flies were so thick. Sandy Taylor heard her, and agreed to help write a petition.

Sandy Taylor and her husband Jim moved here not long ago from the South and before that the Midwest, where Jim had worked for Monsanto for many years. They are exactly the sort of people who revitalize communities by moving in to them. Before long Sandy was helping to organize our town's new library, the first in its history. They became mainstays of Rotary, of the church, of the theater group. They represent everything that is good about a certain American civic ideal, a spirit that is in many ways foreign to this backwoods spot. And it's not as if they are environmentally unaware or unconcerned; Sandy was a guide for many years at the biological research station that Washington University ran in her home town of St. Louis. "Our happiest memories as a family are the camping trips we used to take."

But to her, as to most people, black flies were not a desirable part of nature. "I can't garden, I can't walk in the woods without all this protective paraphernalia that's uncomfortable and hot and irritating," she told me recently. "My legs become a mass of bites, and they don't go away till August." Soon several hundred people had signed the petition she helped draw up, and the town board was busy drafting a set of specs so they could put the job out to bid. Local innkeepers predicted the cost might well be covered by the taxes paid by vacationers who would otherwise stay away. It looked like a done deal, as if our town would soon join the twenty-one other Adirondack communities that treat their streams with Bti.

Against most expectations, however, opposition began to form. Not particularly organized—there was no official group, no "Save our Flies." Instead, questioning letters started appearing in the local paper. Some of the comments concerned cost. "This is going to cost us $40,000, my share will be $56, and I don't even know if it's going to work," said one resident. Others questioned the effectiveness of the plans: Johnsburg covers a vast area, most of it deep wilderness, and since black flies will migrate a good distance in search of the blood they need to lay eggs, all those streams would have to be treated, which some experts said was a dubious proposition.

But most of the opposition was unexpectedly philosophical. For one thing, the messages of thirty years of ecological thinking have begun to really penetrate people's minds. The fact that there are millions of black flies around Johnsburg in the spring, several residents pointed out, means that something must eat them for dinner. Fishermen testified that they had slit open trout bellies to find them crammed with black flies; others worried about birds, or about bats, or simply about whether it was prudent to muck around with Such Vast Systems.

And there were the people who said: this is not such a big problem. Sure, a few days a year, when there's no wind, it gets bad, and so I wear my bug veil or I stay indoors.

And then there was something more yet. A surprising number of my neighbors said—not always loudly, often a little backhandedly, maybe with a shade of embarrassment—that somehow the black flies were a part of life here, one of the things that made us whatever it is that we are. Someone wanted to know, "Could we still have the Black Fly Ball at the local tavern?"

I once did an odd experiment where I found the largest cable TV system on earth, which was at the time a hundred channel operation in Fairfax, Virginia, and I got people to tape for me everything that came across it for the same twenty-four hour period. I took my 2,400 hours of videotape home to the Adirondacks with me, and spent a year watching it, trying to figure out what the world would look like to you were that your main window on to it. And what I found, amidst the many lessons that spewed forth from the six home shopping channels, the four music video channels, the three sports channels, was this one overriding message: you are the most important thing on earth. You, sitting there on the couch clutching the remote, are the center of creation, the heaviest object in the known universe; all things orbit your desires. This Bud's for You.

This is, of course, the catechism of the consumer society—the elevation of each one of us above all else. Sometimes it is described as "human nature," usually by people who would argue that you can't do anything at all about it. But of course in other times and other places, people have managed to put other things at the center of their lives—their tribe or community, their God, nature, or some amalgamation of these things. Sometimes that's been all to the good; visit an Amish community. Sometimes its meant pogroms. All I'm saying is, there have been other choices to offer.

Whether that still is true, however, I'm not sure. We have grown up in cultures so devoted to consumption—grown up so solid in the understanding that you define yourself through certain patterns of consuming—that I doubt very much we can truly shake them. How else would we behave? From "real needs?" Save for the relative few of us who ever experience actual hunger, or actual involuntary exposure to the elements, that sense of reality is as hard to summon as a sense of what it felt like to be chased by sabertooth tigers. Poor people are just as interested in brand names as anyone else, just as devoted to the various cults (convenience, comfort, identity) of this central religion as anyone else.

And so it is no real stretch to say: the drive to eliminate black flies from this small rural town where I live is simply one more manifestation of our deep consumer urge. We want to consume bite-free air; we want to consume our cedar decks and our pools and our gardens free of any complication or annoyance. We want to consume them when we want (not just on windy days), and how we want (barechested, with no damned bug veil). Jim Taylor spent the later part of his career at Monsanto managing the Astroturf division—managing the metaphor, fair or not, for the conversion of the natural into the convenient.

But what about those of us who opposed the black fly treatment? We exemplars of biological virtue, eager to sacrifice ourselves for the sake of that great order Diptera and its thirst for our blood? How explain our escape from the great consumer faith into which we were baptized?

Mainly, I think, by saying that we are just consumers too. Why do I not want black fly larvae killed in Mill Creek where it runs past my house? Partly because I don't want the biology of the stream tampered with; but at least as much because I live not in Generic Suburban America where everything is supposed to be Convenient, but in the Rugged Frontier Adirondacks, where everything is supposed to be a challenge. At some level, I fear that I like black fly season for the same reason I like winter and bad roads; because it heightens the adventure of living here.

I consume inconvenience, turn it into a pleasurable commodity; it becomes the fuel for my own sense of superiority. I don't feel special because I own a particular brand of clothes, drive a particular make of car, smoke a particular brand of cigarette; I feel special because I have a crappy car, because I wear old clothes all the time, because it's twenty miles roundtrip for a quart of milk. I like it when people call up from the city to talk and the power has just failed, or a blizzard has just struck, or the temperature has gone to 30 below. I feel larger because of all that, I think; it pumps me up the way a Nike, a Rolex, an inground pool, a Ford Explorer is supposed to pump you up. Black fly season is a test, something to endure; I come out of it feeling tougher, stronger. Which means, I think, that I'm a superconsumer too. Black fly season is about me.

And in this I am not alone, I imagine. The shift toward voluntary simplicity now underway in some small corners of this culture is in some ways simply a shift toward a new self-image. Instead of defining yourself by what you buy, you define yourself by what you throw away.

There is clearly a sense in which this slightly submerged consumerism is more twisted than its straightforward counterpart. Elimination is a logical human response to black flies, Bti a giant and efficient version of the timeless slapping hand. Consuming fly-free air is, at some level, extremely logical. Finding a way to consume fly-filled air is more than a little nuts.

So is it all just a toss-up? If it's an age of endless irony, when non-consumption is just another form of image-building, does it make any difference how we live? Can you say that one path is better than the other? Can you say we shouldn't kill all the damned black flies?

You can, I think, though you have to say it carefully, aware that your own sense of superiority is more than a little absurd.

The first argument is clear: even if the main reasons you defend black flies or recycle your dental floss have to do with you, they nonetheless benefit the rest of creation. Whereas normal consumption is almost by definition costly to the earth, this more rarefied form is almost by definition cheap and undamaging. Which is a great practical virtue, since the results of normal and everyday consumer life now threaten to wreck everything around us. I've spent much of the last ten years writing about global warming, which is nothing more than the sum total of our lavish devotion to convenience and comfort and power transmuted into several extra watts of solar energy per square meter of the earth's surface. It is human desire translated into planetary physics, and unless we can get those desires under some kind of control the physics will turn impossible. By this analysis, though it may be bizarre to consume by not consuming, it nonetheless is like supplanting heroin with methadone; one's cravings are stilled with minimum damage to the underlying system.

And yet there is something more to it than that. By its very nature, this kind of somewhat silly nonconsuming puts you in harm's way—raises the possibility that you will be exposed to forces that might actually change you, begin to erode some of the conditioning we've carried since near birth. An example: when I lived in New York, I helped start a small homeless shelter at my church, and spent many nights there. This was classic nonconsumer behavior, robbing me of many hours I might have spent in restaurants, barrooms, movie theaters, and boudoirs. But of course I did not do it primarily because I was a good Christian; I did it because I liked the image it provided me (and, I hoped, others) of myself as a slightly sainted fellow.

Over time, however, the mere fact of being there began to change me in certain small ways. I learned that in some fashion it made me feel peaceful to do the small daily tasks of that place—changing the sheets, cooking the soup, delousing the pillowcases. It was one of the paths to learning not to resent housework, one way to cease the innate consumer desire for a maid (or a mother). In fact I sensed, counterintuitively, that this work made me happy—a revelation that would not have surprised any of the long chain of gurus and Christs and other cranks down through the ages, but certainly shocked my suburban system. Having been exposed to some deeper (if transient) joy, I was marginally less of a sucker for the various ersatz appeals of the culture.

Sometimes now I help with the campaign to return wolves to the Adirondacks. They were wiped out here in the last years of the nineteenth century by people who thought of them in the way that realtors now think of black flies—as an annoyance standing in the way of progress. I try not to pretend to myself any more than I have to that my main interest is with the wolves, or with the health of the forest that badly needs a top predator. I know that what I want is to hear a wolf howling in the woods, because it will make this place, and my life here, feel yet more romantic. I will consume that wolf howl, just as my predecessors consumed the quiet of their suddenly wolfless nights. But once the wolf is there, that howl will also carry certain other less obvious messages; and there will be the remote chance of an encounter with this other grand representative of creation, an encounter that might go beyond mere consumption. I saw a grizzly bear this summer in Alaska, not far away on a muddy bank on a foggy night, and the sheer reality of that encounter shook some small part of me out of the enchantment into which I was born.

Black flies accomplish this, too, in a subtler way. They remind you, day after day in their season, that you really aren't the center of the world, that you are part food, implicated in the crawl and creep of things. They are a humbling force, and even if for a time I can involve them in my self-aggrandizing myths, they still exert a slow and persuasive pressure of their own. Over the course of a decade, living in a place dominated by high mountains, wild winters, summer storms, trackless forest, and hungry insects has in fact warped me in certain ways. I am not the same person who came here. I am still a consumer; that was the world I emerged into, the air I breathed for a very long time, and its assumptions still dominate my psyche. But maybe a little less so each year. And just perhaps my daughter a little less than that.

There are times when I can feel the spell breaking in my head—the spell of the advertiser on the tube, even the spell of the mythmaker in my head. There are times when I can almost feel myself simply being.

At least for this year, Johnsburg decided not to use Bti. Instead, they're sending out a questionnaire with the tax bills: if the town decided to treat the streams, it asks, would you be willing to let the workers on to your land? I think quite a few people—by no means a majority, but probably enough to make the plan unfeasible—will say no. Like me, they'll likely do it without quite knowing why. But it's one small sign for me that the enchantment is wearing off, that the incantation sung over our cradles by the TV may be less permanent than some think. That spring may be coming—and with it the biting flies, by God.

Home

Last spring, on a nice day, a flood of water three feet deep suddenly inundated the road that runs past my door, sweeping whole trees out into the lake. It subsided as suddenly as it had risen; within fifteen minutes the road was drying out. I hiked up the stream down which the flood had come, noting the trunks left on high ground, the channels carved by the rush of water. And half a mile back in the woods I found what I knew I would: a blown-out beaver dam that had released five or six feet of pond with a sudden boom. One mislaid branch, one repair put off too long, some small mistake had finally rewarded the water for its patience. But never mind—what was once pond will soon be a green, rich clearing. And the beavers had already moved a quarter of a mile up the stream, ready to start again their endless alterations to the landscape.

An unremarkable event, in the larger scheme of things, except that a hundred years ago there would have been no beavers here. Like most of the rest of the eastern United States, the Adirondack Mountains, where I live, had been cut over and trapped out. The forests had been overhunted; the streams ran brown with pollution from the mills and tanneries, and now the Adirondacks have recovered: most of the animals that were chased from here have returned to great tracts of state-protected wilderness.

Which is to say, I live surrounded by contradiction. Six years ago I wrote a book called *The End of Nature*. It argued that human beings were ending the very idea of wildness—that as our cars, factories, and burning forests filled the skies with greenhouse gases, we had finally become large enough to alter the most basic vital sign of the planet, its climate. As we heated the planet, I said, we would change the flora and the fauna *everywhere;* even at the poles or in the Adirondack wilderness, we now influenced every physical system.

The intervening years have made this argument surer. Only the outermost fringe of scientists now doubt the reality and power of global warming and other large-scale environmental damage. Since the book was published we have experienced the warmest year in recorded history, a small taste of what the climate-scientists say is in store for us. For the first time humans are altering the most fundamental phenomena. We have grown so big that we literally overshadow the earth. Nature as something separate from man has vanished.

Writing that book depressed me, and many of its readers both here and abroad have told me that they were depressed as well. Which is appropriate: it should depress us to live on a planet that becomes less complex and wild with each passing day, and it should depress us even more that we are the cause of that change. Most of this book is devoted to strategies for retooling our societies and economies so they do less damage: that is the hard and unending work that will occupy us throughout our lifetime. It is the particular challenge that history presents those of us who happen to be alive at the moment. If we can't prevent the environmental damage already under way, we can—if we act boldly—limit it. But I no longer think fear is sufficient motivation to make such changes, especially since they involve the most fundamental aspects of our economies, our societies, and our individual lives. To spur us on we need hope as well—we need a vision of recovery, of renewal, of resurgence.

Which is why this book begins where it begins—why it begins, in a sense, with dessert. For as it happens, I live surrounded each day by one form of that splendid new vision. I live on the East Coast of the United States.

The restored wildness of the East, its renewed vigor, seems to concentrate most purely in one patch of the region: my patch, the Adirondack Park of upstate New York. New York, of course, can boast like few other states—capital of world politics, linchpin of world finance, incandescent hub of art and drama. And yet greater than all of these may be the little-known legacy of the Adirondacks, the world's first experiment in restoring an entire ecosystem.

The Adirondacks cover one quarter of New York State. They are bigger than Vermont or New Hampshire; bigger than Yellowstone, Yosemite, Glacier, and Grand Canyon National Parks combined. People came late to this rugged landscape. Even the Indians used much of the land solely as a seasonal hunting area. High, harsh, and cold, its loftiest peak had not been climbed by a white man until decades after Lewis and Clark returned from the Pacific. But when people finally arrived, they did so with a vengeance—loggers, especially, penetrated the very heart of the mountains, searching after pine and then spruce and then whatever. My township was devastated by the tanneries, which cut down hemlocks by the millions to use the bark for curing hides and then poisoned the rivers with the runoff. Elsewhere, the loggers came after saw timber or pulp—the first images of clearcut devastation that Americans ever saw were magazine drawings of the Adirondack streams from the late 1800s.

The horse teams and crosscut saws, the farmers and the trappers, managed to chase off most of the wildlife. They left behind just a few stands of old-growth forest—a hundred thousand acres, perhaps, in the Five Ponds wilderness in the western corner of the Park, along with many smaller patches scattered throughout the mountains. It is splendid to walk in these timeless forests—spruces a hundred feet high, yellow birch and hemlock a dozen feet around at the base, moss-crumbled nurse logs scattered on the forest floor.

But ancient forest is not the real glory of the Adirondacks. It's the new forest merging with the old, the groves thirty and fifty and a hundred years old that are increasingly indistinguishable from old growth. New old growth. Perhaps no place on the planet has recovered as comprehensively from deforestation as these mountains five hours' drive from New York City. The Adirondacks are the Yellowstone of rebirth, the Yosemite of revival, the second-chance Alaska. For conservationists imagining not simply the salvation of what remains pristine, but the restoration of what has been degraded, this is just about the most heartening spot on earth. The Adirondacks offer a few scattered reminders of what Eden looked like, and a million vistas from which to imagine redemption.

Some of the recovery has been purely accidental. In a land where the growing season runs ninety days in a good year, and the first thirty of those are spent swatting black flies, only one generation of farmers tried to cultivate the cleared lands. But much of the credit for the health of these mountains belongs with human beings—with the people of New York who, seventy-five years before politicians anywhere else discovered "ecology," began the process of protecting these hills. Early visitors (the world's first ecotourists, "swells" from the city who journeyed north for the wilderness and soon built great camps and hotels) were appalled by the rate at which the trees were falling; their concern merged with the more hardheaded worries of the state's industrialists that the Hudson would begin to silt up as whole mountains eroded and that the waterways which were the state's economic lifelines would deteriorate. These two factions combined in the state legislature to produce landmark legislation setting up a forest preserve and, in the summer of 1894, declaring that it "shall be forever kept as wild forest lands. [It] shall not be leased, sold, or exchanged, or be taken by any corporation, public or private, nor shall the timber thereon be sold, removed, or destroyed."

The state did not buy every inch of these mountains. It acquired land slowly but steadily, often when timber barons couldn't pay their taxes: by the 1990s, about 42 percent of the Park was actually in public hands. And it is these "forever wild" lands that have served as the backbone of the recovery. Two-thirds of the land in the town where I live belongs to the state of New York. If you walk west from my back door, you hit state land in minutes and can continue on it for days.

If you did so, your trip would be glorious in its ordinariness. Almost everywhere in America we have saved the grand rocks and ice; in the Adirondacks, too, the sheer granite of the High Peaks is well protected and well hiked, some of the trails rutted so deeply you nearly disappear from view. But the High Peaks are barely a sixth of the Park. The rest is the kind of land that in so many other spots has been cut, drained, filled, and developed. Not sheer cliffs, but swamp and spruce thicket and mile upon mile of hardwood and hemlock. You reach pond after pond called "Mud" or "Round" or "Fish" or "Second" or "Thirteenth." There are thousands upon thousands of mountains too short to be bare on top, never climbed by people because there's no reason, except maybe venison, to climb them. If you do stumble to the top, instead of sweeping views you get strained glimpses through the lattice of bare branches. If you find a fire scar or other small opening, the vista is of six or seven or eight or nine lines of ridge, all rounded and soft in the twilight. This place was saved for ecological reasons; it is the nearest we have to an intact ecosystem. Gazing out over it gives me a primeval thrill even more powerful than the view from the top of Mount Rainier or El Capitan: *so this is what the world looked like.*

And could look like again—for a very different Adirondacks are easily remembered by the oldest residents. Crow Mountain, in whose shadow I live, offers a 360-degree view of unbroken forest, save for a few roads and houses and the spire of the Methodist church. "I remember when you could hardly see a tree from the top," one of my neighbors says—with some regret, for he recalls as well the agricultural community that existed ("flourished" would be much too strong a word) here in his youth. But the small dairies have closed, and their pasture reverted first to pine and birch and now to the trailing species, the beeches and the hemlocks and the maples that dominate our forest once again.

With the woods have come the critters that once lived in them. Just as in other areas across the East, there's been a slow but steady progression of animals back to the burrows and dens of their ancestors. Fifty years ago much local excitement attended the first bear seen in town in living memory; now bears seem as obvious a part of the landscape as trees, their berry-dyed scat and their nighttime hooting a common part of life. A decade ago it was the return of wild turkeys that dominated talk at the barbershop; now they, too, are common. Otter swim in the rivers and ponds; fisher and marten have long since rebounded.

At the moment, we are all worked up over moose. The animals reappeared in the Adirondacks in the 1980s, having wandered over from their increasingly crowded homes in Maine, New Hampshire, and Vermont. Some New York conservationists wanted to "reintroduce" them, trucking more moose over to swell the new herd. Most locals—already a little worried about colliding with one-ton ungulates on back roads—argued convincingly that moose were returning on their own, and that the $1 million budget for the project might be put to better use. And indeed the moose have kept right on multiplying. There was one on our creek last week; word soon spread throughout the area, the same peal of exhilaration that greeted the bear two generations ago and that I pray will greet the wolf in my daughter's day.

To me, though, the greatest of all the returned exiles is that large and bucktoothed rodent, the beaver. Once all but wiped out by trappers—its habitat eroded by drying streams—the beaver has rebounded with such vigor that there may not be a stream in the Adirondacks without a lodge: floods like the one described at the beginning of this chapter are commonplace. For years now beaver have had a big dam right next to our house. Our only neighbors—summer people who show up for a weekend every month or two—try to knock the dam down, working hard to dismantle the carefully placed sticks and logs. Within a night, however, the hole is plugged. The trees have died in the new wetlands behind the dam, and its murky, slimy waters are filled with all the many forms of life that thrive in murk and slime. It hums, vibrates with frog and insect. Soon—next year, maybe, since they're running out of accessible trees—the beavers will move on down the stream and make themselves a new pond. Slowly the dam will give way and the water leak out; then the pond will grow into a meadow, and the trees begin to take over once more—shouldering slowly in toward the center like schoolboys around a fistfight. I can take you to a hundred places within walking distance where this transformation is happening. *On some Adirondack creeks, man is no longer the chief agent of disturbance and change.* The stream by my home on which the beavers have built their dam was originally called "Beaver Brook." Its name soon changed to Mill Creek, since it was lined for a brief pulse of history with sawmills, grist-mills, even a calico mill. The mills have long since closed, though, and the beaver has returned; the old name makes more sense again.

And that sweet thought triggers another, which is at the center of this book. In the Adirondacks, and to a lesser extent throughout the rest of the rural East, we have been given a second chance. This reborn wildness is not all that it once was, and we must operate within certain limits—most notably our large population—not faced by the first Europeans to reach this area. But this second-chance world is not completely broken, either; though its soils and forests have been altered by past human practices, though its climate and weather are now influenced by our gaseous contribution to the atmosphere, it still retains sufficient vigor to reassert itself—for its original species to press up through the weight of our settlement and reestablish themselves. "Though we have caused the earth to be seriously diseased, it is not yet without health," writes Kentucky farmer and essayist Wendell Berry. "The earth we have before us now is still abounding and beautiful. . . . The health of nature is the primary ground of hope—if we can find the humility and wisdom to accept nature as our teacher."

So far we can claim neither humility nor wisdom: our good fortune is mostly accidental, and as we shall see, new dangers born of human carelessness and selfishness threaten even the tentative recovery of this place. Still, the hope represented by the East is real. It is transferable, too, to any other place that still has some open space and some rainfall: surely people on every continent can look at it as a hint of the grace of nature if people back off, give it some room and some time. The world, conceivably, will meet us halfway; the alternative to Eden is not damnation.

Home Again

A few years ago, the Adirondack county in which I live decided it needed a new landfill. The consultants said 375 acres were required, in order to store the ash from the hundred-million-dollar incinerator they'd sold the county on a few years earlier. Three hundred and seventy-five acres of landfill lined with two (2) giant rubber sheets, enormous landfill Trojans to prevent unwanted leakage. Three hundred and seventy-five acres that would need to be kept free of trees, mowed twice a year for eternity so no roots would ever rupture the rubbers. And of course the landfill would need huge sodium vapor lights, left on all night.

Anyhow, the consultants conducted a highly scientific search around and about the county to determine the best place for this landfill, and soon they announced their five final sites. And where were they? Not in the southern, urban part of the county—outside the Park—where ninety percent of the residents generated ninety percent of the waste. Four of the five were clustered forty miles from the city, at the very edge of the county, right around the mountain where I live. The highly scientific consultants arranged for letters to go out to all the people who lived on the proposed sites, ninety families in all. Letters that arrived Christmas Eve, informing the residents that soon other highly scientific men would be arriving to drill holes in the land to make sure that the waste wouldn't drop directly into a subterranean stream if the condoms broke.

And we were not supposed to fight. Not supposed to fight, because this is a poor backwoods place and they were offering cash. Not supposed to fight, because we're not that kind of people. It's less apathy than a deep feeling of disempowerment. What I mean by disempowerment is illustrated by the following. There was a meeting at the town hall, where the impartial outside consultants were going to explain the mystery of why it was scientific to truck garbage forty miles into the mountains. It was winter, but all the consultants were wearing suits and Italian shoes without any laces. And if you are sitting there in your Sorel boots, you are allowed to get angry for about a minute; but when the man in the loafers talks in his soothing way about the necessity of it all, you are supposed to sit down muttering and figure that it makes no difference—they'll do what they want; they always do. And if you keep talking, they try to make you feel ashamed, call you a NIMBY (which is short for "not in my backyard"), and make you out as some kind of obstructionist.

I was deeply proud of my neighbors: we fought on anyway. This is a backward place—that is, it was only a generation ago that everyone knew how to fend for themselves off the land, and that connection has been slow to fade. People still *live* here, physically and emotionally, instead of residing in that grinning suburban-California nowhere that flows out through cable TV. That connection to the land came to the fore one cold night in February at the final scene of our battle, a meeting of the regional development agency that was considering regulations which might block the landfill. One after another, my neighbors rose to say their piece.

Kent Gregson, a musician who'd served as something of a bard to a right-wing property rights campaign a year before, had composed a special song, which he performed for the commissioners:

They make the garbage in the south
And ship it to the north
The county budget pays the bill
To truck it back and forth

"Who's going to speak for the withered trees? Who's going to answer for the dead fish?" asked Ron Vanselow, who was working seasonally as a forest ranger. Kelly Richards, an eighth-generation native of the area, said, "We get our water from spring-fed wells. We raise our eggs, meat, and vegetables; tap the sugar maples; harvest firewood; and rear our pets and children on the land. They told us we shouldn't worry because they weren't actually taking our *homes*. But my home doesn't just go to the walls and then stop. That land *is* my home."

Finally the Reverend Daisy Allen stood up. She is a Pentecostal Holiness minister—she just celebrated fifty years in the same pulpit and personifies "beloved" in our town, after a lifetime of attending the dying, comforting the sick, providing for the hungry. She began her testimony quietly, nervously. "There's a beaver dam there," she said. "It's played a large part in giving beauty and a place for fish. Will the beaver lose their home? Will the fish die? . . . There's no florist where we live, but will we lose or find endangered our trillium; our wild oats; our yellow, blue, and white violets? Will we lose our mayflowers and buttercups, daisies and dandelions, cowslips and adder's-tongues? Will the beauty of the apple blossom and the pear tree be gone forever? Where will we pick our Northern Spies, our maiden-blush, crab apples, yellow transparents, duchesses?" She talked about the darkness for a while. "I can walk the country roads at midnight, able to see by moonlight," she said. "I study the Bible, and I'd like to give you an illustration from it. Naboth had a vineyard close to the palace of Ahab, king of Samaria. Ahab said to Naboth, 'Give me thy vineyard that I may have it for a garden of herbs. It's near my house. I'll give thee a better vineyard, or I'll give you money for it.' Naboth refused, because his father had owned it. But Ahab pretended sickness and his wife came in and said, 'Why don't you eat?' He said, 'I can't, because Naboth won't let me have the land I want.' And wicked Queen Jezebel said, 'Why are you so sad? Isn't it within your power and jurisdiction to take whatever you want, no matter whose it is?' And she wrote letters in Ahab's name. And Naboth was stoned to death. Jezebel heard of his death and said to Ahab, 'Go take possession; Naboth is dead.' And he went to take possession, but God spoke through his prophets and said, 'Where Naboth's blood has been licked by the dogs, so will yours be licked.' " The $150-an-hour guys sitting in the back of the room in their Italian loafers didn't say a word.

And we won. The regional agency rejected the landfill, and all of a sudden the county reworked its figures and decided it maybe needed only ten or twenty acres and could probably rent them from the already-built landfill in the next county. As we were leaving the meeting that night, one of the consultants snapped the locks on his briefcase, looked up at me, and said, "We think it would be more mature if you guys didn't deal with this on such a personal level. We try to keep things on a professional basis." But we'd been right to take it personally. It was the place where we personally lived.

The euphoria faded pretty quickly, of course; a dump is a pretty easy thing to battle, and we haven't done as well when it's a new subdivision under discussion. But the victory made me realize anew the power of aroused people working together, even—or especially—if those people are the "locals" or "rednecks" or "woodchucks," which is the Adirondack term. And it helped me see beyond the trees and bears to the other glories of this place. If the Adirondacks were just a walled-off park, the views would still be splendid, and the wildlife might be even better off. But it's the fact that there are people here and throughout the rural East that makes its recovery so special. Long live the beaver; long live Daisy Allen.

Forty-Six—But Who's Counting?

One day in midsummer
while climbing MacNaughton
I ransacked my brain
And found I'd forgotten
Just how many peaks
I still had to bag
Before I could send for
My Forty-Sixer tag
And so I composed
This mountain ditty
To sing in my car
As I drive from the city

Oh I've been up on Haystack and Porter and Street
I've wandered on Saddleback, conquered Gray Peak

Up Rocky Peak Ridge to the summit of Giant
And then through the Wolf Jaws I've stumbled defiant
Up Blake and Emmons and Dial and Nye
They're all on my list in this summer up high

For I'm following Bob Marshall up all the High Peaks
My feet are so sore, and my polypro reeks
I'm flybit and rainsoaked and proud as can be
Before Labor Day comes, a 46er I'll be

I climbed up Mount Marcy and crossed to Skylight
Lugging my stone to the summit that night
Donaldson, Seymour—they're part of my saga
As well as the peak that they call Couchsachraga
I've climbed down from Whiteface to pay Esther a call
Cascade, it caused me no trouble at all

For I'm following . . .

The trio of Dixes and Hough and McComb
Up Gothics and Sawteeth before I came home
Basin and Tabletop, and rocky Wright
I sat up on Big Slide awaiting first light
Santanoni and Allen and Nippletop too
From Colden to Colvin I've wandered right through

For I'm following . . .

Panther and Iroquois peaks I have crossed
On Seward and Marshall I found myself lost
From the top of Algonquin I had a great view
Saw Nippletop, Phelps and Redfield too
Why only last weekend I stumbled up Cliff
And now my notes show I've completed my list

For I'm following . . .

I thought I'd be happy but in fact I am sad
My blisters are healing but my heart's feeling bad
I've nothing to live for
I can think of no goal
Except for to climb them
All again in the snow

Barbara McMartin

Barbara McMartin is quite literally the mother of Adirondack trail guide-books. She's written and edited more than a dozen, covering every acre of the Adirondack Park with four-season, multi-use information for the outdoor explorer (See the Discover the Adirondacks *series, published by Backcountry Publications).*

But her writing doesn't focus solely on guidebooks. Her monumental work, The Great Forest of the Adirondacks *(North Country Books, 1994), documents all the elements that make up the history of the region's forested lands—from tax policy and social history to politics and market economics. McMartin's dogged comprehensiveness seems to have paid off, for aside from raising all sorts of issues about the way these lands have been managed, she has uncovered and catalogued tracts of old growth woods previously unknown in the region.*

Known at large for the forthrightness of her ideas and prose, Mc-Martin, whose work has appeared in publications throughout the region, including Adirondack Life, *lives year-round in Caroga, New York, with her husband, W. Alec Reid.*

The essay reprinted here first appeared in 1999 in the Adirondack Journal of Environmental Studies, *edited by Gary Chilson, a professor of Environmental Studies at Paul Smith's College.*

It's Not a Model; It's a Mess

The Adirondack Park's mix of public and private lands has been called a worldwide model for environmental planning in this day of growing populations and shrinking natural resources. During the Park's centennial in 1992 we reveled in our role model status, and I admit I was one of the proudest boosters of the way New York State has integrated public and private land within the Blue Line. Deeper reflection has shown me just how wrong I was.

My husband and I are really very fortunate; in the past twenty-three years we have visited one hundred national parks and other public lands around the world. Maybe I exaggerate, but we certainly have seen a lot. It's interesting to note just how the Adirondack Park compares to its counterparts throughout the world.

Countries and their parks break down loosely into two categories. There are those where natural resources are really threatened by population expansion; where preservation is essential, not only to preserve biological diversity but to preserve water, soil, and vegetation in order to sustain populations; and where controlling the relationship between private interests and public needs has to confront life and death issues faced by native populations. Examples of this type can be found in Africa where domestic animals compete with wild and often endangered animals in the game preserves, where ecotourism, game parks, and reserves have produced some limited success; or in much of Central America, where forests have been destroyed or harvested in order to make room for expanding farmlands and where failures to limit forest destruction have meant that natural disasters like hurricanes have totally destroyed local economies. In places like this, all the solutions are very difficult.

The second category comprises countries that have succeeded in creating park systems that work. These countries have either set aside whole, protected parks and preserves or integrated public land with private lands in a way not too different from the Adirondack model. It is necessary, however, to further divide this category: those countries that are struggling to create a system of parks and preserved lands and those whose success exceeds or equals ours.

The first category offers many contrasts. Ecotourism probably had its birth in Africa. By controlling people's access to wild animals (safety of viewers is a tremendous concern) dozens of parks were created in Kenya and Tanzania. We have seen prides of lions in Ngorongoro Crater and stood on the veldt in the midst of a migration watching in one sweeping view a million wildebeests and zebras. Zimbabwe's Hwanke

Park is well managed, so are South Africa's parks, but Tanzania and Kenya are struggling. We have seen how in Zimbabwe native leadership has maintained and expanded parks, conserved wildlife, and assisted the country's economy.

We have seen what island extinction can do to isolated islands as on Mauritius where many species of birds and plants are lost. We have seen how pressures for food and fuel have resulted in the destruction of boojum trees of Madagascar and limited the range for lemurs and birds. Places like Madagascar are slipping farther and farther behind. Forest destruction even reaches into the small areas the country has tried to set aside for preservation.

We have walked a little in Nepal (but never learned to like yak butter tea), climbed to Tigers Nest in Bhutan through forests draped with the moss called "old man's beard," and visited Bharatpur in India, one of the most spectacular bird preserves in the world. Forest destruction for fuel in Nepal is appalling and threatens the great Indian and Pakistani rivers with severe flooding. We saw people cutting fuel in a sacred and protected forest near Katmandu. Forest destruction is credited with causing the severe floods on the Yangste that occurred in 1998. Bhutan is trying to preserve forest stands, and their inaccessibility makes that a possibility. But one of my most vivid memories from visiting that country was a day spent at a magnificent Bhuddist festival in Paro. The government used the occasion to inform natives through booths filled with poster displays about birth control, health measures, and forests. For the latter, there was a picture of an old man and his story: "When I was a young boy, I gathered wood to cook the family's dinner in half an hour. Now I walk for four hours to find fuel, often I have to stay overnight to find enough fuel for two days."

These places rarely have the luxury of separating preserved lands from agricultural lands. And, this is probably where the Adirondack example really shines. Because we have that absolute separation between lands that can be logged and lands where no trees can be cut, we provide an economic base for the region as well as environments and ecosystems that are as natural as our state's preservation efforts can provide. There may be conflict between the two kinds of lands, but they are separate and will remain that way. Third world countries might see our form of separation as a model to achieve, but it is beyond their political grasp.

India presents a very different picture, and exemplifies my second category. As I began to categorize different countries' responses to natural resources, it has become apparent that India's efforts reflect the British tradition. Game parks in India have poachers, but they also have enough staff to keep the poachers under control. The parks are separate from agricultural or forest lands where trees can be harvested. Some of the very few bright spots in large animal preservation are found in India. Certainly controlling India's burgeoning population is no easy task, but preserving natural resources is a government priority and an effective policy.

Observing the impact of British traditions around the world, it seems as if England has done more to influence the world than the United States has. Of course, Great Britain had a worldwide colonial empire in which to implant their English traditions. Public and private lands in England have been intertwined since William the Conqueror established Britain's New Forest. With its mix of public and private lands, this could have been a model for our Adirondacks, although it is more likely that our mix of public and private lands owes more to accidents of history than to planning.

Certainly the tradition of setting aside parklands has followed the Empire, and many countries that were once part of the British Empire actually do a better job managing public lands both for preservation and for people than we do in the Adirondacks.

Consider the results of land preservation in Canada; here each province not only has protected lands but goes out of its way to help tourists find history and nature at many levels within the parks and their surrounding developed lands. A visit to any province gateway center will convince you of that. And, Canada has some great parks, the best of which are so tightly managed that their residents often visit America to avoid the controls, which the government has found are necessary to protect their parks.

New Zealand and Australia both have fantastically well-run parks interspersed with settlements. New Zealand has some of the best scenery in the world and some of the most spectacular and well-maintained trails you can imagine. Signs tell you about how long a trail will take to walk and warn you of all the problems you might en-counter. The park service controls the numbers of hikers on the most desirable places. Here are preserved lands that would be perfect, except for one thing—early settlers brought birds and animals from home, and they have wiped out some species and threatened others. (Tree ferns are a favorite food of imported deer.) At first glance, New Zealand appears to be an image of England with little, if any, native flora and fauna. We did get to Stewart Island and a nearby sanctuary on Uva Island where there are no deer and the forest is pristine—and magnificent.

Public lands in New Zealand are managed not just for preservation, but for people to visit and enjoy. Their economic benefits are real, but preservation of natural resources has failed because steps to preserve forests and limit the introduction of exotic species were too late, and the processes cannot be reversed.

Australia, too, fights exotic fauna and has found that once intro-duced, the disastrous results are virtually irreversible. Consider the problems Aussies face trying to eradicate introduced rabbits. Neverthe-less, Australia has fantastic parks from the cold forests of Tasmania to the tropical wet regions of the northern coasts. There are trails every-where with great signs and attention to natural details. One of our rain forest walks was spectacular, with a planned and well-maintained trail, a series of waterfalls, trees (Nothofagus) that were more than 4,000 years old, and leeches.

Great Britain itself has walks of all kinds tying public lands to pri-vate destinations along both public thoroughfares and private paths. These walks integrate wonderful, inexpensive places to stay with his-torical places and spectacular scenery. A long tradition of good guide-books, maps, and a population that appreciates the paths makes it all possible.

Most of Europe has a tradition of trails, and although there is nowhere the proportion of protected lands found in America, there are strong controls on forest lands that aid species preservation. Southern Europe was settled so long before anyone thought of land preservation that most of the great forests surrounding the Mediterranean were cut in the time of ancient Greeks and Romans, and sheep and goat herding since that time have permanently altered the flora. It was only on one of the most remote walks I have ever made, a trek through the Samarra

Gorge in Crete, that we found native forests—the fact that they were too remote and difficult to reach made it impossible to cut them.

Turkey struggles to limit access to its national parks by the sheep and goats that destroy native plants, and, reinforced with attempts to better the lives of people in the countryside, it is beginning to succeed. Still, we found it depressingly difficult to discover how far we had to travel to reach natural and relatively undisturbed sites to see the origins of those plants, like tulips and daffodils that now grace western gardens.

Abruzzi, a park in Italy's Apennines, is an unusual example. The state owns only one percent of the land, yet through planning, government help, and a charismatic leader, the park has protected the brown bears for which the region is famous, reintroduced wolves and the wild chamois they feed on, separated regions used by sheep herders from the preserved areas by compensating herders, trained local people to serve as guides for tourist groups to provide employment and make sure animals and land are protected, promoted the region and increased tourism to a level that makes the local people appreciate their resource and the need to protect both the land and its wild inhabitants.

There is no question that most of the rest of the world lags behind Europe and former British colonies in setting aside public lands and developing them for recreation and economic gain. The biggest exception is, of course, Costa Rica, with fifteen percent of its land protected. Costa Rica has led the way in both Central and South America in setting aside preserves and trying to help natives benefit from those preserves. It is not an easy task, but the government is behind it all the way. Ecotourism works. Resource preservation makes the country a primary destination for foreign tourists who enjoy the jungle trails, mountain paths, and ubiquitous birding walks.

The Chileans have many spectacular parks. Torres del Paine is my favorite and it is spectacularly well run. Still, the country has had trouble protecting the rare temperate forests that are so sought after for lumber and pulp. Seeing mountains of pulp logs waiting for shipment to Japan made us wonder if enough forests had been protected. Fra Jorge, a coastal park in the desert north had one of best short trails in the world. We walked from desert vegetation to rain forest in fifty paces, the changes all caused by patterns of fog rising from the ocean below the park's cliffs.

Argentina's parks along the Beagle Channel reminded us of parks in the western part of our country. The Patagonian coast has important preserves for penguins and sea elephants. In the glacier parks, we had boat rides to fields isolated by ice where strange temperate forests were home to rare plants. That country has not only established preserves, but accommodations for visitors.

Ecuador has park rangers in the Galapagos that really care about protecting that fragile place. Venezuela has parks for birds and rare plants. The Peruvian headwaters of the Amazon basin have wonderful jungle parks—birds and butterflies that are more spectacular than the pictures in travel brochures. Ecotourism is making inroads in the struggle to limit forest destruction.

What does all this have to do with the Adirondacks? Certainly much of the rest of the world has become aware of the need to set land aside and protect it. All these attempts have flaws, as does the preservation effort in the Adirondacks. Here, where we have lost almost no species (wolves and lynx are the main exceptions), we still have problems. The accidental nature of the way we set land aside has meant that some of the ecologically important areas—the Blue Ledges, Boreas Ponds, Preston Ponds) are in good hands, but not within Forest Preserve protection. Some lands that might better serve the forest products industry have been preserved. Small parcels that give access to Forest Preserve tracts have not been acquired. While the total acreage of the Forest Preserve is about right, we may need to swap some lands, but we probably will not. The Third World comparison is most telling with respect to exporting natural resources. The inability of Third World countries to develop processing or manufacturing to boost the economic value of their products occurs right here. Too many of our resources are shipped out without benefiting local people. Sure, we share the mix of public and private lands with parks around the world. We are older than many, but not all. The Adirondacks cannot be a model for those countries that face almost insurmountable pressures from population and lack of resources. Even when we compare the Adirondacks to countries with well-developed park systems, it is obvious that our region is certainly not unique, except in one devastating way. Every other park has a central organization that integrates planning and carries out the goals of preservation, economic development, and people's needs to be a part of nature.

We have done a very good job of natural resource protection. We have done a very poor job of putting people in a natural setting. And here is where the model fails, where what stands out in the management in other parks and mixed areas points up the deficiencies of the Adirondacks. Every successful park we visited had a coordinated management that represented the best efforts of central governments to effect preservation, promote tourism, and serve local peoples.

The contrasts with the best parks in other countries, especially those that were once a part of the British Empire, points up our shortcomings. In the Adirondacks, where preservation is so advanced, very little has been done to place people in the natural areas in ways that protect those areas and enhance people's needs and desires to be a part of nature. The failures are all traceable to our bureaucracies. There are overlapping agencies, split regions, and multiple, competing governmental bodies. We in the Park are governed by entities that are parochial at every level. The only way we are unique is in the mess that purports to govern our most precious resource and the people who need to live and work in it.

Strong words, you say. But it is clear that overlapping layers or fractured entities of government mean that we are not getting the best from established agencies. For example, we have two disparate regions of the Department of Environmental Conservation (DEC), which, in spite of their allegiance to DEC staff in Albany, manage to administer state lands in very different and sometimes hurtful ways. The western region has completed most of its Unit Management Plans and is leading the way in recreation planning for some of its wild lands. The eastern region still cannot produce a plan for the abused and overused High Peaks region and has made virtually no strides in planning for recreation in other areas that could serve to divert use to less threatened and developed areas.

The Adirondack Park Agency (APA) is supposed to oversee planning for our public lands, while the DEC is supposed to do the actual management of those lands. But the APA is already eight years behind in revising the State Land Master Plan, which is notably short in advice for recreation planning in our Wild Forest Areas. The APA has only one staff member responsible for state lands. The APA and DEC talk, but have accomplished little together.

Empire State Development also has split regions. Only the northern and central portion of the Park is within its Adirondack region; the southern portion is tacked on to the Leatherstocking and Capital regions. There is an Association of Towns, but they have little status in talks with state agencies. The Local Government Review Board has status, and increasing input in APA deliberations, but no real part of the planning process. Add to this the overlaps of the Departments of Transportation and Health, and you see the reasons we have a mess.

What could be accomplished if there were better communication and a direct line of organization? For starters, it would be possible to help local communities expand their ties to the Forest Preserve, to foster proper use of it as part of their tourism programs. They could be encouraged to help plan trails from the communities to surrounding state land. It would be possible to have trails from hamlets, vacation centers, and guest accommodations to the beauties of the Forest Preserve. Local government participation in Park planning and organization is essential; it is the best means of providing representation for residents in the context of larger planning and government agencies.

Have other national or state parks done a better job? In this country, all our other parks are contiguous geographical entities, not intermixed public and private lands. Their managers are concerned with them as resources to be protected and as recreational opportunities for the public. Sure, there are problems of buffers and extraction of mineral resources, of overuse and too much building of public accommodations within their boundaries, but these problems can be solved.

They do have some great examples of how to make public lands work for people. Almost every national park has a good visitor center near the entrance (the Adirondacks' centers are remote destinations, not the place to obtain first impressions and an understanding of what may be available both at the public level and at the private level). Many national parks have roads surrounding them or penetrating a part of them, with roadside stops, vistas, and information about what you are seeing. National parks and forests have a range of trails offering short introductory walks, moderate hikes, and long backcountry treks. Every short hike I have tried has been a wonderful sample of what the region offers. (How few such sample trails exist in the Adirondacks! And, the best were not even built by the DEC, but by the Nature Conservancy. That organization built the boardwalk that takes you into Silver Lake Bog; the steep, fern bordered trail to Coon Mountain's summit and its panoramic view; the wetland and views along the trail to Cooks Mountain overlooking Lake George.)

Can you imagine a program like the recent efforts of the Adirondack Regional Tourism Council, which prepared booklets on canoe routes and great walks and day hikes, working together with the DEC to develop new opportunities in the regions where they are scarce? Consider the benefits of a comprehensive plan that will ensure that almost every wild forest and wilderness area in the Park has a short, introductory trail and roadside stops and picnic places on surrounding roads. Imagine how desirable it would be for towns to have trails leading out from bed and breakfasts or motels to special places. Or even enough trails to special places nearby that could act as a magnet for visitors. Most progress toward promoting the Park as a tourist region has come from local tourist offices and county tourism organizations. Such efforts have never been integrated with the DEC or APA.

Further, the organizations that purport to watch over public concerns for the Park are even more fragmented and contradictory than the governmental agencies. Some organizations are concerned almost exclusively for wilderness values and limiting the impact of development on wild lands. Some groups are mainly concerned with acquiring new lands. Others focus on developing access, in some instances in ways that threaten the wild land values. The cacophony of voices, each asking for financial support for their organization, splinters and weakens their thrust. And, in recent years such organizations have proliferated rather than joining together to focus on real support of the Park and its wild land and economic values. The whole Adirondack region is one of the most beautiful in the United States, but all most people hear about are the tallest peaks. It will take a concerted effort to unite all the parts of the Park and to promote them equally. Recent attempts have been piecemeal efforts at best. The DEC's Use and Information Plan, an aborted attempt to use federal funds for recreation planning, failed when it was decided that it was not the venue for really integrating the private sector with the development of public lands. It was a doubly unfortunate misstep in that representatives of towns and tourist agencies were eager to participate, yet thwarted. Still, the exercise did show the possibilities of joint efforts.

The Park is an incredibly complex mix of resources and opportunities. I do not think that real progress can be made toward integrating the needs of Park residents with wild land preservation until all the involved agencies are part of one council that works together. We are in dire need of leadership for the Park. There is a lack of vision that is mired in overlapping layers of government. More government control is feared, but vision would not require or necessarily create more control—it would propose a framework in which all existing agencies could be integrated more effectively.

A more streamlined governmental approach would not eliminate public participation in planning and managing our wildlands; it would enhance it. In fact, it should make it easier for towns and local entities to be effective because they would have fewer layers of government to contend with. A joint agency dealing with all aspects of the Adirondacks could provide a forum for all interested parties—preservationists, conservationists, foresters, down-staters, residents, everyone—to work together openly.

Back to my foreign travels. I marvel that countries with such limited resources have done so much. I appreciate what the western tradition of parks has done for more prosperous countries. I am saddened that the Adirondacks which has done such a spectacular job of preserving natural resources has done so little to make these resources easily available to the region's visitors; that it has done so little to provide the economic base that residents require; that it has not made this "a park of people and natural resources" as we hoped when we planned the Park's centennial.

Roger Mitchell

Roger Mitchell spent his boyhood years in Saranac Lake, New York, where, as a member of the local Boy Scout troop, he tramped around the nearby woods. He went away as a young man to find his fortune, which he did as a scholar, earning degrees from both Harvard and England's Manchester University. He then became a poet and professor of literature at Indiana University, where he published several volumes of poetry and was a frequent contributor to a number of major literary reviews.

He has since come home to the Adirondacks, for his residence and for subject material. Two of his recent works stand out. Adirondack *(BkMk Press, 1988) is a collection of new and "found" poems (poetry based on pre-existing, often ephemeral historical documents), and* Clear Pond: The Reconstruction of a Life *(Syracuse University Press, 1991) is the story of the author's search for Israel Johnson, a nineteenth-century Adirondack settler. One critic declared* Clear Pond *"already a classic of Adirondack literature." Mitchell's tale of obsession won the John Ben Snow Prize for Literature in 1990.*

The poems below are from Adirondack; *the essay "Around Here" is published here for the first time.*

Mitchell and his wife, Dorian Gossey, a novelist, have a home in Jay, New York.

How It Starts

It starts with wanting to know something,
with wanting to stop being the baffled drifter,

with being the baffled drifter, of course,
in the first place, but then wanting to stop.

It's not that I'm angry. It's not that.
In fact it's a nice role, the baffled drifter.
There is so much to be baffled about,
if one chooses. And who wouldn't, or doesn't.

It starts with knowing enough already.
One can know enough already, and not
know it. One can go on knowing and know,
at the end of it, not how to chop wood.

Or to stand still. Sometimes I think
of standing still. For a year. Don't worry,
it's just a thought. But I think it anyway,
standing there thinking of standing there stone still.

Reuben Sanford and John Richards, Surveyors, Make Their Report, October 1827

> . . . where an ordinary surveyor could hardly be paid for the
> exercise of his profession.
>
> —Charles Fenno Hoffman

> . . . the desart place where we were.
>
> —Pehr Kalm

The most easterly line of this tract
is also on land of second quality,
the term, first, being inappropriate
to any we saw in all those weeks.
From the southeast corner to the river,
it is fifty-five chains. Thence,
on very rough steep hills and high mountains,
rocky, and the passage thwarted

on all sides by fallen trees, mossed,
and of great size and age, their criss-
crossing on one another so continual
and inveterate as to be often vexatious.
This is of fourth quality, no more,
where streams and twisted brooks rush down
between the rocks and mountains,
leaving no smooth place anywhere.
One hill or mountain crowds close behind
the other all along, reaching,
at the north boundary and on rough steep hills
a high rocky spruce-bound mountain.
The land, we repeat, is of the worst kind,
but for a few small pieces to the south.
On the west, it is again rocky, broken,
though timbered with spruce, cedar, fir,
some beech and a multitude of birch.
Stupendous rocks and ledges, craggy
and irregular, in many places
kept us from running lines. And the insects.
The locusts of Egypt were a harmonious choir
to these pestilent nuisances.
Animals of every sort abound.
It is a wilderness, no more, no less,
and will not soon cease being such.
How you will convince reasonable men
and their wives willingly to place themselves
in so barren a place, we do not know.
The isolated hunters and hermits hereabouts
do not seem suited to your purposes.
Indeed, they would be hostile to them.
The winters are unforgiving. There are no roads.
Once mined, the ore will lie on your hands.
It is our advice, though not asked for,
to abandon this scheme and seek your fortune
elsewhere. Leave this pathless waste
to the panther and the bear.

I Do Not Know What I Did Do

Poet's note: Juliet Baker Kellogg, 1842–1931, lived all her adult life, per-
haps her whole life, in the village of Minerva, Town of Minerva, Essex
County, New York. She was married first to Wesley Rice, from 1864 to his
death in 1873, then to William Kellogg, who died the year after she did.
She started a diary on January 1, 1865, and kept it, with few interruptions,
for the rest of her life with Wesley Rice. I do not try to present a reliable pic-
ture of the whole of her life, but instead what I imagine was a typical life
for a woman of limited means in this place at this time.

Wesley and Juliet supported themselves in a variety of ways. They
were, first of all, a farm family, but since the growing season was so short
in the Adirondacks, Wesley did odd jobs outside the home, chiefly acting
as a guide for hunters and anglers. Juliet did some sewing for other people,
but she also ran an intermittent boarding house for Wesley's clients. The
Rice home seems to have been one of the early sportsmen's hostelries, typ-
ical of the early days of the Adirondacks. Not a hotel, it would most likely
have been a house with an extra room or two added on. It is no surprise,
given the rigors of the climate and of guiding, that Wesley Rice died in
middle age of pneumonia.

Wesley Goes Out

Wednesday, first: Today
Wesley went out.
          Don't know when
he is coming back.

A Beautiful Morning
Friday, nineteenth:
               A beautiful morning.
I do not know what I did do.
Saturday: Ironed.

Anniversary

February eighteenth: One year ago today
   I was married, yes!
      Tonight, *he*—my husband, promised
to come home
      but he has not
      yet.
I have been very busy   all day,
cleaning house
         and mixing biscuits,
and a little of everything.

Sunday, nineteenth: Reading today
and looking for Wesley.
           But he has not come
at 8 o'clock   at night.
              Oh!
I think it is so wrong to stay
after one has promised to come
such a time.
         Nine o'clock. He has just come.
Had a letter from Rosina.

What I Did Do

Tuesday, twenty-third: Washed.
          Working.
Wednesday, twenty-fourth: Baking.
          Etc.
Thursday, twenty-fifth: About the same.
Friday, twenty-sixth: Ironed.
          Cooked.
Saturday, twenty-seventh: Snow.
Sunday, twenty-eighth: Watched cattle.
Monday, twenty-ninth: Baked bread.

Tuesday, thirtieth: Washed.
Wednesday, thirty-first: Baked all day.
Thursday, first: Cleaned house.
        All day.

        The President's Death

Wednesday: Washing and cleaning,
doing chores.

Thursday, twentieth:
        Made me a waist today
        like my sun bonnet.
Rainy and cold this afternoon.
                        Evening.
Wesley came about 8 o'clock. Told us
about the "President's death."

Friday, twenty-first: Rainy
and cold.
        Not doing much.
Ironed.

        The First Pond Lily

Monday, nineteenth, June:
Picked wool all day.

The first pond lily.

        Washed Wesley

Friday, twenty-third:
Wesley went out.
Picked wool.

Saturday, twenty-fourth:
Ironed in the morning.

Judson, Jane and I went to Beaver Meadow
to bring home bear meat.
Sunday, twenty-fifth:
Wesley came home.

Monday, twenty-sixth:
Washed Wesley.

Tuesday, twenty-seventh:
Washed Wesley.

Wednesday, twenty-eighth:
Washed Wesley.

Thursday, twenty-ninth:
Washed Wesley.

Friday, thirtieth:
                    Wesley went out.

    Going Out of the Woods

Monday, Third, July. Started about five o'clock to go out of
the woods took dinner to Bradley's went in evening to
Dower's went and got
                    a new hat
                              walked up to see Charley
and Currants and baby saw Mrs. and Miss Towsley went to
bed about 12 Tuesday fourth went to picknick took dinner
with Mr. and Mrs. Evans saw the fireworks in the evening
went into the ballroom staid about two hours watching
everything Wednesday fifth took breakfast at
Warrensburgh
          (at half past ten)
                    was at Hadley in afternoon
went with Luther and picked some strawberries Mother
and Father came this evening Thursday sixth washed

this morning went down to Billy's Rosa Lurancy came in
the afternoon and Mary I went home with Rosina Friday
went visiting down to Billy's in forenoon went to Henry's
in afternoon Saturday started for Chester took dinner to
Warrensburgh got to Uncle Jake's about six o'clock Sunday
went up to Sidney Hill
                              had some cherries to eat
                                                      Monday

Wesley started for home I rode up to Aunt Lois's washed and
ironed just at night I went home with Philana Tuesday went
up to Bial Bates helped them pick wool all day took dinner
and tea there staid with Aunt over night Wednesday
Cousin Charles carried me to Horicon I stopped to Mr. Bells
went to cousin Joseph Coons staid to dinner and tea cousin
Sylvia came down to see me I went home and staid all night
with her Thursday went up to Uncle Elie's staid all day
Uncle and Aunt came a ways with me I came to Horicon
Went up to Uncle Jake's Jo
                              carried my satchel up

        About the Same

Tuesday, twelfth, February: Warm,
                                        cloudy.
                                        worked,
        I sewed some,
knit.
        Wednesday: Cleaned house,
worked,
                        knit
                        Thursday:
Worked, knit some.
Friday: Ironed,
        A beautiful day.
                                Saturday:
Mopped.

       Sunday: Read most all day.
                    Blowy,
drifting.
      Monday: Washed.
              Three years today
since I was married.
          Tuesday:
      About the same.

    A Funny Time

Saturday, eighth:
         Went out to a wedding.
         Helped make the cake.
Had quite a funny time
           in evening
putting them to bed.

    Not Much

Friday, thirty-first:
        Not much.
Choring round.

  I Wash the Poor Wether's Fleece of Wool

Wednesday, twenty-ninth, March:
    Very pleasant today. Quite busy
    washing and breaking brows.
    Gathered six pails of sap.

Thursday,   thirtieth: Rainy in the morning.
        Cleared away pleasant
in the afternoon.
             We are alone yet.
I have washed the poor Wether's fleece of wool.
  (Wesley came in

just as I am writing.)
Had a letter from Mr. B
            and also
one from my   *unknown admirer.*

Friday: Went down in the Swamp
after spout timber.

It Was Took Away

Wednesday: Sunny
            but windy.
I washed,
but am in considerable pain.
Thursday, fourth: Morning
            been sick all night.
Have not slept one wink.
Wesley has gone after the doctor.
                    I do not feel much
like living.   Evening he came
and Mr. Jones came with him.
                    Another night
of pain and agony.
Friday, fifth: Another
        day of pain. Oh,
        how horrible.
A night of great anguish.
                    Slept 2 hours,
that is all,
            in this whole time.
Saturday, sixth: Still
            in pain.
In afternoon Dr. Gady came.
                    My child
born dead,   a boy,
                    a very large one.
It seemed to me

soul and body
almost separated.
It was took away
                    by main strength.

        And Now It's Done

Monday, sixth: Washed.
            I don't know why
            I write this down.
        No one will read it.
        Not even me.
                        When I wash
I like to write
                        "Washed."
I did it,
and now it's done.

Around Here

The Adirondacks is not new to me, but Jay is. So, when I'm not driving around looking for a band saw or some citronella candles, I sit at the window or walk around in the field (my wife and I have roughly forty acres of old farmland right up against the foothills of the Jay Range) looking at whatever passes by. What I see is a mix of things, mostly on the surface, but much of it tied to what has been going on in Jay for a long time. Some of it, like the birds, for a very long time.

We have almost no trees. The land in back of us has thirty to fifty-year-old white pines on it. Probably, for this part of the world, it is third or fourth growth. They make a barrier and a backdrop for us, a contrast to our open, exposed sandy-bottomed field. We are glad our neighbor has just logged his land, since it's unlikely he'll do that again for another thirty years or so.

By "sandy-bottomed" I mean that about two inches under the thick carpet of grasses, wildflowers, and alder bushes lies pure sand. When I dug a hole to sink a post for a clothesline two years ago, I got down three feet in about as many minutes. At the back side of the property, though, a wide wall of boulders, some as big as bathtubs, collects lichens and shelters some long stretches of blackberry canes. Somebody stripped these acres of its boulders and rocks with horse and drag so that something could grow here. The pile of rusted farm equipment along the wall suggests it was probably hay for horses and milk cows that grew where now we watch a farm slowly revert to bushy field and eventually, I assume, to recovering forest. Already, in a sort of drainway across the land, a line of poplars, birch, white pine, and alder is making motions toward natural reforestation.

We have friends who say we should keep the field mowed, mostly for esthetic reasons, I think, though the man who mows the few acres in front of our house grew up on a farm only six miles away, and when he looks at the ninety percent we leave unmowed, a squint of regret passes over his face. He feels the loss of a way of life in it, though he quickly admits he would never go back to it.

Open fields are great feeding grounds, so we have a steady company of birds and small mammals. Some live in it, other pass through looking for bugs, mice, voles and other of the plentiful and nutritious forms of life. The deer who drift through in the early morning or at dusk feed on a variety of small hedges and bushes. They are the main reason we have planted neither a flower nor a vegetable garden as yet.

Our companion beasts, as I think of them, keep unpredictable schedules, but this spring we've had almost daily visits from a red fox. He or she seems to have a den on the neighbor's property where there is, as well, a small pond and a large, though now abandoned, beaver lodge and at least a hundred feet of intricate dam. The beaver has moved a short ways downstream and built a new lodge and dam. This year we saw our first coyote out pouncing at the grass. We had a bobcat close to the house one evening after dark. It hung around screeching for ten minutes or more, seventy or eighty yards from the house. And, when we described a strange nocturnal grunting to a friend one time, she said, "bear." Something scratches through our small compost pile, as well, yet it could be anything from the fox to a neighborhood cat to a crow, but not, I think, bear.

I don't know whether to say the lushness of this land lies more in its grasses and flowers (of which I am a slow student), its birds and butterflies (this year's highlight is a pair of resident bitterns), or its views. The fixed view is dominated by the working side of Whiteface, where on a winter morning you can see the headlights of the cats creeping up the ski slopes to tamp down the night's fresh snowfall. Whiteface, though, is only the tallest peak we can see. Its two neighbors to the north, Lookout and Esther, look like shoulders in a lifted wing, while the near hills, Oak Hill to the right, Wainwright and Bassett (which once had a small ski slope on it), and coming left, Ebenezer Mountain and Rattlesnake Knob, though they form part of the western edge of the valley of the east branch of the Ausable River, do not have the storied heritage of the larger mountains. The Jay Range behind our land forms the eastern edge, and when we get an occasional look at it, as in coming down the two-mile hill from Wilmington, we almost envy those who have it to look at every day.

Today (June 4) we are having squalls. Every thirty minutes or so, Whiteface and almost every other land formation disappears as a gray ball of cotton fills up the valley and throws six minutes of very wet rain on us. Ten minutes later, the sun is out. Ten minutes after that, more rain. This is all to say that the sky—the fluid view—is a continuous parade of cloud, sunlight, moon, and star. As they say of snowflakes, no two skies are alike. Every sunset is its own show. We are far enough north that it is little exaggeration to say that the sun sets in a different place each night.

I spent eight or nine of my early years in Saranac Lake, so it might look as though settling in the Ausable Valley was a kind of homecoming. But the Ausable Valley is quite a different place from the valley of the Saranac River. It's also a different time. No place on earth can possibly be the same on the eve of the twenty-first century as it was in the middle of the twentieth, though if it were possible anywhere, it would be here in the Adirondacks. That, too, has been one of the reasons for coming back. But, since none of us can be the same person at sixty that we were at fourteen, this whole experience is in most ways totally new. I see things differently now. I bring a small accumulation of knowledge with me which, for instance, this morning, drove me to spend two or three hours chasing down and identifying the "floater" I've been seeing for days in the grass. It's called a spring azure, a small butterfly whose overwings are azure but whose underwings are a light gray brown with almost microscopic eye-like dots on it. When it flies, it is a flake fallen from the sky, but when it lands and folds up its wings, it disappears in the grass.

Someday, I tell myself, I will learn the grasses. I've spent my life teaching, so I can't help thinking of life except in terms of learning something. I suspect if I were to lie in the grass instead of just looking at it, I might "learn" something else, though that sounds like something to save for an outing from the old folks' home. For now, I content myself with learning the names of the parade of wildflowers that starts arriving in early spring and rolls on through till the first frost. I am still at the point with them that I must relearn most of them each year. Already, by early June, we have seen common cinquefoil, lesser stitchwort, purple vetch, some form of buttercup, Deptford pink, wild rose, bladder campion, blue-eyed grass, dandelion, birdfoot trefoil, orange hawkweed, smoothish hawkweed. At the moment, the blackberry canes are sputtering like sparklers along the field edge. We look forward to pie.

I suspect that my scramble to know these acres more intimately is a response in some way to having, as it were, defected. Maybe I did leave because my father had to find other work back in the fifties when the (TB) sanatoria closed for good, but I willingly took the ramble our upheaving culture considers the norm. I went where the jobs were. A career was more important than a place. Maybe I should have stayed where the last fling of the dice left in me 1975, i.e., southern Indiana, but I have chosen instead a field to "farm" visually for the northern harrier which hawks over the draw every other week or so, where two American bitterns have nested in some secreted weeds at the bottom of the field, where a pair of eastern phoebes have built a nest up under the porch roof and hatched five ravenous chicks, where woodcocks "peent" in the draw after dusk, where deer, fox, coyote, bobcat all pass by, and where one evening we came home to find a ruffed grouse dead on our back doorstep, curled up in sitting position, as though it had come home to die.

You don't get away with romanticisms like that around here, though. As a neighbor, one of the Coolidges, pointed out to me when I told him about it, it probably flew into a window and broke its neck. And it's called a partridge here, not a ruffed grouse.

Tam Lin Neville

A true working poet and writer who grew up in Keene Valley, New York, Tam Lin Neville has been published widely. Her lyric poetry has appeared in Mademoiselle, American Poetry Review, The Massachusetts Review, Ironwood, *and several other literary reviews and journals, and a number of anthologies. Her essays and reviews have been published in* The Three-penny Review, American Poetry Review, the Denver Quarterly, *and others.*

Her chapbook, Dreaming in Chinese, *won Calypso Press's first chapbook competition in 1995, and her first book of poetry,* Journey Cake, *in which the following poems appeared, was published in 1998 by BkMk Press, University of Missouri-Kansas City. The prose poem, "Glistening Slug on a Mountain Road," appears here for the first time.*

Glistening Slug on a Mountain Road

I set a stone to measure its progress and went on up the mountain to come back an hour later and at first not find it. But there it was, a foot on the other side of the marker. The length of it undulated so slowly I had to bend to see how it moved over the crown of the road. The head and shoulders, what pulled this creature along, were bunched and twisted in moving over a stone. The body straightened once past and moved on. By night fall it would enter the woods, the forest floor.

As I went towards home the little flesh antlers with their knobs hung in my mind—and the mute orange spots in the otherwise bare skin of the back, glistening and displaying themselves for no one to see. Small beauty there on a rainy November day. This snail without a shell doesn't know its own skin—the loveliness of her spots and the circles around them in perfect rings, not lopsided or orbiting crookedly. Antennae waving slowly in the misty air, belly sucking itself along by what means? I didn't want to disturb it by turning it over, so little of the creature is protected to begin with.

The grand clouds sail overhead, over the mountains, over the impossible wideness of the road where the slug progresses patiently unaware. I walk home in the falling dark and enter through the back door, into our kitchen. My husband looks up ruefully like a shepherd come in from too long alone in the fields, smelling of sheep and dung and cold grass and wanting a touch of home, the waft of meat from the oven, the steam of soup, a touch of whiskey to stave off winter.

Stirring my tea I thought of the lowly slug who was not even male or female or kin to me, the slug that was now traveling the forest floor without faltering, without thought.

I set out butter and slice the bread. May we partake of the wine of patience the glistening slug has left on the road.

Water

In the middle of the night
all noise falls from the roads,
only the river is moving.
Necklace and belt lie cold by the bed.
Now there is nowhere to go
to escape your gray eyes, your smile.
My tongue is broken and a thin flame
runs like a thief through my body.

I go to my daughter's room
where she stirs in the heat of sleep
and lie by her side. Nothing wakes her,
my blood is nothing new. All night
the smudge fires flicker in the orchard.
Deer come to drink at the river,
their thirst the same as water.
Across the valley, a slow train is leaving
without lights. I don't sleep
though something like sleep
builds a porch around my body
where I lie by my girl, looking out.

Waking Alone in Winter, 5 A.M.

Waking in you
sweet skin
in the only warm room
in an empty house—
the first of the sun's light
streams to firelight
and the trees as they appear
are the queer masts of a great ship
coming in without wind.

Joan Potter

Joan Potter was born and raised in Tupper Lake, and returned to the Adirondacks in 1990 when she and her husband moved to a log cabin near Elizabethtown. There they founded Pinto Press, a small publishing company that specialized in Adirondack books. Joan co-authored the press's first book, The Book of Adirondack Firsts, and edited several others. A regular contributor to Adirondack Life, she wrote the book African-American Firsts, published in 1994, and co-authored the children's book African Americans Who Were First (1997). The selections reprinted here first appeared in Adirondack Life in 1999.

Diners, Drugstores, and Dives

In my teenage scrapbook, which I have carefully carried from place to place over the forty-nine years since I graduated from Tupper Lake High School, I find a booklet with a yellowed paper cover embossed in gold: Senior Class Memories. I riffle through the pages, reading snippets of sentiments from my long-ago buddies: "Remember Willie's dock and the good times we had!" "Good luck to the walky-talky of the third period gym class." And an old saw, "Remember Grant, remember Lee, to hell with them, remember me."

One inscription, in neat adult handwriting, stands out from the youthful scribbles. "You are to be congratulated on your graduation," it reads. "I hope you never graduate from your friends at Maid's Pharmacy." It's signed by John Maid, owner of the drugstore in whose red leather booths my friends and I spent many after-school hours, sipping chocolate Cokes and gossiping about our teachers, boyfriends, and female rivals.

I remember Maid's as a sunny, cheerful spot with a soda fountain; booths along a wall; shelves of ointments, powders, pills, and cosmetics; and a counter for prescriptions. Our other teenage meeting place, the Miss Tupper Diner, was in retrospect more grown-up. Instead of the drugstore scent of chocolate and cologne, the diner smelled like fried eggs and Lucky Strikes. Working men ate there, settled on stools at the counter so they could banter with the cook as he tossed burgers on the grill.

My friends and I sat in booths for hours and always ordered the diner special—toasted sweet rolls dripping with melted butter. I don't remember if we drank coffee and smoked cigarettes. Maybe we did, taking a chance that no relatives or friends of our mothers would push open the door, bringing in a blast of cold icy air, and catch us in forbidden pursuits.

My most vivid Miss Tupper memory is of the evening my girlfriends and I decided to bleach our bangs. The six of us were on the cheering squad—later kicked off for drinking Tom Collinses in a Potsdam restaurant before a basketball game—and were among the most daring eleventh-grade girls. We each had hair of a different color and style, but we all had bangs, and somewhere we got the idea to bleach a streak into them.

At Maid's drugstore we bought the fixings—peroxide and some kind of white powder. Then we headed for the diner. Two by two, while the others waited in a booth, we locked ourselves in the tiny women's bathroom, spread the mixture on our hair, and waited for the magic transformation. It worked—more or less—and each of us emerged with bangs in various shades of blond and orange. But what I wonder is, why did those incredibly tolerant diner owners let six giddy teenage girls hold their bathroom hostage for what must have been an entire evening?

The drugstore and the diner were our weekday hangouts. On Saturday nights my girlfriends and I got dressed up in our twirly calf-length skirts, short-sleeved sweaters and black flats and headed for the Hotel Altamont. There we sat around a table in the dimly lighted Mountain

Room tapping our fingers to the music and waiting for someone to ask us to dance.

Although I clearly remember drinking rum-and-Cokes at the Altamont, none of us had yet reached the legal drinking age. In fact, pasted in the back cover of my high-school scrapbook is a cardboard sign I lifted from the wall of the dance hall the month before I left for college. In thick red letters the notice reads: "No Minors Permitted in Bar or Mountain Room at any Time." Below the message, some jokester had printed "John L. Lewis."

One Saturday evening after I'd left the house, the police chief telephoned my father to warn him that his officers were going to "raid the Altamont" that night and catch all the underage drinkers. "Just in case your daughter's there, Jess," he said, "I thought you'd like to know."

With that news, my mother leapt into action and headed for the hotel. I can still hear the astonished voice of my friend across the table in the dark, smoky Mountain Room. "Joan, your mother just walked in." Unthinkable. My proper mother in this raffish place. But I looked toward the door and there she was, huddled in her woolen coat and motioning to me. We all hid our cigarettes under the table and I rushed over to her. "Chief Timmons called and said there's going to be a raid tonight," she whispered. "You'd better come with me." She gave me just enough time to warn the other kids, and by the time the cops arrived, everybody under eighteen was safe at home.

A police raid was an unusual event; we teenagers always felt quite comfortable at the Altamont. But our ultimate Saturday night destination was the Waukesha, a rambling log roadhouse a few miles south of the village. We headed there whenever we could find someone with a car to give us a ride.

Inside the Waukesha, neon beer signs hung over the bar near the entrance, and lamps on each table in the long main room illuminated the woodland paintings hanging on the walls. At the far end of the room was a space for dancing and a bandstand where Corky Arsenault and his combo played tunes like "Tangerine" and "A Cottage for Sale." I distinctly remember the piano player as a skinny old woman who always kept a mug of beer within reach. Probably, though, she was a lot younger than I am now.

It was at the Waukesha that I slow-danced with my boyfriends and then rushed into the women's bathroom to gossip with the girls about my current love object. It was in that very bathroom that someone described to me just exactly what was meant by a French kiss. And it was at the Waukesha, not long after I graduated from high school, where my friend Arthur celebrated his safe return from the Korean War.

Everybody at the bar wanted to buy Arthur a drink, and he couldn't refuse. Finally he clambered up on the bandstand and announced that he was going to sing "The Marine Corps Hymn." I can still see him up there, singing his heart out and swaying to the music until he fell over backwards, crashing into Corky Arsenault's drum set.

I don't know where Arthur is today, and the wonderful Waukesha is gone, destroyed by fire in 1975. The Miss Tupper Diner was transformed into a more upscale restaurant called The Rose in the mid-eighties, but that has closed too. Maid's—sold to Monakey & Meader, then overwhelmed by national chain pharmacies—is today an optometrist's office. And after the Grand Union Company bought the old Hotel Altamont, a wrecking company came to demolish it, tearing away—according to a newspaper report—eighty-five doors, including the one my mother had nervously pulled open when she came to rescue her underage daughter.

Twenty-Five Years to Life

"Without it, I don't know how the North Country would have survived," says Marjorie Swan, a member of the Chestertown town board and widow of former town supervisor Howard Swan. She's talking about Hudson Headwaters Health Network, which opened its first health center in Chestertown twenty-five years ago this fall. Today, the network—a cooperative effort of townspeople and health-care professionals—has grown to include eleven centers. Eight are in the Adirondack Park, from a little brick building in Indian Lake to the spacious, state-of-the-art facility that was created from an abandoned A & P supermarket in Warrensburg. The Hudson Headwaters staff provides primary, preventive, and specialty care for about 35,000 residents of a 2,400-square-mile area.

The guiding force of this array of medical services is Dr. John Rugge, who arrived at the Chestertown center in 1974 for what he expected to be a short stay, and who now oversees the organization while continuing his practice as a family physician.

"I have sung his praises for years," says Jean Vetter, who organized the Chester Health Center Guild twenty-four years ago and remains an enthusiastic member. John Rugge, she adds, "is absolutely marvelous."

Rugge, a tall, soft-spoken man, reminisced recently about the path that led him to the Adirondacks. Born in Little Falls, New York, where his father was a dairy farmer, he grew up near Cooperstown in a place that he says was smaller than Chestertown. His mother's family was distinguished by a number of physicians, including her father, Harry Vickers, the sole doctor in Little Falls, who used to take her with him to deliver babies, says Rugge, "for company and assistance." According to family lore, he adds, his Uncle Dan, who became a physician, "removed my mother's appendix while he was still in high school."

Despite this background, says Rugge, "I was not about to become a doctor." Instead, he earned a bachelor's degree from Williams College and entered Harvard Divinity School, planning to eventually teach religion. For his field study he chose Massachusetts Mental Health Hospital in Boston, and after a few weeks in that environment decided to become a psychiatrist. "The role of psychiatrist in this real-world setting seemed a lot more attractive than being a religionist," he says.

After staying an extra year at Harvard to take science courses, he entered Yale Medical School, but soon chose not to concentrate on psychiatry. In his third year there he selected a track called "community medicine." Even then, he says, "I was drawn to the idea of a physician caring for a community of people."

From Yale, Rugge went to Albany Medical Center, where he found himself "on a pathway to an internal-medicine program with no clear idea of what to do next." After deciding to take a one-year break from his studies, he rented a farmhouse in Sodom, near North Creek. There he planned to finish writing a book about canoeing and find a nearby hospital emergency room where he could practice before returning to Albany to specialize. (His book *The Complete Wilderness Paddler*, written with James West Davidson, is still in print.)

While Rugge was carrying out his plans, Chestertown was experiencing a crisis. The town had been served by three doctors, including a married couple, Suzanne and Felix Schrenk, who had been there almost forty years. The Schrenks announced that they planned to retire and move to Florida, and at the same time the third doctor suddenly departed.

"We were left with no one," recalls Swan. "My husband, Howard, whose father had been a doctor here years prior, was concerned and formed a citizens' committee. They started a search, went to medical schools and interviewed a lot of doctors. They would come to look over the place, but their wives never liked it."

So when John Rugge went to Glens Falls Hospital in 1974 looking for an emergency-room position, he was sent to a health center in Chestertown that had been installed in the house that the Schrenks had vacated. Along with four newly graduated physician assistants, Rugge found himself the supervising physician of a medical center operated under the auspices of the hospital and located in a building owned by the town. Within a month, he also had become the school physician, town health officer, nursing-home physician, and Warren County coroner.

"It was a short-term response to a potential crisis," recalls Rugge. "I didn't expect it to be more than a six-month or one-year commitment."

By the end of the first year, he was still there and the center was running out of money. Luckily, Rugge got a call one day from a grant writer who had just moved to town. She located the Rural Health Initiative, a federal program that funds primary health-care for communities of great need, and was successful in getting a grant for the Chestertown center. The network is still receiving support from that program today.

This funding, says Rugge, "gave us the ability to bring our centers into the modern era. We were able to update our facilities and equipment and recruit physicians."

Another great boon to the health centers are the auxiliaries whose members raise money and offer other support. Jean Vetter, who organized the Chester guild, recalls that a year or so after the health center opened, she learned that Rugge was trying to find drivers for patients with no means of transportation. A friend of Vetter's who belonged to the Glens Falls Hospital Guild suggested she start a branch in Chestertown.

Guild members have come up with many ways to make money for the center, including publishing cookbooks, making Advent calendars, sponsoring craft sales, and sending out fund-raising letters. They have painted and decorated the facility, raised money for additions, paid for equipment, and furnished an upstairs apartment used by medical students. They still drive patients to the health center.

Not long after the Chester center was established, a number of surrounding towns also began losing their physicians to retirement or illness. Most of the doctors in the area, says Rugge, were Jewish refugees from Germany who had settled in the North Country in the 1940s. "Having all come at the same time, they all left at the same time," he says.

In the fall of 1975 the only doctor in Warrensburg closed his practice. The town and the hospital decided to open a center modeled after the one in Chestertown, and several months later the old supermarket had been refurbished and was ready for patients. By 1978 both North Creek and Indian Lake had also lost doctors and plans were made for health centers there.

North Creek's center, about the same size as the one in Chestertown, is attached to a nursing home. In Indian Lake, the community doctor, Hubert Carroll, had practiced in a building that the town had built for him. Carroll tried to retire three times, says Rugge, "but each time he returned because there was no one to take his place." Carroll was in his eighties when he finally retired for good, and with the town's help the health network renovated and expanded his building. With a waiting room, three examining rooms and a treatment room, the Indian Lake center, says Rugge, "is physically the smallest, but it's the most charming."

As Rugge explains it, "Somewhere along the way what happened accidentally became a strategy. We realized that if we could open a network of health centers, we might be able to recruit doctors who were interested in a rural practice."

In 1981 the network separated from Glens Falls Hospital and became an autonomous, state-licensed diagnostic and treatment center that provided services at four sites: Chestertown, Warrensburg, North Creek, and Indian Lake. The network established a health center in

Bolton Landing in 1985, in Ticonderoga and Schroon Lake in 1993, and in 1998 it added a site at Ticonderoga's Moses Ludington Hospital.

The experience in Schroon Lake was almost identical to that in Chestertown some twenty years earlier. John J. Kelly, who served as town supervisor until last June, recalls the time in the early 1990s that Schroon Lake's only doctor retired.

"Three physicians moved in and opened up, and then about a year later they pulled up stakes and left," he says. "We didn't have any primary care."

To see a doctor, Schroon residents had to travel north to Elizabethtown or south to Chestertown. The town board resolved to somehow provide health care in Schroon Lake. After John Rugge made a presentation describing the Hudson Headwaters Health Network, the board, receiving no opposition from residents, decided to build its own health center and become part of the network.

The Schroon Lake Health Center is owned by the town, which pays the health network $50,000 a year to provide services and collects $25,000 in rent, an arrangement that also exists in Bolton Landing and Indian Lake, where towns pay a stipend to support the centers during winter months.

"Service delivery is excellent," says Kelly. Before the center opened, "recruiting physicians was very, very difficult. Now, the doctors are here because they want to be, and the network does all the recruiting."

The doctors and physician assistants who have become part of Hudson Headwaters represent the kind of medical professional willing to reject high-paying urban practices to work in less-affluent rural areas. Some physicians have received forgiveness for their student loans by working in underserved communities.

Says Rugge, "The physicians initially were people coming out of family-practice residencies, people who generally had some ties to the area; they had visited or camped here. They also were a bit more idealistic than most physicians. They thought the virtues of a rural life were as important as making money."

The network's medical director, Dr. Paul Bachman, is a perfect example of this kind of commitment. For three years before he came to the Adirondacks, Bachman had been the only physician on a section of the Navajo reservation in Arizona. Bachman, who grew up in Buffalo, was in medical school in Syracuse when, he says, "I became interested in working in a rural Third World-type setting. I wanted India or Africa but couldn't afford to go there."

He found the reservation through the Indian Health Service, spent a few months there in 1976 and 1978, and returned with his wife as a full-time physician in 1982, after completing his residency in internal medicine. Their first two children were born on the reservation.

"I loved it," Bachman recalls. "I enjoyed the setting and the Navajo people. But our families were back East. Also, I wanted to work in a larger hospital with doctors I could consult with. Sometimes I felt over my head. I was the only doctor for a hundred miles."

When he decided to leave the reservation, Bachman knew he wanted to continue to work in an under-served area. After looking in Kentucky, Maine, New Hampshire, and Vermont, he and his wife happened to be driving through the Adirondacks on their way to Binghamton to visit her parents.

"In Indian Lake," he remembers, "I saw a sign that said 'Health Center, Hudson Headwaters Health Network.' I saw the same sign in North Creek and Warrensburg. We dropped in on an uncle who lives near Glens Falls, and I left my résumé at Glens Falls Hospital. It got to John Rugge."

Bachman was hired in the fall of 1985 and practices out of the Warrensburg and Chester centers. As medical director of the network, he says he is responsible for day-to-day medical-staff issues; recruiting physicians, physician assistants, and nurse practitioners; and maintaining the quality and continuity of care.

The physician assistants who joined the staff early in the life of the Chester Health Center were pioneers in a specialty developed by Duke University to use the skills of Vietnam War veterans who had been assigned to medical duties. Bill Orluk, a PA at the Chester center since 1975, says he joined the Navy after his third year at the University of Buffalo. Although he had entered college as a math major, he became interested in medicine and had been taking physiology and anatomy courses.

In the Navy, Orluk served as a hospital corpsman, and after his discharge he entered the physician-assistant program at Albany Medical

School. He went to Glens Falls Hospital for his preceptorship and was sent to the Chester center. "I fell in love with the area," Orluk says. "I had never been to the Adirondacks. My wife loved it too; she was from a very rural area in Canada." Orluk, his wife, and their new baby, Thomas, moved into the health center, taking over a section of the house that Rugge had just vacated. Orluk's wife later died of breast cancer, and he remarried ten years ago to a woman with three sons. The family still lives in the center, which makes it especially easy for Orluk's patients to find him.

Orluk says he doesn't mind being so accessible: "It's rewarding to me." He continues, "And after my first wife died, living here, I didn't need baby-sitters. There was always someone to watch Tommy."

The health network now includes twelve physician assistants, but when they first arrived at the Chester center, says Orluk, "Dr. Rugge had to make people see us. Now we're totally accepted. A lot of people choose to see me." In fact, says Marjorie Swan, "We call him Dr. Bill."

Physician assistants, comments Rugge, "have lots of responsibility and professional freedom and do a very broad range of services. But they also have good supervision and backup. PAs and nurse practitioners are indispensable to setting up a medical program."

Today, eighteen primary-care physicians—some part-time—serve on the network's staff, providing family, internal, and pediatric medicine; care of acute and chronic illness; and minor surgery. They are supported by three nurse practitioners and two nurse midwives. The Warrensburg center—with its attractive waiting, examining, and treatment rooms decorated with Adirondack prints and photographs by Hudson Headwaters doctor Daniel Way—also contains a dental office, a physical-therapy room, and a modern laboratory. Specialty care offered at the center includes obstetrics and gynecology, cardiology, mental-health services, and sports medicine and orthopedics. Smoking-cessation and childbirth classes are offered in the Warrensburg office, and a nutritionist travels to the other health centers to meet with patients on demand.

Health-care providers in the network who see some 20,000 individual patients a year, are available twenty-four hours a day, and, explains Rugge, "nobody is refused medical care because he or she can't afford it." As a physician, he says he doesn't know which of his patients are able or unable to pay for services, but, he adds, "as executive director, I worry about it all the time—how to make ends meet. When more than one quarter of our patients are uninsured, how do we find the money to make sure we have a reasonable compensation program to keep doctors here in the mountains?"

On the other hand, says Rugge, as the network has expanded it has become more attractive to physicians, and greater numbers of doctors who specialized in primary care are being drawn to small-town medicine. "One of the pleasures of a rural practice," he notes, "is that you have to get involved in people's lives. It goes to the heart of what it is to practice medicine."

And yes, the doctors and PAs of Hudson Headwaters still make house calls.

John Quenell

John Quenell *first visited the Adirondacks in a peck-sized basket in the summer of 1940. He was two months old at the time, and his parents decided to take him along on their annual visit to the state campsite at Fish Creek Ponds in a container that seemed to fit his diminutive frame perfectly. At Fish Creek that summer he became infected with Adirondack Fever, and since then he has never wished to be anywhere else.*

Having survived public school, boarding school, college, marriage, children, and a career in, by his own account, a "big, dumb corporation," Quenell is now settled happily with his wife, Mike, at Balsam Blister, their camp near Paul Smiths.

In addition to How Cold Was It Last Night?*, Quenell has written the satirical pamphlets* Clothe's For Local's, Johnny Local's All-Purpose Italian Phrasebook, On Entropy, *and* Vole—Benefactor of Mankind or Vermin? Maybe. *He is also a frequent contributor to the* Peasleeville Complainer. *The following work appeared in the* Adirondack Explorer *in 1999.*

How Cold Was It Last Night?

Nighttime arctic chill is one of the hazards of winter life in the Adirondacks, but if your building is tight and your firewood is dry, you might survive. Less certain is how well you will fare the next morning when you visit your local emporium to buy a newspaper, and are drawn into a conversation about How Cold Was It Last Night.

It would be naïve to think that such conversations are intended to be friendly. They are contests, with clear-cut winners and losers, fought by Cold Warriors. The winner is the one who reports the lowest temperature. Ironically, it is the loser who usually has the last word, "Uh," universally construed as an acknowledgment of defeat.

The following suggestions are intended to help you play the game. You will be engaging with professionals, but do not fear. Study their techniques (mostly cheap tricks) and learn not only how to defend yourself, but strike back.

1. The Trap

This is by far the most popular tactic in use today. It is easy and it is obvious. But unless you are really on your guard, it will be successfully used against you again and again.

The conversation between you (You) and your opponent (Opp.) goes something like this:

You. "Boy, it sure got cold last night."

Opp. "Yeah, lots of people been saying that. How cold was it at your place?"

You. "Oh, it hit about 32 below."

Opp. "We had 37 below here!"

You. "Uh."

Analysis. As you can see, The Trap is maddeningly simple. Of course, your first mistake was bringing up the subject of the weather, but the chances are good that if you hadn't, your opponent would have anyway. The key is this: he who goes first loses. Once you have committed yourself, the opponent simply undercuts you. He is lying, of course, and probably you are too, but that doesn't matter. Only winning matters, and you cannot possibly win once you have fallen into The Trap.

Defense. There are two proven ways to defend against The Trap. In reply to the "how cold" question you can say:

1. "I don't know." This dull response at least gets you off the hook. However, it will also brand you as a noncombatant, a party-pooper and a wimp. Not for everyone, but if that's really the way you are, that's okay.

2. "Oh, it was about minus 20 Centigrade." Is this a killer or what? Try not to smirk as your opponent's eyes glaze over and his mouth moves but no sound comes out. Finally, he will recover, and then one of two things will happen: 1) with a shrug he will signal that you are to be dis-

missed as a weirdo; or 2) he will plunge ahead, making the fatal blunder of *going first:* "Well, it hit 37 below here." Now you have him. You say, "Yeah, you must mean Fahrenheit. Twenty below Centigrade is about 40 below Fahrenheit." This is false, but it doesn't matter, obviously.

Caution: never undercut by more than two or three degrees if you want to maintain some sense of credibility.

2. The Pre-emptive Strike

Before the advent of The Trap, the Pre-emptive Strike was the dominant tactic used by Adirondackers, and it is still popular today in some of the more remote communities. Here is a sample:

You. "Sure was a cold one last night."

Opp. "45 below here."

You. "Uh."

Analysis. Now, you and your opponent know for a fact it was only about 20 below, but your opponent's wild exaggeration has thwarted the possibility of any meaningful response. The contest is over before it started, and you have lost.

Defense. Be patient. Don't get mad, get even. The next time it will be your turn:

You. "My God, it was 60 below at my place this morning! I don't know how my thermometer can stand it!"

Opp. "Uh."

If the opponent is worthy, he will even smile a tacit acknowledgment of your rightful place in the circle of Cold Warriors. One caution: if used often, the Pre-emptive Strike can cause *serious credibility problems.*

3. The Wind-Chill Ploy

This can be a devastating tactic if used properly. Just what is "windchill," anyway? In reality, it's not something you can measure, even though weatherpersons would have you believe otherwise. It's just something you feel if the wind is blowing. It makes you feel a heck of a lot colder, for some reason.

"Feel" is the operative word here. A thermometer, like some people I know, does not have feelings. Even though you may have paid good money for it, a thermometer will steadfastly refuse to tell you anything about wind-chill! Ironically, this is exactly what makes the Wind-chill Ploy so useful: the absence of fact leaves a lot of room to maneuver! Consider the following encounter:

You. "Boy, here it is April 24th, and it was 15 below at my place this morning."

Opp. "Well, it was 5 above here, but with the wind-chill it was actually 25 below."

You. "Funny, I didn't notice any wind."

Opp. "It was blowing like hell here for a while. Guess it's stopped now, though."

You. "Uh."

Analysis. You attempted a Pre-emptive Strike with the outrageous claim of 15 below in late April, but your opponent struck back with a clever use of the Wind-chill Ploy. Your clumsy attempt to fend him off by saying you hadn't noticed any wind was easily neutralized. It would have been better if you had said nothing at all.

Defense. When confronting someone likely to use the Wind-chill Ploy, it is best to assume a noncommittal posture. You must be circumspect. Initiate the conversation with questions about the wind—did he notice it blowing last night, where from, how strong, etc. Then tell him how fortunate he was to escape the mini-hurricane that blew through your place, ripping up trees, tearing off roofs, etc. If you do this properly, the chances are very good that the subject of temperature will not even come up!

4. The Instrumentation Innuendo

I have heard idealists say that most of this temperature one-upsmanship would quickly end if only we all had accurate thermometers. They rightly point out that the typical garden-variety mercury thermometer is of questionable accuracy. (If you wonder about this, look at the different temperature readings on a hardware store display rack of thermometers some day.) As for the large aneroid disk outdoor thermometer that you nail to a tree 50 yards from your kitchen window, accuracy is a big joke. (My father once had one that read 10 degrees high in the summer and 10 degrees low in the winter. We indulged him.)

But what does accuracy matter? Even if everyone had a thermometer certified by the National Bureau of Standards, they would still lie about how cold it was last night. It's nothing personal. We are genetically programmed to do this.

In practice, the typical Adirondack Cold Warrior is at least dimly aware that his thermometer might not offer precise information, so he invariably compensates by adjusting the actual winter temperature readings downward a few degrees. This makes him an easy target for the Instrumentation Innuendo! Consider the following:

You. "Guess I'll put up the storm windows today. We hit 9.62 degrees last night."

Opp. "Wasn't that something though? We had 7 here."

You. "Yeah, that's what my old thermometer said too, but on my new Gesellschaft Mark VII recording thermometer with the phase-locked-loop dingus, I got 9.62°. This gizmo is accurate to 1/100th of a degree, guaranteed. Set me back $500."

Opp. "Uh."

Analysis. Your unsuspecting opponent was successfully decoyed by your opening claim and, thinking that you had fallen into The Trap, quickly proffered a sleazy undercut. You then crushed him with the Instrumentation Innuendo, which he richly deserved. He is not likely to mess with you again!

Defense. Although it is a formidable weapon, if someone uses the Innuendo against you, you might at least be able to cut your losses with a rear guard action. For example, flatter him by asking numerous questions about his Mark VII. His small lie will have to grow into a big one and he will become increasingly uncomfortable. Then ask if he could show it to you some day. He will bother you no more.

Summary

Unless you have a really poor self-image and do not mind being trod upon, study these tactics carefully. Practice by role playing with your spouse or the one you love. Hone your skills and go out and win a few. Your ability to survive the long Adirondack winter with some sense of self-worth may depend on it.

Paul Schaefer

Paul Schaefer, 1908–1996, was a visionary leader of the New York State conservation movement from his early twenties. During his long career, he served on countless advisory committees for state and private agencies. He was the recipient of numerous awards and honors, including the Governor's Award from the New York State Conservation Council (1966), the Alexander Calder Conservation Award (1990), and the Governor Mario Cuomo Environmental Achievement Award (1994). He was involved with the passage of the National Wilderness Act of 1964 and for eleven years was the editor of The Forest Preserve. *In 1979, Union College recognized his outstanding contributions to conservation by awarding him an honorary doctor of science degree.*

Schaefer's first book, Defending the Wilderness: The Adirondack Writings of Paul Schaefer *(Syracuse University Press, 1989), documents the campaign of more than half a century to preserve the wilderness in the Adirondacks.*

His Adirondack Cabin Country *(Syracuse University Press, 1993) is a poignant memoir of his life in the wilderness. Three selections from that book, "The Old Log Cabin," "A Day in the Wilderness with Zahnie," and "The Plantations," are reprinted here. Also included is the preface to a book Schaefer edited late in his life,* Adirondack Explorations: Nature Writings of Verplanck Colvin *(Syracuse University Press, 1997).*

The Old Log Cabin

The first time I laid eyes on this old log cabin I fell in love with it. It was situated in a highland meadow that reached to a brook at the foot of a precipitous mountain. A main trail into a vast mysterious wilderness passed its door. It was owned by our mountaineer friend Johnny Morehouse. A combination of family encouragement and the saving of a few dollars from our apprentice courses made it possible for my brother Vincent and me to purchase it in 1926.

It was a simple structure of adz-hewn logs, eight or twelve inches in diameter. Though its logs were weathered by nearly a century of storms and its roof layered patch upon patch, it became our pride and joy at once. It had but two rooms, one with a table, chairs, and a wood stove, and the other with bunks. As we were able, we added a fireplace and then a well with a sweep, rope, and pail to lift the cold, nectar-like water from its depths.

Possession of this Adirondack pioneer's cabin quickly changed my life. My friends from the city now had a place with free lodging in a vast wild region where they could hunt deer and bear and fish for trout. And I had, without cost, free transportation almost whenever I wanted it, in rather ancient open touring cars in which we nearly froze when it got cold.

As we began to use the cabin, the whole country began to challenge us. We found streams and lakes abundant with trout and trails with fresh tracks of deer and bear. The nearby mountains were trailless and exceeded three thousand feet in height. We soon were standing on storm swept peaks looking out to distant horizons. On one mountain, we discovered five streams, one of which was fed by a great swamp and spawned a cataract a thousand feet high.

From the cabin, as well as from all nearby clearings, the graceful Crane Mountain dominated the view. It invited exploration. Several very steep trails rose from the historic Elliot Putnam farm, located three miles back in the woods. They led to a glacial lake in a bowl below its summit and to the forest ranger's observatory. From its isolated peak, we could see most of the Adirondacks, some of the Catskills, and part of the Green Mountains of Vermont. On a rocky rampart of the mountain, we could see our cabin country and the vast wilderness beyond it.

Hunting and fishing became a part of our life. I was lucky to have gotten an antlered buck and a bear by the time I was seventeen, but many of my friends were not so successful. In fact, many of our hunts were magnificently unsuccessful. Time and again we would hunt mountains, ridges, and swamps from dawn to dusk and come back to the cabin and eat pork and beans. At such times, the memory of the taste of fresh venison and its fragrant cooking odor would renew in us the spirit of the chase. Always, there would be a tomorrow when the buck we missed had larger antlers. We were more successful trout fishing, for this most beautiful of all fish was to be found in every stream, in or out of the wilderness, and in all of the lakes we knew but one.

During my apprenticeship as a carpenter, my boss would let me have time off as fall crept into winter and outdoor work became more difficult. One year, he let me take a month off to work with a skilled taxidermist. Usually, I would spend a week during the winter at the cabin. Most of the time I would be alone, but once in a while I would invite a fellow hitchhiker I had met on my journey north to join me. To encourage drivers of cars to pick me up, I always had traps visible in the top of my pack on the way north and a batch of tanned furs visible on the way south.

Sometimes when bitter cold permeated the logs or their interstices, I questioned my sanity. Less than eighty miles distant was a warm home and wonderful meals cooked by my mother. At such times, I would throw another log on the fire, get out my fiddle, and try to make music like old Hugh Lackey.

Those winter days were priceless to me, for I had a haven where I could immerse myself in cooking and read without disturbance. I brought along books by John Burroughs, Henry David Thoreau, Francis of Assisi, and Viscount François René Chateaubriand. Verplanck Colvin's descriptions of some of the country back and beyond kept inspiring me to know the country better. It was in this hermitage that I began to think about writing. It began in the dim light of an oil lamp and the occasional flare-ups of a dry log in the fireplace.

A Day in the Wilderness with Zahnie

One afternoon during the summer in the early 1950s, Howard Zahniser dropped in at my Adirondack log cabin to renew the conversation we had started the night before at his mountainside cabin half a mile away. Howard was the executive director of the Wilderness Society in Washington, D.C., and very concerned about Adirondack issues. He was helping us develop national strategies for our battle to save the Moose River wilderness and its virgin forest located about forty miles to the west. We also had discussed the growing threats to wilderness everywhere by the increasing penetrations of Jeeps and planes into remote areas. I recalled when I met Bob Marshall nearly two decades earlier that even then he viewed mechanized incursions as the major threat to the integrity of the country's vanishing wilderness regions. Bob had founded the Wilderness Society, and now Howard was carrying Bob's ideals forward by crusading for a National Wilderness Preservation Act.

Because we had talked so long into the night, I asked him if he would rather take a hike into Bog Meadow. He agreed, and we headed for the trail that enters the Siamese Ponds Wilderness a scant quarter-mile away. We were leaving a land that slopes gently for a couple of miles to a valley where Crane Mountain rises majestically to fill the view. Close at hand, Cataract Mountain stands precipitously, its ragged spruce etched sharply against the sky. We would go about three miles before we reached Bog Meadow, a small lovely opening in an otherwise heavy forest. The meadow has been an ancient habitat for beaver, and they still occupy it perennially.

Along the trail are clumps of violets, trout lilies, trillium, and an occasional Indian pipe. The forest floor for miles in all directions is lush with ferns. We startled several deer but did not see them. A brightly colored salamander crawled along a moss-covered tree lying alongside the path. The forest's canopy almost blocked out the sky.

As we proceeded, discussing the centuries-old hardwoods and the value of these protected watershed forests, we noticed the sun had vanished and the sky had become overcast. Several days of rain during the previous week had left the trail moist with an occasional pool in low spots. We crossed a cold spring brook, went further, and crossed another one. Their waters would not meet for fifty miles. We reached the height-of-land, about 2,300 feet in elevation, and followed the trail down a gentle grade into the deep woods.

We were in no hurry. For me to be with Zahnie in wilderness was an end in itself, as I had discovered about five years earlier on our first trip into the Adirondack High Peaks. All of nature seemed to take on a new significance when I walked leisurely with him in this kind of country.

We reached Bog Meadow in mid-afternoon. The beavers had again built a dam on the stream. The placid waters of the little pond reflected the sky and the great trees surrounding it. I tossed a grasshopper into the water and it disappeared instantly as a brook trout broke the water's surface. We sat under some balsams at the pond's edge for a while. Dragonflies dipped and soared over the pond. We saw an occasional bird in the treetops. All was still. It was a time when one could hear the melody of silence.

To the north of us was a swamp interspersed with an occasional hardwood hummock. Half a mile away was a tiny sheet of water I called Lost Shanty Pond. We headed for it. At the pond, we startled a deer, which bounded off through the woods. Several small islands, heavy with brush and small trees, floated on the still, dark waters. The islands added additional wildness to the scene. We walked around the pond, looking for some evidence of man. A footprint, a dead campfire, a piece of paper. We found none. There were an abundance of deer tracks and those of a bear. On the west side of the pond, where decades ago I took my first antlered buck, was a boulder-strewn hillside. It invited you to tarry, to sit on a rock and think, or to just sit.

Howard was to leave for Washington the next day, so we reviewed again our strategy for the Moose River fight, which after five years was reaching new legal and political heights. We talked about that greatest of conservation-minded families in New York: Louis, Jim, Bob, and George Marshall. We talked about Robert Sterling Yard, Richard Westwood, and Hugh Hammond Bennett. About Ira Gabrielson, Anthony Wayne Smith, and Pinky Gutermuth, all of whom were involved in our New York conservation battles. We stopped talking and listened to the absolute silence of the wilderness.

Suddenly, I realized that the afternoon had slipped away. An overcast sky had hidden the sun, and we had become unaware of the time. Dusk was falling. We had no flashlights, so we moved quickly toward Bog Meadow and the trail that led to our clearing. It was almost dark when we reached the trail.

Ten minutes later, it was so dark I could not see my hand in front of my face. The trail was rough and rocky, depressed from the adjacent woods so that it was not too difficult to place one foot ahead of the other and make some progress. We noticed something very strange on the trail. Scattered bits of a dull phosphorescent light glowed in the moist parts of the trail. We knelt to examine them. Tiny mushrooms, phosphorescent! We moved cautiously ahead, expecting a quick end to this good fortune. But the strange glow beckoned us on, and we moved at a good pace for some time. At the height-of-land we lost the glow. We continued our pace; the trail ran almost straight down the hill to a clearing above the cabin. We saw an open sky clearing of mist and Cataract Mountain looming despite the darkness.

Before the cheerful light of the cabin's fireplace, we marveled at our experience. We had both seen "foxfire" before, phosphorus in decayed wood, but this phenomena in living mushrooms was something else again. Howard and I had climbed several mountains, been caught in a violent storm atop one, and had known the joy of a deep wilderness campfire in High Peaks. Most of our trips were under adverse conditions of one kind or another. As he got up and prepared to head for his cabin, he remarked that it seemed that something wonderful happened on every trip we made. I watched him from the cabin door, playing the strong flashlight that I had forgotten earlier in the day on both sides of the trail, stopping once or twice to examine something of interest. As he disappeared in the woods, I concluded that Howard was a man who epitomized the movement to preserve the American wilderness.

The Plantations

Below the log cabin was a field. It was full of boulders, scant in soil, and supported sparse grass and goldenrod. It sloped gently to the east toward a valley two miles away and granted a magnificent view of Crane Mountain.

In 1931, I decided to reforest the land. The experts at the New York State tree nursery at Saratoga suggested that I plant spruce and red pine. I ordered 5,000 trees, and I picked them up for ten dollars in the early spring. I had discussed the idea with Johnny, and he was incredulous. "M'by," he said, "Trees is meant to cut, not ta plant. Ye'll spile the view my father made."

When my brother Carl and I showed him the 5,000 seedlings that I could easily hold in my two hands, he scoffed. "Trees," he remonstrated. "Why them things ain't hardly bin born yet." Reluctantly, he agreed to plant them after we showed him how with a mattock. He would have Carl and a neighbor, Willie, help him.

The next Friday afternoon, I was at Johnny's door. "Did you get the trees planted?" I asked him. "Why sartinly," he said. "Can't ya see how they've already shet into the sun?" It had started to rain.

The next day, I walked across the "plantation." Only here and there, among the weeds, could I find a tiny transplant. I began to think I was a fool to think a forest would result.

For several years, it was almost impossible to find the trees, except on a small sandy hill over by the creek where even weeds would not grow. It was that hill that made me decide I was no farmer. But strangely, the trees were growing well there.

During the next years, my conservation activities kept me so busy that I used the cabin only to sleep in and did not roam the land. When I did notice that trees were springing up all over the place, I got some more and established four more plantations of smaller size.

The years rolled on, and the trees began to prosper. Soon, they were as tall as I was, then ten feet, fifteen feet, thirty feet, and more in height. I found that Johnny was right. The splendid view of Crane Mountain was gone.

My conservation activities kept me from thinking about plantations until one winter's day, with snow heavy on all branches, I finally perceived that I did indeed have a forest—as a matter of fact, five of them. The trees just kept growing a foot or more each year until when they were eighty-five feet high, I realized they were fine enough to build a log cabin.

In the early 1980s, I gave friends of mine trees enough to build what is one of the finest log cabins in the Adirondack Park. As Carl and I watched it go up, log upon log, ceiling beams, fireplace mantels, and rafters, we could hardly believe that once they were trees not larger than a wooden pencil that we held in our hands.

After the trees had been cut for the cabin, their loss was not even noticeable in the plantations where all manner of natural things have come to life—canoe birches more than a foot in diameter, princess pine, snows that linger into June, deer, grouse, fox, woodchucks, and snow-shoe rabbits. The view is gone, and we have to climb the hill to see the mountain as we once did. In its place is an infinity of nature that has grown rapidly within my lifetime.

Preface

From *Adirondack Explorations: Nature Writings of Verplanck Colvin*

By the time I was fifteen, I had spent several summers with my family in the east-central Adirondack Mountains. I decided to begin a library about that fascinating country of mountains, rivers, and lakes. My father indicated that there were bookstores in Albany that handled old books and that most likely I could find something over there.

Albany, the capital city of New York, was about twenty miles southwesterly from our home in Schenectady. In those days, a trip of that length by trolley car was usually quite an adventure. I had a considerable walk from our home to the trolley, which took me to downtown Schenectady; there, I transferred to another one that would take me the fifteen miles to Albany.

When the open-sided electric car bound for Albany started to move, it was apparent that the motorman did not want to "spare the horses." He began in a burst of speed that he kept up for most of the trip. There were very few people on the car and they seemed to relish the ride. When the motorman approached a stop on his route and saw that no one was there to be picked up, he stamped on something on the floor, rang a bell, and increased the speed of the car. At some places, the trolley seemed to weave one way or the other. I hung on for dear life.

Eventually, we reached Albany, and I was glad to find myself on terra firma again. I inquired of several pedestrians for directions to bookstores and eventually found myself walking down a narrow street with tall buildings on either side, not far from the capitol. At the foot of the hill, I found a building with a sign on the front: "Scopes' Books."

Many books were visible in the store window. After some trepidation, I finally walked in.

Mr. Scopes was standing there, a distinguished-looking old gentleman, bent with age, with white curly hair. When he heard me enter the store, he looked up from what he was doing, peered over the rims of his glasses, and asked, "What can I do for you, son?" I told him that I had come to find books on the Adirondacks, that I wanted to start a library on the region, and I hoped that I could find some old books here that might make a good beginning for such a library.

He looked at me and said, "I think you mean that, don't you, son? You really want to start a library?" "That's right," I said. With that he turned and went to a tall ladder on wheels that was leaning against the bookshelves. He pushed to a specific place; apparently, he had something in mind. He climbed the ladder, reached to the top shelf, and came down with a small thin hardcover book. He handed it to me, and said, "This, son, is the kind of a book you need to start a library. And look, here is the signature of the man who wrote it." The name was Verplanck Colvin.

I was disappointed in the size of the book, but when I opened it and saw a picture of surveyors on a mountain, it looked to me as if it would be a worthwhile beginning. I finally told Mr. Scopes that I wanted it and asked how much would it cost. "Well, that's an expensive one," he said, "But it's worth it. Five dollars."

By no means did I have that much money on me. I told him that I would get the money to him as soon as I could, hoping he would let me take the book. He must have read my thoughts, for he told me I could have the book when I had paid for it in full. To me five dollars was an astounding amount to pay for an old book. He said that he would hold it for me and keep his eye open for other books that might be of interest. These he would have when I came back.

More than a month later, I returned. Waiting for me was the thin volume, *A Report on a Topographical Survey of the Adirondack Wilderness*, and other books that looked interesting and were of considerably more substance.

Not long afterwards, I found another bookstore in Albany on Spring Street, owned by Harmon Lockrow. Mr. Lockrow also seemed to understand my interest in acquiring more books, and I indicated to him, as I had to Mr. Scopes, that I ultimately wanted to procure a *complete* collection of books—I thought, as many as forty or fifty books—on this wonderful Adirondack country.

I found myself fascinated by this Mr. Colvin, an articulate adventurer, who published essays with accountings of his explorations. As a youth, he had accompanied his father on trips to the nearby Helderbergs to settle property disputes. His father, Andrew Colvin, was a lawyer, deeply involved in defending the tenants in the Rent Wars in the nearby mountains that form the westerly skyline of Albany, arising about fifteen miles from the city. A chain of cliffs near the crest of the range, up to two hundred feet in height, stretches north toward the Adirondacks and south toward the Catskills. Forest heavily covers the talus slope that extends from the base of the cliffs to the level of the relatively open plains a thousand feet below. From any point on the escarpment, it is possible to look out upon this undulating plain nearly fifty miles in diameter, bounded on the north by the Mohawk River and on the east by the sea-level Hudson River and the city of Albany. To reach the Helderbergs in those days, the Colvins traveled by horse and buggy. The long trip across the plains to the mile-long cliffs gave father and son a chance to think about and discuss the origin and uniqueness of the mountain range. There is little doubt that these trips were instrumental in determining the direction that Colvin's life would take.

His early writings included an illustrated article on those mountains entitled, "The Helderbergs," as well as "Narrative of a Bear Hunt"; "Ascent of Mt. Seward and Its Barometrical Measurement"; an article about an Adirondack mountain; and "The Dome of the Continent," an article on the Rocky Mountains. He completed his early work entirely on his own initiative, as a volunteer who had become enamored by what he saw in these mountain systems. All of these lesser-known works were written before he published *A Report on a Topographical Survey of the Adirondack Wilderness*, which was the first of a long series of documents relating to the New York State Land Survey and before he was on the payroll of New York State.

In 1865, four years before "The Helderbergs" appeared in *Harper's New Monthly Magazine,* the eighteen year-old Colvin had explored the upper reaches of the Sacandaga River near Speculator and was talking about the possibility of a park in the Adirondacks. The remote and secluded atmosphere of the whole region undoubtedly attracted him to explore it.

By this time destructive lumbering practices were exposing critically important areas of the watershed forest to the incredibly large consuming forest fires that were soon to follow. By 1872 Colvin decided to dedicate his life to the preservation of the Adirondack forest. He was appointed secretary of the New York State Park Commission and became superintendent of the Topographical Survey of the Adirondack Mountains, a job that lasted some twenty-eight years. It was during these years that Verplanck Colvin completed his most important Adirondack writing that appeared in various reports to the New York State Legislature. As the scope of his writing becomes better known, it is crystal clear that no individual in the history of New York State has contributed more to the preservation of the Adirondacks than Verplanck Colvin.

As a youth, I visited the Helderbergs frequently, going sometimes by "shank's mare" and more often by bicycle. The Indian Ladder region, now known as John Boyd Thacher Park, fascinated me with its deep caves, high waterfalls, imposing cliffs, and the exhilaration I found just walking along the escarpment and looking east and north to mountain country that I knew very little about at that time.

One cold winter day while exploring the Helderbergs, I came to a cave known as the Tory Cave. During the Revolutionary War, Tory spies were supposed to have made their headquarters here. From this cave, one could look southeasterly toward Albany, where one of the headquarters of the Revolution existed for some time. The day that I came to that cave, which is high up near the top of the escarpment, I was amazed to find that the weather had caused seepage or dripping from the high limestone ceiling to the floor of the cave. As a result of the constant dripping of water, ice stalagmites had formed, many of them five and six feet in height, with wide variations in diameter from the bottom to the top, sensitively recording the variations in temperature and weather during their formation. At some early time, a large chunk of the escarpment above the cave had fallen so as to block the cave's entrance from winds, which would surely have destroyed the very fragile ice formations. I was excited by my find, photographed what I saw, and mailed the photograph to *Nature Magazine* in Washington. The magazine printed the picture.

Not long after that (1931), I met John S. Apperson, one of the most important conservationists in New York State. He lived in Schenectady and was in the middle of two battles to defeat amendments to the New York State Constitution: the first one would permit the state to reforest and commercially lumber its lands outside the boundaries of the Adirondack and Catskill Parks, and the second would permit the building of closed cabins on state lands in the Adirondacks and would threaten the wild forest character of the mountains. While the reforestation amendment passed, it was only after more than 1.5 million acres of land had been added to the Adirondack Park; the closed-cabin amendment was defeated. It was during these battles that I came under Apperson's tutelage and became immersed totally in fighting to keep the Adirondack forests wild. I found that my connection with *Nature Magazine* proved to be a vital factor in the defeat of the closed-cabin amendment because of the number of articles that it published on our behalf. Thus, as it turned out, the Helderbergs, the fascinating mountains that first attracted Colvin's explorations, also encouraged my own interest in mountains and wilderness.

Colvin's *Report on a Topographical Survey of the Adirondack Wilderness* started my own Adirondack library. The library has grown, not to forty or fifty books, but to hundreds of books, letters, documents, maps, and other material so essential for a balanced library on the Adirondacks.

Both Mr. Scopes and Mr. Lockrow, over a long period of years, were extremely helpful to me. I found to my surprise in later years that they had included books that I had not had time to read. Searching for information on the early history of the Adirondacks, I recently found on my bookshelves the volumes of Francis Parkman's *Pioneers of France in the New York: France and England in North America,* which Mr. Scopes obtained for me fifty years ago. The first volume records that Jacques Cartier, the French pioneer, reaching the site of present-day Montreal in 1535, was the first European to see the Adirondack Mountains. Parkman writes that Cartier looked out from a mountaintop across the St. Lawrence and saw "east, west, and south, the mantling forest was over all, and the broad blue ribbon of the great river glistened amid a realm of verdure."

Also in my collection is a map made by the British War Office in

London for the invasion armies in North America in 1776, over two centuries after Cartier's time. In the location of the present-day Adirondacks on a large blank area appear the words: "This vast Tract of Land which is the ancient Couchsachrage, one of the four Beaver Hunting Countries of the Six Nations, is not yet Surveyed." Almost another century would pass before Verplanck Colvin set out to fill that void on the old maps.

Central to everything that I was able to acquire on the Adirondacks, from bookstores in Albany and elsewhere, have been the many volumes of Colvin's reports from 1872 to 1898, detailing his explorations of the Adirondacks, the mapping of them, and the political ramifications in which he found himself involved. He was the leading light of the forces that began the struggle in 1865 to save the Adirondacks and finally made significant strides in 1885 with the passage of the "Forever Wild" statute by the New York State Legislature under Governor David B. Hill. Colvin's work and writings played a critical role in the establishment of the Adirondack Park in 1892 and in the passage of the "Forever Wild" constitutional amendment by the 1894 New York State Constitutional Convention that was approved by the people in referendum the same year.

Nineteen ninety-four marked the hundredth anniversary of the passage of that wonderful amendment that gives constitutional protection to millions of acres of wild forest in the Adirondack Park. Looking back over history, there seem to be no comparable activities by other states or nations on this planet that equal the combination of actions by the New York State Legislature and the Constitutional Convention that passed the "Forever Wild" amendment.

Over the years, I have read extensively many books by many authors. None surpass Colvin's vision and his manner of expression. His earlier writings—unhindered by the technical details required in his later work—show the full-flowering of his ability to describe nature and the world as he saw it. He was able to convey vast amounts of information to many people when there were no conservation organizations or "environmentalists." He was able to create an awareness of the importance of our natural heritage. His writings provided the solid foundation for the "Forever Wild" amendment, which has withstood a hundred years of challenge.

Verplanck Colvin has given me the key that unlocks the richness of the hundreds of books that have been written about the Adirondack country. Through the years, because of his knowledge and activities, the devastated woodlands have changed to marvelous lands healed by nature; great forest and watershed values have recovered; and as time goes on, rivers and lakes will continue to benefit from the original ideas that he proposed that would maintain forever the wild forest character of the Adirondack region.

Christopher Shaw

*For years Christopher Shaw worked in the Adirondacks in two quintes-
sential regional occupations: camp caretaker and outdoor guide. That
background has, no doubt, informed much of his later work, which included stints as a contributing editor for the original* Blueline, *a literary
magazine now published at SUNY Potsdam, and more importantly, as an
editor at* Adirondack Life *from 1986 to 1989.*

Shaw's work has appeared in Outside *magazine and the* New England
Review, *to name a few, and his radio essays were broadcast from 1993 to
1996 on North Country Public Radio, an affiliate of National Public Radio
that serves the Adirondack region. His latest project,* Sacred Monkey
River: A Canoe Trip with the Gods *(W. W. Norton, 2000), is a book-length
work about canoeing in the watershed of the Usumacinta River which
separates Chiapas, in Mexico, and Guatemala. A resident of the Adirondacks for more than twenty-five years, Shaw now lives with his wife and
canoes in temporary exile in Vermont.*

"Empty at the Heart of the World" first appeared in the anthology The
Nature of Nature *(Harcourt Brace, 1996.)*

Empty at the Heart of the World

You reach the carry at the western end of Low's Lake by skirting a large
floating bog and threading your canoe through eight or ten acres of
drowned timber and gnarled stumps, known locally as "floodwood."
The place has a terminal quality, like an edge or a dead end, and is
ringed by low forested hills. On clear days, the water reflects the sky's

hard blue and the bright green of maples near shore. On dull, leaden afternoons, the landscape has an altogether different aspect, the bleached
and weather-polished floodwood trunks, like photo negatives of living
trees, triggering grim correspondences in the heart.

State Surveyor Verplanck Colvin searched for a reputed "lost lake"
near here in the autumn of 1872. Colvin, twenty-five, remembered the
place, then called Mud Lake, as "lonely and doleful water," in his first
official report to the New York State Legislature, in 1873. His perceptions were clouded by the observations of previous writers, notably S.
H. Hammond and Alfred Billings Street, who found the whole region
around Mud Lake so depressing that they vowed never to return. Few
places in Adirondack wilderness annals have drawn such complex emo-
tions from their visitors.

By the time Bob Marshall explored the area as a forestry student, exactly fifty years later, it had been ravaged by lumbering and a decade of
apocalyptic forest fires. Standing on the summit of Graves Mountain, a
moderate peak northeast of Low's Lake, in the summer of 1923, Marshall wrote, "It was not hard to understand why the early writers called
this the gloomiest region of the Adirondacks." Marshall had devoured
Colvin's narratives as a boy. Later, as he rowed a guideboat up Mud Lake
on his way to the junction of St. Lawrence, Hamilton, and Herkimer
counties, he once again remembered that those writers "were unani-
mous in calling it the wildest and gloomiest place in the Adirondacks.
So I let my imagination carry me back sixty years to the days when the
wolf, moose and panther were of daily occurrence, while man was almost unknown in the region."

For Colvin, the season and the company of his rough-cut guides and
porters certainly intensified the loneliness of that trip. It was late October, daylight at a premium. A group of surly market hunters were
camped there ahead of them. The seasonal derangement of the color
scheme was over, leaving the hills stark, the color of pewter and storms.
He found wolf tracks in the mud at the head of the lake. His crew re-
sented the low wages he paid—though the money often came from his
own pocket—and his prohibition of alcohol. He may have felt outnum-
bered and surrounded.

It was then a true wilderness by every definition of the time, untrammeled and unmoderated. A few years later, in the 1890s, a man

named Abbot Augustus Low acquired forty thousand acres of the Bog River drainage, including Bog Lake and Mud Lake. Low, whose fortune came from the China tea trade, was a latecomer among industrialists who had bought extensive tracts in the area—the railroad Webbs, Durants, and Whitneys—but not to be outdone. Low built a hobby empire in the woods, damming the Bog River ten miles downstream from the head of Mud Lake for a small hydroelectric plant. The dam raised the level of the Bog River and flooded the land around Mud Lake. It backed up the channels of Grass Pond and Bog Lake. The floating bog at the western end of Low's Lake is the shore of the original Mud Lake, Colvin's "broad, soft, peat marsh." Mr. Low named the huge deadwater after himself.

Low's summer neighbor, a few miles south on Lake Lila, William Seward Webb, ran a railroad spur through the area in the 1890s, to facilitate the removal of hardwood logs too dense for river drives. The line later became part of the New York Central system. Around the turn of the century, the New York Central shunted its obsolete coal burners to the Adirondacks. The engines lacked smokestack guards, and cinders sparked numerous fires in the timber slash along the right-of-way. In the dry August of 1908, according to one account, Low counted at least twenty fires caused by locomotives.

That fall, fires swept over tens of thousands of acres in the big country between Cranberry and Long lakes, and north of Raquette Lake, burning the soil down to bedrock. One burned from near Low's camp on Lake Marian all the way west to a ridge overlooking Cranberry Lake, where residents read newspapers by its light at midnight. On September 27, the fire crowned out and swept over Long Lake West, a logging hamlet near Low's dam on the Bog, destroying the railroad station, school, and post office, stores, lumberyards, freight cars, houses, and the Wilderness Inn, a renowned brothel esteemed by lumbermen for its queen-size French-Canadian whores. The town was never rebuilt.

When Bob Marshall stayed at the summer quarters of the New York State Forestry College, on Cranberry Lake, in 1923, he found traces of the fires and continuing bad logging practices in the surrounding woods. He found other things, which astonished him. The first was a roadless area of a size unparalleled in his long experience in the Adirondacks. The second was an expanse of first-growth eastern white pine and black spruce of nearly fifty thousand acres, in a remote area south of Cranberry Lake which had been acquired from Webb as part of State Forest Preserve legislation in 1886 (passed under pressure from Verplanck Colvin, among others). It remains the largest stand of such primary forest in the northeast.

It humbled Marshall, who wrote, "It was . . . pleasant, as we layed [sic] down to reflect, that we were in the heart of a tract of virgin timber about 40 miles square, absolutely unmaimed by man. And yet, we could not help regretting that there should be so very few of such tracts left."

After the Forest Preserve, the legislature created the Adirondack Park in 1892 ("a six-million acre patchwork of public and private land" etc.) and passed the "forever wild" clause of the state constitution in 1894, which prohibited lumbering on state land. Private lands in the Park were unregulated, however, until the Adirondack Park Agency Act was passed in 1969. (Private land makes up about 55 percent of the Park.) The APA Act also created the State Land Master Plan, designating seventeen separate areas, totaling one million acres, as "wilderness." According to the plan's definition, wilderness areas required a minimum of ten thousand acres, which would be managed to "achieve and perpetuate a natural plant and animal community where man's influence is not apparent."

In the 1970s, New York acquired Lake Lila from Webb's heirs. It is now designated a Primitive Area (essentially, wilderness), surrounded by private timberlands and reached by a long dirt road from Route 30.

In 1966, A. A. Low's widow sold her land to the Boy Scouts, who turned over Low's Lake and nine thousand acres to the state in 1985. The land abutted the Five Ponds Wilderness on the west. Lake Lila was a short carry over private land to the south.

A controversial commission appointed by Governor Mario Cuomo in 1990 recommended that the state consolidate its holdings with existing private parcels in the vast forested reach bounded approximately by the Adirondack Park boundary (the Blue Line) on the west, state Routes 3 and 30 on the north and east, and Raquette Lake and the Fulton Chain on the south, calling it the Oswegatchie Great Wilderness (or Oswegatchie-Bob Marshall Great Wilderness). The necessary private tracts would be acquired slowly over time. When complete, the area would contain more than four hundred thousand acres, or six hundred and twenty-five square miles—a postage stamp by Alaskan or Amazonian standards, but huge for the East, where it would be the largest designated wilderness area north of the Everglades. An environmental bond act that would have funded the first necessary acquisitions was defeated that fall. Few of the commission's recommendations have since been acted on.

The area contains hundreds of ponds and lakes, hundreds of miles of navigable waterways at the headwaters of five rivers, three existing wilderness areas, and the greatest variety and concentration of native species in the state, including the spruce grouse and pine marten, both rare. Where mammals are concerned, it is remembered for its many "lasts": the last moose shot in the Adirondacks, the last cougar, the last wolf. The moose went first, by the 1860s. As Paul Jamieson, author of *Adirondack Canoe Routes: The North Flow,* put it, "the last moose was killed many times there." The other two held out somewhat longer, by dint of reticence and intractability. The last wolf hide was brought in for bounty in 1899. Tradition says that Colvin himself shot the last known cougar in 1896, though one source claims a hide was submitted for bounty in the 1920s.

The northwestern Adirondacks remained a refuge for big mammals, big timber, and Civil War deserters—terra incognita in an industrialized state—for many reasons. It was remote from major timber markets, poor in minerals. It lacked the Wagnerian scenery of the High Peaks and lake country to the east, and the spa culture of Lake George and Saratoga. It was, for the East, big, diffuse, amorphous. Scary.

Sparsely settled, it was traveled intermittently. Oneidas and Mohawks from the south and Algonquins from the north hunted and lived there for centuries. In the colonial era, Iroquois from La Presentation, a Jesuit mission at present-day Ogdensburg, used the Oswegatchie River on their treks between the St. Lawrence and the longhouse country to the south. The "Albany Road" ran between Ogdensburg and William Johnson's Fish House on the Sacandaga River during the colonial wars. In living memory, remnants of the road were said to have made up sections of the "Red Horse Trail" from the Five Ponds south to Beaver River.

In 1771, land speculators using the names of two investors, Totten and Crossfield, acquired more than one million acres from Mohawk representatives, the largest purchase of its kind until then. They paid a little more than a thousand pounds. The following year, a survey crew ran blazes along the northern line, and the owners drew a hypothetical grid of lots and "townships" on the highly inaccurate map. (The survey crew, moving west to east, quit marking the line at the summit of Graves Mountain, where, according to tradition, their rum gave out.) Typically, their grid disregarded topography. After the War of Independence, the land reverted to New York State. The exact location of the northern line was one of Colvin's preoccupations. It cut through Mud Lake and approximated the northern border of Herkimer and Hamilton counties and the southern border of St. Lawrence County.

In 1792, another speculator, Alexander McComb, bought four million acres to the north from the cash-strapped state for eight cents an acre. A few years later McComb went bankrupt, and creditors seized the property to parcel it off. The state slowly reacquired some of these parcels as the Adirondack Park took shape in the 1890s, including the old-growth pine and spruce of Five Ponds.

Timber companies arrived around the same time as Colvin. As they had elsewhere in the Adirondacks, they stripped the forests and let the state reclaim the land for unpaid taxes. Colvin based his pitch to the legislature for an official Adirondack survey on the need to know exactly where these parcels lay. To establish legal boundaries, he proposed starting from fixed points and comparing the blazes and landmarks mentioned in colonial patents and deeds. The area involved was approximately the size of Vermont. It was "an undertaking of the greatest magnitude," Colvin wrote, one which his friends advised him to forgo: it required a huge labor force, to be coördinated over hundreds of miles; expensive equipment; unlimited energy; and, as it turned out, thirty years of his life.

In the spring of 1872, with a paltry handout from the state, Colvin headed north, intending to fix baselines from a federal geodetic survey taking place on Lake Champlain. In one incredibly productive season, using giant reflectors erected on mountain summits for triangulation, and barometric altitude computations, he scaled, surveyed, and measured twenty-two summits in the High Peaks and Saranac lakes. In the fall, he traveled west and up the Bog River from Tupper Lake, intending to complete the work he'd outlined for the year. With a few more years experience, he would probably have quit for the season.

The only child of a prominent lawyer and legislator, Colvin grew up in Albany steeped in the literature of exploration. His reports to the legislature for the years from 1873 to 1898 are neglected masterpieces of the genre, echoing accounts by Lewis and Clark, Henry Morton Stanley, John Wesley Powell, and Charles Darwin. As a surveyor he was self-taught. His narratives routinely chronicled triumphs of the will over obstacles placed by nature in the path of science. His view of the Adirondack wilderness was essentially nostalgic and romantic. The 1873 account of his work in the High Peaks is written with breathless élan.

At the headwaters of the Bog, though, with the vastness of low gray hills and uncut forests confronting him, his prose turns brooding and gloomy. He becomes momentarily fixated on discovering the "lost" lake, a cliché and banal archetype of exploratory romances, revealing a youthful penchant for melancholy and fantasy behind the empirical, the desire for an illusion of encompassing mystery close to home, some unredeemed blankness in the state's encircling frontier.

Late October on the Adirondack plateau can fill the sunniest disposition with spleen. At Mud Lake, Colvin's luck petered out. Things fell apart, especially the weather. Labor relations deteriorated. Food ran out. ("We had food for reflection, but little else.") The party wandered aimlessly west of Mud Lake. It stumbled on Lost Lake unexpectedly soon, became lost itself on the return, and was taken in by a solitary wolf trapper—another archetype—who lived on Nick's Lake. Colvin hired the trapper to guide him west over the divide from the Oswegatchie headwaters to the Beaver River, "against all hazards," then hired as additional porters the entire crew of surly market hunters camped at Mud Lake.

Before heading south to the Beaver, the crew lingered another day in this oddly compelling though "dubious" region, while Colvin determined the location of the St. Lawrence, Herkimer, and Hamilton county corner. It was exactly where he expected it to be.

On November 1, 1872, the party embarked from Mud Lake "directly westward into an unknown region of dismal wilderness," with one bag of flour. Conditions deteriorated further. On November 4, having found old blazes marking St. Lawrence County, Colvin wrote, "Our affairs began to look gloomy." There follows a harrowing narrative of cold, error, low rations, stove boats, and near disaster, as the party worked its way south from the Five Ponds to Beaver River, measuring and surveying numerous "unknown" ponds, lakes, and minor summits. On reaching the Beaver, with snow deepening by the hour, he paid his porters and his guide—presumably in cash—and watched them turn back the way they had come. He then struck out east with his original crew toward Long Lake, thirty miles through the "winterbound wilderness." Despite the conditions, he took time to pursue a cougar that crossed his path. The party eventually emerged at Long Lake on November 21, "none the worst for our trials," as he blithely put it.

Colvin had inadvertently circumnavigated most of the area that in 1990 would be proposed as the Oswegatchie Great Wilderness. With a good deal of backtracking, survey work, and immense baggage, it took him more than a month. (In 1878, he returned and marked the northwestern corner of the Totten and Crossfield Purchase, in the Red Horse Chain.) His route, still blanketed in undeveloped timberland, can be reproduced today, though not without trespassing on private lands.

Colvin's reports and lectures helped establish the State Forest Preserve, the Adirondack Park, and the "forever wild" clause of the state constitution. His personal fortune, as his friends had predicted, bore a sizable cost of the survey, and Colvin was reduced to dunning the legislature in later life. He quit his post in 1900, disgusted with Albany's pettifoggery, his records in disarray and his science in question. He became "a pathetic figure" on Albany streets, according to one writer, muttering in his whiskers about money, and "embittered . . . that politicians in league with the lumber interests belittled his work." His contemporary, the historian Alfred Donaldson, whose own authority has come into question, described Colvin's situation condescendingly: "His office looked more like the dressing room of a sporting club than the repository of valuable records. These, if there at all were apt to be buried beneath a picturesque profusion of snow-shoes, moccasins and packbaskets." Colvin lived into the 1920s, advising younger "conservationists" of the Progressive stamp, who carried on his dream of a "park" in the Adirondacks.

The east-west line separating counties, two big land purchases, and the precolonial northern border of Iroquois territory, bisects the area of the Oswegatchie Wilderness like the lea lines of rural England, or the aboriginal songlines of Australia. North of the line, the boreal ecotype prevails; to the south are the mixed pine and deciduous forests more typical of the state.

A picture by Frederic Remington shows a hunter paddling the dark stream of the upper Oswegatchie in a bark canoe, past a metal stake marking the border of St. Lawrence and Herkimer counties, the shaggy gray silhouettes of old-growth pines in the background. An Ogdensburg native, Remington came often to Cranberry Lake in the 1890s. Among other personality deformities, he was known for taking potshots at resting loons from the porch of a tourist hotel.

The same nebulous section of that line west of Low's Lake that drew Verplanck Colvin attracted the young Bob Marshall. Marshall's family had a summer home on Lower Saranac Lake, and by 1923 Marshall had already climbed most of the state's forty-six peaks over four thousand feet. His father, the jurist Louis Marshall, was an early advocate of Progressive conservation laws. In the dedication of his unpublished guidebook, *Weekend Trips in the Cranberry Lake Region,* now in the Moon Library of the New York State College of Environmental Science and Forestry, Marshall wrote, "Just a couple of months before he died, [my father] took a ten-mile walk in the Adirondacks. His love of the outdoors was the purest of anybody I know. His purpose in going to the forest was single: to enjoy the fullness of its beauty."

Along with his prodigious hiking accomplishments, the quest for beauty marked Marshall's own brief, productive career. Writers have cited his record of 200 day-hikes of over thirty miles, fifty-one over forty, and several of up to seventy miles. These figures sound superhuman. In the Cranberry Lake guidebook, he used a rating system for the area's ponds, calling one on the way to Low's Lake "one of the ugliest bodies of water it has been my misfortune to see." ("He was always rating things," a college friend said.) Bog Lake he judged "nothing to rave about."

Marshall put his legs to serious use that summer of 1923, galloping over the terrain from Graves Mountain to Partlow Lake, marking trails (defacing one mountain summit in the process), bushwhacking, and exploring. He defined the Cranberry Lake area as extending from the

Grass River Railroad on the north (paralleling today's Route 3), the Blue Line on the west, the Beaver River/Oswegatchie divide on the south, and the New York Central line, near Low's, on the east. He visited and described ninety-four ponds in that area. (This represents at least a third of the area covered by Colvin in 1872.) His accounts suggest that he could be a difficult hiking companion. Like Colvin, he was prone to plunge ahead without regard to his backtrail, to lose track of direction and time, to find himself benighted and underprovisioned. More than once he curled up against a rock for the night, in the middle of nowhere. On one trip to the Bog River, he lost his map and went on without it. Another time, he lost his camera and dropped what he was doing to go back and look for it.

Throughout the book, Marshall complains of logging slash and destructive forestry practices. On a long hike south to Lake Lila, he came across remnants of the big burns of 1908, the streambeds all dry, calling it "awful, monotonous country." He valued above everything the presence or illusion of primeval nature. Its destruction angered and depressed him. His standards, conditioned by the High Peaks and Saranac lakes, were exacting. On a pilgrimage to the three-county junction, he camped at Clear Pond, a stone's throw from Big Deer Pond, Colvin's Lost Lake. "It hardly seemed possible," he wrote, "that I was in the crowded Empire State of today. Not a house or a soul was within miles." He found all "as [it] had been when the first pioneer trapper spread his blanket in the uncontaminated country termed . . . the dismal wilderness."

The next day, near Big Deer Pond, he came upon "the first [primeval forest] of any great extent I had encountered in the entire region," though he could not help dismissing Big Deer itself as possessing "mediocre beauty."

Continuing south, Marshall stopped at Gull Lake to meet George Muir, "the last of the great wolf hunters . . . who had killed 67 of the 108 panthers, and 39 of the 98 wolves killed since 1870." Colvin had encountered wolf packs there. The panther and the wolf were not so long gone from the country that a natural and human continuity with the time of Colvin could not be traced.

The Adirondacks, even in their farthest reaches, tend to constrict the illusion or perception of wilderness. Rivers run into unnavigable thickets or private "parks," like Low's or Whitney's, forcing canoeists to turn back. You may crest one ridge to view an extraordinarily wild valley, while the next will lead to a strip mine or cottage development. From his experience with the High Peaks (now a wilderness area of two hundred thousand acres), Marshall knew the disappointments that could lie beyond the next range. He looked for places that yielded intimidating distances beyond the initial penetration, along with the possibility of being eaten.

The prose and sentiments of *Weekend Trips in the Cranberry Lake Region* show us a young person driven to recover the sense of vastness that recent generations had circumscribed. Marshall wrote that as a child he had suffered "terrible depression" when contemplating his lost opportunities for discovery. (The deprivation inspired some of his least rational expressions.) We can presume that his devotion to wilderness causes sought to balance the perceived loss of some primordial condition. One writer goes so far as to claim that Marshall's perception of wilderness had a Freudian tinge, his hyperactivity fueled by neurosis.

We remember him better, however, for his grand gestures on behalf of the outdoors. After joining the United States Forest Service, Marshall studied forest fires in Montana, explored Alaska's Brooks Range, and served as forestry director in the Office of Indian Affairs. He financed an inventory of roadless areas in the United States of more than three hundred thousand acres, with money from his own pocket. In 1928, Marshall's contemporary Aldo Leopold wrote an article recommending that the Forest Service abandon a road planned for the Gila National Forest, in Arizona, and set aside the region for "wilderness" use. The article widened a breach that already existed in the Forest Service between wilderness and logging factions.

Two years later, Marshall chimed in with an article titled "The Problem of the Wilderness," in which he began refining his definition of wilderness as "the last escape from society." Its balm was in alleviating "the terrible harm caused by repressed desires." A follower of Thorstein Veblen, John Dewey, and democratic socialism, Marshall also wrote a book, *The Peoples' Forests*, which called for the nationalization of the entire United States timber industry. Convinced that commercial forestry interests, having devastated the nation's private lands, were sizing up federal land for the same treatment, he began pushing for the creation of a national wilderness system.

Undoubtedly, the country around Cranberry and Low's lakes contributed to his understanding of wilderness as an area of no less than two hundred thousand acres, untrammeled by man, where a person could wander for two weeks "without crossing his own tracks."

In 1935, Marshall helped found the Wilderness Society, and he continued traveling to the Adirondacks to advise its advocates in the evolving politics of wilderness. In 1939, at the age of thirty-eight, he died inexplicably on a train between Washington, D.C., and New York. He had logged a lot of miles by then. One historian has made a case that he was assassinated by commercial logging interests convinced that his bid for socialized forestry would succeed.

After a federal Wilderness Act was finally passed in 1964, an extensive tract of national forest in the Rocky Mountains of Idaho and Montana was named the Bob Marshall Wilderness.

An Oswegatchie Great Wilderness in the Adirondacks would pay generous tribute to Colvin and Marshall (who viewed it idiosyncratically) and the far-reaching consequences of their experience there. Unfortunately, such hopes are mired in complications too Byzantine and mindnumbing for discussion here. They are all too common wherever opposing land-use interests face off. Some recent developments are encouraging, nevertheless. In 1993, New York State passed a bill creating a trust fund for land acquisition and other environmental programs. The fund, though far from adequate, marked a compromise between previously intractable foes and earmarked the fifty-thousand-acre Whitney Park for eventual acquisition, among other parcels. An important piece of the puzzle, the Whitney property has been managed for commercial forest production for a century, but is otherwise undeveloped. Gifford Pinchot conducted experiments in European-style "scientific" forestry there and on the nearby Webb property. Rising taxes and low timber prices have forced the Whitney family to consider subdividing lakefront or selling the property altogether. The land lies east of Lake Lila and is laced with ponds and streams where the author of *Woodcraft,* George Washington Sears, pen-named "Nessmuk" after his childhood mentor, a Nipmuck Indian, made his historic canoe trips in the 1880s. From a purely recreational standpoint, its reopening to public canoe access, with the addition of the carry between Bog Lake and Lake Lila, would expand existing Adirondack canoe routes to rival Algonquin Park and the Boundary Waters. It would also constitute fifteen percent of the total land mass for the proposed new wilderness.

Since the idea first arose, one of the main goals for an Oswegatchie Wilderness has been the return of the moose, wolf, and cougar. Roadlessness and a land mass such as four hundred thousand acres can provide are among the primary criteria for success, along with a large and diverse prey base. But "social" considerations carry equal or greater weight, in practical terms. Even years after the works of biologist David Mech, and wolf advocates Barry Lopez and Farley Mowat entered the public consciousness, predators like timber wolves, grizzlies, and other indicators of authentic wildness arouse some of our least rational fears. Restoration efforts for other species, furthermore, have proved mixed. Eagles and peregrines are back in strength, but a program that released lynx in the High Peaks was jeopardized when some were killed by cars and another was shot raiding a henhouse two states away. Any mention of cougars or wolves brings rapid and hysterical howls of protest from deer hunters, as well as from dairy and sheep farmers on the fringes of the Park.

Yet, to believe reports, all three species have slowly filtered their way back, especially moose. Young bulls have been streaming into the Adirondacks from northern New England for years. A proposal to introduce females for breeding was defeated recently by a local campaign promulgating fears of the two projected traffic accidents per year an established moose population would cause, and complaints that the state wanted to establish an "ecological Disneyland" in the Adirondacks. Cougar sightings are common, especially on the Whitney tract, and a forestry professor at Paul Smith's College, near Saranac Lake, saw one crossing a river near my home in the northern Adirondacks in the fall of 1992. Timber wolves have been reported near Low's Lake by trappers and hunters experienced enough in Alaska and the West to be able to distinguish them from eastern coyotes (which have usurped the wolf's niche in many areas). Experts concede that they may have crossed the frozen St. Lawrence from the Algonquin Park area of Ontario. A technical report for the governor's 1990 commission said that an Oswegatchie Great Wilderness could support a core population of wolves, and a study by the United States Fish and Wildlife Service recommended the Adirondack Park for possible future wolf restorations. It's academic for now. A call I made to the local office of the state environmental agency to ask about the possibility brought a typical response: "Don't bet on it."

It raises the question of definitions. In Colvin's day, everybody knew what "wilderness" meant. Much of that meaning was negative, but this was certain: wilderness was real and it had wolves in it. By Marshall's time, the big scary animals were gone from our temperate wildernesses, and abstract specifics had become necessary. Marshall spoke of compatible uses, minimum acreages, and the tonic effect on the human spirit, a social benefit. Today the poet Gary Snyder defines wilderness as a place where "the unmediated processes of nature are maximized." Snyder supports the big animals' return, emphasizing their positive role in local cultures. Marshall would have, too, though he didn't use them much in his arguments. Aldo Leopold, memorably, watched the "green fire" fade in a dying wolf's eyes and saw there everything ephemeral and nonrational that the wild unmediated world contains—the world of our origins, the world we still live in.

In a 1992 book titled *Forests: The Shadow of Civilization*, Robert Pogue Harrison writes that in literature, "forests begin to appear early on as the scene for what later comes to be known as the 'unconscious' " (or the "subterranean" consciousness). Early humans made clearings in wild places, he says, "that correspond both literally and figuratively to the purely psychic reality of human consciousness." One was safe, the other the abode of danger and insanity.

For a long time, I was perplexed by this disparity between our perception of wilderness and its reality. I lived deep in the woods, unclear about the meaning of that as a rhetorical position or point of view. Once, I drove south and attended a reading by the poet William Bronk, held in a cinder-block college building in Glens Falls, New York. The poet wore a madras sport coat and green slacks. The poems were flinty and dark, as the Adirondacks can also be. When he read a poem called "The Arts and Death: A Fugue for Sydney Cox" and intoned the lines "World, world, I am scared / and waver in awe before the wilderness / of raw consciousness, because it is all / dark and formlessness; and it is real this passion that we feel for forms," I felt like I knew exactly what he was talking about.

In the last century, we have undergone a radical cognitive shift in our relation to wilderness and geographic vastness. Discounting outer space and the oceans (both compromised), it no longer defines and circumscribes us. We surround it. It is no longer "beyond." The global village has become a sprawling megaburb. Tracts of open space where the unmediated processes of nature are left to themselves amount to so many vacant lots. Now the places remotest from civilization are found at the center instead of the fringe.

Outwardly, the biblical process of dominion is complete, yet inwardly we have misgivings, whether we know it or not. We miss the big open. We miss the freedom to migrate, a one-to-one relation with the gods and the land. We miss the adrenaline or endorphin rush just existing in the world induced. The size of our awe is directly related to the size of the vastness, though I admit I speak as an insatiable vastness junkie.

Wilderness isn't supposed to be scary anymore, partly because some of us have accepted our place in the planetary scheme and partly because many of the animals we once considered antagonistic to our presence—the wolves, grizzlies, tigers—have been wiped out or neutralized. Yet the hazards—psychic as well as physical—are real. As Ed Abbey reminded us, a "danger well-known to explorers of both the macro and the microcosmic [is] that of confusing the thing observed from the mind of the observer, of constructing not a picture of external reality, but simply a mirror of the thinker." Bad maps, for instance, resulted. Barry Lopez says that our perceptions of wild land are "colored by preconceptions and desire." Human consciousness has a stake in wilderness. So if it isn't a mirror, it is at least a giant projection screen, and what it shows us is frightening. Our psyches are circumscribed by a darkness. Inside, we still inhabit a plain where carnivores surround us. There exists every possibility of losing the self, of gazing into its heart and being reminded of our ordinariness and eatability, our own marginal importance in the grander design. A desirable consequence, certainly. But there is also the danger of losing sight of the thing itself.

Sheer bigness reduces that possibility. For our wildernesses to attain what the grizzly-bear advocate Doug Peacock calls their "full and former biological glory," they need *depth*, where crossing one range leads to a farther range, and beyond that to another, where bearings fail and the pretense of expertise is ridiculous and all the tugs of civilized comforts and amenities fall away, where the self breaks down into the bits and pieces of its historical prejudices and misconstructions and reconstitutes itself from its basic elements. A place where the eternal caucus meeting in session, unconsciously, in the out-of-the-way boardrooms of the mind, falls silent. Where there is nothing but the presence and the act, and the unmediated unfolding of processes we only dimly comprehend, without justifications of their real, imagined, or contrived use value. A place at the pleasure of which we continue to exist. A place where praise and thanksgiving for the mere existence of its forms and peculiarities whips unceasingly through the pinecones. An offering. A holy and living sacrifice. Wine splashed on the ground.

Colvin and Marshall confronted the amorphous wild between the Oswegatchie and Bog Rivers and were changed. Something in its formlessness mirrored uncertainties that slouched like remnant wildlife through the rational personas they had constructed. One had his feet in the age of conquest; the other tried to evolve a new consciousness and requite a loss. Both were haunted by the existence or memory of vanishing archetypes. Both fought for the wild's perpetuation as for a part of themselves.

The Adirondack Park is still one of the places where our idea of what constitutes wilderness is being worked out (a hazardous undertaking for all involved: the mirror is cracked). For years, its built-in limits frustrated me, until I made the long carry from Low's Lake to the Oswegatchie headwaters one September, a traverse of watersheds which recent acquisitions had made possible. Paddling through the floodwood on Low's Lake, I felt the awe of an approaching vastness, a defining edge, though I knew—at least, hypothetically—what lay beyond. The carry trail wound easily southwest through mixed forest. At the end, I put the canoe down and gazed across acres of alder swamp and beaver dams toward the big pine country of Five Ponds. I had entered a true beyond, the kind of place you might go for reasons more profound than recreation, and knew that if I continued toward the Red Horse country it would yield—instead of a highway, a farm, or the back corner of the mall parking lot—further extents of derangement or enlightenment before I emerged.

Another time I went there to find Colvin and Marshall's "three corners." It suited me as a destination, being hypothetical and therefore imaginary. I also wanted to test the connection between the big empty places in the landscape and the big empty place inside, though I wasn't sure exactly how to conduct the experiment.

I left from Second Pond early one evening, cloud banks floating low and flat on the red sunset, paddled west on the long flow and camped alone on Grass Pond. In the morning, I slipped back down the channel and crossed the flow, leaving my canoe in the shadow of the stark floodwoods that guard the carry. I walked to Big Deer Pond and took a compass bearing west and north. My course took me through a mixed forest of pine and yellow birch, over an easy rolling topography. If any cryptomorphic moose, wolves, or cougars were about, they left no sign that I could see, though bears had clawed the beeches and the chocolate kisses of deer lay everywhere in the runs.

After a short hike, I crossed a creek and struck Nick's Lake, where trappers had entertained both Colvin and Marshall. Its shore was deserted. Here I took another bearing, climbing east and a couple of degrees north. A few minutes later, I stood on the edge of a broad flat, under a canopy of mature forest stretching to oblivion. Planes of sunlight with bugs in them transected the shadows. My feet rested on a soft matte of winter-green, bunchberry, and princess pine. There was no marker, no view, no epiphany, but it was the place. I tried not to think of Colvin with his transit, or Marshall with his loss. I tried to think nothing, in fact—to achieve in this wild heart of the world the resigned acceptance and emptiness of mind that all great teachers tell us is the sole reward and essence of being.

But I couldn't. I was surrounded by wolves. They kept creeping in and crowding the unlit corners of my thoughts like neglected responsibilities, in the dreamy way they do, yellow-eyed and serene, big dogs indifferent to people, patient and unsentimental, as if they had crossed the frozen St. Lawrence of our brief history here and worked their relentless way back where they belonged. In a way, their presence was truer than mine. I was just the vehicle for their lupine reclamation project. I heard a hermit thrush and a white-throated sparrow. A junco rustled in the dead leafage under a tuft of fern. That's all there was, with its implication of everything. Me in my emptiness, surrounded by wolves.

Alex Shoumatoff

*As is evident from the selections reprinted here, Alex Shoumatoff consid-
ers writing a subversive activity. A graduate of Harvard and formerly a
staff writer for* The New Yorker, *Shoumatoff has traveled the world exercising his distinct brand of travel literature and what some critics call literary journalism.*

His work has been published in several publications, including Rolling
Stone, *the* New York Times Magazine, *and* Esquire. *He has authored
several books, including* Florida Ramble *(Harper and Row, 1974),* West-
chester: Portrait of a County *(Coward, McCann and Geoghegan, 1979),* The
Rivers Amazon *(Heinemann, 1979),* In Southern Light: Trekking through
Zaire and the Amazon *(Simon and Schuster, 1986), and* The Mountain of
Names: A History of the Human Family *(Philip Turner, ed., Kodansha
America, 1995).*

*Both of the pieces reprinted here were first published in 1997. "Camp
Life" appeared in* Vanity Fair, *and "The Real Adirondacks" was published
in* Snow Country *magazine.*

Shoumatoff lives in Keene, New York, with his wife and family.

Camp Life

Anyone familiar with the secretive ways of old American money will
suspect the authenticity of the term "great camps" to describe the lavish rustic compounds that began to appear in the Adirondack wilderness of northeastern New York State late in the last century. The term
is too ostentatious for American bluebloods; the same people, after all,

referred to the Gilded Age mansions of Newport as "cottages." Or take Litchfield Hall, still in the Litchfield family; they call it simply "the house." In reality, it is a stone castle, sitting in the middle of 10,000 acres in the central Adirondacks, at the end of a six-mile-long driveway. There is a stuffed giraffe in the main hall. The place stands comparison with such opulent American residences as William Randolph Hearst's San Simeon and George Vanderbilt's Biltmore, in North Carolina.

"No American is supposed to have a toy like this," Bambi Litchfield, the step-mother of Pieter Litchfield, a computer consultant in his mid-forties and the castle's present owner, observed to me recently. (Note the old Dutch spelling of "Pieter." His mother's family was in New York when it was still called "New Amsterdam.") To the west is the 52,000-acre Whitney Park, currently in the hands of the flamboyant seventy-one-year-old Marylou Whitney, a former real-estate broker and actress, and the fourth and final wife of Sonny, whose millions came from the Vanderbilt-Whitney fortune. "Marylou says with a straight face that 'we're neighbors, just across the street,' " Pieter told me. "But it's a long-distance call."

For the most part the owners of Adirondack seasonal homes, no matter how palatial, just call them "camps." The adjective "great" was introduced in the 1970s, when many of the more fabulous places had fallen on hard times and some had burned to the ground (being made mostly of wood, they are firetraps). The aristocratic Wasp families who built them had been in decline since the 1950s. Black-tie and butlers had gone out with the war. Appreciating that the camps represented a unique tradition in American architecture, a building style at once vernacular and monumental, preservationists coined the term "great camps" to distinguish the most elaborate compounds from such lesser manifestations as the grand camp (two or three buildings), the lodge (one big building), the log cabin, the rough or parlor camp (a platform with tents), the open camp (a lean-to), the day camp (basically a picnic site), and the summer camp, where you stash your kids for a few weeks.

About four hundred gems of the Adirondack rustic style, as it is known, are still tucked away in the woods, most of them on lakes, invisible and unknown to the general public, which is exactly how their owners want it. Thirty-five of them are (or were, in their heyday) great camps, self-contained little villages of (in the case of Marjorie Merriweather Post's Topridge) as many as sixty-five buildings, each with a different function: sleeping, dining, bowling, billiards, squash. The buildings were made from the materials at hand—the fireplaces from fieldstone found on the property; the walls, rafters, posts and columns, and stairs and staircases from the trunks of local red spruce, hemlock, yellow birch, white cedar, or white pine; the doors, gables, and railings trimmed with branches, roots, and burls—the more gnarled and twisted the better—in what is variously called twigwork, polework, or stickwork. Birch and cedar bark sheathe the interior and exterior walls, the ceilings, and gable ends. Even the chairs, beds, tables, and cupboards are fashioned from minimally worked native wood.

The Adirondack rustic style is at once an aesthetic phenomenon and an opportunistic one. It is said to be indebted to the Iroquois wigwam, the hunter's shanty, the Swiss chalet, the Russian dacha, the Japanese teahouse, and the Shinto temple, not to mention Victorian notions of roughing it and the picturesque. The official father of the style is William West Durant, who was born in 1850 and died in 1934. His father, Dr. Thomas Clark Durant, made a fortune in the railroads, which he invested in real estate in the northern woods, in an era when the Adirondacks were just starting to become one of the most popular summer-vacation destinations in the Northeast. By 1872 he owned more than 500,000 acres. His son, William, studied art and architecture in England and Germany, and it was his idea to develop the land by building vast, rustic estates for the robber barons. In the process he designed some remarkable compounds, which wound up in the hands of J. P. Morgan and Alfred Vanderbilt, two of the richest men of the day, but also bankrupted himself; he ended his life as a real-estate-title searcher, instead of living in one of his fantastic creations, as he had dreamed.

To a large and underacknowledged degree, though, Adirondack rustic is the product of local woodworkers' getting inventive during long, cold winters, making up the decorative detail as they went along. The Adirondacks remained a roadless wilderness, a forbidding last frontier, until well into this century, long after most of the rest of the country had been settled, so customizing the local wood, no matter how labor-intensive, was more economical than hauling in finished lumber.

The aesthetic underpinnings of the style date back at least 150 years, when European and urban intellectuals started making the pilgrimage upstate to the ancient weathered domes of Mount Marcy—the highest mountain in New York State—and its attendant High Peaks. Winslow Homer and Hudson River School painters Asher Durand and Thomas Cole created big canvases of the sun-shot, verdant Keene Valley floor fringed with the jagged mountains.

One night in 1898 in Panther Gorge, beneath the High Peaks, the radical empiricist philosopher William James, brother of the novelist Henry, experienced "a state of spiritual alertness of the most vital description," he later wrote. "It seemed as if the Gods of all the nature-mythologies were holding an indescribable meeting in my breast with the moral Gods of the inner life." Freud stayed for a few days at Putnam Camp in 1909, but failed to succumb to its rustic charm. "Of everything I have experienced in America this here is probably the strangest," he wrote to his family in Vienna. "There is a group of roughly made log cabins with a name to each. . . . We discovered the existence of special books on camping with detailed instructions about all these primitive appliances."

On a Saturday evening in the middle of last August, high season in the Adirondacks, when the blackflies and mosquitoes had receded and the thousands of crystal-clear lakes warmed to comfortable swimming temperature, *Vanity Fair* contributing photographer Jonathan Becker and I went for drinks at Andrew F. Derr III's grand camp, Hills Rock, kicking off a fortnight that took us all over the six-million-acre Adirondack Park. The park was established by the New York State legislature in the last two decades of the nineteenth century in order to preserve this magnificent wilderness of mountains, forest, lakes, and rivers as "forever wild," but only 42 percent is owned by the state; the rest is in private hands and still encompasses vast, vestigial robber-baron estates from the last century, as well as the huge holdings of several hunting and fishing clubs and paper companies. It was our goal to visit people "in camp," to get a sense of the differences in rustic design and ritual from lake to lake, and to pick up the lore of these secluded paradisal enclaves, which seem still to exist in another era.

In 1888, Andy Derr's great-grandfather Samuel Lowrie, a Presbyterian minister from Philadelphia, built the first house of this impressive complex, Hills Main, described by the architectural historian Richard Longstreth as "somewhat barnlike in appearance, its squat mass capped by a hulking gambrel roof." Lowrie's daughter Harriet expanded the bunkhouse in 1905 to create Hills Garden. His son Walter, an Episcopal clergyman, built Hills Rock across the brook in 1926; it consists of an elaborately trimmed and stenciled chalet, inspired by Walter's summers in the Italian Alps, and an authentic Japanese teahouse in which, at the age of sixty-six, Walter translated the complete works of Kierkegaard.

Gin-and-tonics in hand, we stood on the chalet's porch and watched the sunset pinken a glimpse of the High Peaks between the trees. Some lines in Latin had been inscribed over the entrance to the sitting room: "So the earth too is full of terrors appalling / With caves and great mountains, and forests profound / Which we for the most part are able to shun." Below the chalet the brook flowed down smooth gray basement rock in silent, delicate-fingered streams, occasionally collecting into limpid pools big enough to lie in. Andy is a friendly man of fifty-eight who "packed it in," as they say up here, a few years ago, leaving his father's insurance company to live in camp full-time. He is a good example of the process of what might be called "Adirondackization," which often takes place after a family has been coming up for several generations. Camp becomes where your heart is, the focus of all your yearning for the pure and the beautiful; everything else pales beside summer in the Adirondacks. Finally you pack it in. In season, Andy tools around in a blue 1966 Chevelle convertible that rides like an elegant old motor launch.

John Cheever, in his story "The Day the Pig Fell into the Well," about a family coming up to the Adirondacks over several decades, described the magic of camp life this way: "It seemed as if the summer were a continent, harmonious and self-sufficient, with a peculiar range of sensation that included the feel of driving the old Cadillac barefoot across a bumpy pasture, and the taste of water that came out of the garden hose near the tennis court, and the pleasure of pulling on a clean woolen sweater in a mountain hut at dawn, and sitting on the porch in the dark . . . and the clean feeling after a long swim."

Following cocktails we proceeded to a square dance at Uplands that was a benefit for the Nature Conservancy. Square dancing is a traditional and, at this point, practically extinct camp activity, and Uplands has a huge open living room that is perfect for the purpose. Uplands belongs to the Thornes of New York, who are, as a friend put it, "very old and very rich"—meaning many generations of Yankee money topped off by a turn-of-the-century railroad-and-banking fortune.

Phebe Thorne Marrin runs the camp and is one of the few hostesses in the area who still entertain on a large scale. An administrative-law judge in New York City, she is in the process of packing it in; her husband is chief counsel for the Adirondack Park Agency. The house was completed in 1909 and is gray shingle with green trim. As the architect John Baker has written of the shingle style, of which Uplands is a shining example, "It is an architect's style when fully realized—ordered, disciplined, and comfortable with a sense of casual dignity." The house has a pagoda roof, an eyebrow dormer, long eaves all around to protect the windows from storms, and a breezeway connecting the living room with the dining room, in which a moose head was draped with blazing Christmas bulbs for the benefit. Phebe is emphatic that the Uplands is a great camp, boasting not only a main compound but also a log cabin and a cottage in the woods where her grandmother "practiced the piano, took naps, and got away from her multiple houseguests and seven children."

The fiddling for the square dance had a slightly French-Canadian flavor (like some of the old local families), as couples who lived during the winter in Westchester, Fairfield, New York City, Far Hills, the North Shore of Long Island, Baltimore, and Main Line Philadelphia gaily do-si-doed and allemande-lefted. Their median age was about seventy.

From the square dance we continued to a party at nearby Maple Knoll (not its real name), one of the most original log houses in the Adirondacks, where the twenty-year-old son of the family (which prefers not to be named) was throwing a party for his generation. He had brought over a rock band from Burlington, Vermont, and the party spilled out onto the wraparound porch. The house was built in 1875 for John Matthews, who had made his money from the design and marketing of the soda fountain. This was fourteen years before Durant finished Pine Knot, his first and most beautiful effort, and it is every bit as sophisticated. Maple Knoll looks like something out of Bohemia, Scandinavia, or maybe Russia. You go up some stairs to the porch and a heavy wooden front door. Thick cedar logs, with their bark still on and their butt ends sharpened into stakes, meet at corners. Surmounting the front is a huge, steep shingle tower, which used to have a commanding view, but is now blocked by the maples, which have shot up in the intervening century to more than a hundred feet.

Two summers ago at a party at Maple Knoll, eighty-nine-year-old Mrs. Horace B. Learned, whose family had been part of Mark Twain's Hartford circle, thanked her hosts shortly before midnight: "I think I've had the most wonderful time in my life. I've found the pot of gold at the end of the rainbow." She got into her car and zoomed over a cliff in front of the house. Mrs. Learned died in the hospital some days later. A few weeks before, I had stopped her and detached a thirty-foot branch that she hadn't realized she was dragging along under her car. The woman should not have been driving.

Some of the most pristine remaining scenery and camp architecture is found in the private, 7,500-acre Ausable Club, founded in 1905. Its verandaed, cupolaed clubhouse is one of the few surviving monumental wooden structures in the Adirondacks. Upper Ausable Lake, which is reached by rowing or paddling up the narrow, clifflined Lower Ausable Lake and then portaging a mile, has a number of vintage camps such as Treetops, built in 1912 by steel millionaire Edward S. Harkness, who rarely used it, because his wife didn't care for the place. Now in the hands of Lil Chance and her eight children, a Philadelphia family, it has changed little in the intervening decades. The old coats are still in the closet, you draw your bath in a claw-footed porcelain tub. If you feel like roughing it you can sleep outside on fragrant balsam boughs in a lean-to that holds ten before a bonfire shooting sparks into the star-studded night.

Placid Lake, as the Shore Owners' Association decided to call it in 1993 to distinguish it from the touristy winter-sports village of Lake Placid, is the friendliest and least snooty of the lakes and has an eclectic mix of people and of camp styles. In its heyday there were maybe a hundred impressive camps and three huge hotels on the lake. At the turn of the century it attracted show-business and music people—for instance, Victor Herbert, who composed the 1903 hit operetta *Babes in Toyland.* Herbert built Camp Joyland in 1905. In 1949, Guy Lombardo, the big-band leader, tried to break the world speedboat record in a thirty-two foot craft called *Aluminum First* on the lake. Kate Smith, the voluminous songstress famed for her stirring rendition of "God

Bless America," bought Camp Sunset on Buck Island (one of the lake's three islands) in 1937, renamed it Camp Sunshine, and broadcast her national radio show from the boathouse. The theme song for the show, "When the Moon Comes over the Mountain," may have been inspired by her view.

A longtime camp-dweller recalls that, in contrast with her genial radio and television image, "she was a bitch on the lake. She wouldn't slow down her motorboat for canoes. She had no sensitivity to other people." On a pitch-black, low-ceilinged night a few years ago, Kate's neighbor Mrs. Max Cohen was returning from dinner in a big, yellow fiberglass inboard-outboard when she slammed into an unlighted guideboat, mangling one of its passengers with her propeller. The discovery that the victim was HIV-positive was not made public in order not to cause alarm. Since the virus dies quickly outside the body, the water of Placid Lake remained untainted—so clean, in fact, that the camps still draw from it, as does the town.

The following afternoon, Sunday, Jonathan and I went for a swim at Tapawingo, MacFarland and Margo Fish's camp in a quiet cove near Placid Lake's outlet. Mac's father, who manufactured surgical instruments in Erie, Pennsylvania, started coming up before World War II. As we sat on the dock, a family of red-breasted mergansers treaded by, and Margo recalled how in the old days "the camps themselves were like little citadels. You knew about each other, but there wasn't much exchange. You didn't share your lives, because your own life in camp was so full. We just came and hibernated—read, played music. In the sixties, people began to have large cocktail parties. They invited everybody they knew as a return and maybe there were three of those a year.

"I remember when Mac and I would canoe in formal dress to the Saturday-night dance at the Whiteface Inn. It was a romantic era, when people could have a staff, when John, our caretaker, was there to bring in the logs so we could cook on wood, and to cut the ice during the winter so it would be there [the following summer], covered with sawdust, in the icehouse. There was time for romance, for chivalry, because you weren't scrubbing. But by the fifties the men couldn't have the whole summer off, and there was no staff. The men came up for their month, and the women were here with their children, so in a way it was a matriarchal world."

A few days later Sara Jane Kasperzak took us water-skiing behind her beautiful twenty-five foot mahogany Chris-Craft. Her late husband had founded the company that makes Calphalon, the hard-anodized aluminum used in high-end cookware. She now owns Gull Rock, an eleven building camp that was started by a man from Philadelphia in 1903, acquired by Continental Can king Carle Cotter Conway, and then bought by a family of Cuban refugees that sold it to Otto C. Doering, who had been a top operative at the Office of Strategic Services, the World War II predecessor of the C.I.A. When a few years ago it finally got to be too much for eighty-eight-year-old Mrs. Doering, it was picked up by Sara Jane.

We skirted Pulpit Rock, which plunges precipitously into the lake. It was here, on September 21, 1933, that Mabel Smith Douglass, an educator who founded Douglass College for women at Rutgers University in New Jersey, and who had been institutionalized for suicidal tendencies a year before, apparently rowed out from her family camp, Onondaga, tied an anchor to her neck, and jumped from her skiff, which was found overturned by two local men ferrying lumber to a camp. The lake was dragged and dynamited, but all attempts to recover the body failed, and it lay forgotten and in a near-perfect state of preservation 105 feet down until September 15, 1963, when it was spotted by a scuba diver, who grabbed her arm, which came off. As she was being carefully brought to the surface, a passing motorboat churned the water and her head came off and started to sink. It was retrieved minus the jawbone, which had detached. Mrs. Douglass's skin was like hard, white wax, due to a process known as adipocere formation, but her organs were rumored to be as pink and fresh as those of someone who had died only an hour before.

Many camps have their own ghosts. The Vanderbilt-Whitney camp allegedly had an exorcism of a maid who, distraught by a love affair, had hanged herself, but most of the ghosts seem to be benign, and they even lend a certain cachet. One woman was happy for photographs to be taken of her Jack Russell terrier, her splendid collection of etched fungi (an art form peculiar to the North Country—the Whitney camp has one done by Mick Jagger), her Gib Jaques birch love seat (Gib was the premier rustic cabinetmaker until his eyes went bad a few years ago), and her childhood nanny, as long as we didn't reveal her name, that of her camp, or, most important, that of her ghost—a formidable grande dame who had lived in the house for fifty years and is occasionally glimpsed going up and down the stairs.

"My camp was haunted," a man who owned a camp on Upper St. Regis Lake for six years told me. "I and everyone who was ever there felt the presence of a ghost, and I kept having the same dream, of a face floating under the surface of the water. The face was that of a handsome cousin of the [previous] owners who crashed on Nantucket in the late fifties, but the family camp, being his spiritual home, was where his ghost came to rest. Whenever I had this vision, the room would get ice cold." And Bambi Litchfield told me that Litchfield Hall "has a little-girl ghost, the child of a caretaker who drowned in the lake years back, whom I'm thinking of having exorcised. The girl walks through the house with a little tea set and has been heard singing and fussing with the dressing-table things. There are no droppings, so it couldn't be a mouse. If she annoys me, I clap my hands."

There are no great camps on Placid Lake, only grand camps. To see the big ones, we headed west, toward the Saranac and St. Regis lake chains, a region of endless woods and lakes, kettle ponds (created by lingering blocks of glacial ice), and spruce-rimmed bogs with carnivorous pitcher plants, where there is as much open water as terra firma.

We visited Sandanona, on Upper Saranac Lake, which boasts the oldest surviving cabins in a private Adirondack camp, dating from the late 1860s. Charles Ritchie's grandfather, a Philadelphia banker and partner in J. P. Morgan, picked it up in the early 1900s. It is absolutely vintage—a series of small wooden buildings, seemingly untouched for the last fifty years—as are Ritchie himself, a spry seventy-three-year-old gentleman, and his wife, Pooh. "We've torn down eight buildings, including four sleeping cabins, an icehouse, and a tin-lined storage room, because it was just overwhelming," Ritchie told me as we walked into the exquisite boathouse with Japanese overtones, built circa 1885.

At eight miles long, Upper Saranac is one of the biggest lakes in the northern Adirondacks. Thanks to all its bays and prongs of water, it has thirty-four miles of shoreline, 40 percent of which is owned by the state and is thus "forever wild." There are some 500 camps on the lake, fifty of which are important. "Placid is smaller and doesn't have the depth of tradition," Ritchie told us. "Here there is a core group of fifth-generation families." Placid is also lower-rent: you have the merely rich, rather than the fabulously rich. There is a lot of old wealth on Upper Saranac, not to mention newcomers such as Sandy Weill, chairman and C.E.O. of the Travelers Group. Weill recently bought Camp Green Bay, an elegant complex built in the 1920s, and gave it a complete overhaul that includes an indoor swimming pool.

Ritchie took us out on the lake, where we passed the site of the Saranac Inn, a huge, white clapboard structure that burned to the ground in 1976. The inn had attracted every president from 1900 through F.D.R., and the Hollywood crowd, including Bing Crosby, Bob Hope, and Errol Flynn, in the 1930s. "We were playing tennis when the fire erupted," Ritchie recalled. He also pointed out Prospect Point, built by Adolph Lewisohn. The nonferrous-metals king is reputed to have spent $2.5 million on it between 1903 and 1930. The camp is one of the several masterpieces built by William H. Coulter on Upper Saranac Lake. A consumptive who had worked in a New York architecture firm, Coulter came up in 1896; in those days, fresh air was the only known therapy, and the pure, pinescented air of the northern forest was believed to have special medicinal properties. For Lewisohn, Coulter designed what *Town & Country* in 1904 called "a quaint lodge in the country." Actually, it is a king-size Germanic stone-and-timber chalet whose hulking silhouette we could barely make out among some tall pines. From the lake you can tell the presence of the camps only from the pines planted 120 years ago to hide them, Ritchie explained—and of course from their boathouses. Lewisohn's boathouse is a gem, with Coulter's signature diamond windowpanes and gable ends papered with white birch framed by split-hemlock faux beams, making it look like a rustic Tudor. Just south on the lake was Coulter's equally imposing confection for financier Otto Kahn.

Ritchie showed us the Point, the former Camp Wonundra, commissioned in the late 1930s by William Rockefeller from William Distin, the top second-generation camp architect. Ritchie claimed that Rockefeller's only instructions to Distin were "I know you have a dream house. Build it for me." Today the nine-building compound is a Relais & Chateaux resort. For $ 1,300 a night, a couple can cruise around in a Chris-Craft, drink Dom Perignon, and live like a Rockefeller in camp circa 1930. "They really do a bang-up job," Ritchie said.

• • •

The penultimate Saturday of the season, the one before Labor Day weekend, found Jonathan and me and one of my sons sitting on a dock and watching the Idems Race on Upper St. Regis Lake, the nobbiest of all the lakes. The Idems (Latin for "same") are one of the oldest one-design (meaning you're not allowed to alter the design) sailboats still being raced in the United States. Designed by the naval architect Clinton Crane in 1899, these elegant yachts are thirty-two feet long but have only nineteen feet in the water, and a big gaff-rigged mainsail on a tall, hollow wooden mast. Seven of the original twelve Idems were in the race. Their crews, each usually from a single camp, sail for blood. It's a small lake with lots of islands, very squally, and the wind keeps changing. "Protest flags fly frequently," Ritchie told me, "and occasionally families don't talk for quite some time. There's a man on the sheet, a man on tiller, and a stay person. As you come about, you have to loosen the stay on lee side and tighten the windward one or bust the mast. This is critical."

The Idems rounded a buoy and the leader came right at us, heeling at a 45 degree angle, and at the last second there was a brisk, disciplined rustling of rope and sail, the woman at the tiller plunked her shapely bottom from port to starboard, and they came about.

The next morning St. John's in the Wilderness church was abuzz with chatter about Harlan Crow's post-race party. The lovely stone Episcopal church has a round stained-glass window with an Idem in the center, and it is where the St. Regis set worships. Harlan, the son of the Texas millionaire builder Trammell Crow, had recently bought Topridge, Marjorie Merriweather Post's fabled camp, and had been sinking millions into it. He flew in a bagpipe player and several singers on his private jet to entertain at the party—his way of presenting himself to what Ritchie called "not an easy playground to break into."

An old school friend who summered as a boy in the fifties and sixties on Spitfire Lake, adjacent to St. Regis, recalls "lots of boat races and little activities" and "trying to wrestle bras off girls—a hellish but engaging process. On Wednesday nights Mrs. Post had movies for the kids. We'd all go over in the little ten horsepower boats we'd had since we were fourteen; it would take half an hour." A boatman would help the guests dock at Topridge's boathouse, perhaps the most celebrated

Adirondack rustic structure of all, whose "extraordinary detailing of [cedar] roots, limbs, and twigs . . . surpasses any Durant invention," as Harvey H. Kaiser writes in his book *Great Camps of the Adirondacks.* Its architect was a local builder named Ben Muncil, who also invented "brainstorm," or Adirondack siding—a rustic clapboard that has the wavey edge, the irregular, barked outer surface of the sawed log, still on it. To Ritchie, the boathouse is "an architectural oddity. All the decorative treatment is bentwood, mostly cedar. The railings are all the same and it makes quite an impact."

Then Mrs. Post's guests would take a funicular up a steep slope to the big house. "The main room was stunning," my friend went on. "Mrs. Post had a fine collection of Indian stuff [now at the Smithsonian], including Crazy Horse's warbonnet and kayaks hanging from the ceiling. There was a deck of cards made of human skin, supposedly from scalps, on a side table, and what was reputed to be a stuffed narwhal penis on the mantelpiece. Mrs. Post looked and sailed through life like an empress, but she spoke with a real midwestern snap. One time in the mid-sixties she came to lunch. General Foods [to which Mrs. Post was the heiress] had just come out with a new freeze-dried fruit cereal, and she asked what we thought of it. We said it was perfectly revolting and, in fact, it bombed."

We followed Ransom Duncan, who had been singing in the church choir, in our car to the dock, and got into his breathtaking twenty-eight-foot wooden launch, built in 1909, and sat down in its aging wicker seats. The family flag—a black Maltese cross on a yellow center against a red background—fluttered snappily as we cruised the brilliantly sparkling, wind-whipped Upper St. Regis. Ransom, now in his fifties, is fourth-generation on the lake and a member of the family that manufactured Lea & Perrins Worcestershire sauce in the U.S. In 1984 he left the company, where he was technical director, and is now "fully retired," living in his camp full-time and "trying to keep it from falling in around our ears," as he put it. His wife, Judy, is a Fenn, another old St. Regis family. Theirs is a classic "lake marriage."

St. Regis has some stunners. Pine Tree Point is probably the most architecturally refined camp of them all. Returning from a trip to Japan in 1902, the Frederick Vanderbilts decided that Whiteface Mountain, which can be seen in the distance from the lake, reminded them of Mount Fuji (there is a slight resemblance). So "they hired a bunch of Japanese workers away from one of the world's fairs and Japanned their camp," as Ransom put it. His grandmother recalls that the Vanderbilts even dressed their maids in kimonos. It was from Pine Tree Point that, just before World War II, Standard Oil heir Fred Pratt water-skied in his tuxedo to dinner at Wild Air, the equally sumptuous camp of the Reids, who owned the *New York Herald Tribune.* Supposedly he didn't even get his pant legs wet. The boat dock at Pine Tree Point has the traditional Irimoya roof shape of Japanese temples. Of interest also on the lake were Ransom's great-grandfather's party room on Birch Island, a twenty-by-forty-foot, entirely barked-cedar replica of the Parthenon, and the stone boathouse of the Philadelphia Earles' Camp Katia, which has a series of yurtlike conical roofs.

Milly Duncan, Ransom's mother, took me to Countess Paolozzi's for tea. The countess was born Alice Spaulding to an early Massachusetts family and was an heiress to the United Fruit fortune. She married a titled Italian architect, was one of the founders of the Spoleto Festival with the composer Gian Carlo Menotti, and now lives mostly in New York City. Her daughter Christina was very beautiful and "a bit of a madcap," according to my old school friend. She bared her breasts for *Harper's Bazaar,* which "caused a constant low murmur on the lake through the sixties and resulted in her being dropped from the *Social Register."*

Milly tied her 1940s Century to the dock with what she called "our very nautical knot," a chain of loops that comes apart with a vigorous tug and is peculiar to St. Regis. We found the countess on the porch, a formidable woman "skimming eighty," as she put it, her forearms sheathed in bangles. "I've just come to pay the bills," she told us. "The camp is not open." The countess had been attending an environmental conference in Istanbul.

"My father, William S. Spaulding, had eighteen servants," she recalled. "One man was just for cobwebs. Now there is this great contrast on the lake between the new extremely wealthy and our descendants. Our wealth has been split so many ways that my children are living a very simple life and couldn't afford to keep up a place like this, so I have a problem making out my will. Which of my five boys will I leave this place to? If I leave it to all of them, will each be able to contribute his share of the upkeep?"

We swung down into the South Central Adirondacks—eighty miles southwest of St. Regis—Durant country, where the robber barons had their vast parks. These men were not into community as much as celebrating their self-sufficiency and rugged individualism. Durant sold them on the idea of having baronial estates in the forest commensurate with their consequence. The great camp was a business idea. The land his father had bought was worthless otherwise. In England, Durant had admired the manor houses of the aristocracy. He would make South Central the playground of the rich, ruining himself in the process. He deeded Uncas, the second camp he built, over to J. P. Morgan, possibly to fulfill an obligation on a debt he couldn't pay. After years of neglect it was bought for virtually nothing by a couple who later divorced and divided the buildings and grounds into two hostile sectors.

Uncas, named for the hero of *The Last of the Mohicans*, sits on a peninsula on Mohegan Lake, in pristine wilderness. It was built between 1893 and 1895 from spruce logs which still have their bark on the exterior walls; inside they are hewn plane, with beveled edges and mitered corners, and are finished with beeswax. The ceilings of the main building are oppressively low, with eighteen inch wide logs spaced every three feet for rafters. This is a ceiling you could park a Mack truck on. What grandiosity had produced this heavy-handed bit of Victorian ecological imperialism? we wondered. "Pine Knot and Uncas were the first attempts to create a picturesque aesthetic, a rusticity with all the comforts," Michael Wilson, a historian of the camps, explained. "Historically and culturally we cherish and destroy nature at once. We create the myth of the garden and yet consume it to sustain our style of life. What that ceiling is saying is 'Damn the woods, we've conquered nature.' Getting the biggest and best trees was an extension of the same ethos as filling the rooms with trophy heads and bear rugs."

As Durant's real-estate empire was coming apart—because he had no idea about cash flow and was finally socked with a sensational $750,000 judgment by his sister for mismanaging their father's estate— he built an even greater camp, Sagamore, a few miles away from Uncas, which he ended up selling to Alfred Vanderbilt for far less than it had cost to build. The main building at Sagamore is a gigantic chalet. Vanderbilt had hoped to use the camp as a honeymoon cottage for his wife, Elsie French, but she caught him in a dalliance in his private railroad car. He then married a divorcee, Margaret Emerson, whose father, Isaac, had invented Bromo-Seltzer. Four years later, on May 7, 1915, Alfred went down on the *Lusitania*. Giving his life jacket to a woman, he said to his valet, "Save all the kiddies you can, boy," and that was the last anyone saw of him.

His widow would marry two more times and preside for nearly forty years over an even more elaborate social scene than the also four-times-married Marjorie Post did at Topridge. The guest list at Sagamore included Gene Tierney, Gary Cooper, Eddy Duchin, and Hoagy Carmichael. Dinner was formal; croquet, at which Margaret was nearly unbeatable, was played in whites. Margaret was also fond of shooting skeet off the porch. "I like every game there is," she once told a guest. There is a famous outdoor covered bowling alley and a playhouse, which Alfred had William Coulter design for him in 1901. There Lord Mountbatten and Bobo Rockefeller played roulette and high-stakes poker. A rearing, stuffed crocodile by the Ping-Pong table held a bowl of balls in its claws. The men had their own lodge, the Wigwam, where they caroused and smoked cigars.

In 1947, Margaret bought Uncas from Morgan's heirs, for spillover houseguests. General George Marshall rented the camp in 1949 after hatching the Marshall Plan and hosted Madame Chiang Kai-shek there.

Joe Pierson, who runs Pine Knot, Durant's first camp, as an outdoor education center for the State University of New York College at Cortland, picked us up in his boat at the Raquette dock. Up until World War II, high rollers with camps in South Central would arrive here in their private railroad cars, which they'd boarded at Grand Central Terminal the night before. There were once eleven hotels on Raquette Lake, Pierson told us. In 1877, Durant *père* built, out on a peninsula, the first village in South Central, with the first church and school—Durant, New York. Turning Durant into a model great camp, Pine Knot, was his son William's first project, and it is perhaps the cradle of Adirondack rustic. "By the time he got done," Pierson said, "there were thirty-nine structures, ten of them connected by covered walkways. There was a farm, a lantern house, a blacksmith. This was where Morgan and Vanderbilt were invited and got used to the pristine lifestyle." Durant, in need of funds to build Uncas, sold the camp in 1895 to railroad king Collis P. Huntington, who died there five years later. Huntington's son Archer couldn't bear to return afterward, so Pine Knot sat virtually uninhabited for forty-eight years.

The twigwork under the gable ends of the main building is one of the masterpieces of the style. The upper gable end is sided with a typically English *fin de siècle* sunburst of radiating straight twigs. The lower gable has a lacy screen of cedar bentwood which in the full moon casts a shadow of the initials *WD* onto the floor through a big French window. Inside, the ceiling is white birch bark, which served the dual purpose, Pierson explained, of bringing the outside in and brightening the interior. Pine Knot has the first birch-bark papering and the first knotty-pine interior paneling in the country. Durant's bedroom-and-study cabin, with its wainscoted bathroom, is patterned after his ocean-going yacht, the *Utowana*. Pine Knot is whimsical and enchanting, and it lacks the pomposity of Uncas. The only non-native material used in its construction, Pierson told us, was glass.

We continued south to a 58,300-acre private hunting-and-fishing club near Old Forge, which I agreed not to name. Augustus Shepard, a gifted architect who belonged to the club, designed twenty-nine camps on three of its lakes. He regarded one of them as his masterpiece—Tall Pines, built in 1916, which expanded on six buildings by Stanford White, who was also a member. "Shepard was quite the blade and was well liked by everybody," said Milo Williams, Tall Pines's current owner, who restores guideboats for a living. "Shepard would do a camp, go to Florida for the winter and booze and gamble, then he would have to come back up here and do another one." Williams showed us the Shinto torii door and window lintels and other Orientalia, as well as the birch-barked icehouse.

That evening, at the bar of the club house, also built by Shepard, I struck up a conversation with a young man who had married into one of the club's oldest families, "but they squandered their fortune and lost their camp and now we have to rent a room on the second floor of the clubhouse," he told me. In 1992, Geoffrey Douglas published a harrowing memoir of his parents' disintegration on the lake in the fifties called

Class: The Wreckage of an American Family. Massey Lake, as he disguises the club, was "an enclave of corrupted privilege: backward, incestuous, a confederacy of tortured souls. . . . Half the lake was sleeping with itself. . . . Sex at Massey Lake in the summers of the early fifties, among the nucleus of couples with whom my parents spent their evenings, was a currency of exchange. Sometimes consummated, sometimes leveraged, sometimes only implied, it was the *theme* of those evenings as of a costume ball. It was their point. It was what you got drunk for."

Geoffrey's father, a state politician, swapped wives with the owner of the next camp, a Utica industrialist named Earl. It ended with his mother killing herself with pills, his father marrying Earl's ex-wife, and then Earl putting a pistol to his head in a woodshed above his camp.

The current thinking among scholars of Adirondack rustic style and the great camp is that Durant's status as the creator is exaggerated. The style evolved independently in many places and is indebted as much to the genius of local builders and master carpenters as it is to the camps' architects. One of these carpenters, Donald Beaney, better known by his nickname, Stretch, makes a good case for this. A big fellow, 250 pounds at least, with a walrus mustache, he works for Peter Torrance, the premier rustic-camp builder in the Adirondacks today and the keeper of the tradition. Torrance's camps are aesthetically descended from those built at the turn of the century, but they are fully winterized and have all the modern amenities. Stretch showed me some of the rustic touches he had put on a camp Torrance was building in Keene Valley for a retired New York City couple: birch-barked gable ends with angled hemlock-bark appliqué, a stair of slabs with the wavey edge up instead of down, as is usual, "which gives you something more to look at. To get the bark of the wavey edge to stay on, you cut the tree down in winter and let it lay a season or so. Longer and you start getting the worms and bugs into it and they make beautiful designs. See these scar marks?" He pointed out a delicately worm-eaten log surface.

The spaces between the poles on the upstairs railing had been filled in with what Stretch called "freestyle twigwork. It's just a matter of filling in the void. You look for Y's—crotch branches and stuff. We'll have a big pile to sort through. This one's better here. You can't take too much time thinking about it, because you're not being productive." Stretch was gruffly unsentimental about his twigwork. He would have balked if you had suggested it was art. "We aren't making some kind of statement here," he explained. "We're just trying to transplant Mother Nature."

The Real Adirondacks

The black flies will eat you alive, the natives are hostile, the mountains are low and boring, the trails are muddy and slippery, and the fishing sucks thanks to acid rain. So if I were looking for a place to hike or camp and have a wilderness experience, the last place I'd head for is the Adirondacks. And as a place to live, forget it. The winters are cold and long, the schools are terrible, and about the only place you can get work is in one of our many prisons. The only reason I've been living here for the last ten years is because I can't sell my house. Every morning when I get up I ask myself, what am I doing in this godforsaken forest? So I've made it my personal mission to warn all you downstaters, flatlanders, suburban yuppies, and aging boomers who are thinking of moving up to the country: Don't come to the Adirondacks. Vermont is the place for you. Keep the hell out of here.

As one of my neighbors puts it, Vermont is like Austria, while this side of Lake Champlain is more like Bulgaria. In Vermont everybody is an ex-hippie or a Democrat, and they all drive around in Volvos listening to NPR and shopping at the winery, the cheesery, and the bootery, and it's so quaint and politically correct that you want to barf. Over here, Democrats and ex-hippies are about as common as mountain lions. (There's actually supposed to be a couple of them—cougars, that is—over the mountain from our house.) The native Adirondackers—the mountain people who have been here for generations—are extremely laid-back and would never pass muster in Vermont. They have their old cars and refrigerators and everything else they ever owned in their dooryard, and they haven't finished putting up the siding on their house and probably never will. They're a dying breed; there are only a few families left in our town. I recently asked one of them what his attitude about life was, and he said, "I more or less live day to day and try to figure out how to get the things I want without going into debt or asking anybody for anything."

There's an updated type of native who drives around in a brand new pickup that he keeps spitshined. He has a dish that gets a hundred channels and a lawn that he mows religiously and an American flag that he runs up each morning. He's usually the next generation of the laid-back type and picked up his neatness in the service, or he's got a profession and an image that he has to present. But all of these guys have pretty much the same outlook. Some of them have great senses of humor; others seem to have none at all until you get to know them and discover a wit that's "drier than a popcorn fire," as one man described it. They're sturdy people whose values were forged in a harsh environment and reach back to pioneer days. If one of them dies or burns himself out of his house, the neighbors will pitch in and help. Otherwise, everyone respects each other's space. No one cottons to being told what to do, especially if their property is concerned.

So it comes as no surprise that the zoning restrictions imposed by the Adirondack Park Agency haven't gone over too well with the local population. "The goddam APA," as one man called it, has jurisdiction over what happens within the Blue Line that encloses the Park's six million acres. It controls everything from lakeshore development to the way property can be passed down to your kids. In 1975, someone dumped a truckload of cow manure on the porch of the APA's headquarters in Ray Brook. And in the 1990s, when a commission appointed by then-governor Mario Cuomo proposed even tighter restrictions, a group of protesters blockaded the Northway (the interstate that runs from Albany to Montreal), three APA agents making a site inspection at Black Brook were shot at, and a woman on the APA's board who almost always nixed subdivision proposals had her barn torched in Wadhams. One of our local gas stations put up in its front window a portrait of Cuomo with a toothbrush moustache and labeled it "Adolf Cuomo." But violence is a rare, and I would even say uncharacteristic, response up here. This said, there are pockets of it, like the bleak pass between Keene and Elizabethtown where in the last few years two crusty oldtimers have been murdered. The first was killed by a drifter who saw him flashing a bankroll in a nearby bar, the second in mid-January by his twenty-five-year-old grandson who, according to local speculation, may have been suffering from "a very nasty case of cabin fever."

Forty-two percent of the land within the Blue Line is state-owned and "forever wild." You can't even cut a tree without a special act of the state legislature. The rest of the Park is a patchwork of private property. It's the biggest park east of the Mississippi, bigger than Yellowstone, Yosemite, and Glacier national parks combined, and it's the country's longest-standing experiment in letting people live in a wilderness preserve (the original legislation dates to 1885), which is what makes it so interesting. Not that there is any reason to come here.

"The whole point about this place is to keep it secret," a resident of Upper St. Regis Lake, the snootiest and most exclusive of the Adirondacks' summer communities, told me recently. There are class tensions between the summer people (some of whom have been coming up for five generations) and the locals who have to work for them ("pissing in the soup" as a friend describes it), but the one thing everyone agrees on is that we want to keep the place for ourselves. If the Adirondacks are underappreciated, that's just great.

Our property, at the foot of Crane Mountain, backs up on 14,000 acres of state land. We have bears, coyotes, ermines, peregrine falcons, ravens, luna moths, five kinds of delicious Boletus mushrooms, a rare fern, tiny birds called kinglets, and practically invisible butterflies called ringlets, all within a hundred yards of the house; and 90 million people live within a day's drive. Every few months an impressive act of nature will happen to put us in our place, reminding us that its forces are still in control up here. Three Februaries back, a blizzard drifted over our second-story deck, and we were trapped for three days until Ray Manley came up with his bulldozer and dug us out. But this was nothing compared to the blowdown of July 15th, 1995, when a *derecho,* a rare straight-line windstorm with gales of 100 miles an hour and more, knocked down in less than half an hour the trees in a swath of nearly 100,000 acres, mostly in the remote northwestern Oswegatchie basin. Towns like Star Lake were cut off for days. There ensued a bitter debate about whether the felled timber should be salvaged or left to return to the ecology. The environmental groups favored the latter course of action, or inaction, and found an unexpected ally in the pulp and paper industry, which was concerned that the timber would flood the market, and they prevailed.

The Oswegatchie basin includes 50,000 acres of old-growth pine and spruce that were hit hard; long considered one of the wildest and gloomiest parts of the Adirondacks, it is now even more so. You can canoe for days back in there without running into anything human.

Dead wood is a big part of the forest landscape. Maybe a third of the balsams on my land have been knocked over by wind storms or snapped by ice storms over the years. But that just opens space for seedlings. At Christmas, you look for double-needle balsams (most are single-needle). They make the best Christmas trees.

Then there are the smaller acts of nature, which can wreak serious havoc on your career and your appliances. One morning I was clattering away on my lap-top on deadline for a slick New York City magazine when suddenly the power failed and I lost the whole story. A beaver, it turned out, had dropped a poplar tree over a power line down in the valley, plunging us back into the pre-Edison era for a couple of hours. Poplars, by the way, are known locally as "popples." There are four species in these parts. One is known as "Bommagilia" (for Balm of Gilead, a reference to its nice-smelling buds). I'm always on the lookout for local lingo, of which there isn't a whole lot left at this point. The Adirondack twang is subtler than the grating ones of Vermont, New Hampshire, and Maine, and it takes a while to develop an ear for it. A lot of men have this deep, gruff way of talking so you can hardly make out what they're saying. Sometimes you'll catch an old-timer saying "eaves-trough" instead of gutter, or "I be" for "I am." "Jeezam Crow" is the big North Country swear word; the name of the Lord isn't taken in vain up here the way it is downstate. We're too smart for that. Clyde Rabideau, the mayor of Plattsburgh, our biggest town, has a Jeezam Crow award that he gives every week to an Adirondacker who did something positive for a change. The winner is announced over the radio and can stop by Rabideau's convenience store and pick up his or her prize, a free T-shirt or a touque, which is French-Canadian-Northern-Adirondack for a woolen ski-hat. Everyone perfects his own personal slant to his touque.

Not long ago I called the mayor's office and Rabideau himself answered. I like a mayor who answers his own phone. He told me a lot of locals around Plattsburgh and over to Tupper Lake are of French-Canadian descent, and though they don't speak French anymore they still use French reflexive grammar, as in, "Hey, I remember dat, me," or "You got any more wine, you?" Then he faxed me a hilarious memoir he had written about his *grandpère*, Médor Rabideau, a trapper who used to brew his own dandelion wine. Farther south, by the time you get to Elizabethtown or Keene, the French component is vestigial. It only survives in local surnames like Jacques, LeClair, and Gagnon, and some of the people who bear them look kind of French. The best French-Canadian Adirondack fiddler, by the way, Donnie Perkins, works at Wendy's in Plattsburgh.

Back to the subject of acts of nature (that's another thing that happens if you live in the North Country long enough: you start to digress): Last summer, lightning struck a pole halfway up the hill, traveled up my phone line, and fried my computer. I'd just gotten on the Internet, and so far that's the only significant thing I've gotten from it. I should have learned my lesson, because the summer before I'd lost a TV and two phones the same way, but I didn't.

Probably our most characteristic and awesome natural phenomenon, however, are the slides. A lot of the High Peaks—Dix, Gothics, Giant, Whiteface, and, of course, Big Slide—have them. There's a new slide on Kilbourne, a foothill of the Sentinel Range outside of Lake Placid. To get there (not that I'm suggesting anything), you take the Lake Placid-Wilmington road, park at the plaque commemorating the founding of the Forest Preserve, pick up a herdpath across the road that will soon take you to an old lumber road on which you hang a left, and walk for fifteen minutes through bug- and nettle-infested jungle until you get to a streambed choked with an avalanche of tree trunks, boulders, root systems, and soil. It's a scene of incredible devastation, believe me. Then you make your way up the streambed to a thousand feet of sheer naked bedrock where the stuff used to be growing, until it was loosened by pounding rain and came crashing down. The bedrock is billion-year-old anorthosite, a form of granite unique to the Adirondacks but one of the major components of the moon and some of the oldest rock on earth. About five million years ago, it erupted through the Appalachians in a dome about 160 miles in diameter roughly centered on

Blue Mountain Lake. From the streambed, you can bushwhack over to Copperas Pond, which is a nice place to swim. This takes about half an hour unless you get lost or run into a pack of wild dogs, which you probably will.

I'll tell you two more beautiful hikes, if hike you must, and that's all you're going to get out of me. For the first one, you need two cars and some partners. One group parks at Newcomb and the other at Adirondack Loj, and you both make for Indian Pass. You can meet for lunch and swap keys at Scott's Clearing, a big old clearing left when a beaver dam went out a while ago. Or you might want to go up to Avalanche Pass, which offers some of the most dramatic mountain scenery this side of Yosemite, and climb Colden Dike up to the top of Colden. This is one of the most spectacular climbs in the Adirondacks, but it's a bit hairy in a few places, and if you fall to your death, don't blame me.

The Adirondack Museum in Blue Mountain Lake is one of the finest regional museums in the country. It has some of the most beautiful guideboats, old wooden motor launches, Rushton canoes, and Adirondack chairs ever made. There's Sunset Cottage, a masterpiece of mosaic twigwork from Whitney Park, the private 55,000-acre compound now run by the flamboyant heiress Marylou Whitney (who said at the cottage's dedication that it was where everybody changed into their bathing suits and that she was sure her late husband Sonny had made love to a lot of women in it before she got involved with him). The museum also has the private railroad car of one of the robber barons, among them J. P. Morgan and various Vanderbilts, who built palatial rustic camps on remote lakes in the forest and entertained in black tie.

If the museum is the center of scholarship on the Adirondacks, Burdick's Chain Saws in Jay is where I'd go to get a blast of the local culture. Dale Burdick, who runs the place with his wife, Joy, blows away Leno and Letterman as a stand-up comic in my and a lot of other people's opinions. Bernie Rosio sharpens the chains and has one of those deep, gruff deliveries you can barely understand. I asked him one time where he was from and he answered with two bullfrog croaks. Finally it sank in that he had said "Black Brook."

There's always a lively scene at Burdick's. Two gents with their touques slanted just so stop in for coffee most mornings. One time I met two guys from deep in the northern Catskills who had come up to roast a pig for a wedding. Another time a Lenape Delaware Indian came down from Port Kent with an old beat-up Stihl.

"I need a new blade," he told Bernie.

"You need a new saw, that's what you need," Bernie told him after looking at it.

"I need money, that's what I need," the Indian said.

"Can't help ya with that," Bernie said.

It took several visits before I heard a joke from Dale that was printable, and it wasn't even a joke, it was something that happened: the day Ralph LeClair, who is no longer with us, God rest his soul, lost his favorite dog and his wife asked him for a divorce. Ralph picked up the dog, which was a beagle and had been hit by a truck, off the road, and when he got into the house, his wife had coincidentally just happened to decide that she'd had it with their fifty-some-year marriage and wanted out. "Look, I just lost the best dog I ever had," Ralph told her when she informed him of her decision. "Quit trying to cheer me up."

When deer season comes, "I let all my men out and they all try to kill something with fur," Dale told me. Getting your deer is the defining ritual of the Adirondacks. Between the 24th of October and the first Sunday in December half the work force goes on unemployment, and if you have a problem with your plumbing or electric, you have to fix it yourself, because pretty near every able-bodied local tradesman is in his hunting camp. Until a few years back, the high schools used to let out every boy over fourteen so he could get his deer.

"It's what you looked forward to all year," one of the many Smiths in our valley, who took me into his camp, told me. "Just being back in camp and going hunting." The Smiths were Scots-Canadian and came up the Ausable River from Lake Champlain with the first settlers in 1816. Bucky, as I'll call him, has a full beard and speaks real old-timey: He drinks woine," goes for a "hoike," and abhors "voiolence."

"Long as I can remember, there was the tradition of going into camp," he told me. "You're jess born into it. My dad had me hunting partridge, rabbits, and squirrels when I was eight year old." Bucky's sons are still in town, but they don't go into the woods much, "because they're too busy doing other things." But the ritual of getting your deer is still going strong, even if it has undergone some recent modifications. The modern hunter rides into camp like Rambo, in a four-wheeler with a plastic scabbard for his gun. Some camps have TV. If you don't get your deer, it isn't the end of the world. You play poker and drink with your buddies. "Getting drunk is the true meaning of deer season," says Dale Burdick. And as anyone can tell you, more deer get shot in the bars than out in the woods.

Bucky's dad and his uncle built the camp in the 1940s on land they had leased for ninety years from Finch, Pruyn, the paper company, which sold the land to the state. The state is still honoring the lease, which has forty years to go, so this is a legal camp on state land. There are others that aren't legal. They're known as "outlaw camps." As we bushwhacked up to the camp, we kept passing deer runways with fresh prints, some of them big. Bucky said he'd never seen so many deer as there were this year. "If you know the runs, there's not much of a trick to killing 'em. It's just being there at the right time. I don't shoot anything under ten point. I seen three that were presentable this fall." Bucky doesn't shoot black bear any more either, and he doesn't trap fisher cats and pine martens, which is how he supported himself when he came home from Korea in 1959, because the money you get for their skins isn't worth killing them, and there are so few of them now that it doesn't feel right. Bucky still spends several hours a day wandering in the woods, as I do, collecting useless bits of information like the location of seasonal springs. He knows his trees and shrubs cold—hardhack (ironwood), the preferred wood for ax handles, and the three kinds of "shumack."

The camp, named Hedgehog Den, was a gem, ten by fifteen feet, with six bunks and a woodstove. It had nearly been washed away by the floods a month earlier. That was last year's exciting act of nature—the worst floods in the Adirondacks' recorded history. It started raining buckets on Friday, November 11, and when it finally let up the next morning, bridges had been swept away, roads were gone, and places like Peasleeville and Black Brook were completely cut off. The damage in Essex County alone was estimated in the millions. "The flooding raised hell with the hunting," Bucky told me. "Everybody had to come out and see if his house was still there."

We walked down the brook and an hour later we were drinking beers in Bucky's brother Ronnie's living room. Ronnie had just retired from the Air Force, and he was devoting his retirement to golf. You wouldn't think the Ads (as some of us call them; others call them the Dacks) would be a golfer's paradise, but they boast some of the oldest and most scenic courses in the country. I've played most of them (there are more than forty open to the public) and these are my favorites: the East Course of Malone, Saranac Inn, Whiteface Inn, the Lake Placid Lower, Craig Wood, Westport, Sagamore, and Thendara, and in the nine-hole category, the Ausable Club, the Barracks and Top o' the World. Some of the courses have resident red foxes that follow you around and take an interest in the game, curling up below the tee and almost seeming to roll their eyes when you slice into the woods. A few years ago I smacked a career drive on the sixth hole at Craig Wood, and a fox pup ran out on the fairway and took off with my ball.

The drive from Keene to Lake Placid through the Cascades Lakes is one of the most scenic stretches of highway in the Ads. Rock climbers this July morning are clinging to the cliffs of Pitchoff, off to the right. (Chapel Pond Slab and Poke-O-Moonshine are the other climbing meccas.) The hiking trail up Pitchoff takes forty-five minutes. Two huge erratics, or boulders deposited by a long-gone glacier, are poised on the summit. The flumes—cuts of water through tilted, fractured strata—are another of our natural wonders. Krummholz—the stunted, impenetrably dense balsam-fir forest near the summits of the forty-three "High Peaks" over 4,000 feet—are our most singular vegetation type. There was an old Indian named Henry Nolat who lived in a one-room shanty at the foot of Pitchoff until he died a few years ago. Nolat had long streaming hair and knew the mushrooms, and he used to go up on Pitchoff and cut the inner bark of black ashes into strips of bast that he wove into pack baskets, which is one of our indigenous Adirondack crafts.

I pass a neighbor in his pickup, and we greet each other by raising the first fingers of our right hand off our steering wheels, in keeping with the local etiquette. Half an hour later, I am driving through Saranac Lake, which is very funky and has seen better days like a number of our bigger towns (Port Henry and Malone also come to mind) and is a good example of the habitat a friend calls "deep dark New York." During Prohibition, Saranac Lake was a thriving center for Canadian bootleggers, and it is still full of bars. The liveliest one, the Water Hole, has live music on weekends. Last Saturday, a black woman who had come up from Virginia with her bass player and her drummer played electric guitar and belted out the blues in a style between Lightnin' Hopkins and B. B. King, while several derelict long-haired mountain-men types whirled around on the dance floor like dervishes.

I stop at Chuck Jessie's studio to check out his latest collection of chandeliers, lamps, chairs, and coffee tables, which he makes from tree burls and the antlers of deer and elk. Chuck is Adirondack born and raised, and is a retired Navy Seal. He built his chalet, on a little lake, completely from scavenged wood, but you wouldn't know it because the craftsmanship is so superb. Chuck built his dream camp in his head as he lay awake on long, dark nights in Vietnam. He embodies the Adirondacks' self-sufficient ethos and self-taught creativity as well as anyone I know; and if you want to see his stuff and meet the real deal, give him a call.

I pass a house that had just burned to the ground. The impact of fire, accidental and otherwise, on the North Country's real estate has been horrendous. Most of the grand old hotels and the finest rustic great camps have gone up in smoke, their existence documented only in photographs. Someone, perhaps a disgruntled former employee, has been torching the buildings of the old Lake Placid Club one by one over the last few years, and the local police haven't been able to nail him. I know of one man who burned himself and his wife and their thirteen children out of five houses before he died a few years ago; he kept heating them with green wood that gunked up the chimneys with creosote.

Continuing up to Gabriels, I take the road to a remote outpost in the hinterland called Onchiota, "where the men are men and the sheep are scared," as Dale Burdick jokes. The center of Onchiota consists of little more than an establishment nicknamed Blood, Sweat and Beers, Inc., which used to be a grocery store until Hayden "Bing" Tormey, the guy who owned it, retired. He keeps his tools there now and uses the place as a workshop, and locals still come in to gossip and pass the time. On the way out of town a sign says "Leaving 67 of the Friendliest People in the Adirondacks (Plus a Couple of Soreheads)." This is a little more hospitable than a sign in the equally remote and tiny Hawkeye (down the road a piece from Swastika) that says "We Shoot Every Third Visitor and the Second One Just Left."

If you take a left at Onchiota, there is a nineteen-mile loop my son and I took on bicycles one time through backwoods with lots of lakes that are drained by the Saranac River. Just as you are about to cross a bridge over the river, there is a spring off to the right where you can stop and drink some famously pure and refreshing water gushing out of a pipe. The halfway point of the loop is Loon Lake (not the one in E. L. Doctorow's novel, which is a composite of several different lakes in the central Ads), a once-exclusive summer colony with a golf course that has fallen on hard times. Some of the buildings were designed by Stanford White and are in various states of dilapidation and restoration. On the way back, you pick up Route 3 at Merrill Corners, and after a mile or so you hang a right, which will take you back to Onchiota. While you're there, you want to stop at the Six Nations Museum, created and run by an Iroquois family who care deeply about their heritage and offer one of the most authentic Native American experiences available to the casual tourist that I've ever encountered in my travels. The Iroquois called the Algonquins, who hunted in the Ads in the summer, the Anaducksue, which means Bark Eaters and was not complimentary (the implication being that they were lousy hunters). A great battle between the two nations was fought at the mouth of the Oswego River, as told in a seventy-five-foot-long band of pictographs circling the walls in the museum that is the longest piece of beadwork in the world.

No one lived full-time in the Ads until the white man came. It was a zone of peace, and even after the white man came people were basically supportive of each other because they never knew when they might need each other's help. My theory is that the harsh environment, where the temperature can swing eighty degrees in twenty-four hours, has had an equalizing and harmonizing effect on the people, and this is where the live-and-let-live attitude that is the essence of the local culture came from. But I don't feel like I really have a handle on this place. Maybe my grandchildren will, if they choose to live here, and I wouldn't wish that on anyone.

Natalia Rachel Singer

Not unlike a good many writers in the region, Natalia Rachel Singer is particularly engaged by issues surrounding people and wilderness in the Adirondacks and North Country of New York State. What makes her voice distinct is a lyricism born of a training in the tradition of American letters. A professor of English at St. Lawrence University in Canton, New York, Singer teaches creative writing and contemporary environmental literature.

Her fiction and nonfiction have appeared in numerous magazines and journals, including Harpers, Redbook, Ms., The Iowa Review, and The North American Review. Most recently, she is the editor, with Neal Burdick, of North Country: Essays on Life and Landscape in Northern New York (North Country Books, 2000).

The essay reprinted here first appeared in 1996 in Adirondac, the magazine of the Adirondack Mountain Club.

A Girl in Winter

One recent January a group of colleagues and I took a trip to the Adirondacks to spend some time discussing outdoor education. Our destination was the Sagamore Institute near Raquette Lake, where William West Durant, the son of a robber baron, built a Great Camp which the great-grandson of another robber baron, Alfred Gwynne Vanderbilt, turned into the most luxuriant and well-staffed wilderness resort in the world. I had been there a year before with mostly the same group, and we had enjoyed the well-groomed cross-country ski trails, our contact with the friendly staff, the lectures on natural history, and the delicious healthy food. I was looking for some quiet, and I couldn't wait to slip on my snowshoes and leave the cares of the world behind.

On our way to our retreat, we hiked up Blue Mountain in order to have an "authentic" wilderness experience to reflect on later, around the fireplace. Stocked with notebooks, Polaroids and Chunky bars, we skied up as far as we could, then switched to snowshoes. The sky was blue behind the line of iced firs, and the birches and pines were canopied with snow. In my endorphin-induced euphoria, the trees looked to me like cheerful villagers piling white baskets of feathers upon their heads.

When we got to the top, we drank hot soup from our thermoses and peered down on the world. There was nothing to see but sky and trees and a thin strip of road wrapping itself around the landscape like ribbon. Civilization and its discontents seemed miles—lifetimes—away, and as I slid my way back down, I realized that the exertion of climbing and focusing on each step had kept my mind clean of worries as though an eraser made of snow had wiped my brain empty.

We would remember this moment as the high of our retreat. On the same afternoon we were to encounter a new and very public manifestation of everyone's most terrifying nightmare. Perhaps we should have stayed on top of the mountain a little longer and basked in our optimism.

Famished for dinner and eager to be warm again, my colleague Bruce and I drove into the Sagamore entrance, only to be greeted by the state police. It occurred to us that they might be looking for someone— a fugitive—and that we'd taken the wrong turn onto someone's private road. When we made our way to the main lodge to check in, our hostess told us quietly and grimly that the police were here to dig for the body of the twelve-year-old Sara Ann Wood, the girl who had been kidnapped near Utica the previous summer and whose eyes had haunted me from posters in every airport and post office I'd visited since.

We found out later that Sara Ann Wood's father was staying at Sagamore as well, and as we sat together at meals in the days ahead, discussing our misgivings about the nature-versus-culture dichotomy and post-modernism's impact on the topic, we furtively scanned the faces of the other lodgers for someone's downcast eyes. The staff must have fed Mr. Wood privately in his room, because we saw no trace of him, but we did see a lot of state troopers—a room full of them, to be precise, with badges gleaming, their guns bulging from their belts. Our conversations must have puzzled them, but no more than theirs puzzled us. They were waiting for the big machine to be shipped up from the World Trade Center to replace the more primitive back hoe as they sifted through the frozen earth in search of evidence.

Outside, the bent trees with their babushkas of snow assumed a posture of mourning. Skiing, all I could see were human-like shapes in the wood, the heads bent in grief. And at night, as we drank cognac shots and beer and discussed the tendency of some of us—especially this writer—to anthropomorphize what we see in nature, I couldn't forget that everyone in our group was a parent, and that somewhere, in the main lodge, a father was kneeling by his bed on the hardwood floor and praying.

The last morning before we left I went for a walk alone and followed a ski trail where our informative nature guide, Shelly, had led us animal tracking the day before. Shelly's natural history lesson had actually been a social history lesson, because every tree she pointed out was second growth, or third, and no one, not even the former owners of the Great Camp, had recorded what the Iroquois saw in the forest before the mining and lumber and paper companies stripped 96 percent of it away. I couldn't help but think of our connection to the natural world as the work of a team of serial killers—New York State government repaying its Oneida allies by taking the Adirondacks from them and paying them less than a cent per acre, loggers ravaging the forests and creating soil erosion and siltation of streams, the industries from the Gilded Age to the present leaving behind their legacy in acid rain. I considered the Durants, the Vanderbilts; somehow Sagamore's rich and very American history seemed culpable as well. These robber barons were responsible for bringing the nation's first electricity to the Adirondacks, as well as train carloads of wealthy Manhattan men, up for "gaming" and smoking cigars.

And yet as much as I wanted to condemn the mentality that has made the natural world an object of conspicuous consumption, it was hard not to be impressed with the men's ingenuity and optimism, their faith in technology, their sheer pluckiness. They built their lodges to look like Swiss chalets, always with the idea that no matter how many trees they felled, there were plenty more where those came from. How had our American aristocracy treated the Sagamore staff, I wondered. Were they kind to those skilled craftsmen who built the fireplaces carefully stone by stone, to the daughters who folded laundry and monitored the ice house, to the caretaker's girls who studied spelling in the old schoolhouse? How had America's richest families treated their own daughters?

As I walked along the old logging path, I said a prayer for the family of Sara Ann Wood, and for all the families who have lost their children, and for all the children who have been damaged by their own families and are still not protected by the law. The trail opened up to a large clearing where only one old tree stood watch—a yellow birch, its bark stripped along the base—among a batch of adolescents: some young maple, white pine, and stands of scrappy cherry trees, known for their ability to survive after a forest's devastation and the erosion of a forest bed. Perhaps I should have seen these young cherries as a positive sign, a symbol of rebirth after death, but all I could think of was how much prettier the trail would be if there were trees everywhere, and how the empty spaces made me feel somehow afraid.

When we left that afternoon there were TV crews crowding the roads, and I wondered what I would say if someone asked us to offer our opinions. The earth where the police were working was ravaged, churned up, the dirty snow piled in twiggy clumps around molding stumps of swamp maple and balsam plucked free of their roots. It was snowing heavily, and the weather forecast promised more freezing cold. It struck me as a sad state of affairs that after 100 years of preserving the Adirondacks, the wilderness was, on that particular day, just a good place to hide a girl's body. We drove home silently, watching the school buses drop off children and thinking how trusting we are just to leave our homes sometimes and walk in the open air. The snow fell on the landscape indifferently—over the body of Sara Ann Wood (if it was, indeed, in the vicinity), over the tracks I'd made that morning and the ski tracks up Blue Mountain—burying all of it, even our rich and complex social history, beneath its weight.

Mason Smith

As a working writer and boatbuilder, Mason Smith knows a good deal about joinery. Putting together words or wood while highlighting both form and function has been a passion for much of his life. Smith has advanced degrees in creative writing and English and American literature from Stanford. His creative nonfiction has been published widely, from Gray's Sporting Journal *to* Adirondack Life.

The works included here, "You Hear Loons Calling" (1975) and "Lone Watch in a Gold-Fobbed Forest" (1974), first appeared in Sports Illustrated.

Smith and his wife, Hallie Bond, author of the seminal Boats and Boating in the Adirondacks, *live year-round in Long Lake, New York.*

You Hear Loons Calling

What was the good of it, hunting up obsolete tools and materials that were already scarce sixty years ago, artificially aging your viewpoint, spending about a year learning how to build, and building just one of what you maybe couldn't sell at the price you'd need to live? Then taking a maiden voyage on a stream that would certainly beat it up and maybe break it up?

But when we dropped the handmade canoe into the head-waters, with four days on the best wilderness river left in the Adirondacks ahead—wild trout, unspoiled country, seven carries—it felt as good as if we'd clinched all 2,000 copper nails at one crack. We were making such satisfactory connections: with the Adirondack tradition of travel by water, with the nineteenth-century craftsmanship of J. Henry Rushton, with the source of the river that clatters all winter through our frozen towns down below. This was a lap joint in time, as if the two centuries had been riveted together at their '70s.

July. The water was low. The headwaters were cold and clear, smoke tinted in the deeper places, hueless over the brassy shoals. Brook trout panicked at all angles from underwater grasses that rose from the gravel and flattened along the surface. Often the stream narrowed to a rock pile, or the alders nearly closed it off or a cedar had grown clear across. With woven pack baskets and us aboard, the boat drew five or six inches. The brand-new varnish touched bottom. Half of the time we were in the water, nursing the little cedar boat along. We brought sneakerfuls of water with us when we got back in.

Grasses, trees, sun, water, sky. We had to get over the pang of not taking pictures continually. Had to look at the treasure chest of stream bed and say, "I guess I won't ship that to a museum." Everything we saw was going to be just like the Dewar's in the only bottle of whiskey we were carrying. Gone when gone.

Then suddenly I saw something. A reflection too long and straight, a color too dark green—another bottle, bedded almost completely in the gravel. Only a finger's width was showing.

Not trash. We were too far up, on an estate where the water probably isn't even poached. We paddled back. I put a leg over and stooped to pull the bottle up. It was an old one, hand blown, seamless, irregular in thickness inside its simple form, with a few tiny bubbles and silver darts in its smoky green glass. A rounded lip, tapered inside for a cork. We pictured some swank angler in the '90s, toasting a two-pound speckle with a European wine from a shaded hamper. I rinsed out the gravel and my brother stuck the bottle in one of the pack baskets. That was one thing it seemed all right to snitch. We could let it fill with associations while the other emptied of whiskey.

In the Adirondacks everybody knows the portable rowing skiff called Long Laker or Saranac Laker or simply the Adirondack guideboat, evolved and patiently built in the long winters by the woodsmen who would use it to carry gentlemen through the wilderness after trout and venison and the supposedly curative forest air. It is one of America's nicest creations, equal to, say, the Morgan horse minus the long feet and weighted shoes of the foppish present-day breed. Durable, fast, versatile, graceful, light, even prepotent, true to type: it is instantly recognizable with its tumble home ends, its smooth pine skin laid up on delicate, anthropomorphic ribs cut from naturally curved spruce or tamarack crooks.

But hardly anybody even knows what the word canoe *meant* in the last century, what it meant for the first twenty years the American Canoe Association existed. The principal features of the canoes of the 1870s and later were derived not from the Indian birchbark (open, with minuscule decks and high-pointed ends), but from the Eskimo kayak and the log dugout; and not by white Americans applying modern techniques and materials to the native craft but by our copying the copying of certain Britons. Particularly John MacGregor, a proselytizing advocate of muscular Christianity who brought European boatbuilding to these native forms and made the resulting *Rob Roys* famous through books about his solo voyages in them—on the Rhine, on the Baltic, in the Middle East. He helped form the Royal Canoe Club in 1866, and some Anglophile New Yorkers copied *that* in 1871. They imported their first boats or had American builders work to English plans. Soon their builders tried ideas of their own, and vied with the English to perfect and popularize what were called cruising canoes.

These were slender, shallow, usually lapstrake, decked, with a cockpit, and most often set up to paddle and sail. Small as they were they had flotation chambers, dry storage, and room to sleep in: miniature yachts. They were very well suited for exploration of the myriad remote waterways within the now-closed frontier, and right away were taken on much-publicized expeditions to find the sources of the Mississippi and Columbia, for example, and run these rivers to the sea.

Canoeing was one of those new sports, baseball and football among them, which simultaneously started up around the 1870s when the country rather suddenly found itself peaceful and prosperous enough to need something besides fist-fighting and horse racing. The art of designing and building the canoes flourished for twenty years. Then came the depression of '93, the bicycle craze of '96, the cheaper open canoe that could be mass produced, and now the immortal uglies, the immoral maintenance-free. The gallant wooden lapstrake cruiser is a thing of the past.

So it was the only thing to take us down this river. We couldn't bring hackwork or plastic or aluminum up here. Suppose we met a troll, or a snowy egret, or some other Representative of the Owners? "Riding in something that just does the job, huh? Needs no care, huh? Only cost you a week's wages, huh? *No fishing.*"

"Look!"

Alders dipping into the water at the inside brink of a rocky bend made a sort of shady veranda for a houseful of gaudy trout. One, two, three, four, five, too many to count, mature brook trout well over a foot long moved out and paraded downstream beside us, fully exposed in the sun, their red and blue and gold spots, their black and white and red fins piercingly displayed.

"Did y——! How m——! What do you call that?"

"There they are again!"

As we moved through the tail of the bend we met them going back indoors. What sauce. We stopped. But it must be that I still did not believe we deserved them. "We'll never touch them," I said.

"Why do you say that?"

"Never touch them." I put on a Royal Coachman, dry.

"Why the pessimism?"

"It isn't pessimism."

The leader floated in a rueful meniscus, dappling the bottom with a shadow like linked sausages. Nevertheless, something revolved in the water. There was no resistance when I lifted the rod. The Coachman was gone.

In 1880 a frail, diminutive shoemaker from Pennsylvania named George Washington Sears decided to make his first trip to the Adirondacks. He was an outdoorsman, soon to be famous as the author of *Woodcraft* and several series of letters on his wilderness solos published in *Forest and Stream* under the pseudonym Nessmuk. He didn't intend to see the Adirondacks from the stern of a guide-boat. He was going alone, and since he weighed only 105 pounds, he needed the lightest, finest canoe he could get. He studied the work of the best canoe builders of the day and satisfied himself that J. Henry Rushton of Canton, New York, was the only man to build it. Rushton came up with a ten-footer under eighteen pounds painted; the next year, one of less than sixteen. Nessmuk named his third Rushton canoe after Dickens' voluble nurse who took no water. It weighed just ten and a half pounds. The Adirondack Museum displays it now: the *Sairy Gamp*. Partly through Nessmuk's encomiums in *Forest and Stream*, Rushton became the most famous canoe builder in all the country.

Raised in a remote village on the northwestern fringe of the Adirondacks, at thirty Rushton had not been much of a success at anything but good fellowship. Single, without capital, in poor health. He borrowed a set of forms and built himself a boat to take to the woods in hope of getting the better of his persistent dry cough. Somebody bought the boat. In 1880 he signed the charter of the American Canoe Association on Lake George, one of two builders among the rich sports. In 1886, in a sort of miniature America's Cup race, his *Vesper* sailed rings around the English boats, decisively repatriating the North American native craft's development.

There is a grand collection of Rushtons at the Adirondack Museum at Blue Mountain Lake. They pull at you. The long slender planks of white cedar, beautifully darkened with age, their clear grains in delicate tension with the lines sweeping up to curved stems unconsciously perfect; the intimate, accurate nailing, every inch along every seam, each nail in vertical line with others from gunwale to keel; the joints fitted impossibly tight along those varying curves; the absence of heavy timbers, instead the multiple fine thin ribs only two or three inches apart. You hear loons calling, just looking at those boats. You think you could make one the way Henry James said you could write a novel: it is "too difficult indeed; but there is only one way to master it, which is to pretend consistently that it isn't."

My brother Everett was convinced people would pay the builder of such things a living wage. He read the Adirondack Museum book about Rushton with appendixes by Rushton's son Harry, describing construction methods. He read Stephens' standard *Canoe and Boat Building for Amateurs* (1885), subscribed to *National Fisherman*, talked to John Gardner, assistant curator for small-craft studies at Mystic Seaport. He hung around the museum looking at plans and drawings and an ingenious tiltable bed piece on which molds for a hull could be fastened. He wrote all over the eastern United States and England and Canada to locate copper nails in various sizes.

White cedar was not to be had. It grows plentifully in northern New York, practically a weed, but the big trees you need for clear, vertical grain planking are all gone. He bought yellow cedar, which came from the Oregon coast. He bought oak, too, for keel and gunwales; the other woods—red elm for ribs and tamarack for stems—he went out and found, hauled, had locally sawn.

Most boats are born dead: skeletons first, decently covered, then launched in a ceremony like burial at sea that tosses them back up alive. A lapstrake canoe is a shape before it is a structure, a usable boat before the first rib is put in. Once the keel and stems are in place on the forms, the planks are attached to each other, acquiring strength like an eggshell's, a dome's, a fender's.

Each plank is spiled, cut out oversize to a curve that will allow it to bend into place without edgewise springing and show a fair catenary line from stem to stem; resawed into an identical pair, planed to one-quarter inch, spliced with a twelve-to-one bevel splice and then hand fitted to the preceding plank throughout a five-eighths-inch-wide mating surface from end to end and clinched there, cedar to cedar, with copper nails, ends clipped off so not to split the wood, driven through both thicknesses and against a clinching iron so that the clipped end curls back into the wood and holds.

The first plank my brother put on, when the clamps were released, flew off in splinters. With each pair in place, the winter shortened by a week or more. In fact, it was spring, it was summer before the boat was lifted off the forms, turned right side up, the bones put in. The shop's Round Oak stove was fired up again, an oilcan half full of water connected to a long wooden box hung from the ceiling joists, thin, half-round strips of slippery elm steamed to pliability. Holes were punched through the laps at each of the fifty-four rib positions, nails stuck in them from the outside, ready.

Now craftsmanship couldn't be painstaking, slow. There were only ninety seconds in which to drive sixteen nails into each rib as it was drawn from the steam box, bent into the shell and held in its place as near as the holder could tell with the holes covered and his hands and clinching iron in the way. After a minute and a half the elm was hard and dry again, and would split or would turn back the soft copper nails before they came through to the iron. I crouched beneath the hull to do the driving.

We put on cedar decks, oak gunwales, caned seats. We sponged warm water over the hull to raise the indentations of the hammer, let it dry, sanded, varnished and sanded and varnished again.

Now, every few minutes, we were leaving some of the varnish on a rock.

We carry around a gorge, through high pine plains. There was a great fire here as well as lumbering. The sand has grown to grasses for thousands of acres around the large gray stumps. The pines are coming back now. Someday pine needles and shade will smother out the grass. There will be large white cedars again someday, too.

We are gliding on a long still water. The river is smooth and darker. We learn to read the dimpling water over rocks and logs. We pivot tightly between forested knolls and marshes.

All along we have startled deer bedded in the grass and brush right beside us. Mostly invisible, or we just see the flag. We hear them bound off and stop and blow the scent of us out of their nostrils. Once we come almost up to one standing in the middle of the river, just a big orange body with a three-bladed propeller in place of a head. Everett says that he felt wild there for a moment, felt as if he were a buck, not a man, watching her switch her tail, lift her knee.

Under the exposed roots of the grasses and under the alders the banks are littered with freshwater clamshells. Now and then we see a muskrat slip off the shore; once an otter. There are blue herons, spooking early and creaking off, and an American bittern waddles into the grass from a mudbank with his nose up. Belted kingfishers flee ahead around each bend. This is what the boat was made not to violate. I photograph my foot, a bit of oak-split basket, the blade of my paddle, some planks and ribs and gunwale and some water and greenery. It all belongs.

We drift on, not explorers but archivists, feasting on a vision without wreck, paint, wire, print, or masonry, but instead of opening new country we are zipping it shut, leaving behind the highest altitude, sharpest air, coldest water, wildest fish.

"Wish I had my banjo," Everett says.

• • •

The old books about the Adirondacks are clear on the subject of fish. There were lake trout in the big lakes and brook trout everywhere. Early in the spring and late in the fall you would find them near shores and in rapids, hungry for brightly colored flies like the Parmachene Belle. In July you might think there were none—unless you found a spring hole.

Below our tenting place this night we seek the mouth of a tributary stream the map shows coming from three or four miles away. If it is spring-fed, cold, we may find the big ones.

We pass its mouth, a simple delta with an island in the middle. I sink to the calves in mud, but the surprise is not that. It is the pain.

"Feel that."

"Ho, ho, ho, ho."

This is ice water. The spring must be right here. We fish toward the mouth with dry flies, carefully. Nothing. We fish up as far as we can from the bar. Nothing. We go back and get the boat and enter the tributary, bowman casting ahead. It widens into a basin with another island. Then a narrow channel, alders on the right, grass on the left. Another basin, strangely round, black and still. Nothing, not even rises. Out on the river little fish had been cartwheeling everywhere, most of them shiners, I suspected. Here, a stillness.

No, a fair fish splashed, up a still-narrower channel. Behind that, a swirl. I liked the sound of that swirl. I had on some kind of Ausable River special, new. I let it descend on that place, almost among the alder branches that grew from under the surface. It was sucked in with another shoveling of water.

The fish did not reveal its strength at first. It seemed to think that this fly could not be serious, and simply tossed about in deprecation. But then it gave up mere hope. It was hooked, and it just knew it and became very mad. It wore itself out completely, so that when I took it in my hand it was as safely handled as a two-pound bag of gold. In the gathering dark we looked and looked at it.

The boat isn't a replica of anything, though the methods and features are like Rushton's. The profile approximates a lovely centerboard sailing canoe called *Stella Maris* shown in Atwood Manley's *Rushton and*

His Times in American Canoeing. It is fourteen feet long by thirty inches wide and ten inches deep amidships, fifteen inches at the ends. As Harry Rushton might say, if you chew gum you need two sticks, one in either cheek. Though we have it loaded pretty heavily, it is very fast through the water and very quiet. Beginner's luck, Everett says.

Later in the summer we took the boat to the annual regatta of the American Canoe Association in the Thousand Islands. For the fun of it we entered the boat in a paddling race against sixteen-footers, mostly fiber-glass Sawyers that are knifelike, long rhombuses designed to fit barely within the formula for canoes (thirty inches width, four inches above the keel amidships), mostly paddled by enthusiasts of punishment who use the wide-bladed racing paddles and cadence their strokes and switch sides at a yell from the stern paddler. We lined up in the middle of a field of eight.

At the gun we sprang forward as quickly as the rest. Then some madman paddled too long on one side, and suddenly all eight boats were converging. Those crude coal shovels dug at our hand-carved black cherry paddles, people yelled, "Look out for the cedar, look out for the cedar!" and proceeded to bump into it. We quit paddling, shook our heads.

There was a strong wind, high choppy waves combined with the wakes of inconsiderate powerboaters. Down at the first mark the two leaders were broadside to us, struggling to turn. One boat had already capsized. The others were heading out wide to start their turns early. It occurred to us that we were still in the race. We made right for the buoy, nipped it, turned easily because of our shorter keel and curved stems, and came out of the turn in third, which we held down the long leg and back to the finish, even though we shipped water over the bow all the way.

You can have that way of impressing sweethearts, however. We went across the water (and the international boundary) to the ACA's Sugar Island. We expected to see a gorgeous congregation of old cedar canoes, perhaps Rushtons, Stephenses, Joyners, Eversons, Ruggleses, along with all the recent developments.

Surely the few members of the association who use Sugar Island, the few who come to the regatta (the ACA is dominated by white-water canoeists now, its power is in the West) are *old* enough: about a dozen grizzled eccentric septuagenarians who every year bring up (from Brooklyn, it sounds) their thirty-year-old Peterborough and Old Town canoes which they have stamped with their own opinionatedness in every sort of sail rig and chafing gear and crass arrangement for style and comfort you can imagine. They resemble the English, who lost the challenge cup in 1886 to *Vesper* in that they sail from reclining positions, only their heads in view and now and then a foot with which they shove down or up their single leeboards.

Their canoes would be collectors' items to a lot of people, but these old gents have butchered them up (nicely) so they can sail them frontward and backward. The same guy always wins. He stuck a big aluminum mast in his and a sail that belongs on a Hobie Cat. The others, with their sliding gunters and leg-o'-muttons and lateens, have a moral victory every time they lose to him.

But there is only one old Rushton, *Old Joe*, a Princess model with dumb sails called batwings. Dumb as the sails are, with spars fanning out through them like fingers (sailmakers were not apprised of the airfoil then; babes in the dark), the lone old decked cruising canoe is irresistible.

We camped the second night at the end of the sixteen-mile-long still water. The rapids below were spectacular and looked extraordinarily fishy; deep, aerated water, large pools, swelling slicks between rocks, banks overhung by shade trees. In the first little falls I hooked a strong fish. Something told me I wasn't going to like it when I got it in hand. A good cast and float and take and tussle and thirteen inches and all, but: brown trout. Way up here in the country of the Swiss Guard, this stodgy tank in olive drab, this warm water lounger.

Then it rained. Simply, it was the wettest, noisiest electrical storm I have ever been in. We couldn't sleep. We lay in the tent, listening to the same train bang through the same station over and over, colliding with rock walls all the way. There was great turning on and off of lights. After much too long I said, "Are you as scared as I am?" and my brother said "Yes."

The boat was pulled up on a mucky beach a few yards upstream, since everything else here was rough granite rocks. In it were the rods and paddles. Imagine it floating off as the water rose and humming along past us and over the brink of the falls.

I ran out and stone-hopped to a great boulder in the river from which I could see around the bushes to the little mudbank. The flashlight wouldn't make a hole in the blackness that far. I couldn't see the boat.

Then the lights went on and I saw it clearly, tilted on its side, every rib etched against its pallid skin. I remembered a girlie show at the county fair: a pitch-black stage, then a blue-white strobe on a heart-breaking body, then blackness. I watched a couple more of these cameos and went back to bed.

In the morning the whole world had foundered. The stepping-stones were a foot under water. We splashed to the rock, hopeless, guilty, wanting the night back.

The boat was held to the muck by the water inside it. The river was inches over the bank, but it hadn't floated.

That day we accomplished no more than to get to the foot of the rapids. It rained, we got lost with the boat on our heads, we got skunked fishing. Everett broke the tip of his rod.

The next day we swam the boat down another set of rapids to the bridge where the one gravel road crossed. Below that it was still for another half-mile. Then the river dropped out of sight, shores and all. We carried the pack baskets below the mile-long gorge and hiked back up for the boat.

A boy in hunting clothes stood by the open front door of an old Dodge deep in the grass of an old lumber road. He gave us his profile. Down inside the car an old man was working. Very slowly he backed out and faced us. The gray hair was wild on his head, in his eyebrows. Wire-rim glasses, clear eyes, a couple days' growth, a faint grin possibly humorous, possibly critical. "What club *you* belong to?" he asked.

We were on a leased park now. We explained our presence, told him of our permission.

He said, "What happened to the brook trout?"

I said I didn't know.

He said, "How long's a trout live?"

I said I didn't know that, either.

"Five years." he said. "What happened to the brook trout?"

I said I didn't know what he was getting at.

"It wasn't fishermen," he said. "What happened?"

I didn't know.

"When we had timber, we had trout. When the timber went, we didn't. What happened to the brook trout?"

I knew what he meant now, but wanted to hear the way he would say it. I knew it would be a way I'd never guess. He stood reposeful between the open door and the car, still smiled that critical and friendly smile. He said, "It used to be in November and December, in hunting season, you could go up any of these little feeder streams and in every pool you'd see two trout, this big." The old man held the crescent wrench a foot and a half away from the other thick, stiff hand.

"A female and a male," he said. His smile was friendly now for sure.

That was the connection. The spawning streams were spoiled.

We said we had to get our boat. He said he had to get some oil in his transmission, perhaps a way of poking fun at our idea of necessity.

We float three miles, noticing that the black-cherry trees are blighted as badly as the elms. We carry around the last rapids, then paddle seven miles of meandering grassy channels and a lake to where our home folks have been watching our paddles glinting, in time, in the low sun for an hour.

The children semaphoring on the bank. Wife swirling her pailful of hair and cocking a camera. That blocky orange thing on the hillside which reveals itself to be a dump truck. The suggestion that we take a shower in the camp-ground facility while a picnic is prepared. After four days on the flowing changing river all of it seems like indentured servitude. The boat is upside down on top of a Saab. We realize *we* have been hauled off to a museum.

A young man who restores classic cars for a living in Springfield, Massachusetts, came in August to the antique boat show at Clayton, in the Thousand Islands. He brought, on a trailer behind his car, a Maine rowboat called a Rangely skiff, not in show condition. He was hoping to use it toward a trade. What he wanted was an old decked cruising canoe with sails.

There weren't many there: two. None for sale, none he wanted. Then, in the commercial area, he saw Everett's boat, the varnish retouched, the yellow cedar bright and young-looking beside the deep-aged Saint Lawrence skiffs and Adirondack guideboats, the Ruggles canoe and *Old Joe.*

He stopped and looked it over closely, talked with Everett. He went back and looked at the Rushton, the skiffs, the Nickerson guideboat. He came back and wrote a check to confirm his order: an eighteen-foot canoe with main and mizzen, flotation, a sliding seat, a folding center-board. It will surely take all winter to make. The design is up to Everett, understanding that the young man is going to sail the canoe ten miles out to sea; the basic model in his mind is Rushton's *Vesper.*

Lone Watch in a Gold-Fobbed Forest

Every hunter I knew was gaunt about the ribs. Socially, they were inattentive. The deer hunting in the Adirondacks had been awful.

The sport long ago became another witless mass diversion automatically performed in the autumn by droves of the wrong people, a meaningless commercialized, anachronistic, habitual indulgence, an annual all-points diddle of women, employers, the deer, ourselves. We've learned to live with the mob wheezing and hacking about the woods in search of a hood ornament.

The past several years, but this year, especially, there didn't seem to be any deer. People quit asking each other, "Got your buck yet?" They assumed not. If somebody did get one, he didn't brag. His buck only emphasized the scarcity of others. He parceled out the meat for his friends.

I waited for snow and cold, hoping the deer would start to move, thus making tracks, thus proving their existence. My old hunting area, the hills around Lake Ozonia, had been sold and divvied up—leased, anyway. I trespassed a little with the natives, leaving the posted country to the lessees on the weekends. They probably don't even know where their lines are. Ambrose Stark kept saying we would put one in the kettle. Day after day we saw nothing, not even a doe.

One man I talked to had simply quit. Said he wasn't hunting because there weren't enough deer in the woods. He is glaringly unique to react so logically. Most of us hunt deeper and longer, not less.

Earl Hazen, for example. He has sixty cows to milk night and morning, and his hunting club is an hour away. His whiskers grow, schoolboys come over icy roads on bicycles to do the chores, the corn ground goes unplowed. He sees a buck at last, misses with the first shot, and his gun, neglected, jams. He cleans and oils it, then tries it on a coy-dog pouncing after rodents way off at the top of the pasture, misses, but the weapon reloads properly. He resumes. The schoolboys milk without him.

I felt like Earl about hunting—it had to remain credible. Surely deer existed in the big private holdings hereabouts: Kildare, Whitney, St. Regis, Litchfield, Rockefeller. These tracts of Adirondack forest must provide hunting with the old coherence, craftsmanship, romance. I wanted a few thousand acres to myself, that was all. I would seek an invitation; meanwhile, not to miss a chance, Earl took me to Madawaska Club.

Until around 1940 most of the St. Regis Paper Company land that lay northwest of the town of Saranac was open hunting. But the taxes rose, and St. Regis posted its land, forcing the hunters to lease. To retain the right to hunt a little of the area they used to roam, Thurm Hazen and some local men formed a club to lease 3,300 acres bordering Madawaska Pond. They bought a demonstration Quonset off the grounds of the St. Lawrence County Fair, hired a camp cook, put in a phony telephone to see how guests react when told their wives are calling, and have been hunting together almost thirty years, fathers and sons and friends.

The older men are more cheerful, louder than the young. They have not darkened over the lack of deer. Their poker is rough. Their talk is profane and clean. They appreciate each other. This year a white leghorn rooster is at large in the camp.

Earl and I and Gary, another guest, arrive before first light. Earl slips into the dark Quonset to write down where we are hunting. The rooster goes berserk in the pitch-black bunk room. We can hear it from out there in the pickup. Earl brings out a blob of whiteness in his arms and spills it by the woodpile. Later, two miles deep along the Ross line, we hear it crow for dawn. This trail is a boundary with wealth—across it is a 23,000-acre private park. Deep in, there is a stretch of swamp and timber knolls where deer cross from Madawaska to feed on hardwood slopes.

It is chilly, the leaves are soaked, no snow. Earl has been gone two hours on his dogged quest, forgetting us, it seems. I move along. The line trail is a window in the dark trees where Gary's back slants across the light-brown grasses of the swamp beyond.

His position and color are odd, and I lift my small binoculars. The back drops behind a large moss-covered rock and the head comes up with that lacy canoe of horns, and I say to myself that is not Gary, that is a buck. Not Gary. Buck. Buck, buck, buck.

Not inaccessible and potent as on tavern walls; angelic and sweet, he walks toward me, low-headed, idle. I'm still seeing Gary in him, because where the hell is Gary otherwise? I can't shoot. It's exactly where I meant Gary to be. The eyepieces rattle against my spectacles. Broadside for an instant, he steps up onto Ross and out of sight.

Last night we looked in the record book. Through the 1940s and '50s Madawaska hunters took around twenty-eight bucks a year, and there was never a shortage of camp meat. In the early '60s, only fifteen to twenty deer were killed. In recent years, six or seven. So far this year (1973), three.

Tonight is the occasion of an annual dinner. A biologist from the neighboring estate brings over a bag of smoked trout and joins the club for a venison stew and an evening of poker. The old cook roasts a turkey.

For twenty years the state told us we had too many deer. The woods were overbrowsed. We had to kill back the animals and let the winter range recover. To the bewilderment of many northern Adirondack hunters, who had seen the same winter range support twice as many deer and could not imagine how a scientist who was awake and out of doors could now locate too many, the state authorized a massive harvest of does. Old-fashioned woodsmen limited themselves to bucks as before, but the Day-Glo hordes and poachers were willing enough. The plan was working. The deer became tragically scarce. Then came three bitter winters in a row, ending with the catastrophic snow of 1971–72. What the state had just accomplished, the climate did a second time over.

There is a mystery. Deer breed young and twin more often than not; they have the potential to increase by more than fifty percent a year. The winters since 1972 have been exceptionally mild and there is plenty of feed. But the herds haven't recovered. It's as if the deer were failing to breed. This year it has been hard to tell when, or whether, the bucks were in rut.

•   •   •

I'm invited to hunt for two days on the private lands of the St. Regis Paper Company: The Sunbeam Club, 14,000 acres used by salesmen and customers. Maybe it's different there.

Driving the Blue Mountain Road before light I follow the slow-moving white car of a well-known poacher's wife. She will look for her sign, perhaps an empty six-pack carton hanging in a tree. No one will bother her. If her man has any game, it will probably have been shot between the eyes. The hunter from downstate who buys it to take home may overlook this evidence that the deer was taken at night with a flashlight held along the barrel.

A mile in from the Sunbeam gatehouse three slightly rustic buildings stand at the edge of a still-water stretch of the St. Regis River. A generator drones in the powerhouse. Two deer hang from the buck pole. The manager, Stanley McVean, and four guides are having breakfast, served by two women in white. In a pine-paneled room beyond, with a warm fire, stuffed fisher, bearskin, deerhead, gun rack, radio giving the weather (it will drizzle), the host salesman and his guests in socks, wool pants, and thermal tops are drinking Bloody Marys. I am told a hunting story off the bat:

"You see those deer out there? See the smaller one? Burt here shot it. Went to get it, had only one horn. Went to drag it, horn came off. Looked at the horn: covered with velvet. Guide goes to dress the deer, and the deer is a lesbian."

I am handed an ashtray from the mantel, with a skinny, seaweedy six-inch antler in it, a horned doe. It seems a bad start.

We breakfast in another sitting, never seeing the guides or discussing the plan of the day, praise the indifferent scrambled eggs and go out with jackets, hats, gloves, rifles, some with day-hiking packs, and pile into a school bus.

Wait a minute. A school bus? Inside the humpbacked blue-and-yellow vehicle a sign is stenciled: NO EATING ON BUS. Frankly this type of travel seems a little metropolitan.

But for such hunting, tight, linked, uniform drives with minimum opportunity for the loss of the large accounts, it is the cat's pajamas. McVean will drive along the roads, stop at a runway, say, "Gimme a scope," or "Brush gun," and to the hunter who clambers forward, "Get up on that knoll. Deer will be coming from over here." Then he drives on 200 feet and places the next man. Well, I think, these guys aren't really rich. They're customers.

But on my first watch, after a comfortable half hour of stillness, the deer explode, running, pausing, turning. Seven pass me. Thirteen are seen. On the second drive, two. On the third I see four, weaving under high ledges before me, shouldering together, overrunning each other, finally rock-scrambling up like mountain sheep, knocking down flints that clatter like a bunch of tin plates.

The impression is of things belonging, completing the warm wet day on long hillsides under the pillars and crowns of large poplars. You sense the weight, breathing, warmth of the deer, you see briefly into their lives—even if you do it exactly as a doorman. By God, it is good to see the creatures in this quantity.

The total count is more than thirty deer many of them seen by five or six of us. But that's much fewer than five years ago and no bucks. Some of us walk in after the last drive, and I talk with McVean about the herd.

Terrible. No deer. This was exceptional today. He doesn't blame the winters. He blames the doe permit and the night hunters. The state is responsible for both. The doe permit is some desk rider's dimwit idea, not applicable to this area of the Adirondacks [the state finally realized this, and as of the 1974 season no longer issues such permits], and the poaching goes unpunished.

Stan used to enjoy catching poachers and running them in. "Hunting men is twice as exciting as hunting deer," he claims. "But you can't be afraid to pull a gun on them, and that's just what I am now." Liable to end up talking to a judge himself for threatening human life or some damn thing.

The state people tell him that after all, this is like Appalachia. Venison's about the only meat some people get. It makes a difference. The warden here, great big guy, is afraid of nothing, but he doesn't enforce the law. And these other clubs along the road can't even agree to hire somebody to patrol it.

I am thinking that poaching is more than inevitable in the Adirondacks. It's built in, induced, by the pattern of land ownership. Between the rich and the state there's not much left. The native hamlets scavenge at the edges of great wildernesses—either the 2.25 million acres kept forever wild by state constitution or the million and a third acres owned by, to pick an arbitrary cutoff number, the largest fifty landowners. That takes us down to plots as small as eight square miles.

The guests at Sunbeam seem worried about me, as if I were part of the native infrastructure. Who is this bird with the moth-poached doublet and the Remington .30? The last time the Maryland judge saw one of those guys was when he was in the FBI! A man keeps asking me, "What's the gist of your article, I mean what is the gist of the piece going to be?" He isn't satisfied with "Whatever develops." Leaning out of the gin rummy game, he gives me the theme himself, in case I am not comme il faut:

"Deer hunting's deer hunting. The same everywhere. For rich or poor. The rich don't have it any better than the poor. Isn't that right, Pierre?"

I do realize that I earned this hunter's permanent boredom by asking if the full-length one-piece stock of his Finnish rifle, so smooth and shiny, were plastic. And then whether the same firm also made digital wristwatches. Dear me, what boo-boos.

But he may have spoken the truth. In another day of hunting at Sunbeam eight hunters and five guides saw about seventeen deer, but only one shot was fired, possibly not at an angelic boy. It was the hunter next to me who fired. He broke a leg on a deer that had just passed my test for does: I couldn't put horns on it, as the saying goes. Whatever sex, the deer bled badly and lay down, but got up when the guides went after it and ran right on out of the drives arranged to trap it. The head guide said it would live, till winter, anyway. The broken leg was swinging toe arcs in the snow. No one exaggerated the importance of the thing.

I was glad enough to leave. The Sunbeam woods are very, very fine, but I am not at home with the men. Their conversation is built with jokes, like blocks. They call up their wives at night. They drink as if habitually, without boisterousness. If hunting is a high point in their year, they don't show it.

I realize that all my life I have thought of deer hunting as something that would end. Someday it would be a thing you couldn't just choose to do. As a youth I had not felt I was learning something I would always do in the fall, but learning, before I lost the chance, something people *used* to do.

It surprised me then to discover that I was wrong, and that instead of ending, it would go on and on, mostly as a mode of consumption perfectly characteristic of the new times: managed. It isn't saved, it's changed. And so it doesn't exactly fill the need for something continuous. That is why I yearn to hunt alone in a trackless wilderness.

The end of the season is practically here. Kildare refuses. Whitney refuses. Of course they do. The last thing they want is publicity. What do you think they own all that land for? A reporter is an arm of the assessor.

One day of coherence would be enough. One day of the simple and natural and timeless activity hunting surely must be. Not as a tool of the state to prevent overbrowse, not as an arm of the timber lobby, not as part of the team, not as a client, not as a poacher. I still don't know if hunting is for plain men to *do* any more. I make one last contact, with huge, castled, 28,000-acre Litchfield Park. And the answer surprisingly is, "Come on in."

Litchfield is sure it is right—on land, on timber, on wildlife, on recreation—and glad to have us know it. In the big new steel garage that services Liparco's green Brockway trucks and yellow Pettibone loaders, John Stock, the forest supervisor and a timber-tax expert, explains with the brevity and decision of a man to whom questions have answers:

"Timber growth in a year is about 60¢ an acre. Taxes are around $1.25. You can't grow timber profitably. That's one side. Then there are the deer. Studies show that if you have forty deer per square mile, you get about 150 seedlings per acre of the kind that make good timber. If you have twenty deer per square mile, you get 14,000."

Liparco solves the dual problem of taxes and seedling survival by leasing about 18,000 acres to fifteen small clubs. The rent helps to pay the taxes (until recently paid all the taxes), the hunting controls the deer population, and all the year-round recreational benefits of ownership are extended to others, which is socially good, morally right and not bad PR. The deer harvest on Litchfield is currently eight times what it is on state land, and the bucks are very large and fat. There are about 10,000 acres the company doesn't lease and hardly anybody hunts. Be at the garage at seven sharp, and Stock will take me up on the mountain.

Somehow I've got to steady myself until dawn. I go over to Ray Brook to talk to state officials, to hear their side of the argument over the lack of deer. I might finally take sides, with the scientists or with the hunters. I have an idea who is right, but don't like the idea. I know that the nineteenth-century tradition of plenty is the obverse of an actual record of careless slaughter. Venison all year. Wash-tubs of trout.

The wildlife biologist dares to tell me that his name is Greenleaf Chase. I am sure that any policy he believes in is innocent and good. He admits to being an author of the policy of killing back the herd, and estimates that it was carried on about three years too long. The principle is right, however. Proof is that starvation in 1971–72 was *worst* on the large private tracts which were underhunted, and the recovery there is slowest. Kildare Club, for example: only fourteen men hunting 9,000 acres and only *two* bucks killed so far this year.

The deer will come back. It takes time. The feed had to come back first. But each of the next few years there'll be more. The state game managers would like to educate us to accept killing does and bucks more equally. They would like us to give them the power to regulate the kill as state wildlife officials do in the West, in close local detail, by natural deer areas; even to provoke a harvest, in remote country, by incentives if necessary. It is still blurred for me. I think I see circles in the reasoning that are just about as Malthusian as nature's.

The whole mountain, down to the dark, still water of Jenkins Pond, is within cloud. The light changes eerily. Somewhere a Liparco generator is running—probably at that Bavarian farm with the gambrel roofs, hipped gables, bottoms buried in slopes, that suddenly appeared and vanished on the road in. Over the mountain to the north a chain saw makes long cuts.

Splendid brood trees—giant pines and hemlocks, birches thirty inches through—rule a forest of descendants. Their antiquity, and the deep green mosses, and the single boathouse on the two-mile pond, give this forest an air in common with the towered Litchfield castle somewhere farther in, its great hall full of mounted heads, and with the heroic sculptures of elk and deer on granite pedestals at the gates out near the highway. If a forest can seem gold-fobbed, embossed, this does.

I trust it is all in my mind. I'm alone on two square miles of perfect country. The single day ranges ahead, ample as an ocean. Somewhere near ten o'clock (I don't wear a watch, the sun is lost and the light in the forest fluctuates mysteriously) I stand near one of the two tops of the 2,400-foot hill that shelters the pond on the north. A wind flows up through the dripping fog. Slowly I zip my jacket.

Below me, out of sight and hearing at that moment, a deer approached. Since first light, probably, he had been coming from the swamps this side of Buck Mountain, alone. He ignored the other deer below the ledges. He wasn't following a track.

He passed under the other, higher hill, and between it and a separate green knob where, over granite caves, stalactites of ice dripped noisily. Occasionally an icicle broke off and clattered down with a sound you could mistake for a great tree cracking its hinge as it fell.

Almost silently I unwrapped a Peanut Butter Cup.

Neither of us knew what was coming. The deer must have looked (like me) not nobly masculine but foolish and sad, cursed with filigrees of mortality about his head. Both of us were feeding, listening, going somewhere very carefully.

I slowly crumpled the paper, put it in my pocket, brought up the gun from between my knees, slid the safety back off and moved.

It might have been a couple of horses getting up on hard ground and clomping away. I could hear his lungs drive air out, almost voiced, higher every stride, like a trolley speeding up, as if his fear increased each time his feet struck, loud as the clank of gears. Back down his old track in six bounds, he heaved himself off, up a steep ravine over the notch.

Then the shrouding raining silence of the woods. Hindsight. Notes for self-improvement. For example, run. But it was impossible to regret. The heaviness, the loudness, the nearness, the voice, finally the incredible fact that staring down that slope I could not see him.

I moved respectfully all day. All the deer had gone north. Jenkins Pond at four was utterly still. It seemed separated in time, belonging to itself. I don't want to describe it. I walked a mile back to the car. I thought of unloading my rifle by trigger, as on a Saturday night in the Last Chance Saloon.

I stripped to the waist, washed with snow, dried with a towel from the pack and put on clean shirts. I was elated. Elated that hunting is hunting, as the man who killed the horned doe said. That for another year I wouldn't have to give it up. Elated not to be divided, except by writing, from the men drinking beer and shooting pool and telling about their hunting experiences up on the backside of Rockefeller, in the poor, bleary bars of Tupper Lake.

J. Curt Stager

After earning his doctorate in zoology and geology from Duke University, Curt Stager relocated to the region in the mid-1980s to become a professor of biology at Paul Smith's College. Once in the mountains, he immediately began to convey his love for the natural world in a compelling, accessible voice.

His translations of the mysteries of the outdoors can be found in many places. His nationally syndicated public radio program, "Natural Selections," is produced locally and can be heard weekly on North Country Public Radio. He has also published numerous articles in National Geographic, Science, Wild Earth, Adirondack Explorer, *and* Adirondac. *While Stager's work is focused primarily on the Adirondacks, his research interests have led him to East and West Africa, the South Pacific, Sweden, and much of eastern North America.*

The two natural history essays reprinted here originally appeared in his first book, Field Notes from the Northern Forest *(Syracuse University Press, 1998).*

What Should You Do When You See a Bear?

My first encounter with an Adirondack black bear in the wild took me by surprise. I was driving past Lake Clear on my way to work one morning when a large black hulk lumbered across the road in front of me and vanished into the undergrowth. From behind the wheel, I reveled in that brief glimpse of wildness.

Black bears embody much of the romance of the Adirondacks, a lasting reminder of earlier days when other large predators roamed these woods as well. Their ability to subsist on a wide variety of foods has helped them to withstand hunting pressure and human encroachment more successfully than did the wolves, wolverines, and cougars that were driven to local extinction during the nineteenth century. Even so, you do not see black bears very often. They are usually very timid around humans, and under normal circumstances you are much more likely to encounter indirect signs of bear presence than to see the actual animal.

Black bears *(Ursus americanus)* are quite different from others of their kind. When we speak of bears in the Adirondacks, we are not talking about enormous predatory grizzlies *(Ursus horribilis)* or man-munching polar bears *(Ursus maritimus)* that sling two-hundred pound seals over their shoulders like lunch sacks. Rather, black bears are the ones that guide books call "generally harmless to humans" and "omnivorous" (they will eat your sandwich whether it contains beef or bean sprouts). An autumn-fattened female can weigh 160 pounds, and a male can tip the scales at 300 (the record male in New York weighed 750 pounds). This is far less than the weight of a western grizzly, which often exceeds half a ton. But if you unexpectedly meet a black bear in the woods, you quickly notice that it still outweighs you, and it is difficult to forget that a small but significant number of black bears—all presumably well accustomed to human presence (and garbage)—have been known to attack, kill, and even eat an occasional hiker.

One spring morning I went fishing with my friend Phil. We spent the morning in his canoe drifting down a sluggish tributary of the Saint Regis River, following a narrow winding corridor of overhanging alder thickets as we plucked tiny brook trout from the dark current with our fly rods. The stream we rode meandered through broad open expanses of once-burned land, now covered with lush tangles of bracken fern and blueberry. Sometimes when we rounded a tight curve we sent white-tailed deer crashing away through the undergrowth. We pulled out at Cranberry Rapids, where our other vehicle awaited us on a dirt track that runs through the barrens. "I like to jog out here a lot," Phil mused as we lifted the canoe onto the truck bed. "But sometimes I get nervous running through this place alone. One day I almost ran into a bear that was eating blueberries on a little rise beside the road. Usually when you see one out in the open like that, you mainly get to watch its rear end as it runs away. But this guy was different. He just stood up on his hind legs and stared at me. He wasn't going anywhere, not with all those berries left to eat." It is unlikely that a black bear in this situation would attack a human, but that fact is little comfort when you face one alone and unarmed except for your water bottle. "Basically he got to watch *my* rear end in retreat that time."

Just beyond the barrens, Phil suddenly stopped beside a telephone pole and stepped out of the truck. The pole wore a ruff of foot-long splinters at about head height, just below a "No Trespassing" sign. "This wasn't here before," Phil said as I joined him beside the pole. "Looks like something's been sharpening its claws on it." I walked up to press my fingers into a deep gouge in the dense wood. Alongside the groove, entangled in a spray of slivers, two long black hairs swayed in the breeze. "Must have been marking his territory," Phil muttered. I wondered if it was the work of that same bear who had defended his hill so defiantly—and if that clawed message was intended for Phil.

I once attended a public slide presentation on the subject of bears by Lou Berchielli, a wildlife biologist with the New York State Department of Environmental Conservation. Lou began by pointing out that the average black bear encounter is more of a privilege than a hazard: "Bears usually see, smell, or hear you long before you even know they're around. They know that we humans are predators, and they steer clear of us. You're lucky if you get to see anything more of them than tracks."

Bear tracks are easy to recognize in the soft, fine-grained soil of a stream bank, footpath, or dirt road. Each paw print sports a row of scratch marks dug by five toes tipped with nonretractable claws. According to Lou, it is also relatively simple to tell male from female by the sizes of the prints: "If the heel of the hind print is more than four inches wide, it's a male. If the heel print is smaller than that, it's either a female or a yearling."

Not only are wild bears typically shy of humans; they do not seem to bother other large animals very often, either. Lou offered an amusing example of this: "Black bears in these parts often seem to be more interested in insects than in larger prey. A few years back, I examined a road-killed deer that a bear had been feeding on, expecting to see large pieces of the deer missing. But that wasn't the case. All the bear had done was to claw open the carcass to get at the fly larvae and carrion beetles inside it."

In addition to their utility in feeding, bear claws—essentially just elongated toenails—make passable tree-climbing tools. You can often find old claw marks on tree trunks if you look carefully. They are easiest to spot on trees that have smooth, light-colored bark, especially beeches *(Fagus grandifolia)*.

Normally, changing day length provides the instinctive trigger for denning in black bears, but in years when beechnut crops are particularly heavy ("mast years"), bears often go into their winter dens about a month later than usual to take advantage of that food bonus. Females are also thought to give birth to larger litters in the winters following heavy beechnut yields.

You can pretty much forget about seeing bears in winter, although they sometimes wake up and step outside for a brief stroll. I have seen their tracks in January powder in northern Maine, but that is rather unusual. Although a black bear's seasonal sleep is too shallow to count as true hibernation in a technical sense (Lou Berchielli calls it "periodic sleeping"), bears do experience a drop in body temperature of five to ten degrees Fahrenheit during the winter. Because their body temperature is still relatively high during this down time, it is important for bears to conserve body heat as much as possible. This is probably why their dens tend to be quite small and easy to keep warm in. A typical rock crevice or hollow tree den may measure only one or two feet in height or width. Some dens, however, consist of nothing more than a pile of brush, and some bears have even been found spending the winter curled up right out in the open.

During their long sleep, bears lower their metabolic rates along with their body temperatures, a physiological adaptation that helps them last up to five months without eating. They also gain some nutrition from their own urea by diverting it from their bladder to their intestines, where bacteria convert it into a form that a bear's body can use for building vital amino acids and proteins. And because they do not take in food all winter, hibernating black bears do not mess their beds. A fibrous plug of leaves, pine needles, and fur swallowed just before bed-time corks them quite effectively.

In the case of females, though, their sleeping bodies do occasionally emit other things: half-pound, nearly naked, newborn cubs, and the milk on which to suckle them. There are usually only two cubs in a litter, and they instinctively nestle into mom's thick fur to get at her teats and to snack until spring. A mother bear may or may not be awake at the actual moment of birth, but she often rouses enough to roll onto her back or to sit up and help her newborns to nurse.

Black bears do not normally eat for two weeks or so after emerging from their dens (late March for males, early April for females), but when the animal's digestive system eventually kicks in, the first thing it usually wants is salad. Wet areas are a prime destination then, because some of the earliest spring plants thrive there, such as skunk cabbage and marsh marigold. Later, forest glades and fields feel the press of heavy feet as bears arrive to graze on grasses, dandelions, and wild strawberries. During warmer months, you might come across a rotten stump or log that has been torn apart where *Ursus* has excavated grubs, beetles, ants, or crickets. And when the blueberries, cherries, and raspberries ripen, you can tell that bears have been at work in the berry patches by the crushed foliage and by the large droppings peppered with undigested seeds.

Bears also feed in even less elegant ways, and the surest way to see bears in the Adirondacks used to be to hang out at the town dump. But several years ago our public landfills were closed in favor of recycling and trash export, and local bear society apparently went through a period of upheaval as result. For about a year after the closings, the dump bears, descended from a long lineage of trash scavengers, began showing up at our back doors.

One summer morning in 1992, a bear broke into a house just down the road from my place and emptied my friend's refrigerator while she was at work. My neighbors and I began to wonder if we might be safer living in the inner city. Over in Oswegatchie, about an hour and a half west of Paul Smiths, my fiancée's family's summer cottage was also burgled. The place was almost untouched except for one broken window, its jagged frame edges flecked with crimson droplets and black hairs, and for the remains of a single glass vase that once held a bouquet of fragrant phlox. As we figured it, the bear must have simply followed its nose to the faint scent of last year's flowers.

The rest of that summer did still less to arouse my sympathy for displaced bears. I grogged awake one morning to the sound of heavy thumping at my back door. Then I heard a crash, followed by the sustained tinkle of falling glass. Turning to look through my flimsy bedroom window screen, I beheld an enormous hairy black bear behind making its majestic way into the woods, leaving a broken porch window and a shattered sense of security in its wake. And the next day, the college dean nearly collided with a large bear while driving past the campus quadrangle. She screamed, and the bear bolted; in its terror, it crashed headlong into the chain link fence of the tennis courts, fell, got back up, and lit out for my hillside. All I heard of this commotion was the loud bang of a flying impact against the metal garbage can beside my back door. After my experience of the previous morning, I decided it was a good time to stay in bed.

But one person who lives near me actually encourages bears to visit his house. Ray Fadden is a retired schoolteacher who owns and curates a roadside museum in Onchiota and who is well known in the region as a tireless advocate of Native American rights and culture. It is less widely known that he also feeds bears at his house. This all began when a nearby dump closed and the bears were left without their familiar food source. The kind-hearted old man took it upon himself to look after them and has been at it ever since. Friends often show up on Ray's doorstep with sacks of sunflower seeds for the chickadees and chipmunks, or with trash bags full of raw animal parts. I took seeds last time.

"I've got one youngster this year who's been causing trouble at night," Ray said as we left his back door. His unkempt shock of white hair blazed like a beacon atop his red flanneled shoulders, and I followed it along a path that winds through the woods behind his house. "He keeps breaking in through the screen door to our porch. Most of them wait outside to be fed." Ray did not seem to be worried about his own safety as he told me this; he was more concerned about the cost of fixing that screen door. I got the feeling that I was listening to a father complain that his teenage son had just batted a baseball through another plate glass window.

The heavy odor of rotting flesh sweetened the air as we approached one of the feeding stations. It was just a stump among the trees, but the ground was well packed around it, and a chorus of flies hummed in the undergrowth. They sounded happy to hear us coming. "I leave food out for the bears all summer, and they show up almost every night. But when hunting season starts, I come out here and fire off a single rifle shot. The bears don't come around any more when they hear that. They know it's not safe in these woods then."

I have never sat out at night to watch the bears come to Ray's feeding stations. They know him better than they know me, and I am not sure how comfortable either of us would feel out there in the dark together. Besides, it strikes me as a rather personal, private connection that the old man and those bears share, not the sort of thing upon which outsiders should intrude.

Sad to say, Ray's bears have more to worry about these days than they used to. Not only are the dumps closed and sport hunters hot on their trails each fall, some folks in the Far East believe that black bear gall bladders cure impotence and are willing to pay a thousand dollars or more for a single bladder, enough to touch off a booming illegal trade. Fortunately, gall bladder poaching is less common in New York than in other states, in part because it is legal to sell those body parts here, so they yield much less profit than do the black market prices.

In spite of hunting, poaching, and car collisions, New York's bear population seems to be in little danger of extirpation. We are their only predators; there seems to be plenty of good habitat for them; and because they eat such a wide variety of food, they are not likely to starve if one or more food sources dries up now and then. And it is probably just as well for the bears that our local landfills have closed. Garbage actually comprised only a fraction of the diet of the so-called dump bears, because they generally filled up on wild foods growing near the dumps. Although most of their trash-foraging was apparently out of curiosity and a taste for exotic snacks, it was probably harmful in the long run. Bear droppings around landfills were often full of paper from diapers, paper towels, and picnic plates, and on at least one occasion, an individual was seen with indigestible plastic strips dangling from its rectum. Dump bears also drank heavily from toxic leachate puddles.

Because black bears are pretty common in the Adirondacks, it is probably a good idea to make a list of do's and don'ts for an encounter with *Ursus americanus.* Overall, the best rule of thumb is to use common sense in your dealings with them. For example, avoid doing something silly like spilling tuna oil all over yourself, like I did during a camping trip through Montana's grizzly country in 1976. Do not eat in your sleeping bag, for similar reasons. Rather than invite break-ins by keeping food and other smelly things (including toothpaste) in your tent, stash them outside in a plastic trash bag hung well out of reach on a sturdy line strung between two trees. This will help to keep marauding raccoons out of your gear as well.

As long as we are on the subject of camping in bear country, you may be glad to know that an actual scientific field study purports to have shown that black bears are not attracted to human menstrual odors. Rather than get too graphic about the methods involved in that study, I will just reassure you that nobody was staked out as bait.

Of the few bear attacks reported in the Adirondacks, the vast majority have involved a good measure of human folly. For instance, one teen had his butt bitten when he tried to make off with two cubs; a pretty reasonable and restrained response from a concerned mother, I dare say. Just remember that a bear is not going to act like a human in your presence. It is more likely to treat you like another bear. That may involve swatting you hard with a powerful clawed mitt or giving you a good chomp if it thinks you are getting out of line.

In the unlikely event that you find yourself facing an unfriendly-looking bear (ears laid back, hackles raised, jaws working), I am sorry but I am not sure what to tell you. After searching through several dozen sources, I have collected a perfectly confusing array of encounter strategies from which to choose: stand your ground, back slowly away, lie still, clap your hands, talk gently, and scream your head off while charging the beast. Trying to flee is also reasonable if you have a good head start, but black bears have been clocked running at thirty miles an hour, and they climb trees better than you do. If you are actually being chewed on by a black bear, experts generally consider it to be a good idea to holler and fight back rather than to lie still, because the animal is clearly under the impression that you are suitable food and requires some convincing to the contrary.

So, what should you do if you see a bear in the Adirondacks? For those who choose to avoid this issue altogether, just hang your food at night, keep a clean camp, and make some noise occasionally, and I can almost guarantee that you will never see *Ursus americanus* anywhere but in a zoo, a picture book, or on a roadside. For the rest, I recommend standing very still and savoring the moment as best you can. Before you know it, the animal will probably run for cover and leave you with nothing but a lingering shot of adrenaline and a good story to tell.

Snowfleas

When I came home from work yesterday, the message light on my phone machine was blinking. It was a breathless call from a friend whose house was being assaulted by an army of mysterious little bugs: "They're land-based, but they are okay on water. They look like tiny specks, but then, *ping*, they're gone like fleas. I wonder if you could tell me how I can, um, get rid of them. Besides stomping all over them, I mean. They're trying to get into my door. I don't want them here!"

I called and reassured her that they were nothing more than swarming deadly bloodsucking Adirondack plague fleas. She knew me well enough to know that this meant that they were perfectly harmless. They were not fleas at all, and they did not particularly wish to invade her house. I have seen them swarming against the side of another friend's house in late April, but that was probably only because the house stood in the path of their migration. No, these were not fleas (Order Siphonaptera, translating from the Greek to something like "wingless siphons") but rather spring-tails (order Collembola), and they thought no more of biting anybody than we would of biting them. Nonetheless, these kinds of insects do hop around in a manner so reminiscent of flea-leaps that most people call them snowfleas.

You have probably seen snowfleas (*Hypogastrura nivicola*) at some time or another if you spend much time out in the woods in late winter, but you may not have realized it at the time. They are so small that you are not likely to "see a single snowflea." You normally see *many* snowfleas sprinkled across the snow like dirt or soot. When they are really swarming, the snow can turn gray with them.

One warm day in February, I skied a forest trail that was literally black with them. I could not imagine how many lay crushed in the ski ruts. The sickly odor that rose from the crushed bodies reminded me of fish slime. Perhaps the smell was a sort of warning chemical released by springtails in distress, or maybe it was just the stench of mass insect death.

You have to get a close-up view of a springtail if you are going to see why they are not fleas. A flea packs six legs beneath an almost crescent-shaped, jointed brownish body. It stands tall and narrow, and when it walks, it tends to sway like a galleon on the high seas. You never see fleas in dense swarms out in the woods, except perhaps on the miserable hide of some luckless mammal or bird. A typical springtail, on the other hand, is blue-gray and stands a bit closer to the ground. It has a distinct head with a pair of dark eyes (each consisting of sixteen smaller ones) and with floppy, segmented antennae. It even looks kind of cute. Being a wingless insect, it has six legs for walking, but at first glance you might think it had an extra pair of legs folded under its belly.

That is the spring on the springtail's tail. It is forked, leading specialists to call it a *furcula*, after the Latin word for fork. It works under the same principle as do catapults. When the animal wants to move fast and far, it flicks its furcula against the ground and tosses itself high into the air. A springtail is small, only a couple of millimeters long, but it can jump ten to twenty times its own body length at the drop of a furcula. A furcula is a handy device for a springtail to have, because the little beings are pretty defenseless otherwise. Many of them are distasteful to insect predators, and most are covered with loose scales and bristles that make it hard for predators to grab them. But the furcula is the Collembolan answer to wings. When the animal is not leaping about, it keeps the furcula clasped primly against its third body segment.

If you take an even closer look at a springtail, you will probably also notice yet another structure affixed to its underbelly, this time to the first body segment. It is a tubelike thing, called a *collophore*, that sticks out of the animal's chest and confuses scientists. At first, naturalists supposed that the collophore was used for sticking a springtail to whatever it happened to be walking on. In fact, that is how springtails got their official scientific name, Collembola: *coll* is Greek for "glue," and *embola* means "bolt or wedge," like the one you have sticking out of your chest if you happen to be a Collembolan. The term "collophore" derives from *coll* and *phoros*, and translates as "to bear glue." Unfortunately for the terminology, specialists now suspect that collophores have more to do with drinking than with glue. Should this turn out to be correct, I suppose some earnest young taxonomist will soon suggest changing the official name to "Bibembola."

In fact, some scientists have taken into account the springtail's many oddities and have considered putting it into a class of its own, separate from the insects. They have the requisite six legs, but no other insect has a furcula or a collophore. Furthermore, springtails do not metamorphose from a larval infancy into adulthood, as do most insects. They just hatch out of their respective eggs and get bigger, shedding their armorlike exoskeletons as they grow.

There are many kinds of springtails, probably many more than have been recorded by scientists, and most do not live on snow. I have seen little gray rafts of *Podura aquatica* drifting about on the surfaces of tide pools on the coast of Maine. I have found them clinging to the roots of salt marsh grasses *(Spartina alterniflora)* below the tide line in North Carolina. Those salt marsh springtails were covered with a water-repellent white wool that seemed to keep them dry down there in the wet, anoxic mud of the flooded marsh. I suppose that they breathed through the same air tubes that bring oxygen down to the roots of the intertidal grasses. People have reported finding springtails throughout North America and in Europe, so you can probably find them just about anywhere you bend down and look for them.

Most of my personal experience with Collembola, however, has to do with the ones that darken the snow in late winter and early spring, the ones that everyone calls snowfleas. I wish that I could tell you exactly what they are doing out there on the snow, but I cannot. Nor could anybody at the state museum in Albany when I called them, nor at Cornell University's prestigious entomology department, nor at the Smithsonian Institution. I even tried launching my own half-baked research program to answer the question for myself. As you will soon see, I had plenty of fun but did not discover what I set out to find.

One day in March, we had a brief thaw, and fresh hordes of snowfleas appeared on top of the snow. I noticed that they collected in hollows in the snow, especially in ski tracks and in footprints, and that they seemed to favor the shady sides of rutted tracks. Here was a chance to solve the mystery of why snowfleas appear on the snow.

I began by trying to find out where the creatures were coming from. Wondering if the snowfleas were working their way up through the snowpack, I dug into the snow in a thinly populated section of drift, looking for stray dark specks. I found none, other than the occasional dive-bomber from the cliff edges of the hole. I had thought that the congregations gathering inside footprints and ski tracks might have been evidence of migration within the snow itself, because breaking through the surface with boots or skis would probably expose burrowers. Instead, I learned that the tracks just collected animals that jumped into them and had trouble jumping back out.

By looking closely at individuals inside my own footprints, I could see how much trouble some of them were having. I watched one laboring up the rough face of a snow cliff that I had just made with my right foot. It got a few inches up the wall, then seemed to lose patience. It gave a flick of its furcula, presumably to speed itself along. Of course, furcula flicks throw the animal away from whatever surface it is walking on. Because this one happened to be walking on a vertical surface, the result of the flick was to send it sailing out into space and back to the bottom with a silent crash. I felt like I was watching the torment of the damned, as the insects endlessly climbed and tumbled. Within half an hour, the footprint was shadowed with black flecks.

I went back indoors and came out shortly with a freshly brewed mug of coffee. I sat down on the sun-drenched wooden steps leading to my kitchen door and leaned over to watch a swarm on a glistening snowbank. The bright sunlight poured its energizing warmth into my winter-pale arms and face, making it very easy to stay put for a long look at the wealth of life around me.

Placing a clear sheet of plastic over a patch of snow, I counted the snowfleas under it. There were as many as twenty per square inch of snow, but they can be much more densely packed than that. A book on my shelf claims there can be one hundred thousand of them in a cubic meter of forest soil, and still more when they are migrating.

I set my coffee down and leaned closer to peer through a hand lens in hopes of seeing what the snowfleas were doing down there on the melting snowscape. The ones on the snow itself were crawling and hopping about with no purpose that I could discern. The ones on the part of the steps soaked by snowmelt sat still with their faces pressed against the wood. The ones on the dry parts of the steps milled about like their compatriots out on the snow. Then I noticed that the wooden steps were slippery with something, probably algae or fungi. It looked as though the snowfleas were drinking or grazing on something on the steps.

Maybe the snowfleas were out on the snow in search of food? There are reports of them drowning by the score in maple sap buckets, and Collembola have been found eating pollen and the fibers and spores of certain fungi. But what could they be eating on clean-looking snow? Admittedly, pollen grains are pretty hard to spot with the naked eye, but nothing I know of releases pollen in winter. You can find certain kinds of fungi or algae growing on old snow, but I have seen snowfleas gather on freshly fallen powder.

I walked along the footpath leading into a nearby patch of woods and noticed that they were most abundant under hemlocks (*Tsuga canadensis*). Then I noticed that the wet bark of the hemlock trunks, just above the melting snowline, was packed with tiny gray specks, all apparently munching on water-activated green algae flecks—just as they were on my back steps. The wetter portions of fallen hemlock branches that lay in the snow were generally covered with snowfleas; branches of other kinds of trees were not.

It so happened that this particular snowflea emergence began just when my biology students were casting about for research project ideas. By the week's end a pair of students, Catherine and Missy, were busily probing the depths of local snowflea ecology. They chose a nearby patch of woods that sported a convenient hiking trail. Their research program was simple; leave fresh footprints in the snowy trail and record the density of springtails that accumulate in the footprints in different forest habitats. For several sunny mornings in a row, Catherine and Missy stomped out a line of prints and returned on the half hour to count the snowfleas.

It was not the most rigorous project, but it yielded some interesting results. Their footprints quickly filled with Collembola everywhere they went, but the densest accumulations were always among hemlock stands. Mixed conifer stands came in a close second, and birch groves yielded the fewest. The students also recorded slightly lower air temperatures in the shady hemlock and mixed conifer stands. Did these results reflect some inherent patchiness in Collembola populations, or food preferences, or temperature preferences, or what? As is often the case with field research, this brief glimpse into the private lives of snowfleas brought up more questions than it answered.

After a year of observation and reading, I had yet to answer the central question of what the darned things are doing out on the snow in the first place. They certainly did not seem to be eating anything there, because they always seemed to be moving when they were on snow. They were not mating on beds of snow, either, or at least they never let me see them doing it. They seemed to be crossing the snow, apparently after crawling up tree trunks from the forest floor.

One day I chanced upon a twenty-year-old article by Walter H. Lyford entitled "Overland Migration of Collembola *(Hypogastrura nivicola* Fitch) Colonies." At last, I thought, The Answer. I was mistaken. Lyford was writing about migrations on the forest floor itself. In autumn, no less, as well as in spring. It seems that the readily noticed frolics on snow are just loose aggregations, with individuals generally keeping several millimeters of space between themselves and their neighbors. During the autumn and spring, springtails crowd together by the thousands into colonies that travel as discrete units through New England woods.

Lyford followed several colonies through Harvard Forest in September 1971. Each colony was about a foot wide and usually consisted of at least five hundred thousand individuals. (Another author reported colonies three times as wide as this, made up of several million crawling and jumping insects.) Each colony moved in a straight line atop and within the duff of the forest floor, barring the occasional stump and boulder, and traveled as a unit for up to five days at a stretch. Any given swarm typically covered between three and five meters per day. Being a professional scientist, Lyford tried a few experiments. He covered one colony with a black plastic sheet, casting it in shadow. The mob stopped in its tracks and refused to budge until sunlight hit it again. He blocked the paths of colonies with metal barriers sunk through the litter and into the mineral soil below. After one day of immobility, the stymied animals inexplicably shed their skins. Maybe that is what was going on with my friend's apparent snowflea invasion. I wish I had thought to ask her if the things were molting all over her doorstep.

Again, more mysteries. In spite of his detailed analysis of springtail migration, Lyford mentioned no motive for snowfleas to walk across snow. Given that they might get together in spring and fall for an occasional molting orgy, why would little black insects leave the relative warmth and safety of a forest floor to scamper across icy white expanses?

Finally, after months of phone calls, I located someone who had a firm, if rather disappointing, answer to the mystery. Dr. Kenneth Christiansen, a professor at Grinnell College, happened to be in his office when I called for the fifth time in as many months. He generously agreed to let me interrogate him on the subject of springtails, his research specialty over the last several decades.

So, what are snowfleas doing out there on the snow in the middle of winter? As Christiansen put it: "Nothing."

"They breed in the leaf litter under the winter snow," he explained matter-of-factly. "By midwinter their populations get so big that they just sort of boil out onto the surface of the snow. The ones you see outside like that are just the unlucky ones that got squeezed out of the crowded upper soil layers. They aren't doing anything out there; there's nothing for them to eat on the snow, they aren't mating, and they have no place in particular to go. They just sort of wander around all day and work their way back down to the soil around the bases of tree trunks for the night. Basically, they're pretty unhappy little characters."

Christiansen was full of fascinating tales of springtail behavior and ecology that almost made up for the let-down of his snowflea explanation. Collembola live almost anywhere, often in huge numbers; some say that they may be the most numerous land animals on Earth, after nematodes. There are parts of Antarctica where the only vegetation is lichens, the only animals are springtails, and the soil is made almost entirely of springtail droppings. Although springtails are harmless to humans, they sometimes become aggressive with each other over disputed territories in the soil. One of their standard methods of attack is to bludgeon each other with their floppy, jointed antennae, using them like clubs with which to bop each other over the head. It does not seem to hurt them much, but it serves the purpose of expressing displeasure: "Sometimes you find a pair of them chasing each other around and around in circles, beating each other's behinds with their antennae as they run." Oddly, this aggressive side of springtails seems to vanish when they get crowded, as in the winter population booms.

As I thanked Dr. Christiansen and hung up the phone, I felt a mix of relief—in finally getting an answer to the snowflea mystery from a world expert—and disappointment, as if the pot of gold at the end of the rainbow was full of sand. Now I am going to have to feel sorry for the little creatures when I see them in their teeming masses, wandering like homeless refugees across the frozen wastes of winter.

Bert Stern

Bert Stern, the retired Milligan Professor of English at Wabash College of Indiana, began visiting the Adirondacks in the mid-1970s. Stern, with his wife, Tam Neville, relocated to Keene Valley in the 1990s after he retired from academia.

His books include a critical study of the American poet Wallace Stevens, and most recently, a collection of poems, Silk, the Ragpicker's Grandson, *published by Red Dust, and a collection of essays,* Falling Toward Grace: Images of Religion and Culture from the Heartland. *Stern's essays have been published in the* Sewanee Review, Southern Review, *and* New Republic, *and his poems have appeared in numerous publications, including* New Letters, The American Poetry Review, Poetry, *and* The Spoon River Anthology.

The following poems are published for the first time here.

Early Autumn in Keene Valley

The miller got tired of grinding.
Everywhere, the full sacks, leaking
yellow or white, everywhere
the mice fat on their gleanings.

What would they do with the bread,
the women, their hands ghostly
with flour? Who cared for the cakes,
so much sweetness, to sicken the children.

But autumn had come, he must grind.
Something was grinding the leaves
and the flowers, earth recoiling
its juices, womb cold and dried up.

The stars in their turning were grist.
Who ground it? he wondered.
His body was yellow and sear
as he bent to the stone that kept chirring.

White-Throated Sparrow

There's always a white-throated sparrow
singing on a mountain top, and somebody
there, hearing it for the first time.
That's what you need to believe,
at least, as your eyes stroke the ruffled
nap of Noonmark across the valley
and you hear that sweet call again,
as final as it ever was, leaving nothing
to say beyond the five notes of its saying.

Fisher

I couldn't see the rage in this thing.
It was poking around in the compost,
a little of this, a little of that, scattering
grapefruit rinds and rotten apples
in a wide radius around, glad, it seemed,
not to be knocking porcupines out
of the trees, not to be ripping flesh,
not spitting out quills, swallowing some,
prickly life, to knock the inedible
out of trees as if it were fruit, quills

in your scat. So this is the Ritz for
the fisher, this is catering, my garbage
succulent again.

But tail as long as body,
the way he walked away, odd arch
of the back, quickness in reserve,
sure movement of a beast ready to heave
itself at anything, teeth tearing belly, muscular
fury, teeth meeting through the flesh,
warm drink, warm drink, swilling
that down.

Tea

Evening came, then morning.
Between, three light steps
on the distant stair, and now
their memory over coffee.

Was it you, while I slept,
slipping down in yellow
silk, to feed the stove
with pine, and drink your tea
alone, at dawn, as you like to do?

Fred G. Sullivan

After a childhood of roaming the landscape in and around the southern Adirondack mill town of Glens Falls, Fred G. Sullivan went away to serve in the U.S. Army during the Vietnam War. The Adirondack Mountains remained his touchstone. He relocated there in the mid-1970s with his wife, Polly, and four young children, after filming Of Rivers and Men *(1973), a documentary featuring the major wilderness rivers of the Adirondack region. This led to the first modern feature filmed in the Adirondacks,* Cold River *(1981), which was a critical and financial flop.*

This experience with artistic failure, coupled with the challenge of raising a family in the Adirondacks, inspired, in 1987, his most notable work, The Beer Drinker's Guide to Fitness and Filmmaking. *The quirky and personal independent film charmed audiences at the prestigious Sundance Film Festival that year, where he won a special award for "originality, independent spirit, and doing it his own damn way." With the* Wall Street Journal *describing Sullivan as a "woodchuck Woody Allen,"* The Beer Drinker's Guide *broke attendance records at independent movies houses in New York City and elsewhere.*

Sullivan, who died in 1996 at the age of fifty, worked as a freelance writer while struggling as a filmmaker in the Adirondacks, his writing appearing in the Boston Globe *and the* New York Times, *among other publications. The essay reprinted here first appeared in* Adirondack Life *in 1989.*

What's So Funny?

My next feature-length motion picture will take a stab at Adirondack comedy. Recently, shamelessly, I have infested the nation's theater

392

screens with a character named Adirondack Fred—a man in a deerskin loincloth whose very presence on a picturesque High Peak seems to profane the landscape. Yes, I am he—Adirondack Fred—and he is me.

But like "military intelligence," Adirondack humor may be a contradiction in terms. One writer, claiming that he found year-round Adirondack life depressingly devoid of belly laughs, now returns to his hometown in the South for six months every year for a "yuk-it-up good time," instead of enduring the bleakness of another winter. In the last century, Robert Louis Stevenson echoed those sentiments when he wrote of his brief sojourn in Saranac Lake, "The greyness of the heavens here is a situation eminently revolting to the soul." No belly laughs for Stevenson. But he was preoccupied with chest problems, since he was in Saranac Lake for the cure.

Saranac Lake is where I live, and I too pine for belly laughs, Adirondack-style. Although I have been involved in Adirondack affairs for a number of years, I can recollect few instances of humor that go beyond the personal and touch with laughter on the broader geopolitical scene.

One rare instance occurred in 1975 when some opponents of the fledgling Adirondack Park Agency dumped a load of manure on the Agency's lawn and implanted there a sign saying "We've taken yours for three years, now here's some of ours."

Reverence is so abundant in Adirondack literature and the politics of preservation that chuckles are intimidated and lost. The essence of the Adirondack wilderness—beautiful, unpredictable, inspirational, warm and glorious, wet and cold, savage and impersonal serves human solitude and renews the soul. Solitude is sacred. Reverence results.

But comedy is irreverent. While the wilderness experience is largely expressed in terms of introspection, comedy needs a community. One reflects the indomitable, untamed power of nature, while the other reflects the indomitable spark of the human spirit. Solitude is calming. Comedy is chaotic. Therefore, to combine the Adirondack essence with comedy creates conflict and tension. To my skewed way of thinking, this is fertile ground for art.

Yet it took me fifteen years as a film maker to build the confidence to plunge into the human comedy of Adirondack life. My first film was a documentary called *Of Rivers and Men*. Made in 1972, it was the first film to examine environmental issues facing the Adirondacks. The chronicle of its production was also my first-ever article for a magazine, *Adirondack Life*, summer 1973.

The environmentalists who financed *Of Rivers and Men* gave me free rein to inform, entertain, and I hoped, motivate its audience. The film turned out to be pretty solid, but it wasn't a barrel of laughs. Yet when I view it now I am most pleased by the several scenes in the movie where I managed to provoke laughter, rather than environmental piety. The biggest laughs come when people are seen flipping their canoes during a frigid whitewater race—the slip on a banana peel, Adirondack-style. The method behind this madness was to get them laughing, then slam home the message.

The producer of *Of Rivers and Men*, a noted conservationist and a grand gentleman, encouraged me to continue as an environmental filmmaker. But we were already locking horns over the propriety and effectiveness of including people, let alone humor, in film images of the wilderness. He wanted pure wilderness, its image untrammeled by man. I wanted to put people in the picture, to reflect the emotion that gives human dimension to that portrayed, and, I admit, in hopes of catching more slips on the banana peel. We parted, both to concentrate on our individual ideas of proper Adirondack films. Years later he would express disappointment that my feature films "didn't measure up" to the potential he saw in *Of Rivers and Men*.

I treasure the few moments of humor in my first theatrical motion picture, *Cold River* (1979), an adventure set in the Adirondacks, circa 1923. Yet that movie was a rather massive industrial enterprise and the serious tone of the finished product reflects the chaos and pressures of its making. In the midst of the chaos I had forgotten how to laugh at myself, and any significant potential for humor in *Cold River* escaped my grasp. The movie became earnest, like so much of Adirondackana. It was my turn to slip on the banana peel.

Commercial failure came in tandem with a blossoming family. Thus, my wife Polly and I joined the gritty ranks of that time-honored Adirondack tradition—poverty and kids. Twin boys did it. We had contemplated a perfect third child to complement our previously perfect two little children. What we got was the double-whammy of twins. Who said Mother Nature didn't have a sense of humor?

The whammy put me into a creative tailspin, the jolly partner of financial ruin. I had to find another wellspring of inspiration, get a job, or commit myself to a sanatorium—and the sanatorium tradition in the Adirondacks is history.

Then dawned the light. The chaos of twins had indeed put people in the picture and a bounce in my step. For if humor comes from tension, I faced it, in panic; if humor comes from observation of human foibles, I had foibles, in spades. If humor comes from the endurance of hardships and stress—the way *M*A*S*H* reflected war in Korea—Polly and I faced four children under the age of five. Deflate the dour, puncture the pretentious, slip on the banana peel.

Eureka! It had taken marriage, four children, a dog, failure, and fifteen years before I announced to Polly that I had at last struck a vein of humor uniquely Adirondack. And it was within our very own family. Said sweet Polly "We're going to starve."

Thus began the odyssey that became the tenderly titled feature, *Adirondack Fred Presents The Beer Drinker's Guide To Fitness And Filmmaking* (formerly *Sullivan's Pavilion*, before we changed the title to sell more tickets). Chaos and comedy. True Adirondack life. It was all around me. To its imperatives I have since surrendered.

No alarm need be sounded, nor fear spread. There are plenty who will continue to ponder the Adirondack Mountains with reverence and awe. I seek the brightness. I see encouraging signs.

The jaunty derring-do of the informal Ski-to-Die Club suggests good humor, perhaps fatal. The after-hours carousing of the Gore Mountain Ski Patrol is legendary, and I would like to volunteer my services, even though my skiing is weak. Harry Tucker's Casa del Sol restaurant in Saranac Lake dispenses great margaritas and grand camaraderie, and I consider myself a charter member in good standing—even if Harry did say on National Public Radio that "Adirondack Fred should be taken out and shot."

The reverence for the loon gives me hope.

And I detect a new found spark when it comes to Adirondack names. Formerly, for every moniker like Lake Tear-of-the-Clouds (is the "tear" acid rain?), there were far too many Mud Ponds. Now consider the Adirondack disease with the Latin name *Giardiasis*; it's an intestinal infection carried in mountain water and caused by a parasite (*Giardia lamblia*) in the feces of wild animals and wilderness man.

This scourge has gained far greater notoriety, however, because some mountain wag tagged it Beaver Fever.

Beaver Fever. Hmmm, a sour scourge with a great title. It may not be a belly full of laughs, but it's something Adirondack Fred appreciates. Hey, maybe it can be a new Adirondack movie—about say, sex, politics, and acid rain. *Beaver Fever*—coming soon to a theater near you!

Philip G. Terrie

There have been a number of historical accounts of the Adirondack region published in the last century, starting with Alfred L. Donaldson's History of the Adirondacks *in 1921. Few writers, though, have been able to capture the full cultural, political, social, and economic breadth of the region's history in the manner of Phil Terrie.*

There is a good reason for this. Terrie has made the Adirondacks the focus of his life's work, beginning with his work as a curator at the Adirondack Museum in 1966. He is the author of several books, including Forever Wild: A Cultural History of Wilderness in the Adirondacks *(Syracuse University Press, 1994) and* Wildlife and Wilderness: A History of Adirondack Mammals *(Purple Mountain Press, 1993). He has written several articles on Adirondack history and environmental literature. Terrie, who has a home in Long Lake, New York, is currently a professor of English and American Culture Studies at Bowling Green State University.*

"A Crisis Looms," reprinted here, is the final chapter of Terrie's most recent book, Contested Terrain: A New History of Nature and People in the Adirondacks *(The Adirondack Museum and Syracuse University Press, 1997).*

A Crisis Looms

The threat to Adirondack forests and lakes posed by acid precipitation was one issue friends and foes of the Park Agency could agree on, but it was just about the only one. When it came to the [Adirondack Park Agency's] Private Land Plan the acrimony was even more intense than the feud over the Crane Pond Road. The primary local version of the Adirondack narrative acknowledged that the Park was a place of beauty and natural splendor but insisted that local governments elected by local people were perfectly capable of protecting the Park. This narrative frequently cast the story of the Park Agency and the Private Land Plan into a class-based contest between two groups. On one side were politically powerless blue-collar Adirondack families whose love of the land, based on experience and history, was deep and genuine. On the other were effete, wealthy, politically powerful conservationists from outside the region who were indifferent to the lives and well-being of the year-round residents and aimed only to "use the Adirondacks for their greedy enrichment and elitist pleasure." As Anthony D'Elia, one of the most strident opponents of the Private Land Plan, put it, "It was the age old scenario of the powerful against the powerless, the rich against the poor."

This insider-versus-outsider narrative possessed dramatic political appeal, but it left out at least one important third party—the cadre of developers and real estate lawyers who stood to make fortunes if no restraints were placed on the development of private land in the Adirondacks. There were, moreover, Adirondackers whose families had lived in the Park for generations who supported the Private Land Plan and hoped it would protect a way of life that they felt was threatened by uncontrolled development. Finally, the oversimplified story of rich-versus-poor also failed to note that virtually all of the land in the Resource Management classification, the land most restricted by the Private Land Plan, was owned by corporations, clubs, and wealthy families with bases outside the blue line.

The case of Anthony D'Elia illustrates how recent conflict in the Adirondacks cannot be neatly reduced to a simple story. A leader of the resistance to the Adirondack Park Agency, D'Elia was anything but a poor Adirondacker oppressed by indifferent conservationists. He was himself an outsider, a successful, college-educated businessman and teacher from New York City, who moved to the Adirondacks in 1972 at the age of fifty-two with plans to develop vacation homes around the Loon Lake golf course. When the Park Agency found his scheme to be in violation of the Private Land Plan and denied him a development permit, he took up the banner of home rule and fought the APA, with an energetic combination of zeal and bitterness, until his death in 1990. Far from being the subject of a simple tale of class conflict, the Adirondack Park was becoming a focal point in a debate of national significance: to what extent does a society have an interest in what happens to private property? And what power does it have to demonstrate and protect that interest?

The first years of the administration of the Private Land Plan by the newly established Adirondack Park Agency did nothing to reduce the level of local resistance. The staff was young and dedicated but came from outside the region. Overworked, they had trouble keeping up with permit applications, the guidelines for which appeared cumbersome and legalistic. Local builders, indisposed from the start to accept the very idea of zoning, grew increasingly impatient with the Private Land Plan and with the APA, some of whose staff, according to one account, were "perceived as young, insensitive, and arrogant."

Behind much of the local hostility to the APA and the Private Land Plan were the realities of the local economy. Politicians and business leaders believed that development—meaning, for the most part, construction of vacation homes—would lead to the creation of jobs and the infusion of outside capital into the local economy. And the Adirondack economy definitely appeared to be in trouble. The Temporary Study Commission found an Adirondack economy characterized by relatively low labor force participation rates, high dependence on government jobs, and high unemployment. What jobs there were in the Adirondacks tended to be less skilled and more oriented toward service sectors than in the rest of New York. In 1960, the unemployment rate for New York State was 5.2 percent, while in the Adirondack Park it was more than twice that, at 11.2 percent. Many Adirondack jobs, moreover, were tied to the seasonal tourist economy and were thus unable to provide year-round employment. The median family income in the Park was only 82 percent of that of the rest of New York.

Even though these figures reflected conditions obtaining before the creation of the Park Agency, after 1971 the Agency itself and its restrictions on development were routinely blamed for any sluggishness perceived in the Adirondack economy. But after two decades of the Private Land Plan, a study conducted by the Nelson A. Rockefeller Institute of Government for the New York Department of Labor found that the economy of the Adirondacks was in certain respects faring better than that of either New York State or the nation as a whole. In particular, the Rockefeller Institute observed that both employment and payrolls rose faster in the Adirondacks during the recession of 1989–92 than in the state or the nation. Between 1985 and 1992 employment rose by 25 percent in the Park; during the same period, it actually decreased slightly in the rest of New York.

None of this meant that the Adirondack economy was exactly thriving. As in many parts of rural America, public sector jobs and lower-paying service industries were overrepresented, while higher-paying service jobs were less common than in New York as a whole. But it was clear that during the first two decades of the existence of the Private Land Plan, the Adirondack economy, far from losing ground as compared with New York State, had in fact narrowed the gap. Whether this was a direct function of the environmental protections enforced by the Adirondack Park Agency is impossible to say. But environmentalists insisted that it was illogical to lay regional economic disappointments at the feet of the Park Agency.

The Adirondack economic picture is indeed a complicated one. The local tax base illustrates how different local finances are from those of most of the rest of New York. In many Adirondack towns, the state owns a significant portion of the real estate, in some cases as much as half of the town. Taken out of the base of land available for logging or other substantial development, the Forest Preserve might appear to be unproductive and a drag on the tax base. But, argue defenders of the Forest Preserve, this is not necessarily the case. The Forest Preserve attracts thousands of visitors from outside the region, in all seasons of the year, who leave their dollars with local merchants. So long as the lands of the Forest Preserve remain undeveloped, moreover, they create no demands for municipal services such as police protection, roads, sewers, and the like. Finally, since the very establishment of the Forest Preserve, in order to alleviate any negative impact on the tax base, the state has paid taxes on it to Adirondack counties and school districts. As the Forest Preserve grew, this funding source evolved into a virtual state subsidy of local economies; by 1964 a Joint Legislative Committee on Assessment and Taxation of State-Owned Land could declare, "Taxation of state lands has become a source of 'state aid' for the support of local governments and schools."

One consequence of this (and of the existence of large holdings in private hands that also contributed significant tax dollars to Adirondack counties) was that, despite an economy that still lagged behind that of the rest of the state in terms of employment and income, some Adirondack school districts were among the best funded in the state. Small populations coupled with major sources of tax dollars coming from outside the town led to high per-student school budgets. For example, in 1993–94, the average number of students per teacher in all of New York State's public schools was 14.3; in New York City it was 15.9; in Long Lake it was 6.31. During the two decades after the establishment of the Park Agency, the average student-teacher ratio in all Adirondack school districts improved by better than a third.

In 1992, a State Education Department study found that Adirondack school districts, with a few exceptions, had more library books per student than did districts across the state. The same study showed that per-student expenditures averaged higher in the Adirondacks than in New York state as a whole: $7,624 for Adirondack school districts, $6,908 statewide, with some Adirondack districts way above the statewide average—for example, Newcomb at $18,586 and Long Lake at $11,660. Even though both average household and per capita incomes were significantly lower in these towns than in New York State as a whole, because of the tax payments made by the state and land owners not living in the town, they constituted relatively rich school districts. At the same time, it must be noted, some of the larger Adirondack districts spent considerably less per student than the statewide norm: e.g., Tupper Lake spent $5,414 and Saranac Lake $5,630.

The complexities and paradoxes of the Adirondack economy, if anything, only increased local hostility to the environmental agenda. And environmentalists, in fact, were often themselves disappointed with the Private Land Plan, which reflected a series of compromises demanded by the exigencies of legislative politics and was thus unable to provide the level of protection that they had hoped for. While these compromises may have been politically necessary, they weakened a plan designed from the start to permit (while controlling) development, not stop it altogether. Throughout the 1970s and '80s conservationists warned repeatedly that the forested character of the Park was slowly eroding as developments perfectly legal under the Private Land Plan popped up throughout the region.

In 1989 a powerful article in the *New York Times Magazine*, illustrated with shocking before-and-after photographs, pointed out that during the previous two years alone more than 100,000 acres of forest had passed into the hands of speculators eager to subdivide and resell. The problem was rooted in the economics of the logging industry. Holding onto forest lands and periodically realizing what profits could be derived from conservative logging was beginning to seem much less appealing to many of the owners of the still-undeveloped back country than selling off for immediate profits. Conservationists wondered what would happen to the Adirondacks if the big landowners, wood products companies like International Paper or Finch, Pruyn and Co. (based in Glens Falls, with a history of over a century of Adirondack logging and holdings of some 154,000 acres), under pressure from stock holders to maximize income, simply decided to get out of the business of logging and into the business of selling lots for vacation homes. Even if interpreted in the strictest way possible, the Private Land Plan could not prevent what seemed to many to be a potential environmental disaster.

That same year Governor Mario Cuomo, responding to a growing conviction among downstate conservationists that the Private Land Plan did not provide adequate protection, appointed another special commission to study the Park and recommend changes in policy. As with the Temporary Study Commission, locals argued that this new body was set up from the start to advance a radical environmental agenda with little regard for property rights or regional business interests. After holding hearings throughout the state, the Commission on the Adirondacks in the Twenty-First Century reported to the governor in the spring of 1990. Reflecting the views of many of the New Yorkers who had testified before the Commission, the Report concluded that without serious modification of the Private Land Plan, the Adirondack Park could lose forever the character of forested open space that had defined the region in the popular mind since early in the nineteenth century.

Among other things, the Twenty-First Century Commission called for an immediate one-year moratorium on building in the back country, tighter controls on development along all lake and river shores, and further state acquisition of key parcels of privately owned forests and waters. The initial response from Adirondackers, already exasperated by what they saw as endless attacks on local autonomy, was almost universally hostile, repeating the claim that conservationists were callously indifferent to the economic travails of local residents. Opposition to the Report quickly became a rallying cry for home rule in the Adirondacks. Citizen organizations issued press releases condemning the Report and arguing that if the legislature adopted its recommendations the local economy would be devastated. The Adirondack Fairness Coalition, based in Chestertown, declared that any evidence of a "crisis" was invented by environmentalists.

To demonstrate opposition to the Report, another group, the Adirondack Solidarity Alliance, organized a dramatic protest. On May 11, 1990, vehicles driven by Alliance members and sympathizers conducted a "freedom drive" that snarled traffic and created near total gridlock on the Northway between exits 20 and 28. Supported by several local politicians, including Republican State Senator Ronald Stafford of Plattsburgh, who rode in the lead vehicle, opponents of the Report organized another motorcade on May 25. One thousand cars and trucks caravanned from Exit 34, near Elizabethtown, all the way to Clifton Park, where they turned around before heading north again for a rally near Frontiertown. The sentiments of the drivers were acidly expressed on one of many large banners: "Take this Report and Shove It." Meanwhile, Donald Gerdts, one of the Report's shrillest opponents, declared of the Twenty-First Century Commission, "They want our blood, they want our land, and they want us out of here."

Conservationists struggled to protect at least some of the Report's recommendations, and a local group supporting tighter development controls, the Residents' Committee to Protect the Adirondacks, emerged to counter the claims of the Solidarity Alliance and other groups. The Residents' Committee argued that groups like the Solidarity Alliance did not represent the views of all Adirondackers, many of whom believed that overdevelopment threatened their traditions and way of life but, because of the virulence of the Twenty-First Century Report's foes, were afraid to speak out in its favor. The efforts of the

Residents' Committee and others notwithstanding, however, the Report was dead on arrival. Governor Cuomo appeared not seriously committed to its recommendations, and after several months of acrimony, accusations, and the absence of substantive discussion, the Report faded into regional memory, another chapter in the story of New Yorkers' trying to decide what to do with the Adirondacks. Although the Report's specific recommendations were not adopted, some local moderates hoped that the furor it generated might lead to new efforts to establish better relations between local government and the Park Agency. Whether this hope will become reality remains one of the crucial uncertainties of the contemporary Adirondack drama.

Conservationists lamented the failure of the legislature to implement tighter controls on development, and the slow but steady erosion of the Park's open space continued. A pattern of development and construction that began with the completion of the Northway in 1967 was continuing and even accelerating. Between 1967 and 1987, the Park saw an average of 1,000 new houses built each year; the Private Land Plan appeared to have little effect on new housing starts. Indeed, after 1987, the number of new houses grew to roughly 1,200 per year. In 1995 Park Agency Chair John Collins (himself a fourth-generation native Adirondacker who fervently supported the Private Land Plan) observed that in 1992 the Park had 62 percent more dwellings than it had had in 1967. In his view the open space of the back country and the remaining undeveloped shores of lakes and rivers were woefully vulnerable to inappropriate development. Indeed, in the two decades after the initial approval of the Private Land Plan, 135 miles of roads and sixty-five miles of shoreline that had been lined only with trees had been turned over to real estate development.

A current example of the potential for substantial environmental change in the Adirondack Park is Whitney Park, in northern Hamilton County. First acquired in 1897 by millionaire William C. Whitney, designer of the lucrative New York City streetcar lines, this tract of 52,000 acres and some forty lakes and ponds, incorporated as Whitney Industries, has been owned, enjoyed, and logged by Whitney's descendants for nearly a century. Though heavily logged and crisscrossed with dirt roads, Whitney Park remains largely forested and would make an invaluable addition to the Forest Preserve. W. C. Whitney's grandson,

Cornelius Vanderbilt Whitney—socialite, co-founder of Pan American Airways, backer of the film *Gone With the Wind*, breeder of fine race horses—died in 1992. And his widow and children were faced with the expense of maintaining an Adirondack empire and retiring Whitney Industries' debt of nearly $4 million. If they opt to subdivide the property to pay their taxes, a devastating blow will have been dealt to the forested character of the very center of the Adirondack Park. The state cannot afford to buy the property for the Forest Preserve, and conservationists are frantically trying to piece together schemes involving easements or some other mechanism to protect the undeveloped open space of Whitney Park.

Meanwhile, the Whitney family, interested in subdividing and developing their land for profit, is expressing a hostility to the Park Agency and the Private Land Plan that further belies the characterization of recent Adirondack history as a conflict between working-class locals and wealthy, downstate conservationists. Tightly aligned with the eastern, elite establishment of prestige and affluence—precisely that element of American society identified by some locals as the sinister power behind the Private Land Plan—C. V. Whitney's aristocratic widow and her son from an earlier marriage complain that "ecosocialists" are interfering with their right to develop their property and hope that Republican Governor George Pataki, elected in 1994, will force the Park Agency to tilt toward property-owning developers and away from regional conservation. In the summer of 1996, when the Whitney family announced plans to re-assign title to four large lots on Little Tupper Lake, conservationists feared that this might be the beginning of a gradual dismemberment of Whitney Park.

The Adirondack political scene continues to be one of paradox, a chief example of which is an uneasy alliance between the forest-products industry and conservationists, both of whom hope that tax policies and other instruments can be devised to keep currently forested lands producing trees and not turned over to developers. The chief legal mechanism, viewed positively but cautiously by both conservationists and forest owners, is the easement, whereby a land owner might trade development rights for lower taxes. Such an arrangement might help keep a wood-products company in business, save the jobs of its loggers, and keep the land from being sold off in small lots.

In the late nineteenth century avaricious loggers threatened the landscape loved by vacationers and vital to a healthy watershed; today the logging interests—the modern equivalent of the transportation lobby of the 1880s and '90s—line up with conservationists to protect the forest from uncontrolled second-home development. "The state," declared Twenty-First Century Commission Chair Peter A. A. Berle (who subsequently became President of the National Audubon Society), "must not let the Park be overwhelmed by the short-sighted interests that would destroy the forest industry and treat the Park as a mere piece of saleable real estate."

Berle's muted acknowledgment of the importance of logging to the local economy is a tentative step toward bringing the year-round residents and their fate into discussions of what the Adirondack Park is and can be. While not all Adirondackers are loggers (or developers), they all need jobs and a viable community life if the Adirondack Park is to be a good place for both people and nature. Like rural towns across the country, Adirondack communities face a dilemma of monumental dimensions. As a resident of Essex County put it, "How can we preserve the positive rural environment that we call 'home' and at the same time improve our economic condition so that we and our children can remain here?" Can the economic picture be brightened without sacrificing the rural features that make the Adirondack Park appealing?

While there is no single "Adirondack" identity, no such thing as the typical "Adirondacker," people throughout the Park share a culture that makes their lives distinct. Adirondackers live in a region where the state owns almost half the land and where the Private Land Plan and the Adirondack Park Agency constitute a layer of bureaucracy that many other rural Americans never confront. More important, they live surrounded by millions of acres of forests and trees. Many Adirondackers treasure the life of the outdoors; they hunt and fish, they climb the peaks. As William Bibby of North Creek told photographer Mathias Oppersdorff, "I feel a part of these mountains, and I feel the mountains are part of me."

Equally important, they are profoundly aware that they enjoy a rural life that is threatened by a host of problems. The Adirondack economy remains relatively unstable, and young people are often unable to find work in the communities where they grew up. The stock of affordable, year-round housing is inadequate. While some towns, like Keene Valley or Lake Placid, attract swarms of tourists and their dollars, others, off the main tourist corridors, appear dilapidated and unkempt. Adirondackers deal with driving distances—to grocery stores, medical facilities, movies, visits with friends—that seem more typical of the West than of a densely settled state like New York. But most Adirondackers like their rural life and want it preserved. Both those whose great-grandparents struggled with the uncooperative soil and climate to make a living as farmers and those who have recently moved here, fleeing the crime, pollution, and chaos of the cities, value a life whose rhythms are still largely dictated by nature.

But they also want a healthy economy, and the fundamental dilemma remains of trying to improve economic conditions without obliterating the mix of the rural and the wild that makes the Adirondack Park unique. For a century and a half, the Adirondack region has appealed to people because it seems so different from the settled, developed remainder of New York. The antimodernism of Joel Headley and William James, the environmental concerns of Verplanck Colvin and David Hill, and the current drive to protect forested open space all depend on a certain image of the Adirondacks—an image of nature as either antidote to modern ills or fragile reservoir of valuable resources.

And the difficulties involved in protecting both human and natural values reflect the continuing power of narratives to define the land and influence people's understandings of the land's meaning. Conservationists have their story of what the Adirondack Park is, what its problems and opportunities are, and what should be done for it. Summer mountain climbers, November deer hunters, January skiers, and white-water rafters in the spring have their version of the Park's meaning. Local business interests and developers have another. And thousands of Adirondack families, allied with neither environmentalists nor developers, cherishing the rural life next to the East's last great wilderness but anxious about their economic security and their children's futures, have yet another.

The gap between these distinct and, one hopes, not mutually exclusive understandings recalls the equally profound difference between John Todd and Joel Headley of a century and a half ago. The question of Adirondack history is, whose narrative of the land will prevail? Or to look at it more optimistically, can a new narrative be constructed that seeks accommodation, that sees the Adirondacks as a cultural landscape, with people and nature, and thriving, healthy opportunities and protections for both?

If we return to the conservation era of the 1880s and '90s and recall the failure of the legislature to resolve the dilemma posed by private land in the Park, we may find just the unifying narrative we need to forge a hopeful story for the future of the Adirondacks. The realities of the twentieth century have made public ownership and management of the entire Park impossible. Although it is an accident of history, the unintended mix of private land, villages, and state-owned wilderness can itself be seen as *the* Adirondack story, a source of conflict but also a great opportunity.

In the Adirondacks we have a landscape that could be a model for the world. It is a place where people live and where nature matters, where it is just this combination, this interrelationship between people and nature, that defines the place, provides its meaning, constructs its narrative. If we think of the Adirondack Park as one big place rather than in terms of distinct landscapes within it—the villages and private land on the one hand and the Forest Preserve on the other—then we have a place that can be both functional and protected. If we can say that the failure of the New York legislature over a century ago to decide just what is wanted in the Adirondacks is the beginning of what has become the latest and most promising Adirondack narrative, then the irresolution of 1892 might be seen as a stroke of incredible good fortune.

Chase Twichell

A century ago, Reverend Joseph H. Twichell, a congregational clergyman from Connecticut and friend of literary notables such as Mark Twain and Charles Dudley Warner, roamed the wilds around Keene Valley. How fitting, then, that Chase Twichell, while establishing a successful career as a poet, writer, and teacher, return to her Adirondack roots of sorts and find a home in the same town as her ancestor, in the shadow of the region's highest peaks.

Her poems have appeared in the nation's most prestigious periodicals, including The New Yorker, Ploughshares, The Paris Review, The Nation, and the New England Review, and several other notable literary journals.

Twichell, who has taught at the University of Alabama, Hampshire College, and, most recently, Princeton, has authored a number of books of poems, including Northern Spy (University of Pittsburgh Press, 1981), The Odds (University of Pittsburgh Press, 1986), and Perdido (Farrar, Straus & Giroux, 1991). The poems reprinted here are from her two most recent collections, The Ghost of Eden (Ontario Review Press, 1995) and The Snow Watcher (Ontario Review Press, 1998).

Kerosene

Here comes a new storm, roiling and black.
It's already raining up on Cascade,
where lightning makes the clouds look like

flowers of kerosene, like arson at the end
of the match. Lightning comes straight

from childhood, where the burned-out storms
still glitter weakly, tinsel on the dead trees
in the January streets. Back there a kid is still

learning why her parents need that harsh
backlight to see each other.

Snow

Every day it snows an inch or two,
muting the music in the pines.
Old music.

Snow holds back the dawn—
an extra minute of lying here
while the self sleeps on.

Walking home after midnight,
two miles to go. The snow
is telling a story two miles long.

Dead trucks for sale in the yards.
New trucks plough the roads
of the dying towns.

If ever I flee to wilderness to die,
it will be to snow. Thus this snow
at bed time comforts me.

Visitors

Red fox flashing through the pines,
I see your maleness when it
smacks my headlights.

Poor spikehorn, lashed to the roof rack
under an inch of new snow.
First horns, last horns.

A heron lands on a river rock,
the granite they use for gravestones.
Sharp names in the rough stones.

In spring, ten thousand scents.
The snake flees the scythe
into the uncut grass.

Two squirrels take a pinecone apart,
petal by rough petal. Their tails
say *fuck you!* to hunger.

Walking Meditation

I'm the first tall animal
to walk the trail today.
Apologies to the spiders.

The sapling maple I cut
last year for a walking stick
forgives me this morning.

Galaxies of lichens
on the stones—what's
my life to them?

What do the deer
make of my trail? Sometimes
they use it, sometimes they don't.

The wind is a poor net.
The universe
swims right through it.

Ghost Birches

The road crew worked all afternoon
cutting the dead birches.

Run-off from the road salt killed them,

trapped as they were on the narrow strip
left between the asphalt and the lake,

and rain-weakened. The acid
starts the yellow inflammation early,

the leaves in June already
arthritic in the cells.

We used to call them snow ghosts:

one white hidden in another.
Now they're stacked in four-foot sections,
their branches trimmed away,

and in the lake
the new emptiness heals over.
Then comes the plow of winter
straight down the valley,

pushing its wedge-shaped shadow.
All the lesser shadows move aside
as if still talking to one another,

flexible in wind, assessing their losses,
the future already upon them,

its sky-blue speckled crystals burning
down through the packed snow into the earth.

Maybe a man on the crew
with a truck of his own

will come on Saturday
to haul the white logs away, cut and split
and stack them, and he'll find them

crumbled to embers in his stove
when he comes home late and cold
from plowing after a heavy snow,

their shadows having already slipped
up the chimney to join all the other

shades of the world, the young ones
gone back to lie beside their stumps,

the old ones free to travel anywhere.

The Pools

I used to look into the green-brown
pools of the Ausable, the places
where the pouring cold slowed,

and see a mystery there.
I called it God for the way
it made my heart feel crushed

with love for the world outside myself,

each stone distinct and magnified,
trembling in the current's thick lens.

Now when I can't sleep
I say as a prayer
the names of all the little brooks,

Slide and Gill and Shadow,
and the names of the river pools
I fished at dusk,

working my way upstream through
slow sliding eddies and buckets of froth,

the flume, the bend, Hull's Falls, the potholes.
It's like saying the names
of the dead and the missing—

the Ausable, the Boquet, the Opalescent—

though their waters still
rush down over the gray ledges
toward Lake Champlain.

The flume was always
full of bark-colored shadows,

shafts of green light fallen
from the pines, and the silver swirls

of rising trout where now
the gray-fleshed hatchery fish
feed on the damaged magic.

Sleepless, I call to mind
the high granite walls
scored in the thaws,

the banks of black-stemmed ferns.

I lie again on a warm rock
and feel the hand of God on my back,

and feel it withdraw.
In the exact instant the sun
withdraws its treasure from the water

a tiny dissonance,
like bad news forgotten for a moment
but the shadow of its anxiety holding on,

making a little cloud of its own.

It was the thing outside the human
that I loved, and the way

I could enter it,
the muscle-ache of diving
down into the cold, green-brown spangles,

myself a part of the glimmering blur,
the falling coins of light.

Scraps of that beauty survive
in the world here and there—

sparks of rain in the pine candles,
a leaf turning in underwater currents,

then lost in the smoke of faster water.

Sometimes I glimpse the future
in the evenings. It appears
like a doe on silencing moss,

foraging among pocked leaves,
drinking the last light in the pools.

It doesn't even raise its head
to look at me. I'm not a danger to it,

trapped as I am in the purely human.

Bear on Scale

Even dead,
her weight resists the rope harness—

she is not a pet, not a slave.

Although he knows the bear is female,
the man still calls her *it* or *him*.
Two hundred twenty pounds,

turning slowly in the air.
They weigh about the same.

His fingers ruffle the lustrous pelt,
true black but for the long brown muzzle,

and over the small eyes clouded with refusal,

two faint brown eyebrows.
Bears have been known to climb
utility poles for the bee-buzz in the lines,

but she won't sniff the human trees
or cut her four-claw mark
the beeches anymore,

or gouge from the oak its stinging honeycomb.

On shelves behind the man and animal:
paint cans, car wax, caulking gun.

They're in a garage. The floor is cement.
He'll have to get down on all fours

to scrub away the dark spattering

after he cuts her down,
or maybe he'll leave it there beneath the scale

for no reasons he can think of.

William K. Verner

Bill Verner is responsible in part for the greater awareness of place and culture in the Adirondacks and North Country in the last third of the last century. His list of accomplishments and responsibilities is formidable; included are stints as curator of the Adirondack Museum, editor of Adirondack Life, and director of the Schenectady Museum. His publications included many features on Adirondack history and art history as well as the important and erudite introduction to the Adirondack Bibliography Supplement, an indispensable account of two hundred years of Adirondack writing.

Before his death in 1989, Verner was, in addition to being an editor, writer, and curator, a dedicated advocate of the Adirondack landscape. He was an active member of the Association for the Protection of the Adirondacks, the Adirondack Mountain Club, the Wilderness Society, and the Adirondack Nature Conservancy. The essays reprinted here first appeared in, respectively, Adirondack Life (1984) and The Conservationist (1968).

Early Bear Season

Thirty years ago, in *Adirondack Country*, William Chapman White wrote that "two of the best Adirondack months are ahead. As the Adirondack people say, on a hot September afternoon with a warm wind raising whitecaps on the lakes, 'We keep the best weather for ourselves.' "

Over the past few years, we have come to wonder about that. Not to be piggish about this sort of thing, mind you, not to hog the fall months

418

just for those of us lucky enough to live in the Adirondacks year-round, but something seems to have gone awry in recent years to the detriment, we believe, of both those who live in the Adirondacks all the time and those who visit.

Now, from time to time in the past, the Adirondack region has had something called a special bear season. These seasons usually followed upon the heels of one or more of the following circumstances: a relatively high black bear population, low natural spring and summer food supplies, and a greater frequency of nuisance reports—cases where bears got into people's garbage, onto their back porches, or into their camps or houses. In recent years, however, it would appear that we have been enveloped in a state of total war. Special bear season has become "early bear season," and early bear season has become a permanent fixture on the sportsman's calendar.

Unfortunately, it has also become a permanent fixture on just about everybody else's Adirondack calendar as well.

All right, you may well ask, what then really *is* so bad about special bear season, early bear season, call it what you will? Isn't there room for everybody?

Well, maybe there is, but we wonder. Our own particular experience in recent years has been more or less as follows. Labor Day comes, and Labor Day goes. Quiet comes to Adirondack villages again, if only briefly. Kids are back in school. A sprinkling of tourists, many of them older people taking advantage of the freedom of retirement, move along Adirondack roads at a leisurely pace, stop in at village stores, spend time at local museums. And then, all too soon, comes a weekend in September, when there is an inrush of cars, pickup trucks (especially pickup trucks), campers, and even (this one I remember well) a moving truck, the body of which serves as bunkhouse, living room, and dining room for a party of hunters. These vehicles take their positions at select and not so select spots along major and minor roads, especially in the central Adirondacks and in Hamilton County, where the bear population is the highest in the state. It is especially important to point out, by the way, that practically all of this sudden activity takes place along roads and near trailheads that lie within no more than a mile or two of town dumps.

And so, the first weekend of early bear season passes. The next weekend, the hunters return, but there are not as many of them, not by any means. The novelty has either worn off, or the hunters suppose that most of the eligible bears have been disposed of, or perhaps, inner voices begin to murmur that stalking bears around town dumps really isn't much of a sport. Bear fever, early September's lowgrade version of late October's "buck fever," has abated.

By the third weekend (for, you see early bear season does go on and on) there is practically no activity, at least not along roads and near dumps that we are personally most familiar with. About all that lingers, in fact, is the knowledge that it is early bear season still, that there *may* yet be some hunters out there in the woods, and that, *maybe,* it would be just as well not to go venturing out on a hike, the attraction of highly colored fall woods notwithstanding, because you might just get shot at, if not shot. Of course, the odds of getting shot at, much less getting shot, are low, very low, indeed. There is no rational reason why one shouldn't go out into those woods and enjoy that color and that last warmth of summer. But who said anything about rationality? A sense of unfair competition—the unarmed walker and the heavily armed hunter—lingers. No, I'll stay home, or close to home.

It used to be that one could count on having free and psychologically unencumbered access to the woods up until Columbus Day and even after that for a week or two. Muzzleloading and archery seasons really presented no great threat to peace of mind because of the relative paucity of such hunters, because those who hunted in these ways were, one suspected, more than a little experienced, and because such modes of sport demanded close-range identification of targets before the unleashing of missiles. The odds of being dropped by mistake were pretty slim.

I've often wondered about special, now early, bear season. How it came about may be understandable, but how it became a permanent fixture is another matter entirely. Have we gotten ourselves, and the bears, on some sort of biological treadmill?

I wonder about the boosters of local economies. Does a perennially early bear season really help the local economy very much? Isn't it just as possible, more likely, in fact, that such a season hurts the local economy by discouraging the free-ranging fall visitor?

And then, I wonder about the broad spectrum of hunters, most of whom, I suspect, are more than satisfied with the nearly forty days and forty nights afforded by the normal hunting seasons—days to be out in leafless open woods enjoying the chill air, evenings with friends around the warmth of a camp fire telling tales, tall and short. I often wonder if most hunters really think this early bear season, year in and year out, is the way to tackle the bear problem, whether it helps the name of hunting, and whether it really does the Adirondacks—the region's economy, its reputation—much good.

I doubt it, but I may be wrong.

The Adirondack Painters

The roster of American artists who worked in northern New York's Adirondack region is so extensive that, if by some extraordinary catastrophe all American paintings except those pertaining to the Adirondacks were to be lost, it would still be possible to reconstruct a good deal of the history of American painting.

That such a reconstruction would be biased towards landscape goes without saying, but the long tradition of Adirondack art also includes a good deal of genre—scenes of hunting, fishing, trapping, and camping and views of some of the early settlements nestled in mountain valleys—and it encompasses portraits, particularly of some of the guides. There is also a scattering of important historical subjects; indeed, this is where the history of Adirondack art, itself, begins.

The earliest known work of art pertaining to the Adirondacks happens to be the first which deals with New York State as well; it concerns the first white men known to have set foot in the State, Samuel de Champlain's party, which entered from Canada on an exploring mission in 1609. On July 30th, they encountered a band of hostile Iroquois near Ticonderoga and had at them with their arquebuses, an action which was to have a long-term effect upon subsequent history. In Champlain's *Voyages*, published in 1613, there is an engraving of the battle which was probably done after a sketch by Champlain himself.

Another important early historical subject, one which the distinguished historian of American painting, E. P. Richardson, regards as the "first historical print engraved in America," showed "A Prospective

Plan of Battle Fought Near Lake George, Sept. 8, 1755." Thomas Johnston did the engraving from sketches by Samuel Blodget.

The mainstream of Adirondack art and its strongest reflection of American art in general, however, was a phenomenon of the nineteenth century. As had been the case with the Champlain and Johnston engravings, most of even the early nineteenth century paintings and engravings which have come down to us dealt with the periphery of the Adirondack region. It was not until the 1830s that the first views of the Adirondack interior were published in the lithographs of J. H. Bufford, after originals by C. C. Ingham, Ebenezer Emmons, and perhaps others. These plates were used to illustrate part of the State Geological Survey Report which was issued early in 1838, and for this reason they bear a number of interesting associations. One of them is that the report had to do with the first ascent and naming of Mount Marcy, the state's highest peak (artist Ingham made it to the top, too, but not without fainting a few times on the way). Another link is that the report (and one of its illustrations) was the earliest publication to employ the name "Adirondack" in conjunction with the northern New York area. Emmons, who was leader of the survey party, had proposed that the region's high mountain range be called the Adirondack Group. The interest aroused by the report and by articles dealing with the Marcy ascent in the press probably had a good deal to do with attracting what was to become a steady stream of representative American artists to the area.

Throughout the nineteenth century there were some illustrative artists who came to the region as part of scientific survey parties. The young J. W. Hill accompanied Emmons to the Raquette Lake area in 1839, and a generation later Verplanck Colvin, besides lugging the theodolites, barometers, and camp equipage necessary to his topographical survey of the Adirondacks, also packed along drawing materials. At least one artist is credited with doing some exploring on his own, for T. R. Davis, an illustrator and a designer of the White House porcelain service in the 1870s, made the first recorded ascent of Santanoni Peak in 1867.

Most artists who worked in the Adirondacks, however, were there simply to get away from the summer heat of the city—usually New York City where many of them had studios in the same building on Tenth Street—or to find source material for the creation of "that wilder image" which was such an important characteristic of nineteenth-century American landscape art. On a more pedestrian level, others were there looking for new and colorful material to satisfy the appetite of a seemingly insatiable art-buying public.

In the late 1830s and during the '40s the region was visited by such figures as Thomas Cole, founder of the Hudson River School of Painting, by the dean of American engravers, Asher B. Durand, and by the artist-writer, Charles Lanman. A Frenchman, Regis Gignoux, may have barely shaken off the after-effects of an Atlantic voyage before being spirited away to the mountains because there exists a Hamilton County scene by him dated 1844, the year he arrived on these shores.

Arthur Fitzwilliam Tait, famous for his sporting scenes and Currier & Ives subjects, reached America in 1850 and within a few years had become a regular visitor to the Adirondacks, first to the Chateaugay area, later to Long Lake where, in fact, he resided year around for a while in the 1870s. John Kensett, Worthington Whittredge, the Harts (William and James), and Sanford R. Gifford were also active prior to and during the Civil War, and William J. Stillman helped organize the famous "Philosophers' Camp" of Ralph Waldo Emerson, Louis Agassiz, James Russell Lowell and others. He painted these distinguished gentlemen playing at pioneering in 1858.

Following the Civil War, the publication of W. H. H. ("Adirondack") Murray's *Adventures in the Wilderness* stirred a "rush to the wilderness" of "Murray's fools," some of whom were artists curious to see what all the fuss was about and anxious to gather material for the illustrated weeklies such as *Harper's, Franks Leslie's* and *Appleton's.* Among them was one of the illustrators of the Murray book itself, Harry Fenn, who did practically all of the Adirondack subjects for William Cullen Bryant's massive two volume *Picturesque America* (1872–74). The Smillies (James and George), N. A. Moore, Arthur Parton, David Johnson, S. W. Griggs, and Fred Vance represent just a few of the artists active in the period. The most famous, of course, was Winslow Homer, who worked in the Hudson River watershed of the Adirondacks from about 1870 to 1902. By coincidence Homer had been an apprentice lithographer in Boston for that same J. H. Bufford who, twenty years before, had done the first plates of the Adirondack high peak region (Homer regarded his term at Bufford's "slavery"), and he had studied briefly with Frederic Rondel, another artist of the Adirondack scene.

Levi Wells Prentice, a native of Lewis County, was perhaps the last of the devoted Adirondack landscapists of interest, and there is much about his highly individualistic career that is definitely out of the mainstream.

An attempt to single out any one painter in the vast tradition of Adirondack art as having caught the region most successfully in paint is bound to be highly subjective. This is not just because the interpretation of a work of art is necessarily subjective—which it is, but also because judgments as to just what the Adirondack landscape itself may be all about differ from one another considerably. Nevertheless, the Adirondack work of Homer Martin is striking in the manner in which it captures what James Thomas Flexner has called "God's unedited beneficence." Even so seemingly straightforward a work as Martin's "Two Anglers," perhaps painted in 1876, strikes an intriguingly uneasy balance between the ordered and the disordered, between the simplicity of two figures heading down to a river's edge for some fishing and a nature which for all its placidity includes meandering tree trunks and ragged limbs, a fallen branch across the path and a flash of autumn upon it. There is a certain insecure dynamism in the relationship of the figures and the landscape, and it is possible that one who has had the opportunity of spending some time deep in the Adirondacks even today may recognize something of his experience in this painting.

Jack Wikoff

Born in Massachusetts in 1922, Jack Wikoff spent his childhood in the Adirondacks, where his grandfather was a guide and hotelier. During World War II, he was an alpine instructor to the famous Tenth Mountain Division, and much later, after opening and managing a ski lodge in Lake Placid, he was named the official poet of the 1980 Winter Olympic Games, which were held in his home village. He died the following year, after more than a decade of reading his work and lecturing widely in the United States.

Not surprisingly, his poetry is as robust as the adventurous life he led. He studied with Robert Frost and Van Wyck Brooks, and his work recalls the vigorous voices of Whitman, Ferlinghetti, and Hart Crane.

The poems featured here are collected in Adirondack Portfolio: Poems, published posthumously by Station Hill Press in 1983.

When It's Carrion Time in the Adirondacks

This 20° below morning
by the Ausable, my
heart leaped
           to hear the
first birds of spring
               rejoicing
blithely across a
        delicate
rose-streamered dawn; raucous ravens,

425

cawing coarsely
                    at their own crude jokes,
crass
        carrion eaters
reveling in
the death of winter, numerous
small animals,
                    perhaps too
of mine,
                and
I laugh:

Death
            is a beginning.

It
                    says so
right here.

Two Existentialists

My Grandfather,
                    The guide,
Who could level a beam, or
                        Straighten
A line, square a corner,
                    At a glance;
Being himself level,
Straight
Square;
        Lies dead
Under a stone
At the brow of a hill
                    Overlooking two rivers;
Countless footsteps,

Following
This quiet game trail, flushing
That bronzed partridge
From the darkling spruce, deftly
Catching wary speckled trouts from
                   The chill brook:
A proud
        Silent man,
Who did right
          Because right
Was right to do: his
Only unsurmountable barrier
             Separated
Wrong from right, him,
           Ever-uncomplaining,
From pleasure, from
        Plump
Eurydice.

   My Grandmother,
           Doughty doughnut maker,
Baker of pies,
          Terrorizer and
Feeder of tramps,
            And happy children,
                Lies

Beside him;
       The only place she
Ever desired to be,
         Sharing still
Her strength with his, sharing,
His pain her pain,
        His love too, knowing withal,
Blending
       Beneath the wind-blown daisies,
Sharing . . .

        Always giving.
Together
My grandparents lie under a stone
At the Brow of a hill
           Overlooking two small rivers.
One from the Handsome Maple,
             The other
From Marcy,
        That joined together flow
Into Lake Champlain.

Acknowledgments

Permission to use the following material is gratefully acknowledged:

Russell Banks, excerpt from "Mitchell Stephens, Esquire," from *The Sweet Hereafter*, copyright 1991 by Russell Banks; excerpt from *Cloudsplitter*, copyright 1998 by Russell Banks. Reprinted by permission of HarperCollins Publishers, Inc.

Thurston Clarke, "The 1812 Homestead," copyright 1997; Elizabeth Folwell, "Why We Bagged It," copyright 1994; Edward Kanze, "Rite of Passage," copyright 2000, and "An Adirondack Wilderness: West Canada Lakes," copyright 1995; James Howard Kuntzler, "The Man Who Would Be King," 1987; Joan Potter, "Diners, Drugstores, and Dives," copyright 1999, and "Twenty-Five Years to Life," copyright 1999; Fred G. Sullivan, "What's So Funny?" copyright 1989; William K. Verner, "Early Bear Season," copyright 1984, reprinted by permission of *Adirondack Life Magazine*. All rights reserved. "Opening Camp," copyright 1994 by Anne LaBastille, appeared in *Adirondack Life* in October 1994, and is reprinted with permission.

Richard Beamish, "Adirondack Smithsonian," reprinted by permission of *Adirondack Explorer*, copyright 1999.

Michael DiNunzio, "Islands in the Sky," from *Adirondack Wildguide: A Natural History of the Adirondack Park*." Copyright 1984 by the Adirondack Council, Inc., and the Adirondack Nature Conservancy/Adirondack Land Trust. Reprinted by permission.

Phil Gallos, "The Vanishing Cure Cottage," from *Cure Cottages of Saranac Lake: Architecture and History of a Pioneer Health Resort*, copyright 1985 by Historic Saranac Lake. Reprinted by permission.

Alice Gilborn, "The Proving Grounds," "Birds," and "Transit" from *The Woman in the Mountain: Reconstructions of Self and Land by Adirondack Women Writers*, edited by Kate H. Winter. Reprinted by permission of State University of New York Press. Copyright 1989 by State University of New

York. All rights reserved. "The Proving Grounds" appeared in the Winter/ Spring 1986 edition of *Blueline*. Reprinted by permission.

Sue Halpern, "The Place of Solitaries" and "Solo" from *Migrations to Solitude*, copyright © 1992 by Sue Halpern. Reprinted by permission of Pantheon Books, a division of Random House, Inc.; "Civic Literacy: The Johnsburg Library," reprinted by permission of The Orion Society, copyright 1997.

Excerpts from *An Adirondack Passage: The Cruise of the Canoe* Sairy Gamp, written by Christine Jerome and published by the Adirondack Mountain Club, Lake George, N.Y. (copyright 1998 by Christine Jerome) are used with permission of the author.

Bill McKibben, "Deeper Twilight Still," from *The Age of Missing Information*. Copyright 1992 by Bill McKibben. Reprinted by permission of Random House, Inc. "Home" and "Home Again," from *Hope, Human and Wild*. Copyright 1996 by Bill McKibben. Reprinted by permission of Little, Brown and Company, Inc.

Christopher Shaw, "Empty at the Heart of the World," from *The Nature of Nature*, edited by William H. Shore and published by Harcourt Brace and Share Our Strength, 1996. Reprinted with permission.

Alex Shoumatoff, "Camp Life" and "The Real Adirondacks" reprinted by permission of Ellen Levine Literary Agency, Inc. Copyright 1997 by Alex Shoumatoff.

Natalia Rachel Singer, "A Girl in Winter," excerpted from *Adirondac* magazine, copyright 1996 by the Adirondack Mountain Club. Reprinted by permission of the Adirondack Mountain Club.

William K. Verner, "The Adirondack Painters," from *The Conservationist*, copyright 1968 by the New York State Department of Environmental Conservation. All rights reserved. Reprinted by permission.

Excerpts from *Reflections from Canoe Country: Paddling the Waters of the Adirondacks and Canada* by Christopher Angus (1997); *Adirondack Cabin Country*, by Paul Schaefer (1993); *Adirondack Explorations: Nature Writings of Verplanck Colvin*, edited by Paul Schaefer (1997); and *Field Notes from the Northern Forest*, by J. Curt Stager (1998) reprinted by permission of Syracuse University Press.

"A Crisis Looms," by Philip Terrie, from *Contested Terrain: A New History of Nature and People in the Adirondacks*, published by the Adirondack Museum and Syracuse University Press. Copyright 1997 by the Adirondack Museum. Reprinted with permission.